Central Colonies Chronicle

THE FREEMEN, THE SERVANTS, AND THE GOVERNMENT

1722–1732

Compiled by

Armand Francis Lucier

HERITAGE BOOKS
2015

HERITAGE BOOKS
AN IMPRINT OF HERITAGE BOOKS, INC.

Books, CDs, and more—Worldwide

For our listing of thousands of titles see our website at
www.HeritageBooks.com

Published 2015 by
HERITAGE BOOKS, INC.
Publishing Division
5810 Ruatan Street
Berwyn Heights, Md. 20740

Copyright © 1998 Armand Francis Lucier

All rights reserved. No part of this book may be reproduced or transmitted in any form or by any means, electronic or mechanical, including photocopying, recording or by any information storage and retrieval system without written permission from the author, except for the inclusion of brief quotations in a review.

International Standard Book Numbers
Paperbound: 978-0-7884-1060-4
Clothbound: 978-0-7884-6242-9

CONTENTS

List of Contributors..............................v

Foreward..vii

1722..1

1723...33

1724...67

1725...97

1726..129

1727..171

1728..209

1729..265

1730..303

1731..347

Index...386

CONTRIBUTORS

The American Weekly Mercury. Philadelphia. Printed by Andrew Bradford. 1722-1732.

Boston Gazette. Boston. Printed by S. Kneeland for Philip Musgrave. 1722-1725.

Boston Gazette. Boston. Printed by S. Kneeland for Thomas Lewis. 1725-1726.

Boston Gazette. Printed for Henry Marshal and Thomas Lewis. 1726-1727.

Boston Gazette. Printed for Henry Marshal. 1727.

Boston Gazette. Boston. Printed by B. Green jun. for Henry Marshal. 1727-1732.

The New England Courant. Boston Printed by J. Franklin. 1722-1723.

The New-England Courant. Boston. Printed by J. Franklin. 1722-1727. (J. Franklin was banned from publishing because of past articles that appeared in his public print and printed under his brother's name Benjamin.

New-York Gazette. New-York. Printed by William Bradford. 1725-1732.

Maryland Gazette. Annapolis. Printed by William Parks. 1727-1732.

The New-England Weekly Journal. Boston. Printed by S. Kneeland' 1727.

The New-England Weekly Journal. Boston. Printed by S. Kneeland and T. Green 1727- 1732.

FOREWARD

This is an attempt to make American History entertaining as well as informative, for the scholar and the layman alike.

Feel the pulse of the people by reading the same items and advertisements presented in their weekly newspapers; the same words, the same spellings, the same compositions as they were written by Colonial compositors and publishers. (In some cases, minor changes have been made to improve clarity and consistency.)

The following pages are filled with newspaper abstracts concerning run-away slaves and indentured servants, the near frontier, piracy, ships and mariners, plantations, land and home sales, and many more happenings and items of interest to the highborn as well as the common tradesman. Sit down and let the pages of this book transport you back in time to the 1720's and join the people in their daily lives; share their cares and fears, which form an important part of our American Heritage.

1722

PHILADELPHIA Jan. 2. Our General Assembly are now sitting, and we have great Expectation from them at this juncture, that they will find some effectual Remedy, to revive the dying credit of this Province, and restore us to our former happy circumstances.

PHILADELPHIA Jan. 9. The Governor's Speech to the Assembly of the Province of Pennsylvania, January the 2d 1722.

Mr. Speaker, and Gentlemen of the Assembly, You have prudently chose the most reasonable Time of the Year, for the Dispatch of Publick Business, when it will least interfere with your private Affairs in the Country: And I hope I have been so happy to speak your Sentiments with my own, as often as I have lately had Occasion to assure many of the good People of this Province, That we will, at this Time, give an attentive Ear to all their Complaints, and most diligently apply our senses, to restore the planters, Credit without discouraging, the Merchants, by whose Industry clone our Trade must be supported with a sufficient Currency of Cash.

My Mind is so fully bent upon doing this Province some effectual Service, that I have lately form'd a Design of a considerable Settlement amongst you, in order to manufacture and consume the Grain, for which there is at this Time no profitable Market Abroad. And although this Project will doubtless at first prove very chargeable and expensive to me; if it meets with your Approbation and Good-Will of the People, I am well assured it cannot fail of answering my Purpose, to do a real Service to the Country and every Interest of concern of mine shall ever be built on that bottom.

Gentlemen,
If in the Prosecution of your Affairs this

Session any thing should happen, wherein my private Advice or Assistance can be serviceable to you, be assured I will readily and cheerfully meet, as often as they shall be occasioned, any Committee you think to appoint: For, as I am persuaded the Publick Good will be the rule of Thoughts, we may reasonably expect the best issue from united Councils.

PHILADELPHIA 9. About the 13th of November a Ship was cast away on the Middle Ground in the Bay of Chesapeake: She was a Pink belonging to London which loaded in the Head of the Bay, and had on board about 600 Hogsheads of Tobacco.

About the 25th of November, two outward bound Vessels one belonging to Barnstable and the other to London, both bound to London drove on shore from their Anchors: Barnstable Man, being in Lyn-Haven Bay, came to no damage, except only being drove, by the highness of the Tide and a hard Gale of Wind, into four foot water, where it is thought she will be got off after she is lighted, by the Assistance of the Hands on Board one of our Men Of War there, which the Honourable Captain has readily granted. The other, the London Ship, was cast away on Cape Henry, and by the impetuous Breakers was soon beat to Pieces, only 2 Boys and one Man being save of the whole Company.

Also the Sloop Content, William Lyford Master from South Carolina, was cast away upon Cape Charles in the Bay of Chesapeake, the 22d of November. The Men on Board were all saved, and the Sloop and Cargo lost.

There is a Brigantine arrived in the Bay of Delaware, and is hauled up into Prime Hook, to avoid the Driving Ice. She is supposed to be Capt. Simmon's Brigt. from London; from whom we hope to have some Advices to insert in our next.

NEW-YORK Jan. 13. It is excessive cold, and the River full of Ice from the Narrows to New-York. Yesterday a great many People went upon the Ice from New-York to the Ferry on Long Island.

PHILADELPHIA Jan. 16. On the 3d Instant the Honourable House of Representatives of this Province made the following Address, in answer to the Governor's Speech of the 2d, Instant last Week.

May it Please the Governor,

'Tis with great Complacency this House receives the Governor's fresh Assurance of his Regard to the People we represent, in such affectionate Expressions and Zeal, to restore the Planters Credit with just Care of the Merchants, who of late (with others) equally lie under the great Disadvantage of want of a sufficient Currency of Cash; as appears to us from the Melancholy Complaints of the People; and we will readily fall in with any scheme, as shall appear to us conductive to a remedy.

We gratefully acknowledge the Governor's Consideration to acquaint this House of forming a Design to manufacture and consume the Grain of this Country: We hope the Success will answer the Governor's Expectation, bu a fruitful Advantage of his interest, and consequently that of the Country; which are inseparable.

We heartily thank the Governor for his repeated Offers, in condescending cheerfully to assist and advise this Assembly in what may be for the Publick Good.

NEW CASTLE Jan. 16. This Day arrived here the Pink Elizabeth and Cathrine, Cornelius Davis, from Milford, in a passage of 14 Weeks hither. She met with a great Storm to the Westward of Cape Hatteras, which obliged them to cut their Mizen-Mast and Main top Mast clear away, for the Preservation of the Vessels and Lives. The Sea ran very high, and washed overboard from the Deck their Boat and two Men, which were entirely lost.

PHILADELPHIA Feb. 1. These are to give Notice, to all Persons who may have the Appearance of Copper, or other Mines, on their Lands, and are not inclined to go on with the Work themselves, That John Johnston of Pert-Amboy and Company, will hire the Land of the Owners, and give them One Sixth Part of the Produce of the Mine, clear of all charges, and in eighteen Months, or sooner, be obliged to provide Miners, and go on with the Work.

You may direct your Letters to Dr. J. Johnston

in Pert-Amboy, and Time and Place shall be appointed to meet, in Order to agree concerning the above Proposal.

PHILADELPHIA Feb. 13. A Lot for the 13 Years to come, from the 26th of March, 1722, on the West side of the Front-Street in Philadelphia, being 51 Feet in Breadth, with 4 Brick Tenements on the said Front-Street, and in length to the Second-Street, 326 feet, with two Tenements on said Second-Street, bounded on the South by a House and lot now in the Tenure of Mr. Richard Walker, and on the North by Clement Plumbstead, dwelling House and Lot, &c. and pay 15 Pounds per Annum, Ground Rent. Taken in execution by Owen Roberts, Sheriff of Philadelphia, &c. and are to be sold at Publick Vendue at the Coffee House, the 24th of this Instant February 1722.

PHILADELPHIA Feb. 20. Broke out of Common Goal of Philadelphia the 15th of this Instant February, the following Persons:

John Palmer, alias Plumin, alias Paine, Servant to Joseph Jones, run away and was lately taken up at New-York. He has a Cinnamon coloured Coat on, a middle size fresh coloured Man. His Master will give a Pistole Reward to any who shall secure him, besides what is here offered.

Daniel Oughtopay, a Dutchman, aged about 24 Years, Servant to Dr. Johnston in Amboy. He is a thin spare Man, grey Drugget Wastcoat and Breeches a light coloured Coat on.

Ebenezer Mallary, a New-England-Man, age about 24 Years, is a middle size thin Man, having a Snuff colour'd Coat, and an ordinary Tucking wastcoat and Breeches. He had dark brown strait Hair.

Mathew delany, an Irish Man, down look'd swarthy Complexion and has on an Olive coloured Cloth Coat and Wastcoat with Cloth Bottoms.

John Flemming, an Irish Lad, aged about 18, belonging to Mr. Miranda, Merchant in this City. He has no Coat, a grey Drugget Wastcoat and narrow-brim'd Hat on.

John Corbet, a Shropshire Man, a run away Servant from Alexander Faulker of Maryland, broke out on the 12th Instant. He has got a double breasted Sailor's Jacket an lined with red Bars, pretends to be a Sailor, and once thought School at Joseph Colling's in the Jerseys.

Whoever takes up and secures all, or anyone of these Felons, shall have a Pistole Reward for each of them and reasonable Charges Paid by
John Wilson, Goaler.

PHILADELPHIA March 10. James Davis, aged about Twenty six Years, on his Solemn affirmation, says, That he served Henry Badcock of the City of Philadelphia, in the Province of Pennsylvania, Brewer, three Years and a half. And soon after the Expiration of his Servitude with the said Badcock, he hired himself unto George Campion of the said City, Brewer, and wrought in his brew-House about six Months; during which time, and in the Month of May last past, Samuel Boud of said City, Son-in-Law of the said Campion, sailed for Carolina, in the Sloop ——— Thomas Glentworth Master; And the said Campion put on board the said Sloop, for the voyage aforesaid, several Barrels of Beer, to the best of Deponent's Remembrance, Thirty Barrels. And this Deponent says, that George Campion and Samuel Boud aforesaid asked him, to brand the said, Barrels with Henry Badcock's Mark, viz. HB. which Mark this Deponent knew the said Badcock used all the Time of his Servitude, and many Years before, as he had heard. And this Deponent further says, That the said George Campion told him, if he (this Deponent) did not care, or would not get a Brand made, and brand them with HB. Samuel Boud should. But this Deponent at that time refused either to get the Brand or Mark aforesaid made, or to use it when it was made. That he, this Deponent, went about branding or marking the Barrels aforesaid Mentioned with the proper Brand or Mark of the said George Campion, viz. GC. as aforesaid, he said Campion and Samuel Boud aforesaid forbad him to proceed, he having at that time branded or marked, to the best of his Remembrance, four or five Barrels, and the Remainder of the Thirty Barrels aforesaid were put on Board the said Sloop, Thomas Glentworth Master, unbranded; and the said Campion added, if the Deponent wou'd not brand the said Barrels with HB. That Samuel Boud should, and this Deponent further says, That one Capt. Codd arriving to this Port of Philadelphia from Carolina, the said George Campion received a Letter from the aforementioned Samuel Boud. Which Letter, directed and sign'd as aforesaid, this Deponent read, wherein the said Boud advised the said Campion to ship more Beer, and brand the Barrels with HB. because no Beer would sell well there, unless the Barrels were so branded. And this Deponent further says, That since the Receipt of the Letter aforesaid, George Campion aforesaid shewing him a Branding-Iron HB. which the said Campion desired him to put upon some Barrels of Beer, saying, they were for his Daughter Henney Boud, which this Deponent refused to do, suspecting the Design was to counterfeit the Mark or Brand of his former Master Henry Badcock aforesaid, which the said Campion had often tempted him to do. To this his affirmation he hath set his Hand, this Nineteenth Day of February in the eight Year of his Majesty's Reign, anno; Dimini, 1722. Affirmed and Signed before me Char. Read.

James Davis.

  NEW-YORK March 12. They are but four Whales killed on Long-Island, and little oil expected this Year.

  BOHEMIA MARYLAND March 17. This Night there broke out a dreadful Fire at the Plantation of Samuel Byard and Benj. Sluyter, which laid in Ruins two very large Barns, in one of which were a young married Woman and a Negro Girl, together with 28 Milch Cows and Calves burnt to Death and Consumed; and in the other 5 fine Horses and some Sheep destroyed.

  MIDDLETOWN March 20. To be sold on very reasonable Terms, A Tract of Land containing near 300 Acres, pleasantly situated at Middletown in Buck-County; together with a good Plantation-House, a Fulling-Mill and all Appurtenances, a large Orchard of 400 Trees, besides other Fruit Trees, Barn, out-Houses &c. It is very rich land, well Water'd and Timber'd, and 30 Acres of up-Land cleared. Belonging to Daniel Jackson of

Middletown aforesaid, where any Persons may treat with him for the same.

PHILADELPHIA March 21. Run away the 10th instant from Daniel Martin, living at Absaham Pride's in this City, a Servant Man named John Lee (commonly known by the name of Giff), of a middle Stature, fair Complexion, brown Hair. He has a black Hat new dress'd and Camolet Coat, with two Rows of Buttons on the Breast, and one below, and three Jackets, one dark Drugget with red lining, another Striped Holland lined with checker'd lining, and the 3d of Ozenbrigs, and Leather Breeches with Buttons covered with Leather, grey woolen Stockings, and good round toed Shoes. Any Body securing the said Person shall have 40s. Reward paid by Daniel Martin.

PHILADELPHIA March 22. Ran away from Gabriel Stelle of Shewsbury in Jersey, on the 5th of this Instant March, 1722. A Servant Man called Samuel Harding; he has a Mould upon one of his Cheaks (it is thought to be his left) like a Blackberry, dark bushy Hair and reddish Beard. A short Fellow; he has a homespun Kersey Coat on, a Serge Wastcoat and Leather Breeches. He is a Cooper by Trade. Any Person who shall take up and secure the said Servant, and convey him to his said Master, shall have Forty Shillings Reward, besides reasonable Charges.

PHILADELPHIA March 28. Notice is hereby given to all Persons in the Province of New-Jersey, That are indebted to David Lyell and William Bradford, on account of the Excise, That within six Week they apply to said David Lyell at his Plantation or Mr. John Barclay in Amboy and discharge their Bonds, or else they will be put in suit against them.

For the ease of those that lives in the Western Division, their Bonds are left at Andrew Bradford in Philadelphia.

PHILADELPHIA April 5. There is to be sold by John Smith Chocolate-Maker in Chestnut-street, very good Chocolate, pure nut, at Twenty three Shillings per dozen, being made from a choice Parcel of Nuts lately bought.

PHILADELPHIA April 19. On Tuesday in the Afternoon an Accident happened in this City, a

Butcher who came from Frankford, very much in Drink, stript his Cloaths off to his Shirt, ran into the River at the Arch Wharf and was there drowned, he could not be found that Night, and Yesterday was discovered by a Fish hook catching hold of his Leg and so haul'd up.

Whereas about Twenty Years since, there came into these Parts of America, with Mr. Charles French, who lives at Ancocus-Creek in Burlington County, in West-Jersey, one Samuel Lacy born in Northamshire, These are to give Notice, That if the said Samuel Lacy be living and will come to Henry Flower, Postmaster of Philadelphia, he may be informed of something very considerable for his Advantage; And further, if any Person can give any true and satisfactory Account of Proof of the said Samuel Lacy's being now living, shall have a Reward of Five Pounds current Money of the Province paid them by the said
                                            Henry Flower.

NEW-YORK April 21. About three in the Morning Mrs. Burnet, our Governor's Lady, was delivered of a Son upon which all our Vessels in the Road displayed their Ensigns, Pendants, &c.

BRISTOL April 23. Ran away from Thomas Wathell a Servant Man named Thomas Over, aged about 21 Years of middle Stature, fresh Colour and light brown Hair. He is marked with Gun-Powder in the flesh Part of his Arms, with the Jerusalem-Arms, and two first Letters of his Name. He has a new felt Hat, a light coloured Pea-Jacket and Leather Breeches, one Ozenbrig Shirt, grey woolen Stockings and good round toed Shoes. Any Person who shall take up and secure the said Servant and give Notice to his said Master, shall have Forty Shillings Reward, besides reasonable Charges, Paid by me,   Thomas Wathell.

NEW CASTLE April 24. At the Court of Oyer and Terminer and Goal Delivery held at this Place for the County of New Castle upon the Delaware, before Col. John French, Samuel Lowman, Benj. Shurmer and James Steel Esqrs; Eleanor Moore and Elizabeth Garretson received sentence of Death upon being convicted of the Murther of a Bastard Child born of the Body of the said Eleanor Moore.

PHILADELPHIA April 26. Strayed away from Philadelphia about 3 Weeks since, a White Mare about 14 Hands high, Shod before the Shoes turned up, never Shod behind, has an O branded on her near Shoulder, Whoever can give such Account of her as she may be found shall be well satisfied by, John Copson.

PHILADELPHIA May 3. All Persons who have any Claim or are indebted to the Estate of John Davis of Philadelphia lately deceased, are hereby speedily desired to come and settle their Accounts with the Widow, at her House in the Second Street.

The said Widow has two Servant Men to dispose of, one of them by Trade a Taylor.

PERTH-AMBOY May 6. His Excellency's Speech to the General Assembly of New-Jersey, at the breaking up the Session, the 5th of May 1722.

Gentlemen,

I Have so many reasons to thank you for your Proceeding, in this Session, that should I mention them all Time would not suffice me.

Two I cannot but acknowledge in a most particular Manner; The Acts for the Cheerful and honerable Support, and for the Security of his Majesty's Government in this Province.

I cannot but say, That look upon the latter and on the Nobler Present of the Two, as to think Honour always more valuable than Riches.

The World will now see the true Cause of our Misunderstandings in the last Assembly, and that though we met in the Innocency and Simplicity of our Hearts, that the Enemy had sown such seeds of Dissension among us, that defeated all our good Purposes, and made us part with wrong Notions of one another. It has pleased God now to discover the Truth, and no Man in his sober Senses can doubt, that the Hand of Joab was Busy, as it is now certain that it has at this Time.

It is particular Honour to me, to be thus justified in all my Conduct by the Publick Act of the whole Legislature. And God knows my Heart, that I am not fond of Power, that I abhor all Thoughts of revenge and that I study to keep a Conscience void of Offence toward God and toward Man.

After the Publication of the Acts I desire you to return House and after having enter'd this Speech in your minutes to adjourn your selves to the first Day of October next, that though it is not probable that we shall meet soon, it may not be out of our Power, if Occasion should be,   W. Burnet.

Philadelphia May 9. Whereas Thomas Burridge of the City of Gloucester, who came over to New-York in one Capt. Torteided of Bristol in the Year 1713 who I hear is married and lives in some part of the New Countries, either in Pennsylvania or the Jerseys, if he will come or send to Obediah Hunt of New-York, he may be informed of an Estate fallen to him, likewise a Legacy to a Sister of his, who came over some time after him.

Philadelphia May 10. On the 8th Instant, 12 of the Clock at Night, a Fire broke out at Bristol, which burnt down a House belonging to _____ Moor, a Bolting-House and two other Houses. Two men were Burnt one to a Cinder, the other languished some time and since Dead. The Goods in general of all that went to the Fair from Philadelphia are consumed, and R. Robinson of this City hurt very much by a Fall from a Window.

NEWCASTLE May 10. The last Speech of Eleanor Moore at her Execution on Wednesday the 9th Day of May instant, who received Sentence of Death at Newcastle upon the Delaware the 24th Day of April last, together with Elizbeth Garretson, for the Murthering a Female Bastard Child born to said Eleanor.

Elizabeth by reason of the Confession of the said Elianor was respited.

I Elianor Moore am brought hither to suffer for that unnatural Crime, whereof I was legally convicted and justly condemned. I have endeavoured, to my great sorrow, to mitigate my great Offence, by unjustly charging the Fact upon another. God has been graciously pleased to stop my Cancer and rebuke my Madness in this Particular: And therefore, as I render him Thanks for his Grace bestowed upon me, to speak the Truth from my Heart, so I do freely and without

Reserve confess, That what I laid to the charge of Elizabeth Garretson, at and before our Tryal, she the said Elizabeth Garretson, was not Guilty of, for she neither delivered me of the Child, nor conveyed it away, nor buried it.

I was delivered ('tis with great Concern I speak it) out of Doors, by myself, at some Distance from the Dwelling House of said Elizabeth Garretson, near a Hog-Pen, and afterwards laid the Child by the side of a fallen Tree, being satisfied it was born alive by my hearing it once cry; from which place I removed it, and buried it my self, without the knowledge or advice of the said Elizabeth Garretson, she and I having no manner of Discourse about the said Child, or how it was disposed of; otherwise then that she would be now and then relating me what was commonly reported amongst the Neighbours about me. And I heartily ask God and the said Elizabeth Pardon and forgiveness of impeaching her so grossly, and Imposing upon my Judges, so as to rank her in the same Transgression with my self. And I beg that this my Confession may be looked upon as the true and genuine Sense of my Soul, notwithstanding my presumptuous a Manner, and I pray: that this publick Satisfaction which I am now to pay to justice, may be a Caution to those who may come to the knowledge of my grievous Sin and fearful Punishment, to apply themselves in their Youth to remember their Creator, and to avoid loose Company and Sabbath-breaking, which by sad Experience I now find must need in Sorrow and Disgrace.

By what I have said, I hope, you charitably believe I am penitent, and as such I beg your prayers for me, that I may find Acceptance at the Throne of Divine Mercy, through Him that died for my Offences, and rose again for my justification, even Jesus Christ, that one Mediator between God and Man; To whom, with the Father and Holy Ghost, be Glory and Honour for evermore, Amen. Lord Jesus, receive my Spirit.

PHILADELPHIA May 17. For London directly. The Charming Sally Galley, James Gruchy Master, Burthen about Two Hundred Tons, having very good accommodations for Passengers, and will sail with all Expectation, two third thirds of her loading already on Board.

Any Persons that will ship any Goods, or want a Passage, may agree with the Master on reasonable Terms at the Coffee-House, or on Board the said Ship at Capt. Richard Anthony's Wharf.

NEW-YORK May 21. On the 17th arrived here a Flyboat of 400 Tons and upwards named Goronne of Port Louis in France, Capt. Peter Burat, Commander, from Cape Francise to Nants, forced hither to repair, being at Sea so leaky and in such real Distress, that they could hardly free her. She had about 50 Frenchmen and Women on board. 'Tis said, she is much worm-eaten, and will stand need of Repair. She had Sugar on board, but half loaded, and but 2 Cask of Indigo. She went from France to Mississippi with upward of 200 Passengers, who were taken by Pyrates a great many of the murder'd, and the women barbarously abused. They were carried to Saminau Bay, and some time after had the Ship delivered back to them; from whence they went to Cape Francoise, and took in these Sugars. They were stript of most of their Rigging and Sails, and they say, there is not above 50 of the 200 left alive.

PHILADELPHIA May 22. The Speech of his Excellency Sir William Keith, Bart. Governor of the Province of Pennsylvania, &c. to the General Assembly of the said Province, after passing several Bills, May the 22d.

Mr. Speaker, and the Gentlemen of the Assembly, When we reflect upon the Accident and Difficulties that have occur'd to us during this Assembly, and the candid, friendly Intercourse and Manner by which they have been at last happily composed, we must perceive and be convinced, that not only the form of Civil Government, but even Justice itself cannot be upheld and duly administered, without such a Share of Humanity and Condensation, as is necessary to beget a sincere Confidence between me and the Representatives of the People.

Every just and Good Man, before he undertakes any Office in Government, ought well to consider the End and Design of that Trust wherein he is to be employed, which he will constantly prefer to all Views and appendant Advantages whatsoever. It being therefore the Purport and natural Tendency of all Civil Government, to promote the Prosperity and to secure the Peace and Happiness of the Governed: And we being convinced by Right Reason, as well as instructed from Experience. That there is not any better Means can be proposed for attaining this End, than by adhering steadily to the Execution of the Body of admirable Laws, which have been composed, and so carefully transmitted to the Brave and Free People of England, by the Wisdom of their Ancestors, it follows, and so I hope we shall ever conclude, That the fastest and most satisfactory Way, to promote and secure the Peace and Happiness of the good People of Pennsylvania, will be, to administer impartial Justice in all the Cases whatsoever, according to the known and established Laws of the Land. And as this will be our best and surest Defence against the outrages of the Wicked; So this Excellent plain Role will, one time or other, most certainly bring to Light and overcome the hidden dark Projects, and mistaken Wisdom of Ill-designing Men, if they be any such amongst us.

Gentlemen,
I Heartily thank you for the Support you have given me this Year: And while I am Concious to my self, that I have all Things relating to the Duty of my present Station, faithfully served the King, and at the same time have omitted no Opportunity to maintain, establish and transmit to Prosperity, the just Liberties and Privileges of the free People whom you represent, I shall never doubt their cheerful Inclination and hearty Good Will to grant me, from Time to Time, an honourable and reasonable Support.

NEW-YORK May 23. We are preparing to celebrate this Day in the most splendid Manner we are capable; the Garrison and Militia will be under Arms, the Artillery will be discharged at the Fort and all the Vessels in the Road. At Night the City will be finely illuminated, and a publick Bonfire and Wine at the charge of the

Corporation, to drink to the King's Health, Fireworks and a Ball, and a fine Entertainment at the Fort by his Excellency our Governor, &c.

PHILADELPHIA May 24. There is to be sold by Mr. Scot and Mr. Oliver Galtree's on High-Street near the Prison, Philadelphia, All sorts of Medicines, Drugs, &c. for ready Money, and any Person may be there supplied with Lancets for Bleeding, at very reasonable Rates. They are very choice, and lately came from England.

SUMERSET COUNTY MARYLAND May 24. Run away from Benj. Cottman a Mulatto Slave, aged about 25 Years, called by the name of Lawrence; a thick short, well set Man with bushy Hair, thich in Speech, and speaks Dutch. He spreads very wide at the knees in his Walking. If any Person can secure the said Slave, so that the Owner may have him again, shall have two Pistoles besides reasonable Charges, paid by me, Benjamin Cottman.

CECIL COUNTY MARYLAND May 24. Last Night about two of the Clock there arose a Gust and a clap of Thunder, which enter'd close by the Cock Beam of the East End of the House of Abel Van Burkello, tore the Roof to Pieces, raised the Garret, stove down all the Gable Ends, and coming through the Floor into the Chamber melted a Sword in the Scabboard and a Looking-Glass which hung at the Gable End, shivered a Partition below. In the Room where the Gable End was carried away were Mr. Burkello and Spouse, James Henry, Esq; and Mrs. Ariana Fusby, Capt. William Robertson, three Children, &c. In all Ten Persons, who received blessed be God, no Hurt, except one Child about 3 Years old, but not dangerously.

PHILADELPHIA May 31. A Letter came to us last Post, dated from Hemstead Harbour Long Island, requesting a particular account of the New Bath or Mineral Water found in the Great Valley about 30 Miles Westward of this City, for the Satisfaction of the Publick in general, and of several Gentlemen in particular who are inclined to come to it from those Parts for Relief; though we have by us several Instances of remarkable Cures done by the said Water, we are obliged to defer answering the Gentlemen's

Letter till another Paper, when we hope to give a true and demonstrative Account of the Virtues and Cures.

PHILADELPHIA June 7. To be Sold, A Tall Negro Man, about twenty five Years of Age, and speaks indifferent good English, fit, and has been used to all Sorts of Plantation Work. If any Person has a Mind to purchase him, he will be disposed of at a very remarkable Rate, by Mr. Richard Bermingham near New-Castle.

PHILADELPHIA June 12, Run away from John Sutton of Frankford, two servant Men; one named John Earle, of a middle Stature, about Twenty Years of Age, wearing a Sailors Jacket, Leather Breeches, no Stockings, a Pair of New Shoes, his Hair lately cut off, with a Wollen Cap under his Hat. The other named Peter Roads, a Taylor by Trade, very swarthy Complexion and hath been lately sick; about the Age of Twenty One Years, having on a light coloured Coat and Breeches, and no Stockings. Whoever can secure the said Servants, so that their said Master may have them again, shall have a Pistole Reward for each of them. By me, John Sutton.

PHILADELPHIA June 14. John Housman, Upholsterer, in Market-Street, Philadelphia, leaving off Trade and going to England, will sell what Goods he has very reasonable; consisting chiefly of Standing Beds, Feather-Beds, Quilts, and Blankets, stuffs for Curtains, Chairs, Looking Glasses, Couches, &c. All Persons indebted to him are desired to come and make up their Accounts, and those who have any Demands on him may come and settle the same.

Any Person who have any Buck-Horn by them, or for the future will preserve them, may dispense of them to good Advantage to Mr. John Copson Merchant in Philadelphia.

There is now published and sold by Andrew Bradford at the Bible in Philadelphia, an at William Bradford in New-York, the long and expected Book, calculated particularly for the use of the Publick, entitled, Conductor Generalis; or the Office Duty and Authority of Justices of the Peace, High Sheriffs, Constables, Under-Sherrifs, Goalers, Coroners, Jury-Men,

Overseers of the Poor, and also the Office of Clerk of Assize and of the Peace, &c. Collected out of all Books hitherto written on these subjects, whether Common or Statute-Law.

To which is added, a Collection out of Mathew Hale's Works, concerning the Decent of the Lands. The whole alphabeticalls digested, under the several Titles, with a Table directing to the ready finding out the proper Matter under those Titles.

CECIL COUNTY MARYLAND June 15. Run away from his Master William Cox, at the Head of North-East Maryland, a Servant Man named Henry Toffo, a Swede, Newcastle County Born. A little short Man, having on a Felt Hat, Ozenbrig Shirt, blue Jacket and old Drugget Breeches, with his Hair lately cut off.

Whoever takes him up and secures him, so that his said Master may have him again, shall have a Pistole Reward.

DELAWARE FALLS June 17. Runaway from William Hunt of Bucks County, a Servant Man named Benjamin Hillyard, a Blacksmith, aged about 25 Years, Pretty lusty and Tall, with grey Broadcloth Coat, and brown Home-spun Drugget Coat, an Ozenbrig Jacket, Leather Breeches, with Glass Buttons, black Stockings with round toed shoes, wearing a Wig or Cap, having no hair on. and the said Hillyard hath stolen or taken with him a lusty well set Negro Man, belonging to Samuel Beaks, called Qwam, aged about 22 Years, having on a brown short Kersey Coat with Horn Buttons, a fine red striped Vest, and Breeches grey Stockings: Castor Hat and Garlicks Shirt, having his Right Hand burnt, between his fore Finger and Thumb when a Child. Whoever can take up the said Servant Man and Negro, and secure them so that their said Masters may have them, and give notice to their Masters, shall have three Pounds current Money paid by them
                    William Hunt and Samuel Beaks.

PHILADELPHIA June 19. Ran away from the Iron-Works near Sasquehannah in Maryland, one John Foulks, a Welshman, and a Joiner and Cabinetmaker by Trade, and above 28 Years, middle Stature, short sandy Hair and red Beard. He has a new dark coloured Cloth Coat, Wastcoat and Breeches, with Brass Buttons. He has time passed followed Sawing. It is supposed he had counterfeited a Pass.

Whoever secures him, and brings him to the Iron-Works aforesaid, or to Mr. John Copton, Merchant in Philadelphia, shall have two Pistoles Reward, besides what the Law allows,
Witness my hand   Stephen Onion.

PHILADELPHIA JUNE 28. Run away from the Reverend Mr. Daniel Magill, A.M. at the Head of the Elk River in Maryland, the 17th of June, 1722, a Servant Man named Denis Makenulty, about the Age of 19 Years, a black swarty Visage, and very short black curly Hair, low Stature. Clothed when he went away with Damask Breeches and Vest, and black Broad Cloth Vest, a large double-Breasted Broad cloth Coat well worn, and of a Copper Colour, lined and trim'd with black. He took with him a middle size sorrel Horse, snipt on the Face and switch Tail, carrying with him a large Wallet of very fine Linnen, Shoos and black Stockings, with several Papers which he robbed the House of.

Whoever takes up and secures the said Servant, with the goods, and bring him to his said Master, or send him sure Word, shall over and above all Expences, have Two Pounds current Money.
Given under my Hand,   Daniel Magill.

PHILADELPHIA July 5. To be sold at very reasonable Terms, Two Plantations lying at the Head of Apequininanek Creek in the County of Newcastle, formerly belonging to Capt. Hillyard and Wardman, now the Estate of Sylvester Garland, deceased, joining upon one another, both containing about 500 Acres of very rich well-water'd and timber'd Land, with two very fine large Orchards, a considerable Quantity of clear Land one a very good new House, Barn, Out-houses Fences, Ect. If any desire to buy one or both of the said Places, let them apply themselves to Ebenezer Empson, Esq; near Brandy-Wine-Ferry in Newcastle County, or the Reverend James Anderson in the City of New-York, by whom they may be further informed, both as to the Advantage of the said Land, and the Condition of Sale.

PHILADELPHIA July 12. We hear from Lewis Town, That a Brigantine has been observed to stand in and off our Capes about 2 Leagues Southward, for two or three Days together lately; the Wind being Southerly and blowing an easy Gale. She is supposed to be a Pyrate by most Persons there, having her Main-sail down, her Foresail clued up, and standing under her Topsails; being seen by a great many as they were at Harvest Work, at a Plantation near the Sea-Shore.

PHILADELPHIA July 19. We have Advice from Virginia, That a New Governor is daily expected there.

Ran away from William Webb of Kenner Township in Chester County on the 8th Instant, a Servant Man named John Wilson, aged about 23 Years of a middle Stature, swarthy Complexion, Short Hair, he has on a frize pea Jacket lin'd with Red, a striped woolen Jacket, a Cotton and Linnen pair of Drawers and a pair of White Stockings, and a felt Hat. Who ever takes up and secure him so that his said Master may have him again shall have Forty Shillings as a Reward and Reasonable Charges.

PHILADELPHIA July 22. Arrived a small Sloop; Jonathan Swain Master from Cape May, by whom we have advice, That a Pyrate Brigantine and Sloop have been seen cruising on and off both our Capes for about Three Weeks. They several Times sailed up the Bay Ten or Twelve Leagues; and on the 8th Instant brought a large Sloop down with them, which they took up high in the Bay. That Night they anchored in the Bay about a League and a Half off Shore, beat Drums all Night, and seemed to be very full of Men. What Vessels they have took we know not, none of the Prisoners being sent to Shore.

PHILADELPHIA July 26. Run away on the twenty seventh of June last from Armitage. Smith near the Welch-Tract Apprentice Boy, between 14 and 15 Years of Age, Named Nathan Gumly having some streight Hair, full set face of a fresh complexion thick well-set, having on when he went away a brownish grey Drugget Coat and Wastcoat, the Coat lined with white Flannel and the Wastcoat with stripes, Buckskin Breeches with one

Button at each Knee, Yarn Stockings one thread of Black and the other one White, a felt Hat. Whoever takes up the said Boy and secures him and gives notice thereof to his said Master so that he may have him again shall be well Rewarded for their Pain.

PHILADELPHIA Aug. 2. On Monday the 3d of August at the Court House in Philadelphia, will be exposed to Sale by Publick Vendue, a very good Negro Woman and her Child, a Boy about 9 Years of Age, for the Term of 22 Years: All taken in Execution by, Owen Roberts, Sheriff.

PHILADELPHIA Aug. 9. Yesterday in the Afternoon His Excellency Sir William Keith, our Governor, some of his Council, and several other Gentlemen, set out for New-York, intending to meet and accompany the Governors of York and Virginia to Albany, in order to treat with the Indians there.

Philadelphia Aug. 16. On Sunday Night last several Indentur'd Servants and some inhabitants of the City under suspicions of Debt, went away in a Fishing-Boat, which they stole for that Purpose.

On Monday Night a young Woman was taken up and committed under Suspicion of having been delivered and murdering her Bastard Child.

Yesterday a boy about 17, was executed at Chester, for setting his Master's House on Fire and willfully burning three Children in it, We hear, tho' he is so young, he has confess'd his Course of Life to have been bad so long, that he seems to have been prone and practicing Villainy from his cradle, in a constant series of times to this last. His Speech and Confession being so peculiar, we hope to get it in print.

We have an Account of the safe arrival of his Excellency our Governor at New-York, and Col. John French, as Commissary on the Proper Account of the three lower Counties. On Friday last Andrew Hamilton, Esq; and on Saturday following Richard Hill and Isaac Norris, Esq; three of Governor's Council, appointed by that Honourable Board, with the Approbation of the General Assembly, to attend our Governor to Albany, set hence to meet him in New-York, to proceed on their Journey.

NEW-YORK Aug. 15. On the 15th Instant the Brigantine Mackworth Isaiah Everty Master arrived in 15 Weeks, from Swanzey, in Wales, who has brought a Company of Miners.

PHILADELPHIA Aug. 23. The Speech of the Boy hang'd at Chester is the following:

I William Battin, Son of William Battin of White-Parish in Wiltshire in Great Britain, do think it necessary to leave a few Lines behind me, that the World may in some Measure know something of my past Life, and what ill Use I have made of the time that God was pleased to bestow upon me in this World.

I had my Education under my Parents, and their Care was much over me; but I dishonoured and rebelled against them, and regarded not their Care for me; and through the insinuation of the Enemy I neglected their Business, by wandering abroad. So without due Regard to which is good, I gave up my self to the Devil, and to obey his Voice by yielding to his Temptations; which were Lying and picking and stealing other Mens goods. I shall briefly mention some of the gross Actions which I have committed before and after the Time of my running away from my Parents; which was chiefly stealing of other Mens Goods.

The first thing that I stole was, to the best of my remembrance, a Whalebone Whip from one Henry White, next a Cane from my Uncle John Battin, next a Knife and Fork from one Lawrence Tuck, a Great Coat from a Man in White Parish, and several other Things which were found out by my Parents; For which I was severely Chastised by them.

One Day late in the Afternoon I happened to be at a House of John Neves, there came a Pedlar to ask for Lodging; which was granted to be in the Barn, and I went to shew him the way. After I had stay'd with him a considerable Time he wanted some Drink and so asked me, whether I could get him any? I said Yes; then he would give me a Row of Pins. I searched for Drink and he gave me the Row of Pins; but as he was opening the pack to get the Pins, I spied some Money tied up, and took hold of it: He perceived me,

and asked, what I meddled with it for? After it
was dark, I endeavoured to get the Money again,
but could not; however I got a Parcel of Pins,
and went away with them as fast as I could, and
got home before my Father. Next Morning the
Pedlar miss'd the Pins; when my Father came to
hear of it, he suspected me, and asked, What I
had done with the Pedlar's Pins? I told my Father, that I knew nothing of them; but he did
not believe me, told me, he would ask the Pedlar, and I knowing my self to be guilty, and
that it was likely to be known, made an escape
for several Weeks, for fear of being beaten.
This was the first Time of my running away from
my Parents which Practice I afterwards followed
during my Stay in England.

It's to tedious to mention every Thing I
stole, but the practice very much followed, and
am more guilty that way than you could imagine
a Person my Age could be; of which I shall give
one or two passages more.

On Saturday in the Time of my running away, I
went to a barn, where there was a Man Threshing;
I asked him, if he had another Flail? He told
me, He had. The flail being found, I began to
work: The he asked me, where I had learned to
Thresh? I made Answer, with my Father, And Further I told him, if he would lend me a Silk
Hankerchief to wear the next Day, I would work
with him until Night. He told me he would. When
the Night approached, he desired me to stay in
the Barn all Night, as if any come to steal the
Oats, to acquaint him of it, and he would give
me a Silk Hankerchief the next Morning; but no-
body came, and to make it appear as if there had
I took a Shovel that was in the Barn and made a
Hole in the Oats, and flung them about. The Man
came in the Morning, and seeing the Oats so much
scarttered, asked if nay body had been there?
For the sake of a Silk Handkerchief I told a
Lie, saying, That my own Uncle, John Battin,
had been there in the Night to steal Oats: It
evidently appeared to the contrary, for which I
was apprehended, put into Prison, whip'd and
set at Liberty again.

The next thing I stole was a Silver Watch of

the Value of Five Pounds, from one that I intended to serve as an Apprentice with, and about an Hour after I had stole it, I sold it to a Man for an English Half Crown; when my intended Master came to understand that I had stole the Watch he put me in Prison, and after three Days he took me out again and whipped me very severely: But I took no Warning, and soon found an Opportunity to make my Escape, taking with me a Beaver Hat, a Suit of Clothes and a Shirt; since which he never saw me.

This was the Course I followed when I was in England.

My Father seeing that there was not any Good like to come of me, ordered me to be brought over a Servant into the Province of Pennsylvania. About 7 or 8 Days after the Ship, which brought me over, was safely arrived here, I was sold to one John Hunam of Concord in Chester County. I had scarcely lived with him but three Months before I fell again into my old Practice of stealing and running away; for which cause, after I had lived with said Hunam about one Year, he sold me to Joseph Pyle, (of Bethel) in the said County, with whom I continued in the old Practice of Stealing &c.

And now, as the Word of a Dying Person, I give this further Information, to satisfy all that desire to know concerning the burning of the said Pyle's House, and his three Children Viz. Robert, aged about 6 Years; Joseph. aged about 4 Years, and Ralf Pyle, aged about 2 Years; which I declare to be the whole truth.

On Saturday about Sun-set my Master and Mistress went from Home, to the House of Nathaniel Newlin jun. of Concord aforesaid. About an Hour or something better, after they were gone I put the Children to Bed, and the two eldest in one and the youngest in another; when I had, so done, I took the Candle and went up Stairs to get Apples, near which they lay a great Heap of Flax, whilst I was taking Apples, it immediately came into my Mind, through the Insinuation and will of the Devil, to fire the House, and burn that and the Children together, thinking thereby to have better Opportunity to run away, from concluding others would imagine myself were also burnt. To Accomplish this barbarous and wicked Design, I fired the Flax with the Flame of the Candle; and after it had burnt a little while, my Heart failed, so that I could not offer to make my Escape, believing I should be caught, this made me, whilst the Fire was increasing to run down the Stairs to get Water to quench it, which, as I then thought, I had effectually done, and so vent down stairs and laid myself down by the Fire, to wait for my Mr. and Mrs. coming Home. After I had slept a while a great Noise like the Firing of a Gun awakened me, which made me run up the Stairs, where I found the Fire had revived again and the Flames raging through the Roof of the House. I Endeavoured to quench it again but it was beyond my Power so to do; As I came down stairs, the youngest child got up, I asked him what made him rise? He told me, he wanted his Mummy; I gave him a Slap with my Hand and put him to Bed again. After I found I could not quench the Fire, I then thought of taking the Children out of the House but the Devil put into my mind to leave them to be burnt, I need not care whether they were saved or not. I then Ran to the said Newlin's, about a Mile and a Half off, to acquaint my Master and Mistress that the House was burning; they presently asked me, Where the Children were? I made answer, hearing them Mourning lest their Children should be in Danger, that they were out of the House. Then was I smitten with Terror concerning them, whom I had unmercifully left to be destroyed by Fire, being afraid it was too late to rescue them from it; which indeed it was, to the great Sorrow of their Parents and others.

The Villainy I endeavoured to conceal as long as I could: But knowing myself to be Guilty of the Blood of these innocent Children, it lay with such heavy Conviction upon my Conscience, that I confess'd to the Truth of this Wickedness in Part, being also strongly importuned by several so to do. And since this, I have been guilty of the vile and abominable Sin of buggery with a Sow.

I had a fair Tryal, and also received great Favour beyond my Deserving, by being allowed so long Time to crave Forgiveness for my Sins; but I have made such bad Use of this Favour, that before my Tryal, at the Time of it, and afterwards, I continued in Obstinacy, and denied the Truth which I had before confess'd, till within these few Days.

My Judge and Jury had done nothing but Justice, and according to their just Sentence of Death pronounced against me, I am brought to this Place of Execution.

I am just now, good People, going to make my Appearance in the other World, where I must give an Account of all the Actions of my past Life. My Sins are so atrocious and so many, that I can hardly expect Forgiveness such admittance in the Favour of God.

I greatly desire all Youth may take Example by me, and have a Care how they disobey their Parents; when if I had not done, I should not have been here this Day, not brought to this untimely End.

I declare, in the Face of the World, my hearty Abhorrence and Detestation of my Sins; and I trust in God, of his infinite Mercy, through Jesus Christ who died for me, that he will pardon my Transgressions. I also ask forgiveness of my Master and Mistress, whom I have greatly injured, by being instrumental to the Death of their poor Children; and others whom I have offended.

You who are Standers by, I desire your Prayers for me to God, that my Sins may enter before me to Judgement, and that they may not be laid at my Charge.

I yield my Body to this shameful and ignominious Death This 15 Day of August 1722. being about Seventeen Years of Age, hoping that God will have Mercy upon my poor Soul. Lord Jesus receive my Spirit.

This Speech and Confession was taken in Prison by William Davies of Chester, Schoolmaster, in the Presence of Thomas Griffing and John Hughes, signed with the Mark of William Battin, and read at the Gallows before his Execution.

PHILADELPHIA Aug. 30. We have information of a considerable Merchant here, who finding what an Ill Character our Flour has gained in the West-Indies, by the villainess and fraudulent Ways of some Traders, designed to lay out his ready Money in another Province for their Flour, which, he has got here by selling his Goods. A Practice which, if Follow'd must soon ruin all our Trade; and yet who can blame the Merchant, without they have a mind he thought meet with the same ill fortune and loss as S. M. & J. A. This is publish'd to deter the Persons guilty from the Practice, lest they should be publickly exposed. We are in some Hopes, that the Act lately made against shipping off Flour not Merchantable will retrieve our Character of sending the best Flour to the Islands.

PHILADELPHIA Sept. 6. Committed to the Custody of John Hall, Esq; Sheriff of Bucks-County in Pennsylvania, A Young Man, (aged by his own Account 22 Years) has on a thick woolen Jacket and another under it of Cotton, an Ozenbrig Shirt, and Breeches and a pretty good Felt Hat, is of a short stature, red Hair sanquine Complexion. He says he belongs to John Garner a Gardener at Chapham-Point on Petapsko-River, about 13 Miles below a Ferry kept by Thomas Hugh.

He says he left his said Master the 27th of December last, and had lived since with the Sheriff of Newcastle, till he had hanged a Woman there, after which Service he gave him a Pass, since which he came to Chester and hanged a Boy.

This is to give Publick Notice that the said John Garner, in order that he may have his said Servant again.

PHILADELPHIA Sept. 6. Made his Escape from the Sloop Benjamin, Samuel Borrows, Master, from Jamaica, after he lay at Marcus Hook a Tall Negro Man named Archard, aged about 45 Years, having a Scar under one of his Paps. He talks very good Portuguese, and pretty good English, bleeds well, and he is a good Diver. He jump'd overboard and swam down with the Tide of Ebb, having on only a Pair of Breeches.

Whoever shall apprehend him, and bring him to Mr. Joseph Lloyd, Merchant in New-York, shall have 3 Pounds Reward and all Charges defray'd.

PHILADELPHIA Sept. 13. A Tract of Land at Shewsbury in the County of Monmouth, to be sold, containing about 217 Acres, with a great Parcel of Meadow and Upland cleared; Bounded on the East by the Land of John Clayton, on the North by the Never-Sinks-River, West by a Highway, and South by W. Bickley and Abraham's Meadow. Lately in the Tenure and Occupation of Nathaniel Milner, Merchant deceased.

Any Person who has a Mind to purchase, may have an undisputable Title made to it. Enquire of Mr. William Chancellor in Philadelphia, or Richard Wright in Burlington.

PHILADELPHIA Sept. 14. Run away the 2d of this Instant September, from Ambrose Barcroft of Solebury near Buckinham-Meeting-House in Bucks-County, Pennsylvania, Thomas Rolse, He is a short-set middle ag'd Man, with short sad coloured Hair, and took with him a Fustian Frock, a Snuff coloured Cloth Coat, a grey Kersey Wastecoat, one pair of Buck-skin Breeches and a Pair of Linnen Drawers, and several Pairs of Stockings, all much wore; likewise one old speckled Shirt and 3 white Ones. He has a small Scar upon his Lower Lip. and a large Scar upon his upper lip.

Whoever can secure him and give Notice thereof to Ambrose Barcroft abovesaid, shall have Forty Shillings Reward and reasonable Charges, paid by   Ambrose Barcroft.

NEW-YORK Sept. 17. Richard Hill, Isaac Norris and Andrew Hamilton, Esqs; three of the Council for the Province of Pennsylvania, who were appointed Commissioners to attend His Excellency Sir W. Keith, Bart. Governor of the Province, to Albany, on a Treaty with the Indians there, arrived this Morning, having had amicable Meeting and Treaty with the said Indians, and renewed the Covenant Chain with them, to the Satisfaction of all Parties. Col. John French, Commissioner of the same Service for the Lower Counties of Pennsylvania, is also arrived; and His Excellency W, Burnet, Esq; our Governor,

Col. Spotwood, Governor of Virginia, and Sir, W. Keith, Governor of Pennsylvania, are expected here in a Day or two.

FREEHOLD Sept. 26. Broke out of Monmouth Goal in East-Jersey, One Edmund Mackandres, age about 30 Years: A lusty round shouldered Fellow, with dark brown Hair. He is a Pale faced Man. And one William Connar, age about 24 Years. A short thin favoured Man, a little bandy-legged, wears a Wig. And also one John Emans, a well set Man, aged about 30 Years. He has a dark brown bushy Hair, a ruddy Complexion, and has a little of the Dutch Accent.

Whoever secures them, or any of them, shall have for each three Pounds, besides reasonable Charges, paid them by High-Sheriff of the said County.

PHILADELPHIA Sept. 27. Run away from James Heath, at the Head of Sassafras in Maryland, a Negro Man named Jack. He has worked at Carpenter Work. He is a short well-sett Fellow his nose Rising, and has with him a brindled Dog. If any Person can and will secure him, and give Notice to Mr. Charles Head in Philadelphia, Dr. Ryley at New-Castle, or Mr. Andrew Peterson at Apequinimanch, so as he may be conveyed to his Master, shall not only be well paid for the same but also have all reasonable Charges allowed and paid by   John Heath.

NEW-YORK Oct. 1. On the 27th Capt. Greenock arrived in a Schooner from Virginia, who says, That about 200 Negroes near the Mouth of Rastahenack River in that Colony (some which belonged to one Mr. Churchell) got together in a Body Armed with an intent (as it is said) to fall upon the People when in Church, but they being discovered the same Negroes made their escape into the Woods, only five being taken.

PHILADELPHIA Oct. 3. Capt. Owen in the Ship Hanover from Holand, but last from Cowes, who lies in sight of this Port, having on board above 130 Palatine Passengers, who are come to settle in this Country, and we are inform'd that a Vessel with 600 more designed for this Port.

NEW-YORK Oct. 8. On Friday last about Twelve

a Clock at Night, a House full of Tanner's Bark, a Smoke House and a Work-House were burnt Down, All belonging to Samuel Weaver of this City, Tanner; The loss is upward of 2 Hundred Pounds, and is believed to be done willfully: 2 Persons are committed on Suspicion.

PHILADELPHIA Oct. 25. Ran away the 30th of September 1722 from Philip Taylor, David Danis, Richard Bavenson, and Thomas Marshal of Chester County in the Province of Pennsylvania, 4 Servant Men one named William Varill, aged about 23 Years, pretty tall, Fresh coloured, black Hat, brown Hair, brownish Coat and Vest, lined with Shaloon, new linnen Drawers and old Shoos and Stockings. Another Man named William Beaumont, aged 23 Years of a middle Stature, black bushy Hair, thin Visage, Pimples on his Cheeks, new Felt Hat, dark brown Home-Spun Coat old Leather Breeches, grey Yarn Stockings, and New Shoos. Another Man named John Chapman, old Felt Hat, short black Hair, striped Jacket, linnen Drawers, Ozenbrig Shirt, 2 Pairs of Stockings, one old the other one new, and a new Pair of Shoos. Another Man, low Stature, named Edward Cooke, reddish Hair and Beard, a new Felt Hat, striped Jacket and Breeches, new Yarn Stockings, Shoos going back at the Heels.

any Person or Persons that can take up and secure the said Servants, or any of them, so that their said Masters may have them again, shall have 30 Shillings per Head Reward, and reasonable Charges, paid by their respective Masters.

PHILADELPHIA Oct. 25. Several Sorts of Household Goods and Houses to be sold by Sarah Redman. All People that are indebted to the Estate of Joseph Redman, lately deceased, are desired to come to her at her house, and settle their Accounts and pay forthwith.

NEW-York Oct. 29. Arrived here a Pink from Harwich with 200 Palatines taken in Rotterdam in Holland.

PHILADELPHIA Nov. 1. General Post Office. Whereas Masters of Vessels and Passengers do, upon arrival in the several Harbours of North America, deliver many of their Letters and

Packets to the Persons they are directed, instead of the Post Office, to the great Prejudice of His Majesty's Revenue, and contrary to a Clause in the Act of Parliament of the 9th of Queen Anne, which inflicts a Penalty of Five Pounds Sterling for every Letter or Packet delivered contrary thereunto.

These are to give Notice, That from hence forward the Clause before mentioned will be put in Execution against such Masters of Vessels and Passengers, as shall not deliver their Letters and Packets to the Post Master in the several Ports; who have Orders to pay the Bringer a Penny Sterling for every Letter or Packet delivered to them, or shall be equal there unto in the Currency of the several Governments where such Letters are delivered, according to the Course of Exchange.

And whereas many Letters and Packets at times are brought by Passengers travelling the Post Roads, and Masters of Coasting Vessels in North America, and by them delivered to the Persons they are addressed, to the manifest Prejudice of His Majesty's Revenue, and contrary to the before-mentioned act, which inflicts also a Penalty of Five Pounds Sterling for every Letter or Packet carried and delivered as aforesaid.

These are to forewarn all Persons, That the Post-Office Act will from henceforth be put in Execution against such as shall carry and deliver Letters and Packets in the Manner before Mentioned.

  John Lloyd, D. Post Office Master General.

PHILADELPHIA Nov. 8. The Speech of His Excellency Sir William Keith, Bart. Governor of the Province of Pennsylvania, and the Counties of Newcastle, Kent and Sussex, October 22d 1722.

Mr. Speaker and Gentlemen of the Assembly, As my Treaty with the Indians at Albany, which had been lately published, give you an Opportunity to Judge of the Importance of that Service, so it likewise gives me Occasion to acquaint you, That I was in the Management of the Conduct of that Business, very faithfully assisted by the Ability and indefatigable Application of your Present Speaker, who, at my Request, readily undertook the Fatigue of that Journey, to take care of and represent the Interest of these Counties, at a Treaty which he rendered the whole People of the Government much more considerable, in the Esteem and Hearts of the Indians, then ever they were at any time before.

It having pleased God therefore to crown my Endeavours in the Publick Service, even with unexpected Success, it will, I doubt not, occur to the Justice of your Thoughts, That some reasonable Care ought to be taken by the People Representatives, so to express their Satisfaction with a Service of this Kind, that, instead of suffering the Officers therein employ'd to be oppressed with the Burthen of the whole Charge and Expence, they be rather rewarded, in such a Publick and Handsome Manner, as will not only encourage them in the Prosecution of their Duty, but others after them to their good Example.

It was indeed my thoughts, to have called the last Assembly together before I went to Albany, in order to have made some Provisions for the Expence of the Journey; but when I considered the Inconveniences that would have attended their own Homes at that busy time of the Season of the Year, and especially when I reflect on the happy Confidence and perfect good Understanding, that was last Year re-established me and the People, and finding Col. French as ready as my self to rely upon the Justice and Gratitude of this Assembly, rather than put the Country, at that Time, to be Troubled and Charge of Calling the Representatives together, I took Resolutions which most happily succeeded hitherto, and which, I hope, have give you all the Satisfaction and Conduct you can desire.

Gentlemen,
It only remains with me to assure you, That I am come here, at this Time, with a Heart entirely disposed to grant every Thing you can ask of me, for the Happiness and Service of your Country, and to assist you therein to the utmost of my Power.

NEW-YORK Nov. 11. Col. Taylor and other Gentry (with our Mohocks) are returned from the

Eastward, could not meet with any Indians; but found a Letter left for them, The Eastern Indians will not have any Peace with them.

PHILADELPHIA Nov. 15. Ran away from William Yard of Trenton in West-Jersey, the fifth Day of November, a Negro Man named Fransh Manuel, but commonly called Manuel, of pretty tall Stature, and speaks indifferent English. He wears a dark coloured Home-spun Coat, an Asenbrig Jacket, old Leather Breeches, Sheep-russet Stockings, new Shoes and an old battered Hat. He pretended formerly to be a Freeman, and had Passes; but he did belong to one John Raymond of Fairfield in New-England, and I bought him of the said Raymond. And the said Negro has told since he has run away, That he found a Body of ore for his Master, and that his Master has given him free. Whoever takes up the said Negro secure him and bring him to William Bradford of New-York, or to Mr. William Burge of Philadelphia, or said Master at Trenton, shall have forty Shillings Reward besides reasonable charges paid by me,   William Yard.

PHILADELPHIA Nov. 23. Run away from Ezekiel Balding of Hempstead on Long Island, one Indian Man Slave, named Dick of middle Stature and a smiling Countenance. He speaks English pretty well, and no other Language. He can read. He has a big Nose, and has white Scratches on his Arm, and a blue spot on the inside of one of his Wrist, a little above his Shirt wrist-bands. He ran away about the beginning of September and had a Home-spun Shirt and a dark coloured Drugget Coat. We have been informed, that he had intended to get into Indian Habit, Other tell that he said he would go towards New-London and Rhode-Island, and so to Sea.

Whoever can take up the said Indian Man, and secure him, and give Notice to his Master so that he can be had again, shall receive Three Pounds Reward besides reasonable Charges.

PHILADELPHIA Dec. 18. Thomas Denham to his good Country Friends advertiseth, That he Hath some likely Servants to dispose of. These are to give Notice, That One Hundred Palatines will be disposed of for Five Years each, anyone paying their Passage Money at Ten Pounds per Head. If any of their Friends the Dutch at Conestogoe, have a mind to have or clear any of them, the Ship lies in Elk-River, which is nearer to them than Philadelphia; but in about a Fortnight's Time they will leave the Ship and come to this Port of Philadelphia.

PHILADELPHIA Dec. 18. Run away William Hunt at Falls-Ferry in Bucks-County, a Servant Man named David Rives, aged about Twenty Years, fair Hair, fresh Countenance, wears an old Felt Hat, or a woolen Cap, a speckled Shirt, a dark coloured Sailors Jacket lined in blue, course Kersey black and white Yarn Stockings, round toed Shoos, speaks West Country, by Occupation a Farmer. Whoever takes up the said Servant, and brings or sends him to his said Master, shall have a Pistole Reward, with reasonable Charges paid by me   William Hunt.

Run away from his Master William Hayes of Philadelphia, Shipwright, Andrew Kees an Irish Man, short Stature, dark brown Hair somewhat curling, aged about 25 Years by Appearance, and round Visage. Whoever shall discover and take him, so as his Master may have him again, shall receive Thirty Shillings and reasonable Charges paid by me   William Hayes.

NEW-YORK Dec. 24. Yesterday was Fortnight a Brigantine from Ireland, one Holmes Master, with about 100 Passengers and Servants bound for New-London, run ashore at Mannisquan about 14 or 15 Miles from Sandy-Hook the People were all saved, but the Vessel lost.

Also a Brigantine bound from Antigua to New-Haven one Tammago Master, run ashore on the South side of Long Island with Salt and Rum &c. It is supposed the Vessel will not be got off again.

PHILADELPHIA Dec. 26. The New-York Post designed to perform his Stage for the Winter-Quarter only once a fortnight; so that every other Paper during that Time, will contain material Advice he brings.

Very good English Pease and Spanish Snuff, to be sold by Andrew Bradford.

1723

PHILADELPHIA Jan. 1. Publick Notice is hereby Given, That in or about the Month of August Anno. 1721 George Fraser then Master of the Sloop William lying at Anchor at Amboy in New-Jersey, having one of his Men Run away who had received a Months pay, William Cox of Middlesex (who was part owner of the sloop) advised the said Master to leave a Power of Attorney to sue the said Sailor, if he cou'd be found. whereupon the said George Fraser being then just weighing Anchor the same day to sail, had not time to make a Letter of Attorney, but signed to a blank sheet of Paper with two Witnesses to it, to wit, Henry Longfield and Jacob Illison, in order for the Cox to write a Letter of attorney above it, to impower him to sue the said Sailor, that was run away. Upon the Return of the said Sloop, the said Fraser demanded his blank sheet of Paper of Power of Attorney, but the said Cox, put him off, pretending he could not find it, some time after he told him he had seen it among his Papers, and now again says he has lost it. These are therefore to give Notice, that if any Person have found the said Paper (and not received it from the said William Cox) and will bring it to the said George Fraser or to Mr. Andrew Johnson in Amboy, they shall be very well Rewarded for the same. These are also to advise and forewarn all Persons that they be careful not to pay obedience to any Power of Attorney that the said William Cox may produce to recover any Debts so due to the said Fraser, and that if the said William Cox should offer to sell or dispose of any Land or part of Vessel or Vessels belonging to the said George Fraser, that they desist buying of him the said Cox, he having no Power so to do, nor has he any Bill or Bond or other Paper of the said George

Fraser, but only the Blank sheet of Paper above mentioned, to which there are as Witnesses, Henry Longfield and Jacob Illison as above mentioned, And it is to be hoped the said William Cox will not make any ill use of the said Blank sheet of Paper altho' he does not deliver it up, nor give any Release of Acquaintance of or for the same, upon earnest application to him for such Relief or Acquaintance.

PHILADELPHIA Jan. 1. We hear the Snow said to be bound here from Holland is safe arrived at the Porr of New-York with their Palatine Passengers on Board.

Ran away from Samuel Dennis jun. of Shewsbery in Monmouth County, the 18th of December 1722, a Servant Man named James McCurdy, aged about 22 Years. He came from Ireland in the Vessel that was Cast away the 9th of this Month in Mannisquan. He is of a low Stature Indifferent thick set. Speaks English and Irish, he can read and write, He has with him some Books, two or three Shirts, a large felt Hat, an old yellow Wig, black short Hair, of a pale Complexion, a thread bare blew Coat and Button Holes bound, a Cinnamon coloured Vest, an old pair of Leather Breeches, Sheeps coloured black Stockings with several holes in them, an old pair of round toe Shoes. Whoever can take up said Servant and secure him so that his Master may have him again shall have a Pistole Reward besides reasonable Charges.

NEW-YORK Jan. 7. Last New-Years Day at Night, Widow Lawrences Shop was broke open, and about 60 or 70 Pounds worth of Goods stolen. Two Days after the Goods were found in the Chest of a Stranger, who has been a Sea faring Man. He says he came last from Barbadoes, wears a long Beard, and went about Town begging. He is committed to Goal, and a special Commission is granted for trying him and another young Man belonging to New-Jersey, for breaking open a Boat the same Night, and stealing a Parcel of Money.

PHILADELPHIA Jan. 14. On the 4th of this Instant, one David Drewry was hanged at Gloucester in West-Jersey. He was whip'd out of the City not Three Months ago for Thievery, and confessed several facts of the like Nature since, besides that for which he was executed. He was a Man who had a faculty so propense to Stealing, that he would steal for no thought of Profit, and give it away the next Hour; and some say he never made a Farthing of any thing he ever stole, but was so unfortunate that he was catch'd and whip'd for Thievery at all the most most noted Towns in this and our Neighbouring Colony. But at last had so much Grace left in him as to die penitent.

PHILADELPHIA Jan. 15. These are to give Notice, That the Palatines who were before Advertised to be at the Head of Elk-River in Maryland are now come up to Philadelphia, and will be disposed of for Five Years each, any one paying their passage Money at Ten Pounds per Head. If any of their Friends the Dutch at Conestogoe, have a mind to have or clear any of them, may see them at this Port.

PHILADELPHIA Jan. 29. Lost or Strayed away, about the 14th or 15th of November last, from Mr. Dickinson's Nich, near Frankford in Pennsylvania, a large and dark coloured Mare, formerly belonging to Robert King, Collector of Amboy, and bred by Sam. Nostrict of Aneccos Creek in West-Jersey, whither she strayed sometime before, and was found by George Matlock, who lives between Gloucester and Salem. The said Mare is branded on each Buttock with two S's and is particularly remarkable for white Hair of the side of her Nose. Whoever shall secure the said Mare, and bring her to Mr. Hunlock of Burlington, or Mr. Bagley of New Bristol, or Mr. Stevens at Amboy, in order to be returned to the owner, shall have a Pistole Reward, besides all reasonable Charges defrayed.

Stray or Stolen away from Israel Pemburton of Philadelphia the 23d of last Month a Dun Horse with a large black Mane and black list down her Back, a short switch Tail, with a large Brand on her near Buttock in the form of a Sheeve Mold; He paces well. Whoever brings said Horse to Israel Pemburton in this City of Philadelphia shall have 20 Shillings Reward.

All Persons who have any Demands against the

Estate late of Maurice Lifler, deceased, are desired to bring their Accounts to Mary Lifler, Widow and administratrix of the said deceased, at Henry Baderk's: And those that are indebted to the said Estate, are desired to pay with speed, to prevent Trouble.

PHILADELPHIA Feb. 12. There is lately arriv'd in this City a Person who freely offers his Services to teach his poor Brethren the Negroes to read the Holy Scriptures, &c. in very uncommon, expeditious and delightful Manner, without any Manner of Expence to the respective Masters or Mistresses. All serious Persons, whether Roman Catholicks, Episcopalians, Presbyterians, independent, Water-Baptist, or People who are called Quakers, who are truly concern'd for their Salvation, may advise with the said Person at his Lodging (relating to the Time and Place of his so instructing them) at the Dwelling-House of John Read, Carpenter in High-Street Philadelphia every Morning till Eight of the Clock, except the Seventh-Day.

All Persons who have an Account with Edward Carelon, late of Philadelphia, Merchant, are desired to bring them to John Harrison, living in the Second Street or Benjamin Pascal at the lower End of High Street in order to adjust the same. And those who are indebted on the same Estate of Edward Carleton, are desired to come and pay the same with speed, or expect further trouble.

PHILADELPHIA Feb. 19. On Thursday the 7th Instant there happened in Bucks-County a violent Storm of Wind and Rain, attended with several Claps of Thunder and Lightning, which struck the Pole in the middle of a Hay stack, set it on Fire, and consumed the Hay Immediately.

All Persons who are indebted to Samuel Hackney in the High-street near the Market, are desired to come and pay the same, to prevent speedy Trouble; and those to whom he is indebted are desired to bring their Accounts, in order to be adjusted by reason of designs to leave this City of Philadelphia and depart for Great Britain in about a Months Time.

PHILADELPHIA Feb. 26. Publick Notice is hereby

Given, That the Post from this city of Philadelphia to the City of Annapolis in Maryland, will set out (God willing) about the middle of March next. All Merchants and others, who have any Letters or Parcels to send, are desired to put them in the Bag for that Purpose at the Post Office in Philadelphia, whence they will be carefully convey'd to the respective Places and Persons to which they are directed. From the middle of March next ensuing, the Post is designed to keep a constant Fortnight Stage to and from the said City of Annapolis to Philadelphia.
William Atchison.

A very likely Negro Woman, fit for all sorts of House Business to be sold by Andrew Bradford in the Second-street Philadelphia.

PHILADELPHIA March 7. Broadcloth, Druggets, Doroys, Serges, Glass-ware, Tin-ware and Hardware, to be sold at 75 per cent. as shall appear from the true invoice, for Paper Money, Gold or Silver, by Celeb Jacobs, in High-street near the Market, in Philadelphia.

Very good Red Clover Seed, at 12 d. per Pound, or 10 S. per Dozen, to be Sold at the Shop of Frank Knowles in High-street, near the Market Philadelphia.

PHILADELPHIA March 14. Ready Money, at a good price for all sorts of light and gray Hair, by George Sheed, Perrywigg-Maker in the Front-street, near door to Vitner's Arms, in Philadelphia.

this is to give Notice, that there is a Tract of Land to be sold in Ridly near Darby in the County of Chester, containing 290 Acres about 90 cleared, well fenced, and also good coveniency for making Meadow; the Land formerly belonged to Jacob Simcock, and will be sold by William Smith and John Wood of Darby, and John Crosby and John Dutton of Chester-County, of which Persons those that are inclined to buy may enquire, it will be sold at very reasonable Rates.

PHILADELPHIA March 21. To be sold at a store on Redman's Wharf. All sorts of Scotch Linnens and other Goods very Reasonable, by Wm. Dunlop.

PHILADELPHIA March 24. Run away from Rev.

Daniel Magil of London-Tract, on New-Castle County, a Servant Lad named Denis Macanoully about 18 Years of Age, of a swarthy Complexion, with a brown Coat and Sailors Jacket, a Beaver Hat, Leather Breeches, Canvis-Drawers under them, without any Hair on his Head. Whoever shall secure the said Run-away and bring him to his said Master, shall have 20 Shillings Reward besides the Allowance according to the Law of the County.

CHESTER March 27. Made an Escape last Night out of the county Goal of Chester, one William Pricket, of a large Stature, well limbed, brown Complection, short black curled Hair, and is Main'd of his left Hand by the firing of a Gun, has on a narrow brim'd Hat, a brown fashionable cloth Pair of Breeches, square to'd Shoes and dark grey Stockings. Whoever takes up and secures to said William Pricket, that he may be forth-coming, shall have Five Pounds Reward Paid by   John Taylor Sheriff.

PHILADELPHIA March 27. By advice from Sumerset County in Maryland, we have the following Relation, that on the 23d and 24th of February last, there was a great Storm of Wind and Rain, which occasioned the overflowing all the Meadows, and drowned several Hundred Cattle, (some say about 1000 Heads) Several Storehouses were wash'd away by the Sea, and most of their dry Goods, particular Pork, were carried away by the Inundation: Some of that in Barrels, was recover'd again; but as for that in bulk it was all lost. The same Time the Rev. Adams, Mr. Stotre the Collector and Mr. Deskele with several others were drowned as they were passing in a Boat from Weeckaco------ to Annapolis.

PHILADELPHIA March 28. Publick Notice is hereby Given. To all Persons who shall want any large or small Quantities of Lime, merchantable and well-burn'd, that, they may be furnish'd with the same by Nicholas Scull, at the Sign of the George in the Second-street, Philadelphia, at a very reasonable Price, and at the first Hand, the Limeburner of this County having employed him as their Factor.

PHILADELPHIA April 4. Last Saturday the General

Assembly of this Province adjourn'd to May next. the first 5 of the following Acts were passed the 22d and the other 8 on the 30th of March.

An Act for making Current 15000 Pounds in Bills of Credit.

An Act to rectify proceedings upon Attachments.

An Act for Vesting the Lands and Lots of the Free Society of Trade in Pennsylvania, in trustees to be sold &c.

An Act for Respiting Executions upon certain Judgements of Court.

An Act directing the Process of Summons. against Freeholders.

A Supplement Act to the Act for making Current Bills of Credit.

An Additional Act to the Law of Excise.

An Act for Encouraging Trade.

An Act for Regulating and Establishing Fees.

A Supplement Act to the Act for making good Flour, &c.

A Supplement Act to the Act of making good Beer.

An Act for Establishing a Ferry over the River Schuylkill, at the End of High-street.

PHILADELPHIA April 4. Run away from John Gooding of Ready-Island in the County of New-Castle a Servant Lad aged about 18 or 19 Years, swarthy Complexion and slender, having short Hair, an old Hat, Homespun gray Kersey Coat, and Breeches and a blackish Vest with Pewter Buttons. Whoever shall take up said Run-away, and secure Him so that his Master may have him again shall have 40 Shillings and reasonable Charges paid by,   John Gooding.

PHILADELPHIA April 11. We have advice from Jamaica, That the Hoy Delaware, S. Hayman Master, bound from this Port to N. Carolina, in July last was taken by a Spanish Pirate, and also a New-England Vessel which they Burnt, and carry'd the Hoe into Barraco, on the North side of Cuba. It is also Reported that they are fitting out from Barraco 3 or 4 Spanish Privateers, or Pirates, to come on our Coast this Spring.

Ran away the First of this Instant, from Mr. William Chapman and Mr. Richard Hill (both of

London-Town in Maryland,) Two Servant Men viz. Richard Wooten by Trade a Carpenter of Middle Stature, he wears a Horse-Hair Wigg, a Dark coloured Coat, a Black Caliminco Vest and Breeches. Joseph Beckett, by Trade a Bricklayer, ne is Tall and Slender of Stature, Pockfretten, has a Mole with Black Hair on his Face, and a Scar on his Arm, he wears a New suit of Sagothee Cloaths and a Blew Duffils loose Coat, and has a light Wigg. Whoever will secure them and give notice to Richard Hill of Philadelphia shall have Five Pounds Reward.

PHILADELPHIA April 18. We have advice from Amboy, that on the 11th Instant, a Brigantine and a Sloop were seen to come into Sandy Hook, the Brigantine came to anchor but the Sloop stood up of New-York, but it not yet Arrived there, and it is much feared they are Pyrates.

This Morning Capt. Butterfield arrived in 16 Days from Bermuda, he saw lying at an Anchor off Senepuxon two Sloops and a Brigantine, one of them fitted out a Pereauger and sent after him, which came pretty near him and then he fired two Shots at the Pereauger and when they at Anchor saw it, one of them immediately weigh't Anchor and gave him Chase, If they be pyrates as they seem to be, our Vessels which are now Daily expected are in great Danger.

To be Sold by Mr. Alexander Woodrop in Waterstreet near the Crane on Abraham Bickley's Wharf, a Parcel of very likely Negroes viz. Two Negro Boys and one Negro Girl. Also Several sorts of good Cordial Water at 5 s. per Gallon by the Quanty.

Whereas about 3 Months ago a Certain Number of Palatines (being all Indentured Servants) were Imported into this Province, several Family's of them ask'd leave of the Importer to go towards New-York, to seek their Relations in order to get Money to pay for their Time and clear themselves from Servitude, which was granted them on promise to return again in a Month's time, which they have neglected to do; These are therefore to give Notice that if they return not before the 10th Day of May next, that they shall be prosecuted as run aways, and strict search made after them. They are required to apply themselves to Mr. Gearge M'Call Merchant in Philadelphia, and their return, or send their money, which is due, to him, within the abovementioned time.

NEW-CASTLE April 25. The Speech of his Excellency Sir William Keith, Bart. Governor of the Province and Counties of New-Castle, Kent and Sussex upon Delaware. To the General Assembly of the said Counties at New-Castle.

Mr. Speaker and Gentlemen of the Assembly, I Hope this Session will give the People a freshly and singular Instance of our unanimous disposition to answer their Inclinations, as to Comply with all their reasonable Desires, which indeed I ever Understood to be the Duty of General Assemblies in America: But as the Happiness and Prosperity of the Government is no less Concerned in the Due Execution, that in the just framing of wholesome and good Laws, I must recommend to you, Gentlemen, who are more immediately Intrusted with dispensing the Benefits and advantages Intended by the Legislature to the People; That after having Discharged your Conferences by taking such care of the Publick Interest under your Management, as the Act for Emitting a Paper Currency directs, you will then suffer your selves to be moved with a Christian and tender Compassion for your distress'd neighbours, and Unanimously Rejoice the Providence has put it in your Power, To give them some Relief without any berthen to you or Prejudice and hurt of any other Person whatsoever.

Gentlemen,
I Most heartily thank you for the Consideration you have had of my Trouble on this Occasion, I receive it kindly at your hands, and will use my best Endeavours to give entire Satisfaction in those Particulars, which you have left to my care.

PHILADELPHIA April 25. Whereas on the 13th of this Instant April, Two Negro Boys the one named Tom and the other Kent, aged about 16 Years each, with Azenbrigs Britches and Shirts, and a Negro Girl named Cleo, about the same age, all of them Marked on the Right Shoulder with a red hot Iron R. T. and the shape of a Heart over the Letters, belonging to Hugh Hughs and Henry Munday, were Inveagled or Stolen away from Philadelphia, and supposed to be carried up Delaware River. And it appears by several Affidavits made in this City, the said Negroes were seen in the Possession of one Lawrence Pophanche. These are therefore to give Notice that if any Persons shall secure them so that the said Masters may have them again, or will bring them to their said Masters, shall have two Pistoles Reward for each and Reasonable Charges, and all Persons are by this Publick Advertisement forewarned not to buy them.

   This is to give Notice that there is a Tract of Land to be Sold lying on the West side of Skuylkill about Twenty five Miles from Philadelphia, commonly call'd Pickring's Mines, containing 344 Acres, a New House and some Cleared Land and a good Conveniency for making Meadow. To be at a very Reasonable rate by Sarah Thomas of Philadelphia.

   On Wednesday the first of May next, the Old Prison and Yard-Wall in Philadelphia City will be sold at Publick Vendue, at the Court-House, about the Hour of two in the Afternoon, all persons Inclined to buy may then see the Condition of Sale.

   PHILADELPHIA May 2. We have the following Account in the London News-Papers of the 23d of February last, concerning one William Riddlesdon, who was Transported to Maryland and married at Annapolis a Woman he had brought with him, after he had committed divers Rogueries there, he fled from thence, left his Bail, and came to this City with his Wife; and hiring a House here, set up the Trade of Tallow Chandler and Soapmaker, and pretended to give learned Advice in Law.

   William Riddlesdon, An Attorney, who was formerly condemned for Robbing the Chappel at Whitehall, being lately returned from Transportation before the Time limited by Law, married a Gentlewoman of considerable Fortune in the County of Cambridge, in Seign'd Name of Cornwallis; but being discovered, he was committed to the Goal of the said County; and orders are gone to bring him to Town, in order to his more effectual Transportation.

Being arrived safe and brought up by Habeas Corpus from Newgate, he moved to be admitted to Bail, which the Court would by no means allow: He Haragued them for some time, and, among other Things, said, he was returned in order to be called to the Bar as a Counsellor; but the Court have ordered him to the Bar in another Capacity to take his Tryal: He was also remanded back to his old Mansion of Newgate.

A News-Paper of the late Date says, That he was charged, in Custidy of the keeper, by the Gentlemen of the Bank of England, for a Misdemeanor in putting off Counterfeit Bank Notes in France &c.

PHILADELPHIA May 2. Two Prisoners confined in the Dungeon of the New-Prison of this City, has like to have made their Escape last Night after the following Manner: Having Invited the Keeper to drink with them, he accepted the Offer, and, Imagining the Prisoners to be secure enough in Irons, opened the Door, and entering in, one of the Prisoners having got off his Fetters loose took up the bottle and struck him on the forehead, intending to have beat out his Brains, and so make their Escape by means of the Keys: for such a weighty Body of Iron, managed with Force, could have been supposed to have done less than Murder: But not answering their design, the Keeper threw himself back, and had but just Time enough to fly up stairs, unlock the Out-Door and slip out for Assistance having none but himself except the Prisoners in the Goal, and going to shut the same, the said prisoners being come up to it, strove to hinder him: but he overpowering them clos'd the Door, and in doing of it Jam'd one of their Hands between the Door and Door frame, so that they are now safe; but one of the Prisoners having barred himself in the Dungeons, refuses to surrender himself, and threatens Death to any one who shall come near him; for which reason he is closed up in Darkness, and debarred from either Victuals or Drink, till his daring temper shall be abated.

PHILADELPHIA May 9. Ran away from Garet Scank of Middletown in East-New-Jersey, on the 15th of April, A Servant Man Named Cornelius Linch, by Trade a Shoemaker, he is a middle Siz'd Man, pretty well set, aged about Twenty Years, he is Pock fretted in his Face, has Streight light Coloured Hair, he has on a dark Irish frize Coat, Vest and Breeches near the same Colour, a homespun Shirt, and square to'd Shoes, he is an Irish-Man. Whoever shall take up the said Servant and Convey him to his said Master or to Isaac Stelle in Allen Town shall have Forty Shillings Reward besides Reasonable Charges. by
                                        Garet Scank.

PHILADELPHIA May 16. All Persons who have any Demands on John Brooks, of Philadelphia, Baker, living in Strawberry Alley, are desired to come and Receive the same, and all Persons who are indebted to the said John Brooks, are desired forthwith to come and settle their Accounts and pay the same in order to prevent further Trouble. He being Resolved to leave his Business to his Nephew John Bryant.

PHILADELPHIA May 23. Publick Notice is hereby Given. That there is lately arrived in this City one Mrs. Rades who will teach any Young Ladies or Gentlewomen to read & write French to perfection, She will give constant Attendance at her Dwelling-House in the Second Street in the Alley next Door to Dr. Owen. She likewise teaches to flourish on Muslin after the most expeditious Way, and at a very reasonable Rates. She likewise draws all Manner of Patterns for flourishing on Muslin, and those in Fashions on lace which is very pretty quickly learned. She likewise draws Patterns for Embroidering of Petticoats, &c. And those who have a Mind to learn, she will teach very reasonable. She hath very good Orange-Oyl being very good for the Wind-Cholick and Stomach, and fit for many other Things. And likewise Sweat-Meats, as Lemon and Orange-Peel, very well made; it will be disposed by the Pound, Half-Pound, or Quarter, cheap.

N. B. She gives Attendance from Nine in the Morning till Twelve, and in the Afternoon, if any Gentlewoman requires it, at their Houses. As she is but a New-Comer to this Place, all Persons who have a Mind to know more, may enquire of Mrs. Renier in Chestnut Street and she will inform them.

On Monday last was Imported from Bristol in the Ship Philadelphia, Thomas Bourne, Commander. A Parsel of choice Servant-Men, Women and Boys, being Trades-Men, Husbandmen and dairy-Maids; To be seen on Board the said Ship in the River Delaware; also a Parcel of suitable dry Goods Cheap for present Pay, at Robert Rllis's Wharf.

N. B. Those who are disposed to buy may apply to Mr. Thomas Lawrence, or said Master.

NEW-YORK May 31. Tuesday last being the Anniversary of his Majesties Birth-Day the same was observed in the following Manner. At Noon upon Drinking his Majesties, the Prince and Royal Family's Health, a Round of the Guns in the Garrison was fired and was answered by the Vessels in the road, The Soldiers (and with the Officers all in new Cloaths made a handsome Apperance) fired three Vollies, as did our Militia who were under Arms, together with the with a new Artillery Company being all dressed in blew Cloaths with Gold laced Hats, the Company consisted of Masters and Mates of Vessels, at night there was a Bonfire and Plenty of Wine at the Charge of the Corporation, there were Rockets and other Fire Works fired from the Walls of the Garrison, the whole Town was illuminated and the whole was concluded with a fine Ball and handsome Entertainment by his Excellency our Governor.

PHILADELPHIA June 12. Yesterday Capt. Greenman, in the Sloop Hopeful Betty, arrived here in Order to refit, who was taken on the 5th of June last by Low the Pyrate, about 45 Leagues E. S. E. from the Capes of Delaware, bound from this Port to Surrenam. The Pyrate took considerable of their Cargo from them, with most of the Sails, Anchors, and almost all their Water. Low himself abused the Captain very much, and cut him in several Places. They heard by them the Day before they had taken Pitman in a Pink bound from Virginia to London, who was discharged whilst they were ravaging the said Capt. Greemman. The Pyrates informed them, that they had taken 16 Sail of Vessels on the Coast, and seemed then in a great hurry, supposed to be occasined from the Items they had of the Men of War, from Boston, York and Virginia being on their Cruise after them.

PHILADELPHIA June 13. This is to be Sold a Plantation in the Township of East-town in Chester County within 14 Miles of the City of Philadelphia, but within 14 Miles of Navigable Water, Contains 300 and odd Acres that may be made and Improved with a Constant stream of Water, with very little charge, a Dwelling House and a good Large Barn, and an Orchard lying at the Eastern End of Loadstone Barren, very convenient for an Out-let of Liberty. Whoever shall be inclined to view the said Farm may repair to Thomas Edwards, the sight Owner thereof and Dweller thereon, and may be further informed concerning the premises, who will sell and make a good Title to the said Land upon reasonable Considerations to Buyer.   Thomas Edwards.

The following Lands and Tenements, being part of the Estate of Jonathan Dickinson Deceased; are to be Sold by Isaac Norris, James Logan and George Clanpole, Executors of the last Will of the said Jonathan Dickinson viz. Five Hundred Acres of Land in the County of Philadelphia. One Hundred and Thirty three Acres lying on the Road from Philadelphia to S. Blunston's Ferry commonly called Duckett's Land. A House on Society-Hill where John Bettison now dwells, with Eleven lots. A House in Chestnut Street where Charles Brocken lives. A Lot standing on the back thereof; and several other adjoining Tenements, Fifteen, two and Thirteenth part of the Grist-Mills, and Saw-Mill on Chester Creek Commonly called Chester Mills. And one moiety of the Plantation adjourning, which was formerly Celeb Pursey's. As also sundry valuable Household and other Goods.

NEW-York June 17. On the 10th Instant about 30 Leagues from Sandyhook to the Eastward, Capt. Morine and all his Passengers and Saylors heard

Great Guns from Eight in the Morning till Twelve at Noon, which gave us hopes our Man of War had engaged the Pyrates, but hearing nothing from her, some will have it the Pyrates were celebrating the Pretenders Birth-Day.

PHILADELPHIA June 20. To be Sold, three very likely Negro Girls being about 15 Years of age, and a Negro Boy about 14, all speaking good English, enquire of the Printer hereof.

PHILADELPHIA June 27. Yesterday there happened a strange accident on Board of Capt. Annis, as they were unloading and getting a small box out of the Hold of the Vessel in which was Agua-Fortis one of the Bottles happened to break and set Fire to the Ship which soon got out, but the Saylor that went into the Hold to find the box, as it was burning, is since dead with the Suffocating smell. There was on board the Ship at the Time about 150 Cask of Gun Powder.

Deserted the 21st of this Instant June, from the Ship Richard and Mary at Philadelphia, one William Meredith, by Trade a Joyner, of about 21 Years of Age, about five foot high short curl'd Hair, Eyes deep in his Head a Lowring Countenance, he has a mull'd Cap on his Head without a Hatt. Pee Jackrt and no Stockings, he was said to take the New-York road, he carried with him two Joyners planes. Whoever brings him again to the said ship or to Samuel Dicker at Philadelphia, will have Twenty Shillings as a Reward besides all Reasonable Charges.

PERT-ANBOY July 2. Publick Notice is hereby given that one John Wilson Mariner being on board the Sloop William, William Fraset Master belonging to Amboy, who was taken by the Pyrates, the said Wilson was forced on board the Pyrate sloop against his will, and when the Man of War took the Pyrate sloop he was carried along with the rest of the Pyrates and put in Prison in Rhode Island.

PHILADELPHIA July 4. All Persons who are indebted to Anne Jones at the Plume of Feathers in Second Street in Philadelphia, are desired to bring in their Accounts in Order they be adjusted: She likewise designs to dispose of the Lease of her House, as also all sorts of her

Household Goods at reasonable Rates, she designing to go for England in a short Time.

NEW-YORK July 4. These are to give Notice that whereas the Snow Unity belonging to New-York, whereof Robert Leonard was Master on the 25th of January last, at the West part of the Island of Bonira, was taken by a Pirate Scooner and Sloop, whereof Edward Low was Commander, who forced 2 Men belonging to the said Snow go along with them the said Pirates, towit, Richard Owen and Fredrick Vander Scure, both of them belonging to the City of New-York, and have Families there. To the truth of which the said Capt. Robert Leonard & Richard Statts the Mate of the said Snow have made Affidavit before Philip Courtlandt, Esq; one of the Aldermen of the City of New-York.

Our General Assembly are adjourned till the 1st Day of October next, to have raised upward of 2000 Pounds for making good Deficiencies of the Revenue, and to encouraging a Trade with a farr Nation of Indians &c.

NEW-YORK We have Account, that one Josiah Quimby a Quaker living in the County of West-Chester in the Province of New-York has invented a Machine Instrument, which (he says) will move and turn round upon, its own Axis with a quick Motion, for a Thousand Years together, and he has made an agreement (under Hand and Seal) with four Gentlemen of the City of New-York, in the Sum of Three-Hundred Pounds, that he can demonstrate the Feizableness of the Motion of the said Machine or Instrument to two of the Mathematicians, (whose names are therein mentiones) in these parts; or else will demonstrate the Truth of his Proposal by making the said Instrument and putting it into Motion. And it is said Quimby has so far demonstrated the Motion of the said Machine to the said two Mathematicians, that they have given it under their Hands in the Favour whereby he is entitled to the said Three Hundred Pounds.

His Proposal is as Following, viz. That he will make 22 Wheels (more or Less) in a Room of a House, each of which Wheel shall run round upon its own Axis, and shall turn for a

Thousand Years or longer, continuously, with a
swift Motion, without any other force to turn
it round than that which is at first given it
with a Hand or some other force applyed to it
so, the Space of two Days or less, and what it
shall afterwards obtain from others of the same
22 Wheels, the Influence of the Motion of the
North-Star, the Moon, the Sun, the Eclipses of
both Sun and Moon, and from the Planets (provided that allowance be to amend the Materials
of all the Parts of the Instrument or Engine,
when they wear or decay.) That for the obtaining
Of Influence of the Sun Moon and Stars, he is
to be permitted to make a three inch round hole
through the North side of the Room (wherein the
the said Wheels are placed,) toward the North
Star; and likewise a hole two Inches in bredth
and six Foot in Length thro' the South side of
the said Chamber but towards the southing of
the Sun. The said Quimby shall likewise have
liberty to make 3 or 4 more holes through any
Part of the said house to gain Influence from
the Earth and sea, Sun, Moon, Stars and Planets
in their Natural Course, if he shall see cause
so to make them; and shall have the liberty of
digging a Well under the said Instrument of what
Depth he pleases, and of making use of the Common Heat and Moisture of the Air, and of the
air it felt, provided that there be no living
Creature to attend the Instrument, to supply
any thing to it, but the Instrument by the very
make of it, after it is once set a going. He
says he will not be held, that it shall move in
a violent Frost. But that the said Instrument
shall be of such Force and use, that it shall
raise Water with a Continual Stream, during the
whole continuance of the said Instrument (Except in Time of Violent Frost) Ten Twenty or
more Feet higher than the Surface of the Water
from whence the Stream is taken: As for Example
suppose there was a Well dug at low Water Mark
in the North River, he will raise the Water out
of the said Well (by means of the said Instrument) the hight of a Post of 20, 30, or 40 foot,
set perpendicular in the said Well, by a Spout
going up the said Post. He also Prays this

Explanation, that some of the Wheels will not go very swift but others of them at the same time shall go very swift. He proposed to have the Choice of a Room to put up the said Instrument in, provided that be in the City of New-York; and that the said Instrument shall be made and put up at his own Cost and Charge, and that he will have liberty to use Quick Silver or Oyl upon said Instrument. The said Quimby will not give the name of the Perpetual Motion to this Instrument, but an Instrument or Engine that will run round and do work for the Time and in the Manner above Mentioned.

PHILADELPHIA July 11. There is to be exposed to sale by way of a Lottery, a New Brick Dwelling House and Lot, a good Kitchen, Wash-Room, Oven, half a Well, Necessary-House and a handsome Garden, valued at 230 Pounds, being under yearly Ground-Rent of Fifty Shillings per Annum; now in the Tenure of Dr. Francis Gandouit, and situated on the East side of the Third Street near the Market Place in Philadelphia.

The Proposal are six Hundred tickets of Ten Shillings each will be disposed of, Five Prizes to be drawn, the highest Prize is the House and Lot, and whoever draws it is obliged when the Title is made to pay the other Prizes, one of Twenty Pounds, one of Ten Pounds and two of Five Pounds each.

Sufficient Security will be given to the Government by the Managers and Trustees that the whole Affairs shall be carried fairly and honestly and a firm Title made to the Drawer of the greatest Prize. The Lottery is intended to be opened for the dispensing of Tickets by the Middle of this Instant July or sooner if Possible, and if the said Tickets are not all taken out by the last Day of December next nor likely to be soon after, then the sureties oblige themselves to reimburse all the Money as the Tickets are returned. All Persons inclin'd to try their Fortune in this Affair may be Supplyed with Tickets by the Manager and Surities Viz. Philip John at the Rose and Crown in the Front Street, Edward Warner Carpenter living at James Foultis in Second Street in Philadelphia.

PHILADELPHIA July 18. Run away the 15th of this Instant July, from Nathan Watson of the Burrough Bristol in the County of Bucks, two Servant Men, the one named John Amyet, aged about 22 Years, he is West Country Man, of a Middle Stature and goes stooping, he is a Sickly look'd Fellow, short brown Hair, an old Felt Hat, he hath on a Saylors Jacket, light grey Stockings and round to'd Shoes. The other named George Clift, aged about 19 or 20 Years, a thick set strong Fellow of a swarthy Complexion, sour look'd, when he went away he had on only his Shirt and Breeches, an old Hat, a pair of round to'd Shoes. Whoever takes up the said Servants or either of them shall have a Pistole reward for each besides Reasonable Charges.

Run away on the 14th in this Instance June, from Philip Davis of New-Monster, on the Branch of Elk-River, a Servant Man named Morris Harnus aged about 40, Years, he is a Palatine, and speaks but little English, he has light Brown Hair, a thin Face but very Tawney, he has two Jackets with him the one Blue and the other Brown and an old pair of Trowsers. Whoever takes up the said Servant or secures him, and gives Notice to James James Esq; of the Welch Tract, or to his said Master shall have 25 Shillings as a Reward and Reasonable Charges.

NEW-York July 25. At a Common-Council held at the City Hall of the said City on Tuesday the 25th Day of July, Anno Dom. 1723. Presented, Robert Walter Esq; Mayor &c.

This Court having taken into their Consideration the great Service lately done to this Province in particular. as well as to all other of his Majesty's Good Subjects in General, by Capt. Peter Solgard, Commander of his Majesty's Ship Greyhound, the Station Ship of this Province, who lately on a Cruize upon the Coast, in the due Execution and Discharge of his Duty, upon Intelligence given him, sought for, Pursued and Engaged Two Pirate Sloops, Commanded by Low, (a Notorious and Inhumane Pirate) one of which Sloop he took after a Resolute Resistance, and very much shattered the other; who by the favour of the Night Escaped. Twenty-Six of the Pirates so taken being Executed at Rhode Island: not only eased the City of Providence of a great Trouble, but a very considerable Expence, &c.

It is Therefore Resolved (nemine Contra Dicente) That this Corporation do present the Capt. Solgard with Freedom of the Corporation as a mark of the Great Esteem they have for his Person, as well as for the aforesaid Great and Good Service; and that the Seal of the said freedom be inclosed in a Gold Box; that Mr. Recorder and Mr. Brickley do draw the draft of this said Freedom, signifying there in the grateful Sense this Corporation for to signal a Service, to the publick Benefit & Advantages of Mankind, The Alderman Hip and Alderman Cruger to prepare the said Box; That the arms of the Corporation be Engraved on one side, and a Representation of the Engagement on the other, with Motto, (viz.) Quasitos Humani Generis Hostes, Debellare Superbun 10. Junij 1723. That the Town Clerk cause the said Freedom, to be handsomely Ingross'd on Parchment, and that the whole Corporation do wait upon to Present the same. per order of the Common Council,

       Will. Sharpas, Clerk.
    City of New-York

Robert Walter Esq; Mayor, and the Aldermen of the City of New-York. To all to whom these presents shall come send Greeting.

Whereas Capt. Solgard Commander of his Majesty's Ship the Greyhound (the Present Station Ship of this Station) in his Craft, having Intelligence of two Pyrate Sloops of considerable Force in Consortship, under the Command of one Low a notorious Pyrate, that had (for upward of Two Years committed many Depredations, Murders and Barbarities upon many of His Majesty's Subjects and Allies,) lately come upon this Coast, both with great diligence and amongst Application, Persued, Overtaken, and after stubborn Resistance, Vanquish'd and overcame both of them, taking one and driving the other from our Coast, which Action as it is Glorious in it self, so it is Glorious in the Publick Benefit and Advantages that flow from it (to wit) the Safety and Freedom of our own Trade and Commerce as well as all the Neighbouring Provinces on the Continent: Such signal Services done against the Enemy of Mankind merit the Aplause of all Good Men, but more immediately from those of this Province who are Appointed his particular Care and Danger. We therefore the Mayor, Aldermen and Commonalty of the City of New-York Assembled in Common Council to Express our Grateful Sense and acknowledgement to the said Capt. Peter Solgard for the Noble and Faithful Discharge of his Duty, and as a particular Mark of the Great Esteem and just Regard we bear to his Person; do unanimously Present him, and beg his kind Acceptance of the Freedom of the Corporation of the City of New-York and that he will please to become a Fellow Citizen with us. These are therefore to Certify and Declare that the said Capt. Solgard is hereby admitted, Received and Allowed a Freeman and Citizen of the said City of New-York, To have, hold, Enjoy and partake of all and singular the Advantages, Benefits, Privileges, Franchises, Freedoms and Immunities whatever Granted or belonging to the said City.

In Testimony thereof the said Mayor hath unto Subscibed his Name and cause the Seal of said City to be affixed the Twenty-Fifth Day of July in the ninth Year of the Reign of our Sovereign Lord George by the Grace of God, King of Great Britain, France and Ireland, King Defender of the Faith, &c. Annog. Dom. 1723.

R. Walter, Mayor,   Will. Sharpas, Cl.

PHILADELPHIA July 29. This Day we had a violent Storm of Wind and Rain, the Wind being North-East in the Morning and continued shifting till about Noon, at which Time it blew very hard at South-East, which occasioned a great deal of disorder among the Shipping, and blew down several Chimneys, and occasioned such a high Tide here as had not been known these many Years, the Storm continued about 2 Hours and a half, in which Time it wash'd away a Wharf and very much Damaged several others, but has done no great harm to the Stores, it has blown down a great many Trees and very much damaged the Fruit.

NEW-YORK July 30. Yesterday about 8 or 9 a Clock the Wind came up here at the North-East, and vered about more to the South-East, and from 12 a Clock till 4 it blew very hard, with Rain, insomuch that it has broke up all Wharfs from one end of the City to the other, drove all the Vessels (except three) on shore, and three Sloops are broken all to pieces: the water came up into the City higher ever was known before, and has done abundance of Damage to Sugar and other Goods in Merchants Cellars, the Market House before the Coffee-House is blowned down and several other Houses, and the Tyles and Covering of many Houses were blown off, And if the Storm had continued till the next High Water, all the Houses by the Water side would have been destroyed. All the Wharfs around the great Dock is drove away. And in the Slips there is such a vast quantities of Boards, Timber, Boats, Canoes, Staves and other Rubbish lies in heaps, in such a manner as was never seen before. A Pyrate Sloop which Capt. Solgard brought in, was forced to cut her Mast and is drove-away.

PHILADELPHIA Aug. 1. These are to give Notice to all Persons as have purchased Land of the Pennsylvania Land Company, and that have sent Deeds over to England to be Executed by the Trustees of the said Company, the which are duly performed and returned by their Agent who am, or some Body in my Behalf to be Spoke with every Seventh Day of the Week at Henry Hodges, Merchant in Philadelphia, John Estaugh.

PHILADELPHIA Aug. 8. Whereas on the 5th of June last, the Sloop Farley, Thomas Calder Master, belonging to Mr. James Harris of Maryland, Sayled from Piscataqua in New-England, being bound for Maryland, was on the 14th of the same Month, met with at Sea near Nantucket Island by a Sloop belonging to William Clark of Boston, with her Sails Fluttering, her Rigging cut, her Hatches flung over board and a hole cut in her ceiling, she having been attempted to be sunk, the Liquor on board being Destroyed and left in Buckets on the Deck, there was not one soul on board, by which it was thought that the Men were forced away by the Pyrates. The Master Thomas

Calder is a Scotch Man short and set, black Hair, of a whitish Complexion, talks pretty thick, about 30 Years of Age, the Mate Peter Carr pretty tall of a dark Complexion of a middle Stature speaks pretty thick. what other Hands were on board I know not they being ship'd in New-England.

PHILADELPHIA Aug. 8. To be Sold by William Bettredge of Philadelphia, a Lot 24 foot front and 40 Foot deep, with very good Brick House thereon, 15 foot front and 35 deep, and three story High, Likewise a Shop on the remaining part of the said front, they being situated on the East Side of Second Street near the corner of Chestnut Street. Any Person Inclined to Buy the said House, Shop and Lot May treat with the aforesaid William Bettredge about the condition of Sale at the said Shop or his House in Mulberry Street near the Quaker Burrying Ground.

PHILADELPHIA Aug. 22. We have Advise that the Sloop Robert and James, Robert Bird Master, who come out of South Carolina in Company with Capt. Slyfield and was feared lost in the Storm of the 29th of July, she lost her Mast and was drove on Shore about 20 Miles to the Southward of Sene Puxon, but all the Men and Cargo saved, the Cargo very much Damaged.

There is to be Sold by Joseph Best Goldsmith in High-Street Philadelphia a young Negro Man and Woman any Person disposed to buy both or either of them may apply to their said Master.

A Very likely Servant's Time to be disposed of by John Annis Commander of the London Hope.

A Likely Negro Lad about 15 Years of age, to be Sold by Thomas Polgreen in the Front-Street over against the Printer.

Run away Robert Alexander, of Philadelphia Merchant. Three Indentured Servants, they being Palatines and some of those who were Imported about Five Months ago in Maryland, the first namen Peter Kures, a middle aged Man, Tall of Stature and swarthy Complexion, the second John Jerick Garlach, aged about 30 Years, of a middle Stature and brown Complexion, the third named William Smith, a middle aged Man, Tall of Stature and slender, of a brownish Complexion, he pretends to be a Miner. It is supposed they are about New-York.

Whoever takes up the said Servants and secures them, and gives Notice thereof to Mr. George M'Call Merchant in Philadelphia, shall have Forty Shillings as a Reward for each, and reasonable Charges.

PHILADELPHIA Aug. 29. These are to give Notice that William Bradford of New-York takes Paper Money, and on Reasonable Terms, supplies Travvellers, and others, that want the said Paper Money.

Run away from John Keyll of Cristee-Creek in New-Castle County on the 18th of this Instant a Dervant Man Named James McCurdey, aged about 21 Years, a little Man, fair Complexion, pretty fresh Coloured, fair short Hair, he had on a Frys Coat, a brownish Cloth Jacket and Mohair Buttons, a pair of Buck-skin Breeches and brownish Stockings, a felt Hat. Whoever takes up the said Servant and convey him to his Master shall Have a Pistole Reward and Reasonable Charges paid by me   John Keyll.

PHILADELPHIA Sept. 6. Yesterday were tryed at the General Quarter session for this said City and County, James Smith alias Spurling, Isaac Barger alias James Shranbery, upon Indictment for Endeavouring to pass Counterfeit Bars of Gold of which they were found Guilty, and received Sentence to stand in the Pillory for the Space of one Hour, on Saturday next, and then to be tied to a Cart-Tail, and receive 20 Lashes through the Town, and never return again.

PHILADELPHIA Sept. 12. These are to desire the Country Gentlemen that are indebted, to Thomas Denham for Servants, and otherwise to make payment directly, in order to prevent further Charges the said Denham, being bound for England this Fall.

For London Directly, The Ship Richmond, John Richmond Commander, he will be near to take in Goods by the first of October, and is intended to Sayle by November Fair, any Persons disposed to Transport themselves, or Merchandize, may Treat with the said Commander or Thomas Griffitts of Philadelphia.

PHILADELPHIA Sept. 19. Ran away from the Honourable Sir William Keith, Bart. a Servant Man named Richard Chamberland, by Trade a Taylor, of a middle Stature, thin Visage, he wears sometime a black Coat sometime a dark Coloured one, grey Stockings, an old Hat. Whoever takes up and secures the said Servant so that his said Master may have him again shall have Three Pounds as a Reward besides Reasonable Charges.

For Jamaica directly, The Ship Globe John Mackey Commander, Burthened about 150 Tons, and Mounted with 12 Guns, if any Gentlemen or others have a mind to Transport themselves of Goods, they may agree with the said Master at the Sign of the Crown from 1 to 2 a Clock in the Afternoon, or at the Coffee-House, he hath two thirds of his Lading already Engaged. The said Master hath some Palatine Boys to dispose of.

PHILADELPHIA Sept. 26. If any Person or Persons may have occasion to pass or repass, or convey Goods from Philadelphia to Trenton and backwards, their Goods may be secured at the House of John Wollard in Trenton, in order to the Mill there, or at the Crooked Billet in Philadelphia. Passengers may come, and Goods may be convey'd from Trenton, every Monday or Tuesday, and from Philadelphia every Thursday and Friday.

Ran away the 26th of April last, from Jonathan Hanson of Baltimore County in Maryland, a servant Man named James Juery, aged about 30 Years, of large Stature, he has a large red spot on his right Cheek about the bigness of an English Half Crown, he is a Fuller by Trade, and is likely to be found at some of the Fulling-Mills. Whoever shall take up the said Servant and secures him in any Prison, and give Notice thereof to his Master, so that he may be had again, shall have 4o Shillings as a Reward and Reasonable Charges.

PHILADELPHIA Sept. 26. By an Act of General Assembly of the Province of Pennsylvania, made at Philadelphia on the 22d day of March in the Ninth Year of his Majesty's Reign, and in the Year of our Lord 1723. The Lands and Lots commonly call'd the Lands of the Society of Trade of Pennsylvania, are vested in Charles Read, Job Goodson, Evan Owen, George Fitzwater, and John Pigeon, to be sold for the Payment of such Sums of Money as were paid into the Publick Stocks of the said Society for Purchasing the said Lands and Lots, and carrying on the Trade designed by the said Society.

These are therefore to give Notice to all Persons concern'd, that it is Ordained by the said Act, that there shall be two Dividends made of the Money arising by Sale of the Said Lands, at the Days, and by the Persons Appointed in the said Act, at the City Hall in Philadelphia, amongst all Persons having Rights to the same in proportion to the Sums paid by them, or the Persons who they represented, into Stocks of said Society.

The first Dividend to be made on the 25th day of March, which will be in the Year 1725; and the second on the 25th day of March, which will be 1730. And in the mean Time that all Persons having right to any of the said Moneys, may have an Opportunity to make out their respective Claims, they are directed to apply to the Justices of the Orphan Court at Philadelphia who are by the said Act enable to audit and Judge of the several Claims Exhibited to them, and to allow of all such Demands as to them shall seem justly due to the respective Claimants, and a Certificate of such allowance will be a sufficient proof to entitle the Persons producing the same to their Share or Proportion of the said Moneys at the Time and Place aforesaid, Appointed for making Dividends.

PHILADELPHIA Oct. 10. A very good Negro Man aged about 30 Years, lately imported from South Carolina, to be Sold on reasonable Terns enquire of Peter Bayton or Robert Ellis in Philadelphia.

Deserted, the 7th of this Instant September, from the Brigantine Ceasar, Robert Abbot Commander, one Henry Harmson, a German, but speaks indifferent english, of a Middle Stature, pale Complexion, about 23, Years of age, he had on a brown bob Wigg, a light coloured Drab Coat, a Cinnamon coloured one underneat, and a Pair of Breeches the same colour, made French Fashion, he is by Trade a Watch-Maker. Whoever takes up the said Henry Harmson and secures him, and give Notice thereof to Thomas Sobers Merchant in Philadelphia, shall have Forty Shillings as a Reward besides reasonable Charges.

PHILADELPHIA Oct. 10. We have advice from Maryland, that last Week 30 or more Convicts Run away with a Sloop from Annapolis, they being well arm'd, that the Governor has sent an Express to Capt. Solgard at Williamsburg in Virginia, to stop and pursue them.

NEW-YORK Oct. 10. All Persons to whom the Estate of the late Reverend George Macnish of Jamaica on Long-Island is indebted are hereby desired to give in their respective accounts to Joseph Smith jun. of Jamaica, or to John Nealls of New-York his Administrators on or before the First Day of December next. Also to give Notice to all who are indebted to the said Estate, forthwith to bring in their respective Debts, to the said Administrators, as they would not be prosecuted against.

New-Castle Oct. 23. The Speech of His Excellency Sir William Keith, Bart, Governor of the Province of Pennsylvania, and the Counties of New-Castle, Kent and Sussex upon the Delaware.

To the Representatives of the Freemen of said Counties of New-Castle, Kent and Sussex.

Mr. Speaker and Gentlemen of the Assembly, If we seriously consider that unlimited freedom, which it has pleased the Almighty Creator and Absolute Lord of the Universe, to bestow upon Mankind, we may from that Fountain easily deduce the Roles by which Peace and good order is to be maintained in Human Society for since by this Great Privilege it is most certainly in our Power always to do that which is Right and equal to each other, we cannot otherwise cry in our Duty, but by affirming an Irregular and undue Prerogative over our Selves and others, to the Destruction of that Principal, which God and Nature design'd for our greatest Honour and Happiness.

I speak to you after this Manner, because I observed with Pleasure, that the Country have made Choice of such Representatives, as will not distinguish their own, from the People's true Interest, and as I cannot be more solicitous about any thing that the Publick Credit of these Counties should be maintain'd as become a just and Free People. I hope some Enquiry will be made concerning such Persons amongst ourselves, as have been officiously busy to lessen the Credit of your Paper Bills, and that you will think proper Methods to Inforce the Value of them for the Time to Come.

Gentlemen,
As I have no reason to doubt your care in supporting an Administration, which I flatter myself has been hitherto both useful and acceptable to the People who you Represent, I have nothing more at this Time to recommend to you but Unanimity and Dispatch.   W. Keith.

NEW-CASTLE Oct. 24. The Address of the Representatives of the Freemen of the Counties of New-Castle, Kent and Sussex upon Deleware, in the General Assembly, To his Excellency Sir. William Keith, Bart. Governor of the said Counties and Province of Pennsylvania, in answer to his Speech of the 23d Instant.

May it please Your Excellency,
As we do most sincerely Concur with Your Excellency in acknowledging the Great Goodness of our most Beautiful Creator, for having so well freed and dispos'd the very Frame of our Nature, to the several Duties and Necessities of Civil Life; that whoever shall duly reflect on the Powers of his own Mind, may learn from thence, what becomes heard in every Relation; so shall we ever esteem it a singular Instance of the Divine Favour to the People of this Colony, that these who have not the skill to frame Rules to themselves from the foregoing Principle, may collect them as profitably for Your Excellency's wise and just Administration.

Your Excellency hath expressed your satisfaction in the Choice this Colony hath made of Representatives, in Terms so much to our Honour, as we should appear to all the World, as regardless of our Reputation as the Publick Interest (with which we are intrusted) should we neglect and support the Credit of the Species now current amongst us, by the most effectual Measures we can devise, or to discourage and set a lasting Mark of Infamy and Reproach on all such wicked and Pernicious Practices, as tend to weaken or blast the Reputation thereof.

Our sence of our Excellency's Government over us, will be best discover'd by the Provisions we shall make for it's Support, which we shall not fail to take care of for, in such Measure and with such Unaninimity and Dispatch, as shall at once demonstrate our Care of those we represent, and evince us to be a most grateful People to the best of Governors.
Sign'd by Order of the House,

       John French Speaker.

PHILADELPHIA Oct. 24. There is a School in New-York in the Broad-Street near the Exchange, where Mr. John Walton late of Yale-College, Teacheth Reading, writing, Arethmatick, whole Numbers and Fractions, Vulgar and Decimals. The Mariners Art, Plain and Mercators way; also Geometry, Surveying, the Latin Tongue, the Greek and Hebrew Grammars, Ethicks, Rhetorick, Logicks, Natural Philosophy and Metaphysicks, all or any of them for a Reasonable Price. The School from the first of October till the first of March will be tended in the Evening. If any Gentlemen in the Country are disposed to send their Sons to the said School, if they apply themselves to the Master he will immediately procure suitable Entertainment for them, very Cheap. Also any Young Gentlemen of the City will please come in the Evening and make some Tryal of the Liberal Arts, they may have opportunity of Learning the same things which are commonly thought in College.

Strayed away the 23d of September last, from Nicholas Gateau, commonly called the French Cook, Two Horses, the one a dark Bay Horse, about 6 Years old, branded with E.P. on the Shoulders, a long Main and switch Tail, Cid is swell'd like a Stone-Horse. The other a gray Horse, about 4 Years old branded Y. half his Main trim'd, switch Tail, he is shod all around. They both Pace. Whoever takes up the said Horses and bring them to their said Master, shall have

30 Shillings as a Reward and reasonable Charges.

PHILADELPHIA Oct. 31. Run away the 17th of this Instant October, from William Chancellor of the City of Philadelphia, a Negro Woman named Nan, aged about 32 Years, having a Stiff Gown and a new Bonnet Lined with Red Silk: She is supposed to be about the said City. Whoever takes up this Negro, and brings her to her said Master, shall be Rewarded.

For South-Carolina directly,
The Carolina Packet Robert Palmer Commander, will be ready to sail by the middle of November next. All Persons that have any demands on the said Robert Palmer are desired to come and adjust the same, and those who are Indebted to him, are desired forthwith to come and settle the same, he designing, to take his Family out of this Province with him.

NEW-CASTLE Nov. 2. The Speech of His Excellency Sir William Keith Bart. Governor of the Province of Pennsylvania, and the Counties of New-Castle, Kent and Sussex upon Delaware.

To the Representatives of the Freemen of the said Counties.

Mr. Speaker and Gentlemen of the Assembly, Since the natural Situation of these Counties and Practice of out Neighbours, has laid on under the necessity of coming into Paper Currency: I am extremely Pleased to observe the Case which you have a Product to Export and sell to others, it will be a certain Truth, that your Bills of Credit will rise and fall in proportion to the value which they generally bear at the Time amongst your selves; and that again will of it self be regulated according to the distance of Time, in which they are surely to be sunk, and in due proportion or quantity of Bills struck, which ought not be more, than is truely necessary to circulate your Trade, or the bare Exchange of your Product, from one hand to another.

I Take the Opportunity to assure you, Gentlemen, That as I have ever been ready to distinguish with Respect, and Encourage those who generously prefer the publick Good, to any particular Interest whatsoever, so for the future

I will esteem it an essential part of my Duty, to remove all such from Office of Trust or Profit that are in my Power, who shall be convicted or having used any Means to lessen the Publick Credit.

Gentlemen,
The Addition you have made this year to the Support of Government calls for a particular Thanks and when the People come to feel the Benefit of those things, which at the same time you have done for their Ease, it is to be hoped, they will be fully Convinc'd that a Prudent Wise Assembly, can never be at a lost to make Frugality confident with what is just and Honourable, and a harmonious Friendship, will only be always less changeable, but in every Respect preferably to Disorder and Contempt.

W. Keith.

The Address of the Representatives of the Freemen of the Counties of New-Castle, Kent and Sussex upon Delaware, in General Assembly met this 2d day of November, 1723.

To His Excellency Sir William Keith, Bart. Governour of the said Counties and the Province of Pennsylvania, in answer to his Speech, at passing of Laws.

May it please your Excellency,
The Great Happiness we enjoy under your Excellency's Administration, cannot be better exemplify'd, that by the care and Tenderness you make appear in ever Circumstance that tend towards our Welfare and Prosperity. Your regard ceases not with granting us such Laws as we are truely for our good, but the same is continued by causing them to be duely put in Execution, and avowing your Disregard to such as shall be found virtuous enough, either to elude the Acts of abate the Credit and Force of them.

When you consult on Inclinations, and reflect upon our present Condition, we must acknowledge that we are under a Necessity of denying the one to comply with the other; yet, we beg your Excellency to believe, that as we have the greatest and most dutiful and also a most profound Regard for our Person and Character, so what our Circumstances would allow, which

was unanimously and cheefully granted.
Sign'd by Order of the House.
                              John French Speaker.

   PHILADELPHIA Nov. 7. We have Advice from Maryland that one Capt. Bead is arrived from London in Petuxon River, that he was taken by a Pirate Sloop off the Capes of Virginia and plundered by them.

   Run away from Nicholas Asborn of North East Cecil County in Maryland a Servant named Joseph Somper, aged about 17 Years of middle Stature, slender Body'd; full Faced with a mole on his Right cheek, his Hair about half an inch long, he wears a Hat and Cap, a short Jacket, a Coat of dark coloured Kersey, yellow Stockings Russet coloured Shoes, he has with him a Gun with a Square barrel and a large young Dog light Brindl'd a white stroke on his Face, with a long Tail, and Crop'd Ears, he rides a middling sorrel Horse, branded with NH on the near Buttock, with a large Star and in the Stae a sorrel spott, and a little above the Tail a Spott, got with burning, the said runaway has a bag with several things in it, which he stole from his Master and the Neighbours. Whoever takes up the said Servant and Secures him so that his said Master may have him again, shall have 3 Pounds Reward and all reasonable Charges.

   Philadelphia Nov. 21. Notice is hereby given to all Publick-House-keepers, and other Persons Licensed to Retail Liquor within the Province of Pennsylvania, who have neglected to make due Entryes and Accounts, and pay the last half Year Excise that if they continue in such Neglect Ten Days from the date hereof they may expect to be proceeded against as the Law Directs, by
                              Charles Read.

   Run away from Thomas Hynson and Daniel Pierce of Kent County in Maryland, two Servant Men the one Robert MacDaniel, he is a Doctor or Mountebank, his Hair is of a light Colour, he has on two Coats the one a Dark Coloured Druggett being trim'd with Black the other a light Grey Kersey; a felt Hatt, a pair of Yarn Stockings, two pair of Shoes the one Wooden Heel'd. The other named Alexander Arnett, by Trade a Cooper, he speaks broad Scotch, Yellow Hair, a kersey Jacket, linned Breeches, Yarn Stockings, wooden heel'd Shoes, a Caster Hatt, and Ozinbrig Shirts. Whoever takes up the said Servants and secures them, so that their said Masters may have them again, shall receive for each Fifty Shillings with reasonable Charges.

NEW-YORK Nov. 25. We have advice from Madeira dated October 18, That Capt. John Parker in the Snow Henry of Philadelphia, off the Bar of Lisbon, either going in or coming out, was met with an Algerian Rover who plundered him of several Trifles and then left him, and afterward in his sight made after a sloop. Capt. Parker is since gone to Holland.

PHILADELPHIA Nov. 29. Whereas several Bills of Credit have been of late Counterfeited (that in the one and two Shillings turned into Ten) these are therefore to desire all Persons that receive any Bills to take particular Care by Reason the Heads of each sort of Bills differ, there is a Vote of the Present Assembly for giving a Reward of Ten Pounds to those that shall discover the Counterfeits.

PHILADELPHIA Dec. 5. Ran away on Friday Morning the 29th of last Month from the Ship Joseph now in Philadelphia, John Bennet Master, Neil Tomson a Highlanderman, of a middle Stature with sandy coloured Hair, he speaks broken English, wearing a Light Brown Coat, with a Yellow cloth Jacket and a greyish coloured pair of serge Denim Breeches. Whoever shall take up the said Man and secure him or send word to the said Master or to Mr. John Franklin Merchant in Philadelphia, shall be very well Rewarded besides Reasonable Charges.

PHILADELPHIA Dec. 10. Whereas Mathew Burne of Chester County served John Cann two Years (that is 10 or 12 Months) at Stocking weaving and other work, during which time John Canns stocking bore many Reflections and now the said Mathew Burne goes about selling Stockings in John Canns Name as though they were his make, which is false and not True.

Whereas one Samuel Keimer, who lately came into this Province of Pennsylvania, hath Printed and Published divers Papers, Particularly, one Entitled, a Parable, &c. in some Parts of which he assumes to use such a Stile and Language, as that perhaps he may be Deemed, where he is not known, to be one of the People called Quakers: This may therefore Certify, That the said Samuel Keimer is not one of the said People, nor countenanced by them in aforesaid Practice.

Signed by Order of the Monthly Meeting of the said People called Quakers, held at Philadelphia, the 29th Day of the Ninth Month, 1723.

Samuel Preston Cl.

PHILADELPHIA Dec. 14. This Day the General Assembly of this Province adjourn'd to the 17th of April next. At which time, the two following Acts were passed, viz.

An Act for Emitting and making Current Thirty Thousand Pounds in Bills of Credit.

An Act for Laying an Excise or Duty on all Wines, Rum, and other Spirits retailed in the Province, (under the Quantity of 35 Gallons.)

PHILADELPHIA Dec. 17. Lately Imported into this City a Choice Parcel of Jesuites Bark, and Squire Grand Elixir, and choice Lime-Juse, to be sold by Capt. Bignal or Andrew Bradford at the Bible in Second-Street, very Reasonable.

Run away about the Middle of June last, from John Joyce at the Head of the Eastern Branch of Potomack River in Maryland a Negro Man named Robin, of a middle Stature, aged about 21 Years, he Looks very Young having no Hair on his Face. Whoever shall take up said Negro Man and bring him to his Master, so that he may be had again shall have three Pounds as a Reward with reasonable Charges.

1724

PHILADELPHIA Jan. 7. A very likely Negro Girl to be sold by Joseph Richards in Chestnut Street.

To be Sold, a very likely Negro Woman fit for all Manner of House Work, as Washing, Starching, Ironing, &c. Enquire of Andrew Bradford.

Not any Thing is arrived here since our last but a Brigantine from Jamaica. Our River is very free from Ice.

Philadelphia Jan. 14. John Ross (late of the Ship Little Jack) Mariner, came this Day before Me, and made oath on the holy Evangelists, that a Pirate Scooner, on the Banks of Newfoundland about the beginning of July last, came along Side the said Ship, and mann'd out her Boat, and plunder'd the said Ship; and forcibly took and carried away James Stanton Carpenter, belonging to the said Ship; Saying at the same Time, they wanted a Carpenter and Doctor, and further said not.   John Ross.

Jur. cor. me. Jan. 1723.   Jephson Busteed.

PHILADELPHIA Jan. 21. Sir, As I always find, of late, the front of your Paper employed in giving lectures upon several Subjects, which are not only often very diverting, but always very profitable. I hope you will not deny this Letter a place in your Mercury, since it can be predudicial to none, and maybe the preserving me from Ruin. As you always avoid Scandal Falsity's, I am the more desirous my Case should be seen in your Paper.

Know then, I am the Daughter, and only Child, of a Gentleman of _____ Pounds a Year, and being arrived at near Twenty Years of Age, several have made their Advances to me, but none so successful as the only Son of a Wealty Tradesman: As he is entirely pleasing to me, I

have return'd agreeableness with a Modest Civility; but my Father being biggotted to the very Name of Gentleman, and having an innate Aversion for Traders, opposed my choice, and declare his Blood shall never be tainted by my Wedding a Machanick. This his Priciple arguement together with his saying, If I disobeyed I shall not Inherit. He recommended to my bosom an aged Gentleman of Sixty, but of a superior Fortune and ancient Family. Alas! Mr. Bradford, he little knows the sweetness of the young Trader or Machanicks Conversation, or the melting Musick of his Voice. How dull will be the Days, if I Marry the old Sire! the Light of the Sun will be tedious to me. When we are with a Person we like, the most trifling Object can afford delight, but with him we hate the Groves have no pleasure, and the gentle Voice of Birds is nothing agreeable. Oh! that I could give my Father my Eyes, or else see with his! 'Tis Shocking to my nature to disoblige my Parent; but I must affront him, or Injure my self. If Self-Murder is as Criminal as the Murder of another, then an Injury done to one's self is as great a Fault as one done another. Tell him, Sir, the Riches are not essential to Happiness; That a Person may be no Gentleman, tho decended from Lords, and the Tradesman have the Soul of a Gentleman, with the birth of a Machanick. Grandure and Insignificence are not incompatible, any more than meanest and Virtue. Oh let me rather Dye than Marry my Aversion! Therefore it is, Sir, That I call you to my Assistance. Tell my Father, that Tradesmen are not only advantageous to themselves, but Seviceable to the Nation in General; That there's not only profit but real Pleasure attending Business. Also advise him, how dull it is to be a Gentleman; and ask him which is best, To get Money, or to have nothing to do but spend it; and add, what else you think will lessen his over fond Opinion of Gentlemen, and increase his esteem for Tradesmen, which if you can do, you'll Oblige her who is Sir Your Servant.   Lavina.
   PHILADELPHIA Jan. 28. To be Sold, a very likely Indian Woman fit for all manner of House

Work, and Sewing, Washing, Starching, Ironing, &c. Enquire Andrew Bradford.

PHILADELPHIA Feb. 4. On the 16th of this Instant January William Sinton, committed to the County Goal of New-Castle, for forging the Paper Currency of the Government, Broke the said Goal and made his Escape; The said Sinton being a short fresh Coloured Man, about Twenty three Years of Age, wears a light bobb Wigg and Cinnamon coloured Cloaths, by Profession a Quaker. Whoever shall apprehend the said Sinton, and bring him to the Sheriff of New-Castle aforesaid, shall receive the Reward of Ten Pounds from   Rowland FitzGerald, Sheriff.

PHILADELPHIA Feb. 4. By Special Command of the Honourable Sir William Keith Bart. Governor of this Province, Publick Notice is hereby given: That there is to come to his Hands, a Writ of Hue and Cry, under the Hand of the Honourable Hugh Drysdale Esq; Governor of Virginia, and the Great Seal of the said Province, after one Thomas Glascock of Richmond County Virginia, Planter, for having barbarously Murdered William Forrester of the same County, Surgeon, by secretly stabbing him with a knife, as he entered the House of the said Glascock, to which he was invited in the business of his Profession, and of which wounds he instantly died. And that by the said Writ of Hue and Cry, under the hand and Seal of afore said, there is promise a Reward of Forty Pounds Sterling, to any Person or Persons who shall apprehend and secure the said Thomas Glascock so as he be brought to Justice: He is a man of middle stature, about 50 Years of Age, Well set, his Face bloated of a pale Complexion and much Wrinkled, his Hair dark coloured and almost Streight, his Eyebrows large and more than usual winking with his eyes, his Beard growing in patches and of a grayish hue, his Legs large and swelled with the Dropsie, his Garb uncertain, having carried several Suits of Cloths with him. Also he carried with him his Son named Gregory Glascock, about 21 Years of Age, a lusty well set Fellow, with Streight brown Hair, a swarthy Complexion and pretty much Freckled. It is also earnestly

Recommended to all Persons whatsoever, in any of His Majesty's Colonies or Plantations, who shall see or hear of the said Glascock; that they use their utmost endeavours to apprehend and secure him; that so notorious crime may be brought to Justice.

PHILADELPHIA Feb. 11. These are to give Notice, That there was stolen out of the Printing House in Philadelphia 5 or 6 sheets of 20 s. and 5 s. Bills of the Impression Paper Money, some of which were Sign'd and uttered by one John Jones, who was apprehended on Thursday last and brought before the Mayor of this City, and Confessed the Fact, some Bills being found about him unsigned, and as the Officer was carrying him to Goal he made his Escape from him, leaving his Coat behind him. He is a Tall Slender Lad, of pale Complexion about Eighteen Years of Age, he wares a light Bobb Wigg, but is uncertain what other Cloaths he has on. Whoever takes up the said John Jones and bring him to Philadelphia Goal, shall have Fifteen Pounds as a Reward and all Reasonable Charges, paid by

Andrew Bradford.

Likewise all Commanders of Vessels that are bound out, are hereby cautioned against carrying off the above said Jones, as they shall answer the same.

A Servant Man's Time, for 2 Years and 9 Months to be Sold, he is a Barber and Perriwigg-Maker by Trade, and a very good workman, a very brisk Young Man about 22 Years of Age, and fit for any sort of City or Country Business, The Chief reason of his being Sold is his Master's having two more Workman and not Employ for them all. He will dispose of very Reasonably. Enquire of George Sheed Perriwigg-Maker, in Second-Street in Philadelphia.

PHILADELPHIA Feb. 14. Strayed away, about the beginning of the Week, from Andrew Bradford, a Large light Bay Horse, with a star in his forehead, a black Main and Tail, and a black list down his Back, his Feet large and very Bushy, having no shoes on. Whoever takes up the said Horse and bring him to his said Master in Philadelphia, shall be very well Rewarded for

for their Pains.

PHILADELPHIA Feb. 18. To be Sold by Mathew Garrigue at the Sign of the Prince Eugene, in the Second-street in Philadelphia, a good new Billiard Table with its Appurtenances, for a Reasonable Price. All Persons that are Indebted to the said M. Garrogue are desired to pay the same with all speed, he designing to go to the West-Indies, with all his Family, next Spring.

PHILADELPHIA Feb. 25. Whereas the Fence of Francis Neef and Herman Tunen in German-Town, has at diverse Times in the Night been taken away, once 5 or 6 Pannels carried into a heap and Burn'd. These are therefore to give Notice, that if any Person who will inform against the Offenders so that they may be brought to Justice shall have Three Pounds as a Reward, paid by us,   Francis Neef and Herman Tunen.

PHILADELPHIA March 3. A very likely Negro Man by Trade a Baker, he can make Doe, and break Doe, Mould, Drive and Set. To be Sold by Theophilus Spurviter over against the Tons in Chestnut-Street.

PHILADELPHIA March 9. The Honourable Col, Peter Schuyler late President of this Province, dyed at Albany, the 18th of last Month.

On the 5th of this Instant dyed here William Carter, Esq; late Comptroller of His Majesty's Customs of this Port, in a very advanced Age.

REDFORDS FERRY March 10. These are to give Notice that the Commissioners for the County of Monmouth in their Return from Amboy to Redfords at the Ferry-House in the Night had taken out of the room they slept in, one of their Bags of 2033 Pounds out of which Bagg was taken 344 Pounds 1 s. but on the Monday following they found all the Money but half a Book of Bills of 12 s. and 15 s. each, in all 100 Bills, from 22100 to 22200, of which all Persons are desired to be careful not to receive any such Bills; but to apprehend and secure such Person or Persons who shall offer to Ulter them, and they shall have a Reward on Conviction of such Person or Persons the sum of Five Pounds. And any Person who shall bring the sais 100 Bills to Mr. David Lyall, shall have a Reward of Twenty

Pounds.

PHILADELPHIA March 17. Run away from Joseph Coleman of the Township of Whitland, in the great Valley, in the County of Chester, the first of this Instant March, a Negro Man named Franck, aged about 40 Years, he Talks good English and French, having on a white Eustian Frock the upper dubbel Breasted lined with a Lead Coullard Shalloon, leather Breeches, Tallow Stockings and Shoes, he having Swathe about one of his Leg's of the outside of his Stockings, he carried with him an Indian Blanket. Whoever takes up the said Negro and secures him and gives Notice to his said Master shall if taken in the City of Philadelphia or within 20 Miles of the said Colmans House 20 Shillings if 40 Miles 40 Shillings, and if further Three Pounds and all Reasonable Charge.

These are to forewarn all manner of Persons, not to lend any Money, nor sell any Ware; or Commodities, to Ann the Wife of Owen Hugh of East-Town in the County of Chester, upon the Account of her said Husband, for she hath Departed from him without lawful Occasion, and he will Pay no Debts that she Contracteth in his Name, to no manner of Person or Persons. Dated East-Town March the 3d 1724.   Owen Hugh.

PHILADELPHIA March 26. At a Court of Oyer and Terminer, held at Dover in the County of Kent upon Delaware, on the 19th of this Instant, one Francis Maciboy and Irishman received Sentence of Death, for Barbarously Beating and Wounding his Servant Lad of which soon Dyed.

These are to give Notice, that there was left at the House of Owen Humpbery's Sign of the White Horse in High-Street, about eighteen Months ago, a Box with several sorts of Goods as Spectacles, Needles, &c. Whoever shall describe the Marks, and pay the Charge, may have the Goods again.

To be let by Nicholas Gateau (commonly called the French Cook) a good convenient House with a Kitchen, Oven, and three Acres of Clover-Grass Land, fit for Mowing, on the Road to Andrew Robinson's Mill, about a Mile from the City of Philadelphia.

PHILADELPHIA April 2. Whereas there are several large Tracts of Land in the Province of East-Jersey, as well as Lots in the Town of Amboy, in the said Province, yet unsold belonging to the heirs of the late William Dockwra of the City of London Merchant, one of the Proprietors of the said Province; This is therefore to give Notice that Thomas Humphrey's of this City of Annapolis, in the Province of Maryland, who is legally Impowered to sell and dispose of the said Lands (as may appear by the power of attorney, recorded in the Secretarys Office, in the Town of Amboy, aforesaid) will give his attendance from the hour of Eleven to Four in the Afternoon, at Mr. Stephens of Amboy, from the Twentieth of April to the Twentieth of May next, in order to sell and dispose of the Land aforesaid.

A Plantation on Newton Creek in West Jersey, about 7 or 8 Miles from Philadelphia, to be Sold, Containing 520 Acres of Land, 40 thereof in Fence and Cleared, with a Dwelling House, and a large young Orchard and about 20 or 30 Acres of Meadow unmade the Land High and well Timber'd, with Oak and Hickery, and hath a Convenient Landing in the said Creek, clear of all Quit-Rents and Incombraces. It was formerly Robert Mungumery's. Inquire of the Widow Ellis, hard by Peter Barnet's at Maiden-Head, or Joseph Antrobus in Philadelphia.

PHILADELPHIA April 16. General Loan Office of the Province of Pennsylvania, April 8th 1724.

Whereas several Persons, have either by themselves or Friends made application, and got their names entered in the general Loan Office of this Province, for the taking out upon Loan certain Sums in Bills of Credit made current by the last Act, for emitting 30,000 Pounds which Persons either declined their Intentions or neglected to persue their said Application to Effect. These are therefore to give Notice to all Persons concerned, that unless they do forthwith come to the said Office and produce such Surritys as said Act Directs, whereby they may be certainly Entitled to the several Sums which they have Respectively applied for, that the whole Sum directed to be let out upon Loan by the said Act, will be put out to such Persons who do or may apply for the same, without any Regard or Respect to any former Application.

NEW-York April 27. Having Information of a Pirate Ship and Sloop being upon these Coasts, whereupon the Greyhound Man of War made a Dispatch, and sailed Yesterday Morning, and below the Narrows met a Sloop and Commanded her to come and give all account of what she had seen, but she refused, then he sent his Boat aboard the Sloop, but the Sloop's Crew best them off; whereupon they went back again, and the Greyhound fired upon the Sloop and chased her, but the Sloop endured this fire, for near six hours altogether, which much alarmed the Town, it being in sight of the Town; in the Evening a Boy came up and gave an Account that it was Capt. Tirkle Master from S. Carolina, his Men were afraid of being pressed & prefered to make the best of their way ashore. There was one Passenger named John Wilson kill'd in this Battle.

PHILADELPHIA May 7. Ran away the 12th of April last, from Philip Raynold living in Mausemond at James River in Virginia, a Negro named Scipio, (but now calls himself John White) he is a short Fellow, Cole black and round Fac'd, aged about 24 Years, he wears a black Wigg and a Cap, he has on a light coloured Drugget Coat trim'd with black, a black Damask Wescoat, and a pair of Cinnamon coloured Breeches, he hath a hole thro' his left Ear, and sort of a Scar between his Shoulders on his Back, he is a Glasier, a Spoon Maker, and a Tinker, and plays on the Violin.

Whoever takes up the said Negro and brings him to his said Master, or Andrew Bradford, Printer in Philadelphia, or secure him and gives Notice to either of the said Persons, so that his Master may have him again, shall have Five Pounds as a Reward besides all Reasonable Charges paid by   Philip Reynold.

There is another lusty Negro (supposed to be with him) called Harry, belonging to Colonel Diggs at York River, he is a CoachMan, if any Person will bring him to his said Master will be rewarded for their Pain.

PHILADELPHIA May. 7. By Permission of His Excellency Sir William Keith, Bart. Governor of Pennsylvania &c.

This is to give Notice to all Gentlemen, Ladies and others, That there is newly arrived to this place to famous Performance of Roap Dancing, which is performed to the Admiration of all beholders. 1st, By a little Boy of seven Years old, who Dances and Capers upon a strait Roap, to the wonder of all Spectators. 2dly, by a Woman, who Dances a Corant and a Jigg upon the Roap, which she performs as well as any Dancing Master does it on the Ground. 3dly, She Dances with Baskets upon her Feet, and Iron Fetters upon her Legs. 4thly, She walks upon the Roap with a Wheel-Barrow before her. 5thly, You will see various Performances upon the Slack Roap, 6thly, You are entertained with a Comical Humour of your old Friend Pickle Herring.

The whole Concluded with a Woman turning Round in a swift Motion with seven or eight Swords Pointed at her Eyes, Mouth and Breast, for a Quarter of an Hour together, to the Admiration of all that behold the Performance on the Stage to large here to mention.

The above performance are to be seen at the New-Booth on Society Hill, To begin on Tuesday next being the last Day of April, and to continue Acting, the Term of Twenty Days and no Longer. The Price upon the Stage is Three Shillings, in the Pit Two Shillings, and in the Gallery One Shilling and Six Pence. To begin exactly at Seven a Clock in the Evening.

PHILADELPHIA May 14. Run away on the 24th of March last, from Mr. Patrick Creagh, Painter, and Mr. William Rogers, both of the City of Annapolis in Maryland three Servant Men, the first named Thomas Robinson he is tall Fresh Coloured Man, he hath on a Yellowish Double Breasted Pea Coat Jacket, and Leather Breeches, he has long brown Hair, and his talk be an Irish Man, the Second a little Man named John Smith by Trade a House-Carpenter, he had with him two Pea Jackets to one Dark Grey, and the other light Coloured with a Red Vest, two pairs of

Breeches, the one Dark Cloth Drugget, the other Silk Drugget, two pair of Wosted Stockings, one Grey and the other Black; the other named Morgan Rogers, by Trade a House-Carpenter, he hath brown Hair and is much Pock fretten, he hath on a Brown Cloth Drugget Coat and Vest, they are supposed to have Stolen some Carpenters Tools and carried with them. Whoever takes up and secures the said Run aways so that their said Masters may have them again, shall have a Reward for each of them Five Pounds per Head, Paid By,
                                    Patrick Creagh.

PHILADELPHIA May 21. On Sunday last, being the Sixteenth of this Instant, we had a violent Storm of Wind, with very hard Showers of Rain and Claps of Thunder, which lasted abour eight Minutes, it has done very considerable Damage to our Orchards, and has killed several Cattle by the fall of the Trees, and in some parts of the Country they had very large Hail-Stones which they say destroyed whole Fields of Corn.

PHILADELPHIA May 28. There is a farm fronting the Sound divides betwext the Main Land and Staten Island, adjoining to Perth-Amboy in New-Jersey, containing about Two Hundred Acres, besides a large Quantity of Salt Meadow, inclosed by Water on two sides and on the other two good Post and Railes Fence, belonging to Mr. George Willock of Philadelphia, To be Sold on easy Terms, any Person that is inclined to Purchase it, may apply to him, or Mr. George Leslie in Pert-Amboy.

NEWCASTLE UPON DELAWARE May 28. This being the Anniversary of his Majesty's Birth-Day, Sir William Keith, Baronet, our Governor, came to the Court-House, attended with the principal Inhabitants of the Place, and after having cause the King's Charter to be publish'd for erecting the same into a Body Corporate and Politick, with many valuable Privileges, by the Name of the City of Newcastle, he made the following Speech to the Corporation.

Mr. Mayor and Gentlemen of the Corporation, Altho' I have comply'd with your desires at this Juncture, and always find a very agreeable Situation within my self, when it is my power to contribute any Thing towards the Happiness and prosperity of a People, who are immediately under my Care, yet I must put you in Mind, that your Gratitude on this Occasion is principally, and I may say wholly due to the benign influence of a most gracious King by whose Authority you are now happily posses'd of many Valuable and Great Privileges, and whose Royal Pattern of Love and Tenderness to all his Subjects, must inspire such as have Honour to be Employ'd under him in the Administration of the Affairs of Government, with some Share of the mild but Just and Steady Conduct, which so eminently shines from the Throne in a much greater Lustre, than has been known to this, or any former age.

When we consider the happy Period unto which the Wisdom of his present Majesty has brought not only the Affairs of his own Dominions, but of all Europe, it is impossible for us to withstand the Force of our Duty to such a Prince, who Rules and Commands terminates in the particular Happiness of his own People, and general Benevolence to Mankind.

A frequent and grateful Remembrance of many Blessings, We enjoy under the present Reign, must certainly stir up in us a very Sense of the common Benefits that attend in Equal Just and Free Government, where the Magistrates are esteemed and respected in their several Degrees, according to the Opportunities which they have of maintaining the Rights of Liberties of the People which Regard to that Legal Constitution upon which they are Founded, and by which only they can be preserved.

Nature simply considered, without the Improvement of Civil Government, does indeed put Mankind on a perfect Equality; but since the absolute Necessity of Human Society proceeds from the reciprocal Obligations which in the Course of Life Men cannot avoid receiving from each other; it will follow, that the Government of any Society is only the voluntary Establishment of an artificial, but just Force, upon every individual Person; to discharge such Obligations as he has received from the Publick and his Neighbours, with Justice and Gratitude: as any Magistrate therefore who will presume to exercise the Authority of his Office, beyond the equitable intent and plain Sense of the general Rule, may doubtless be charg'd with Injustice and Partiality; so on the other Hand, what person soever shall take upon him to vilify or detract from the Character of my Prince, Governour, or other inferior Magistrate in Authority, who evidently make the equitable Principle the Rule of the Actions; he will be distinguished, by every just and good man, either as an open enemy to the common wealth, or as an abject Slave to his own vile and unruly Passion, which not only render him incapable of doing or intending any good to the Publick, but even of receiving and enjoying the common Benefits which a Right appertain in the Freedom of an English Government.

The long Acquaintance which I have had with the principle Inhabitants of this Place, Encouraged me to hope, that a due Reflection of those Things which I have now recommended to the present Magistracy of this City, will in some Measure assist them and their Successors, to Act in their several Stations from Time to Time, as becomes, Loyal Subjects, Faithful Magistrates and affectionate good Neighbours: Always considering that their own Honour, Interest, and Reputation must be built upon the Ease and Happiness of the People under their Care, and on no other Foundation whatsoever.

The Gov. and his Lady were afterwards entertained at Dinner by the Magistrates, where the King's Health, his Royal Highness the Prince of Wales and all the Royal Family, with many other Loyal Healths drank, with several Discharges of the Cannon belonging to the Place.

NEWCASTLE UPON DELAWARE June 1. The following Address was presented to Sir William Keith Bart. In answer to his Speech of the 28th of May.

To His Excellency Sir William Keith, Bart. Governor of the County of Newcastle, Kent and Sussex upon Delaware, and Province of Pennsylvania.

The humble address of the Mayor, Aldermen, and Assistants of the City of Newcastle.

May it please your Excellency,
The many real Advantages, Privileges and peculiar Blessings which the present glorious Reign of the most Royal Sovereign, bestows on the Subject, are not wholly appropriated to those only who have the Happiness and Pleasure of being more immediately under his Majesty's Eye, but even we who are far distant and remote from his Sacred Person feel the benigh and deffusive Influence of his most Just and steady Administration, in the full Enjoyment of the ancient Rights, as well as in the considerable addition made thereunto, by granting us at this Time the Privilege of a Body Corporate and Politick.

As with unseigned Hearts and the greatest Gratitude, we humbly acknowledge our sense of His Majesty's Bounty, by your Excellency's means conferr'd upon us, so we hope in our several Stations to Improve the Royal Favours, by justly and impartially executing the Powers granted to us, in manner which we may be best suit the Place, Happiness, and Interest of those who are immediately concern'd therein.

And While our Breast are thus full of our Royal Sovereign's Benevolence to Mankind in General, and to us in particular; We are very well assured it's impossible. That any Power granted to us in his Majesty's Name, can be so Misaplpli'd, as to injure or molest even the meanest of out Fellow-Subjects.

We should be unworthy of our Care, Sir, and highly ungrateful, if we did not also acknowlege the last singular Instance of our tender Regard for our Welfare; and as by the just Application of the Privileges you are daily obtaining for us, we shall endeavour to render the Body of the Corporation more and more worthy of the same; so shall we ever continue to pray, That His Royal Majesty's Favours to the People of this Government, may be Long and Late be distributed from Your Excellency's Hands.

We are your Excellenc's Most Humble Servants.

PHILADELPHIA June 11. Whereas several Persons the last Year took upon Mortgages divers Sums; Bills of Credit, out of the Loan Office pursuant to the directions of the Act for Emitting

15,000 Pounds &c. Most of whose first payment are Due, and all will be in about two Weeks; these are therefore to give Notice to all concerned, that the Attendance will be given at the said Office, at the House of Charles Brockdon, from the Hours of Ten to Twelve in the Foernoon, and from Three to Five in the Afternoon, every third and fourth day of the Week, commonly called Tuesday and Wednesday, in order to receive in the said Payments until the Time allowed by Law is Expired, after which those who neglect to pay in, may expect to be proceeded again't, as said Act Directed.

N. B. Any Persons that have of Bills of credit which were Emitted last Year, may have some Changed for better Bills on the Office Days.

By Advice from Annapolis in Maryland, we have an account of a sad Misfortune that happened there to Capt. Lux, Master of a Ship who Unfortunately got a Fire and burnt down, she was laden with about 300 Hogsheads of Tobacco, and was to sail about two Days for London.

PHILADELPHIA June 11. Run away on the 21st of May last, from Philemon Lloyd Esq; of Maryland, two servant men the one named John Kersey by Trade a Carpenter, he's a tall slender Man of a Dark swarthy Complexion, small Visage with short black Hair, aged between Forty and Fifty years, he had on a dark coloured Kersey Coat, a double breasted grey Kersey Jacket, a pair of Cotton Breeches, a long Musquetoe Trowsers of brown Ozenbrigs, with a Felt Hat, a Speckled Shirt, and Country made Shoes and Stockings.

The other named William Thorton by Profession a Husbandman, aged about Thirty years, of a middle Stature, ruddy Complexion, with Red Hair, grey Eyes and Sandy Beard, he has on a Dark grey Kersey double breated Jacket, a strip't Flannen or Lindsey-wooly under vest, a pair of Leather Breeches, speckled linnen Shirts an old Hat, and Country made Shoes and Stockings. Whoever takes up the said Runaways, and secures them so that their said Master may have them

again, shall have Ten Pounds Reward for each of them, with Reasonable Charges, paid by me
                                    Philemon Lloyd.

NEW-YORK June 15. On the 28th past, (being the Anniversary of His Majesty's Birth-Day) the Officers and Soldiers of his Majesties Garrison at Fort George, (handsomely Cloath'd) appear'd under Arms, as did the Militia of this Place, at Noon His Majesties and other Royal Healths were Drank under the Discharge of the Cannon, and three Volleys of the Soldiers, at Night the Houses were Illuminated and there was Bonfires and plenty of Wine at the charge of the Corporation, where the Royal Health were likewise Drank the whole concluded with a fine Ball and Entertainment by his Excellency William Barnet Esq; our Governor.

PHILADELPHIA June 18. These are to give Notice that there is taken up at the Plantation of Joseph Wood near Delaware Falls, a brown Mare mark'd with an S and a Heart, on each Shoulder. If the Owner of this said Mare will come to the aforesaid Plantation he may have her again paying Reasonable Charges.

PHILADELPHIA June 25. The Noted ——— Mr. Riddlesden an Attorney, as he calls himself formerly Transported into Maryland and Married there, went to London, Married a great Fortune there, after that he was taken up and committed to Newgate, and ordered a Second Transportation he has been noted in several English Prints, is now arrived in this Province, when he was here before he went by the name of Van Riddleden, but now calls himself Cornwallis.

NEW-YORK On the 26th Arrived here his Majestys Ship Greyhound, Capt. Solgard Commander from his Cruise; She has been at Virginia, but mist the Spanish Pyrate not above two Days, and the Virginia Man of War, 'twas thought was within six Hours Sale of her but mist her, those Pyrates have taken several Vessels, two Brigantines from Boston Bound for Virginia, Capt. Jones from Guinea bound to Virginia, from whom they took 40 of the best Slaves, and about 100 Pounds and would have carried the Ship off, but feared meeting with the Man of War Capt. Ver, whom Capt. Jones had parted with the Night before. The Pyrates, had 12 Guns and 100 Men, and tis said belongs to the Governor of Havanna; They have taken several other Vessels, one or two from England.

PHILADELPHIA July 2. All Persons that have any Demands on the Estate of Leson Loftus Deceased, are desired to bring in their Accounts to his Widow for being Executrix to the said Will, And all Persons that are indebted to the said Estate, are desired to come and Settle the same.

All Persons Indebted to Owen Roberts of Philadelphia are hereby desired forthwith to Account with and pay him their several Debts, the better enable him to Discharge his, otherwise he will be oblige to proceed in Law, against such a Delay.

NEW-YORK July 6. Four Spanish Pyrates arrived here Friday; from Lewis-Town, and were Examined before the Governor and Council and there is a Commission Granted for their Trial.

PHILADELPHIA July 9. John Rice Mariner, Commander of the Sloop Mary, on his Oath of the Holy Evangelist of Almighty God, Deposeth and Saith, That on his Voyage from Boston the Virginia; Off the Capes of Virginia, in the Latitude of 36 degrees 49 min. He was taken by a Spanish Pirate Ship, called the Francises, Commanded by one _____ on the 11th of June last, that the said Pirate eight or ten Days before he took this Deponent, took a Topman Ship called the Godolphin one Theadola Beer Commander, bound for Virginia, and sometime before that had taken a Guinea, man, Commanded by Jones loaded with Negroes to York-River; that the said Pirate kept this Deponent till the 15th, and then put him on board the Topman Ship with twenty negroes they had taken from the Guinea man; that the Deponent Intended to have made the Cape of Virginia, and to have carried the Ship to the Owner thereof, (the said Beer) who was put on board the said Jones, but the Wind not favouring he resolved to make the best of his way for Philadelphia and being at Anchor near Ready Island, and having two Brothers at Salem, he went with 3 Hands thither, to fit himself with some

Necessaries, that Mr. Rolse the Collector there, having heard of this Deponent being taken by Pirates, Enquired this Deponent of the matter, that this Deponent gave him full and true Account thereof. Whereupon the said Rolse put this Deponent into Sheriffs Custody, and Seized the Vessel.   John Rice.

We have q Report that the Virginia Man of War was taken by the Pyrates after an Engagement of five hours, it is said there is a Letter come to New-Castle (others say she was taken at Anchor, but we want a true Conformation how taken.)

NEW-YORK July 13. On Friday last the Spanish Pyrates were tryed here, at a Court of Admiralty for trying of Pyracys, and Robberys, whereof they were accused and Received Sentence of Death Accordingly, who are to be hanged at such time, and place, as his Excellency (the President of the court) shall appoint, 'tis said his Excellency will Reprieve a young Malatto fellow as an Object of his Majesty's Mercy.

PHILADELPHIA July 16. Ran away the 9th of this Instant, from Alexander Morgan, Pensauken Creek, in the County of Glouster in West-Jersey, a servant Lad named Richard Boon, a well set full Fac'd, short brown Hair, Aged 18 Years; also a Negro Boy named Ceazer, aged about 10 Years, they took a Wherry with two Sails, the White boy has on a homespun brown Kersey Coat a felt Hat, and a Leather Jacket. Whoever shall take up the said Lads and secure them again, shall have 40 Shillings as a Reward for each and all Reasonable Charges.

PHILADELPHIA July 23. Since our Publishing the Deposition of John Rice, Master of the Sloop Mary, who was taken by the Spanish Pirate; we have received a more particular Account thereof which is as follows;

We Sailed from Boston the 5th of May in the Sloop above mentioned, but met with contrary Winds for 5 Weeks; on the 11th of June, just after Observation, being 11 Miles to the Southward of Cape Henry, and, as was reckoned, about 20 Leagues to the Eastward, we Spyed 2 Sail which being Ships and standing from the Land, we judged to be homeward bound, Virginia Men; therefore kept on our Way, Intending to enquire what Distance the capes bore: They hung but English Colours, we the same, and soon we came within Gun Shot, one of them fired a Ball of which came between our Mast and Boom; the other came ranging along Side, and gave a Volley of Small Arms, which, Blessed be God; hurt none; they ordered the Master to go on board the Commodore; which he with 3 Hands did, 5 of their Hands came back with the Boat, examined John Copson what the Loading was; which he gave them an Account of; except the dry Goods; They replyed to him they wanted none such; Dry Goods and Water was what they sought for, So on their return, the Master and Hands was sent back, and ordered to sail on his way; which he did for near an Hour, when we perceived one of the Ships tack about and stand after us; we endeavered to make a way from her for some time, but finding she out sailed us, and fearing their Cruelty, brought to, and lay by until She came up; She, we found, was not the Ship which released us before, but the Prize Godolphin, in which they had put a Lieutenant of the Pirates, as Captain, with 14 or 16 Men, all Spaniards except one French Man. The Lieutenant who is called Capt. Machads, ordered the Master and Owner to come on board him, which they Obeyed, presently after the other Ship came up, and called to that we were in, hot words passed between them; the Commodore being Angry that they came after us when he had released us. In the midst of their Dispute, they saw a Sail, which seemed a Large Ship, this put an End to their Quarrel; they thinking She was a Man of War; was by a great Consternation, And Examined thereupon, and tho' the Master and Owner assured them, they had not seen the Man of War, yet they beat the Master; and flung John Copson head long down the Hatchway. The Ship as soon as she made them Plain, tacked about and stood to the Northward, being as much a fraid of them as they were of her. At Night they shut the Master in the Hold, and locked John Copson in the State Room, into which place next Morning they brought the Master and kept them confined there until the 15th following during which time they unloaded the said Ship, of all her Goods, part of which they put on board the Pirate Ship, the rest on board the Sloop, they being straightted for Water, put 20 Negroe Slaves on Board the Godolphin; which Slave, they took the 5th of that Month from one Captain Jones bound from Guinea to Virginia, after they had loaded the said Ship, they suffered the said John Copson to depart with the Master of the Sloop, and his Men in the said Ship Godolphin; the Wind Comencing still Westerly, the first Land they made was Long-Island 2 Days after which they came into. The Capes of Delaware, the next Morning being the 2d of June they came Anchor in the said River, when the Master, the Mate and 2 Hands, went on Shoar to Salem for some Refreshments as they said, John Copson refused to go with them, was left with one White Man, and the Negroes on board, they promised to return on board directly, and did Design to do so, but was Stop't by the Collector of Salem: Mr. Rolse, who next Day came on board, and Seized the said Ship, and carried her into Salem, then she was on Pennsylvania side, and designed to be brought up by the said John Copson, and his People to Philadelphia, to be secured for the said Owners, until Advice could be sent to them thereof.

John Copson aforesaid, besides the loss of the Sloop, and the Cargo, which was Considerable, was by the said barbarous Villains Stript almost Naked, and otherways Misused.

The Ship is a Gard della Coast, or hired out as such by the Government of Cuba who owns her, she is Called St. Francisco Della Vel; The Officers names are as follows.

The Ship Prancisco Della Vels, owned by the Government of Cuba 97 Men or there about 23 Guns, Officers, Capt. Signor Don Beneto, Lives in St. Christophers, Cuba, near one Port del Primcipi. Lieutenant Captain Machads, lives in Havanna, near the House of Capt. Refendo, Pilot or Master, Benjamin Evans, formerly of London, but now lives in St. Jago in Cuba. Quarter-Master, Richard Holland, born near Dublin, in

Ireland, now lives in the Havanna and is Married to the Daughter of Juan Duran. These Particulars attested by Juan Magan one of their Crew.

NEW-YORK Aug. 7. Youth Qualified for Business and carefully thought; Writing in it's Theory and Practice; Arithmetick and eusie and store way, Adapted to the meanest Capacity. Merchant Accounts, and Book-keeping now in use, and practiced by most Eminent Merchants and Trades in Europe. By Mitchell Somerset, writing Master in Hanover Square, in the City of New-York. Youth Boarded and all manner of Scriveners Business: also those that desire it, may be instructed at their Houses.

PHILADELPHIA Aug. 13. Richard Wall, a Smith or Candlestick-maker of Burmingham in Warwhickshire, England, having been absent from Ann hall his Wife this five Years, and is being four years since he wrote last to her, he being then a Servant in Mr. Thomas Billinger in the Township of Everham in Surrey Pennsylvania; it's supposed he is dead: Therefore the said Richard Wall (if he be living) or the said Billinger (if said Walls dead) desired to write forthwith to the said Ann Wall (who now lives at MacClesfield in Chesire, England) for the said Richard hath a Relation Lately dead, who hath left him a considerable Legacy. And if the said Wall be living, and is not inclined to come to England, he is desired to send over a Letter of Attorney to his Wife, to impower some Friends of his to receive the said Legacy for the use of his said Wife and Child.

N. B. If the said Richard Wall will apply to Andrew Bradford within this fortnight, he may be supplyed with Money, or other things, in order for him going to England.

PHILADELPHIA Aug. 15. The third Instant, about the Hour of 12 (at New-Garden in Chester) there began a most terrible, and Surprizing Whirl Wind, which took the Roof of a Barn and carried it into the Air, and scattered it about two Miles off, also a Mill that had a large quantity of wheat in it, and has thrown it down and removed the Mill-Stone! and took a Lath of the Barn, and carried it into the Air, which fell

with such force down that it stuck fast into a
White Oak Stump, so that it is very hard to get
it out, it also carried a Plow into the Air,
and at the fall thereof, Pitch'd one end of the
Beam, and stuck into the Ground quite up to the
Coulter, so that they were forced to dig it out,
it killed a Parcel of Geese and three or four
Hawks, which were found dead about the Fields.

From the County of Philadelphia we have the
Following account.

At Plymouth, a violent Wind, or Hurricane,
took off the Roof of a large Barn, and carried
it to an adjoining Field, as also half a Roof
of a Store Dwelling House, belonging to the same
Owner, and carried that some distance: It is
likewise said, that among some other things
taken out of the said House Garret, a Woman's
Petty-Coat was taken, and afterwards found in a
Field about 7 or 8 Miles off. Near the branch
of Neshameny, three Men perceiving the Gust coming got into a strong Logg House lately built,
and shut the Door upon them to avoid the Violence of the Storm? but soon perceived themselves in Danger, two of them got out the Door,
and were both taken off the Earth, and one of
them drop'd in a Furrow in a Field, hard by,
where with great difficulty he Escaped, being
Taken away another fell by a Stump; and took
hold of the twiggs growing thereby but the Wind
had too great a Power over him, for it took his
Body from the Ground! but by his fast holding
he escap'd being carried away, the 3d Man upon
the Wind taking up the whole House? some foot
from the Ground, attempted to make his Escape
under the Sill, but it taking the Roof from the
Loggs, they drop'd upon part of the under Pinning, and catch'd him in some Vacancy under
them, who was afterwards Dugg out by his Companions, without any great hurt; the Roof was
carried some Miles off, and broke to pieces,
there was a Chest of Cloath taken out of the
said House, part of the Chest was found a Considerable Distance off, but the Cloath not yet
heard of. It tore and scatter'd round the
Fields, three Stacks of Corn near the aforesaid
House, where they saved some, it took up almost

all the Apple Trees in the Orchard by the Roots and Carry'd them some Distance; a Horse standing at the Door with a Cart or Stead to him; the Cart was Tore all to pieces, the Horse was found some distance off Intangled among a Heap of Trees, that were blown down, but receiv'd little Damage.

We have also an Account from Bucks County that it took up a House from the Ground, where the People was in, and lifted it so high that the Man was making his escape under the ceil, with a Child in his Arms, and the House fell upon him, but has not hurt him very much, but the Child was carry'd away with the Wind? It also took the Water out of the River Delaware, (above the Falls) at the Ferry call'd Camby's Ferry. It had taken very large trees up by the Roots, some about 6o or 70 foot Long, and carried sole Poles from their Place, and twisted them off, it has taken up Fences and scarterred them all about; and it has done much more mischief which I have not particularly Accounts of yet, it went over into the Jerseys above the Falls, but how far we have no particular Account of Yet, it is gone through the Province. We desire all Persons to send in the Particulars to the Printer hereof, to be inserted in our Next.

PHILADELPHIA Aug. 20. On the 17th, 18th, and 19th of this Instant, we had a violent Storm of Wind and rain which has caused such a Fresh in our Creeks and Rivers that it broke several of our Best Mill Dams, in this and other Neighbouring Provinces, (particularly Coll. Trents, the Mill at Penepack,) and the fresh is so strong that our Vessels in the Road have not Winded; Such a Fresh has not been known this Twenty Years.

Run away the 16th of this Instant August, from his Master Walter Nevil, (of Queen Ann's County Maryland,) a Servant Man nam'd Simon Moore, he hath black short Hair, and had on a large Kersey Coat, it has 3 Buttons on the Breast; also a close bodied Duroy Coat, of a blewish Colour lined with the same; a Jerkin Jacket Trim'd with Black, and lined with black Shallon, a pair of shag Breeches with Pewter Buttons a pair of Worsted Stockings, and several other pairs with him. Whoever shall take up the said Servant, and bring him to his said Master, or Caleb Cash in Philadelphia, shall have 50 Shillings as a Reward with reasonable Charges.

PHILADELPHIA Aug. 27. We have further Accounts of the Whirl-Wind, of Hurricane, from the Great Valley, where it took up very large Trees, by the Roots, but particularly one of about 3 Foot over, and carried it up in the Air a great height, so that when it fell, stuck very deep upright; it made clean work where it went, took up all as tho' it had been Grubed, and where it went a cross the Roades, it laid Trees so thick that it is very difficult to Travel, it made a Road of about 40 Pole in Breath and in some Places it parted then met again about two Miles off.

PHILADELPHIA Aug. 27. A well accustomed Shop, and a convenient Tenement; being the late Dwelling House of Joseph Oade deceased, in the Second Street, near the Market Place in Philadelphia, to be Lett together with a Still-house, a soap-house well fixed, with Stills, Worms, Furnaces, and other utensils, and materials, necessary for the carring on the Soap boyling, and Distilling business, also an Engine for cutting of Tobacco, with all things necessary for that Work, which moveable together, with a good quantity of Tobacco, and Divers sorts of Goods are to be Sold very Cheap: For farther Information Enquire at the aforesaid House.

Ruth Norton, who came into this Province about 17 Years ago from Ireland, in the Station of a Gentlewoman's Servant, and is supposed to have been since married to one Thomas Brown, a Sea-Faring Man, may repair to John Brown, Clerk to John Moore of Philadelphia Esq; and be inform'd of something very considerable for her great Advantage.

PHILADELPHIA Sept. 3. We have an Account from East New-Jersey that the great Flood (as mentioned in our former Papers,) has done a considerable Damage to the Mill-Dams, and Bridges and especially Crosswicks and South-River, which were very large and strong; but particularly in the County of Monmouth, it carried away about 40 Mill-Dams, and quite ruin'd some of the Mills, and so likewise in other Counties, but we have not the Particulars of it yet.

All sorts of Household goods, to be Sold very reasonable by the Widow Jones, at the Sign of the Plum of Feathers, in Second-Street, and likewise the House to be Let, She designing to go for England as soon as possible.

A very Strong Negro Man, about 25 Years, fit for all manner of Country Work, as Plowing and Carting &c. To be Sold Enquire of William Rakestraw in Philadelphia.

To be Sold by Thomas Vanbuskirk of Hakensack and George Ryerson of Peguannock both of Bergen County, a certain Tract of Land (commonly call'd or nam'd Bolens Lot) containing about 1500 acres Situated in New-Jersey in the County of Hunterdon, lying on both sides of a Branch of Pasayuck River, called Rokerway River, about two Miles above Humprey Devenports consisting more than half low land, (fit for Raising Wheat) with good meadows: and the rest, generally good high Land, well Timber'd. Those who are inclined to Purchase the same, may Treat, and Agree, with the Persons above mentioned, they being in Power to Sell the same.

NEW-YORK Sept. 7. Yesterday the Custom-house Scooner sailes against Humphry Clay's Passenger boat from New-York to the Narrows, and so back again: In which sailing, the latter had the Advantage, and won the Wager of One Hundred Pounds current money of New-York.

On Wednesday a Man in black Cloaths, and a Light Wigg, riding through Statten-Island, came up to some Children that were at play, and asked one Boy whose Son he was? The Boy answered, I am Isaac Laceman's Son. Whereupon the man Delivered a large Pacquet, he found some New-Jersey Bills, amounting to four Pounds and six Pence. All the writing was, Take this and use it as your own.

PHILADELPHIA Sept. 10. We have Advise from Cape May, that there was a Sloop drove a shore there as a wreck, her Hands having left her at

Sea, and was late Arrived at Lewis-Town: She was commanded by one Capt. Thomas Moufield from Boston, Loaded with Rum and Molasses (the sloop is since got off, and safe at Cape May.

PHILADELPHIA Sept. 17. On Saturday Night last Arrived here Col. Spottwood, (late Governor of Virginia) who was met by our Governor Sir William Keith at Darby, with about 60 Horse from this City, and was welcomed by the Discharge of the great Guns of the Place, and the Vessels in the Road.

PHILADELPHIA Sept. 24. Run away the 3d of this Instant, from his Master Alexander Morgan of Pensauken Creek, in the County of Glouster, in West-Jersey, a Servant Lad named Richard Boon, he had with him a gray Kersey Coat lined with Blew, a dark brown Kersey Jacket lined with white Plannel, brass Buttons. (he went with a Popular Cannoe.) Whoever takes up the said servant, and secure him so that his said Master may have him again, shall have 40 Shillings as a Reward and Reasonable Charges.

PHILADELPHIA Oct. 15. Run away from the Plantation of Cornelius Van Horne, on Rariton River, a Maligasco Negro Man, named Tom, he is a black likely Fellow, pretty Tall, a grave Look, has a homespun brown Jacket, and lined with the same, has Brass Buttons. Whoever takes up the said Negro and Delivers him to his said Master Cornelus Van Horne, in New-York, or in Amboy Goal, shall have Three Pounds as a Reward and reasonable Charges.

PHILADELPHIA Oct. 29. Run away from Benjamin Vining near Salem, the 22d of this Instant, a Servant Man named Edward Burrows; Aged about 35 Years, by Trade a House-Carpenter, middle siz'd, swarthy thin visage with black curl'd Hair, (he is much pitt'd with the Small-Pox) his knees and Toes much pointing one from the other, with a very Slothful Gaite, he had on a white Shirt, a gray dark Broadcloth Jacket, with course Thread Button Holes of another colour, an old blue Camblet Coat, and Leather Breeches; good Shoes and Stockings, a new Hat, he is suppose to be gone into lower Counties of Pennsylvania. Whoever takes up the said Run away and bring him to his Master, or to Mr. Abraham Vining in Philadelphia, shall have 40 Shillings as a Reward and all reasonable Charges.

A good new House with a large lot of Ground, in the Third-Street in Philadelphia, To be Sold. Any Person who are desirous to Treat for the same may Enquire of John Heap and know farther.

These are to Certify to all Persons that have any Accounts Depending upon Samuel Carr deceased they may apply themselves to John Eyera, who is the Administrator.

PHILADELPHIA Nov. 5. Run away from Abraham Porter, of Porters Field in the County of Glouster, in West Jersey, two Servant Men, viz. One named William Young, who went away the 25th of last October, Aged 22 Years or there about, of a fair Complexion and slender, a middle Stature brown Hair lately cut off, and took with him a Gun; he had on a fine Hat, a bob Wigg of brown Colour, and brown Dragget Coat, with a double Breasted brown Kersey Jacket, pretty old, one fine Shirt, and one Ozenbrig Shirt, with Leather Breeches, a pair of grey Yarn Stockings, and good round toe'd Shoes.

The other of said Servant named John Martin, who went away the 29th Day of the same Instant, he's a well set Man, middle size of a redish Complexion, with red Hair lately cut off, Aged about 38 Years, and had on a Felt Hat, with a knit Cap, an old brown Coat mended on both Shoulders two Ozenbrig Shirts, a pair of Leather Breeches, an old brown pair of Stockings, a brown Drugget Coat, and a pair of round Toe'd Shoes with low Heels. Whoever takes up and secures the said Servants and brings them to their said Master, or give Notice thereof so that he may have them again, shall have 30 Shillings as a Reward for each and reasonable Charges.

PHILADELPHIA Nov. 12. Taken out of the House of Richard Grafton in Newcastle, the 5th of this Instant November, a Silver Pint Mug and Spoon, also a Spoon about a Month ago, all are Mark'd G. Any Person that can give intelligence of the said Plate so it may be had again shall have 30 Shillings Reward for the whole, or in Proportion for any part thereof with resonable Charges, or in proportion for any part thereof with reasonable Charges, or if offer'd to sale are Desired to stop them.

Strayed or Stolen away from Joseph Pennel of Egmouth in Chester County, on the 25th of October last, a bright Bay Horse marked with a Half-Penny on the far Ear, and branded with RP on the near Shoulder, and a small saddle mark, and a long switch Tail. Any Person that can take up the said Horse and bring him to the Owner, or William Tidmarsh at the 9 Tunns in Philadelphia shall have Twenty Shillings as a Reward and Reasonable Charges.

PHILADELPHIA Dec. 3. There will be exposed to sale by Vendue on Tuesday next, being the 8th of this Instant December, at 3 a Clock in the Afternoon, at the Coffee-House in Philadelphia: The Ship Fame, Burthen of 300 Tons and mounted with 25 Guns, together with all of her Guns, Ammunition, Apparel and Furniture, and likewise a large Quantity of Arrack French Brandy, also Rhenis, Cherry and French Wines; which said Ship and Goods were taken in Execution (in pursuance of Judgement of the Court of Common Pleas, held in Philadelphia,) for the use of the Sovereign Lord the King, &c. by Owen Roberts Esq; High Sheriff of the City and County of Philadelphia, at whose Office in the said City, the Inventory of the said Ship, Guns, Apparel, Furniture &c. and all the other Goods so taken in execution, as foresaid may be seen by any Person who has a mind to Purchase.   Owen Roberts, Sheriff.

Run away from Thomas Hill of Salem, in West Jersey, and Indentured Servant lad named Jonathan William (formerly a Servant to William Baldwin of Namans Creek, Miller) Aged 18 Years or thereabout being a short well set Lad, of a Brown Complexion, with short Hair, an old Beaver Hat, a dark gray Kersey double Breasted Jacket, a Dragget lair of Breeches of a dark Yellow, a pair of Trowsers; a pair of home made Stockings, and round Toe'd Shoes with Steel Buckles. Whoever takes up and secures the said Servant, or bring him Home to his Master, shall have a Pistole Reward besides reasonable Charges.

PHILADELPHIA Dec. 10. Papers relating to an

Act of the assembly of the Province of New-York for the encouragement of the Indian Trade by and for Prohibiting the Selling of Indian Goods to the French, viz. of Canada. 1. A Petition of Merchants of London to His Majesty, against the said Act. 11. His Majesty's order in Council, Referring to the Lord Commissioners for Trade and Plantations. 111. Extract of the Minutes of said Lords, concerning some Allegations of the Merchants before them. 1V. The Reports of the said Lords to His Majesty on the Merchants Petition, and after Allegations. V. The Report of the Committee of Council of the Province of New-York, in answer to the said Petition. V1. A Memorial concerning the Fur-Trade of New-York by C. Coldell, Esq; with a Map, whereon is laid down the River of St. Lawrence, Quebec, and Montreal, New-York, Hudson-River and Albany; the Mohawk River, and situations of the Settlements of the Five Nations of Indians as also the Lakes and how they are situated with Respect to Canada, New-York, Pennsylvania and Maryland. Printed and sold by William Bradford in New-York.

PHILADELPHIA Dec. 15. On Tuesday Night last was Married Sir William Kieth's Daughter to Mr. Yeilds a Gentleman of the Island of Jamaica.

The same day we had a violent storm of Wind and Rain which rose the Tide very high so that it overflowed most of our Wharfs and Stores, but it being in the day time there was very little damage done, it was much higher than the Great storm we had some time ago, it has also two of our outward bound Vessels on shore, but they will be got off again, its hoped, without very much Damage, two Outward bound Vessels are waiting for fear of the Ice, of which our River is now very full.

PHILADELPHIA Dec. 22. We have Advice that there is a Brigintine from Jamaica, and a Ship from Ireland going into our Bay, but the River being full of Ice they are no Vessels come up or gone down since our last. There was also a Ship from Bristol in the Bay, but she is put out to Sea again.

Just Published and Sold by William Bradford

in New-York, and by Andrew Bradford in Philadelphia.

An Esay on Scripture-Prophecy, wherein it is Endeavoured to Explain the Three Periods contain'd in the XII Chapter of the Prophet Daniel. With some Arguments to make it Probable, that the First of the Periods did Expire in the Year 1715.

Advice received from London of Oct. 12 that Twenty one Felons from Lincolnshire and Nottingshire, that were on Board the Ship Robert and Mary to be transported to Maryland, mutiny'd against the Captain and Seamen the 26th past, and having seized the Boat, made their Escape on Shore near Hatwich.

PHILADELPHIA Dec. 29. On Friday the 25th of this Instant, One William Trent Esq; Chief Justice of the Province of New-Jersey, departed this Life (being ceased with a Fitt of Apolexy) at his House in Trent Town. He was one that was universally Belov'd, and is much Lamented.

We hear from South River that the Bridge there which has been down some considerable time, (to the great trouble of the Travelers) is now put up again, being much stronger now than ever it was before.

Run away the 28th of this Instant, December, from Lawrence Reynolds of Philadelphia, Currier, an Irish Man named Hugh Masterson, speaks much upon the Irish Tone or Accent, about five Feet nine Inches high, wears a bob Wig tied behind with a string or thread, thick Eyebrows, pretty large Nose, a dark brown Coat on, and square Toe'd Shoes. He hath stolen and taken with him, a Silver handled Sword broad shoulder Blade and a Silver Chase to it, but 'tis supposed he has broken the Blade. He has also taken one pair of Shoes, a new Muslin Neckcloath, one Shirt and divers other things. Whoever secures the said Person, and give Notice thereof to the said Lawrence Reynolds, shall have 40 Shillings and Reasonable Charges.

The General History of the Pyrates from the first Rise and Settlement in the Island of Providence to the present Time. With the remarkable Actions, and Adventures of two Female

Pyrates, Mary Read and Anne Bonny. To which is added, A short Abstract of the Stature and Civil Law in Relation to Piracy, by Captain Chas. Johnson. Sold by William Bradford in New-York.

1725

PHILADELPHIA Jan. 5. Whereas by the late Excise Act, all Retailers of Wine, Rum, &c. are obliged once every six Weeks, (or after if there unto Required) to make Entry &c. pay six Pence per Gallon for all Wines, Rum, and Brandy and other Spirits, which they shall Vend within that Time. Notwithstanding which sundry of the said Retailers are considerably in Arrear for excise, which renders the Collector thereof incapable to make Payments to the Treasurer, as is Required by the said Law. These are therefore to give Notice as well as those who form the said Excise as to others, that Unless they pay in their Arrears, on or before the 14th Day of February next, they will be proceeded against as said Law Directs.   Chas. Read. Coll.

PHILADELPHIA Jan. 12. The Speech of Sir William Keith, Bart. Governor of the Province of Pennsylvania, and the Counties of New-Castle, Kent and Sussex upon Delaware,

To the Representatives of the Freemen of the said Province of Pennsylvania in General Assembly met, Jan. 5, 1725.

Mr. Speaker and Gentlemen of the Assembly, The good Agreement which has so easily and Cheerfully Subsisted between the Governour and the people's Representatives in Assembly, for so many Years, has under the Influence of God's good Providence, been very Instrumental towards the obtaining of many good Laws, which have increased our Commerce, and rendered the generality of the People perfectly Easy to what they were some Time before.

Nevertheless, such is the Imperfection of Human Affairs, that even the greatest Blessings are not thought of of, and acknowledge in the same manner by all Men; for the same acts of Benevolence, which one are amiable to Justice and Good Nature, become hateful to the Envious Proud Man; and that Generous Disposition, which leads good Men to be contented with sharing the common Benefits of Life freely and Equally with their Fellow Creatures, in most Detestful to those, who sooth Ambition, and thirst after Power, under the conceited Pretence of subduing Ignorance by their own superior Knowledge.

If the Peace, Interest and Prosperity of a People be (as I have always Understood it) the true End of Government, where any reasonable Ground of Discontent to be found amongst us?

You that are the People's Representatives, and Guardians of the Liberties, the best Councellors to any Governour, and the proper Judges of all publick Grievances, say, Whose Property have I at any Time Wronged? Or whose Petition have I refused? What part of the publick Service have I neglected, and at what Time has our Sovereign Lord the King, the Proprietor or the Country Suffered by any Action or Mis-Conduct of Mine? It is to be charged as a Crime for the Government to concur with your House, into Laws? To Maintain the King's Legal Prerogative, and to support the Proprietor's Just Rights, consistent with the Privileges which he has been pleased to Grant you by Charter? It is a Crime to commiserate the Distress of the Poor, and to provide for their Relief? To encourage Industry and to promote Trade? Is it a Crime to do equal Justice unto all Men, and to appear boldly in defence of the Constitution, and Liberties of our Country?

I say, if these things, Gentlemen are to be charged upon your Government, and an Act of Male-Administration? it is high Time for you to your selves, and Endeavour to ward off the blow, by modestly Asserting your lawful Priviledges, as English Men, and Loyal Subjects, to the best of Kings, as well as Dutiful Tennants to the Proprietor's Families.

The whole Country feels at this Time an agreeable Effect of a most Happy Unanimity, and undisturbed Concord, between the Governour and Assembly, for above seven Years last past; it has the lovely Prospect, I thank God, of continuing Firm like a Bulwark, that is not to be broke down: We have no Chimerical Scheme and New Prospects on Foot, wherewith to Teaze and Surprise one another; our Duty is Plain and Easy, with ready Wills and contented Minds, wherefore we have no just Reason to apprehend the Consequence of any Event, but serve those whose Consciences are less free, to be Afraid.

W. Keith.

To Sir William Kwith Bart. Governour of Pennsylvania, &c.

The Address of the Representatives of the said Province, in Answer to the Governours Speech.

Upon this fresh occasion of the Governour's Speech to us the 5th Instant, We must sincerely and Thankfully acknowledge the favourable Dispensation of Divine Providence, from time to time, to the People of this Province whom we represent; among which we are Obliged in Gratitude to acknowledge the Governour's ready Concurrence to such Bills as in his Judgement appear to be for the Interest of this Province, and particularly such as really do contribute to the Increase of Trade, and render the People easy.

We are nevertheless sensible with the governour, of the imperfection of Human Nature, and that there are in the most Governments some Tempers, that cannot be satisfyed short of unlimited Power; but such are not apparent to us under the Governours Administration.

We cannot concur with the Governour, in observing the solid happiness that attends Unanimity and Concord, (without which no Government can be happy) which we shall always endeavour to promote; and to the utmost of our Power shall be diligent, and careful to suppress every unjust cause of Murmuring and Discontent.

We hope also, that we shall acquaint ourselves Loyal and Dutiful to the Proprietors, and also at all Times with courage, Assert the Privileges of the free born Subjects we represent.

As the Governour has not thought fit to Recommend any thing further to us in his Speech, for a foundation of our Proceedings; we shall apply our selves to consider, what the Exigencies of the Country may at this Time require us, in which shall hope for the Governour's favorable Concurrence, all likewise shall not be wanting to supply the Governour with Honourable Support. Signed by order of the House,

William Biles, Speaker.

PHILADELPHIA Jan. 19. Run away the 28th of December last, from Richard Dobson at the Head of Elk-River, a Servant Man named George Lesley, aged about 19 Years, Fresh Coloured, young Face without a Beard and thick Lip'd. He had on a gray Coat with Redish Buttons, white Linsey Wastcoat. He Stole and took with him a black Horse with a Star in his Forehead, and Branded with a figure of 2 on the near Shoulder and with I.I. on the near Buttock. Whoever takes up said Servant and bring him to his said Master, so that he may have him again, shall have Forty Shillings as a Reward and Reasonable Charges.

PHILADELPHIA Jan. 26. There is a large square of Ground, to the upper end of Chestnut-Street, a little above the House of Dr. Charles Sobers, over against the Post-House belonging to Mr. Anthony Duchee: The said Ground to be let out for ever on Ground Rent, on Reasonable Terms, Enquire of Sarah Story.

PHILADELPHIA Feb. 2. Ran away the 19th of January last, Thomas Parke of Kent-County, two Servant Men, the one named Richard Burk an Irish Man, aged abour 26 Years short Stature, short dark Hair, fresh Complexion; he had on him a yellowish Drugget Vest, and under it a Course blue serge Wastcoat, with Eylit Holes laced to his Body, a pair of Leather Breeches, an old Hat, round toe'd Shoes, white stockings, and two new Ozenbrig Shirts.

The other named Peter Barber, an English Man, Aged about 22 Years of short Stature, short black Hair, and fresh Complexion; his Apparel is a dark Colour'd Drugget Vest, and a striped Holland Vest and Breeches, and a striped Ticking Vest, a pair of Ozenbrig Trowsers, and a new Shirt of the same, an old Hat narrow Brim'd round Toe'd Shoes and a pair of dark Coloured Yarn Stockings.

They have stolen a new dark Coloured Kersey Jockey Coat, a large Silver Spoon and several other things.

Whoever secures the said Servants so that I may have them again, shall have 5 Pounds Reward or 50 Shillings for each of them, paid by me,

Thomas Parke.

Strayed or Stolen away, the 2d of December last, from the Plantation of Thomas Boals in the Township of Freehold, in New-Jersey, a grey Horse about six Years old, he is about 13 Hands high having no artificial marks but two spots of Hair taken off by the Saddle one of them before and the other behind, also his off fore Leg is a little Swollen by some former hurt. Whoever takes up the said Horse and brings him to his aforesaid Master or to Andrew Bradford in Philadelphia, shall have Twenty Shillings Reward.

PHILADELPHIA Feb. 9. The Trustees of the General Loan Office of Pennsylvania, will attend at their Office, on the usual days appointed by Law, being every Third or Fourth day in the Week, commonly called Tuesday and Wednesday in order to receive in the annual Payments of both the First and Second Acts for Emitting Bills of Credit, of which all Borrowers and others concerned are desired to take Notice, and bring in their respective Payments accordingly. When and where broken Bills may be changed for better.

Run away from James Sykes and John Curtis of the City of New-Castle, two Servants the one a lusty tall Fellow, named Mathias Barry, his Hair frisly and sun burnt, he had on a good brown Kersey Pea Jacket with white Mettle Buttons, Breeches of the same, a pair of white Stockings and new Shoes, aged 25 Years.

The other a short well set Fellow, named Stephen Ouldisworth aged abour 25 Years, very short Hair having lately wore a Wig, having a Jacket and Breeches the same as the other, brown Stockings good Shoes with Hobnail in the Sides, he pretended to be a Clock Maker by Trade, Tis supposed they have stolen a bright Bay Horse with a Bob Tail, branded on the near Buttock with the Letter N. a new Saddle with a Broad

Cloath Housing, also a gray Mare.
Whoever takes up the said Servants, or either of them, so that they may be delivered to their said Master, shall have Forty Shillings as a Reward for each, and Reasonable Charges.

PHILADELPHIA Feb. 9. Whereas Thomas Byerly Esq; one of the Proprietors of West-Jersey intending next Summer God Willing, to Transport Himself &c. to Great Britain, having several large valuable Tracts of Land in the said West New-Jersey, and wishing to depose of the same before Departure. These are therefore to give Notice to all Persons that have in Mind to buy said Land, or any part thereof, that they may speak with said Byerly Esq; at any Time at his Lodging at Wood-Bridge, in Middlesex County who will by Draughts of said Land discover the Scituation and Quality of said Land, and sell the same at reasonable Rates; or if they apply to Alexander Mackdowall of Perth-Amboy, he will discover to them the Draught (or if need be by Surveys,) the Scituation, and Quality of said Land.

N. B. The said Thomas Byerly Esq; is invester with two who proprietories in the Western Division, in Right of Robert Squibb deceased, who held his Rights of Edward Byllinge, one of the Parties to the Indenture Quinte Patite, which is the third conveyance from King Charles the II. All which may appear to any that have a mind to purchase by Thomas Byerly's Original Deed, now in the Hands at Woodbridge, and Recorded in Burlington, lib. A. A.

PHILADELPHIA Feb. 16. On the 10th of this Instant was Tryed here at the Court of Oyer and Terminer, held before David Lloyd Esq; Chief Judge of this Province. John Murry for the Murder of one Thomas Williams, in the beating and Bruising him very much about the Head and Stomach, of which said Bruises he Languish'd 14 Days, and then Died. He was found Guilty of Man-Slaughter, and burnt in the Hand. Also Ann Robinson, was try'd for Burglary for breaking into the House of George Campion, but was Acquited.

Philadelphia Feb. 23. Several Tracts of Land being in Maryland, all being in Navigable

Rivers, being 5700 Acres in Dorset County, 2100 Acres in Talbot County, 1950 Acres in Cecil County, 750 Acres in Ann Arrundel County, being late Estate of Nicholas Painter Esq; deceased. To be Sold at reasonable Rates by Mr. William Cornwallis the Owner at Mr. Reynolds Currier in Chestnut-Street Philadelphia.

Philadelphia March 4. Ran away on the 16th of this Instant, from George Rescarrick of the County of Middlesex, in the Province of New-Jersey, three Servant Men, the one named William Hide of a middle Stature, lightish Coloured Hair and curls very much, of a fair Complexion, an English Man born, he is Cloathed in an old Shirt of lightish Coloured Drugget, with good Shoes and Stockings. Another Servant John Miller of a small Stature, black Complexion, having his Hair cut off, and wears a Cap under his Hat, having on a Suit of dark gray Home-spun Cloaths made plain, and but little worn, he wears over them and old Drugget Coat, fashionably made, of a light Colour, good Shoes and Stockings, and has with him a pair of Cinnamon Coloured Drugget Breeches, and wears an old Beaver Hat. The other named Thomas Showthrip, of a middle Stature, a thick well set Fellow, with very short redish Hair, a Yorkshire Man and talks broad, he has a suit of very light gray Home-Spun Drugget Cloaths being quite new, and made Fashionable, with good Shoes and Stockings, and a Half worn Beaver Hat with broad brims, a Carpenters by Trade. Whoever can secure the said Servants so as the Master may have them again, shall have Ten Pounds for all, and in proportion for one or two of them.

PHILADELPHIA March 18. Publick Notice is hereby given to William Burne, Shoemaker, late of Lancashire in Great Britain, That there was about 5 Years ago left him by his Uncle, a Legacy of Value, which if not demanded within 18 Months will be entirely Lost to him. If the said William Burne be living, let him make his Application to John Passmore of Kennet near Brandy-Wine, in Chester County Pennsylvania, and he may be further informed as to the Particulars.

Whereas Evan Morgan of Chester in the Province

of Pennsylvania: Designs (God willing) next Spring to go for Great Britain. These are therefore to desire all Persons that have demands on him to bring in their Accounts that they may be Adjusted, likewise all Persons that are Indebted to him to come speedily and pay the same, that they may save further Trouble. He has all sorts of European Goods to be Sold, as Linnens, Woolens, Stuffs, Shalloons, Camlet and all sorts of Haberdashery ware, likewise Sugar, Molasses and Salt for ready Money, at wholesale or retail. Also a new Brick House of two Story, with a well Accustom'd Shop; a good Brick Kitchen, a Well, a good Garden, and a young Orchard of 3 Acres of Ground, in the Town of Chester. To be Sold or Let for Term of Years. Any Person that is inclined to buy, or rent the same, may apply their selves to the said Evan Morgan, at his House and know farther.

PHILADELPHIA March 25. To be Sold several Houses and Lots of Land, late of Thomas Peters deceased, viz. Two Houses and Lots at the Center, one the late House of William Rakestraw deceased, the other lying in Mulberry-Street, somewhat near Schuylkill. One House and large Lot in Walnut-Street. One House on the Back of Front-Street, over against the Coffee-House, with a Lot and Shop in King-Street. Any Person that hath a mind to Purchase any of the above Houses or Lots, may apply to Rese Peters at Abington, or Thomas Peters in Chestnut-Street, Executors of the said Thomas Peters.

PHILADELPHIA April 8. Run away the 22d of this Instant, from James Morris, sawyer, in Philadelphia, an Irish Servant Man, named John Hayes, of a middle size, aged about 22, pretty round favour'd with brown Hair, having on a dark coloured Irish Cloath Coat, 2 Jackets, one blue the other striped, and two Shirts, one Home-spun the other Exenbrigs, a pair of white Blanketing Breeches, dark coloured Yarn Stockings, pretty good Shoes, and a good Felt Hat. Whoever secures the said Servant so that his said Master may have him again, shall have Forty Shillings as a Reward and reasonable Charges.

NEW-YORK April 12. A Sloop bound from the Bay

of Boston, was some days ago Cast away on the South Side of Long-Island, The People and Cargo were saved, they had a very short Passage, and say that Sprigg the Pirate has five Vessels with him who are all Pirates.

Burlington April 16. A Large Brick House, the now Dwelling House of Col. Thomas Hunloke in Burlington, together wirh a Garden, a large Yard and two Stables, to be let for the Term of three Years from the date hereof. The Furniture Suitable for so large a House, and all Sorts of Liquors used in these parts, also 200 Bushels of Oats, are to be Sold. Any Person that has a Mind to hire the aforesaid House, may apply themselves to Thomas Hunloke aforesaid.

PHILADELPHIA April 29. There is to be Sold at Thomas Chalkley's Store, Sash Windows of the best Crown Glass, ready Painted Glaz'd and Hung, with Choicest Lines, and Pully's just fits upon into Buildings, at 3 Pounds per Pair.

For London Ship Hannover, Braden Wallis Commander, now Lying at Carpenter's Wharf, half of her Loading being already on board, any Person that have a mind to Transport themselves or Goods may apply to Branden Wallis or C. Lodwick Spicer in Philadelphia, where they may agree on Reasonable Terms.

PHILADELPHIA May 6. We have Advice, that the Sloop Mary, Laborious Pearce, Master of this Place, was lost, off of Cape Hatteras, in her Voyage from Saranam to Virginia the People were all saved.

The Brigantine Dove, H. Norwood, Master of this Place, in her Voyage to Virginia, lost her Anchor and Rudder, and with much ado got into York River in Virginia.

Run away the 25th of this Instant, from Edmond Thompson of Edgmont, in Chester County, in Pennsylvania, a Servant Man, named Timothy Higgins, aged about 22 years, with short coloured Hair, fresh full Fac'd of a middle stature and speaks good English, he had on a large brim'd Hat, set up in three Corners, dark coloured Coat and Vest, Leather Breeches, with Brass Buttons, mint coloured Stockings, old Shoes, and 2 course Shirts. Whoever takes up the said Servant and brings him to the Owner, shall have 5 Pounds Reward, besides reasonable Charges.

PHILADELPHIA May 13. General Loan-Office of Pennsylvania the 28th of the 2d Mo. 1725.

All Persons who have Mortgages on Land, Tenements &c. in the said Office the last Year, or Year before, are desired to take Notice, that if they make Default of this Respective Payment, mentioned in their several Mortgages two months after the same becomes due, that the Trustees are empower'd by the Act for Emitting, Thirty Thousand Pounds, as enter upon the Mortgaged Premisses, and make Sale thereof without any further process. And all Persons concerned can expect speedily to be proceeded against accordingly; several having already elapsed that Time, and others very near it.

Whereas it was appointed by the Court by the Orphan Court, held at Philadelphia, the 25th of March last past, That all Persons who had any Claims or Shares in the Stock of the Free-Society of the Traders in Pennsylvania, should apply themselves to Charles Read, Clerk of the said Court, with whom they were required to leave an Account of their Claims, in order that they may be exhibited before the Justices of the Orphans Court, for the making of the first Dividend as the Law (in that behalf lately made) doth direct.

Publick Notice is hereby now given, by the Treasurer for the said Society to the said Claimants, that they bring in their several Claims as aforesaid, without any further Delay, otherwise they will be Excluded from the first Dividend.   Francis Rawle, Tres.

PERTH-AMBOY May 25. His Excellency's Speech to the Assembly of the Province of New-Jersey met and conven'd at Perth-Amboy.

Gentlemen,
I have the Satisfaction of meeting you as soon as the Affairs of the Loan-Office would permit some of the Members to attend; and it is with Pleasure I Congratulate you upon the Punctual Performance of the Payments that the Borrowers were to make for the first Year. There is nothing can support the Credit of the Bills so much

as a sacred Observance of the Terms of the Act by which they were inserted. This Act is a kind of Covenant between the Publick and Private Persons, of which therefore neither of the Parties bound by it can in Honour of Justice break thorow, and when they do, it is no wonder if the Credit of the whole suffers by it, how much soever some Persons have given occasion to much Complaint, I have no doubt but you came determined on your Part, to do nothing that may weaken, but, if possible, whatever may Strengthen your first Engagements, and such steadiness in your Proceedings, and the gradual Decrease of the Quantity of the Bills, cannot fail to support their Credit, and even in time, to restore them to the Intrinsick Value of Silver, for which they were Struck.

The Expiration of the last Support of Government is so near, That I depend on your care to Renew it for the like Term of Years, and to continue an ample and honourable Provision on for the Officers of the Government, and for your Agent in Great Britain. You will judge whether you have any reason to Repent of Confidence you have hitherto placed in the Administration, and if you have grounds to Change your Opinion at this Time.

I am very well perswaded that you will pursue the Interest of the People who who you Represent and all your Deliberations, and that you will lay aside all Resentments and Party Disputes, and be guided by Calm and Solid Arguments only: You will, no doubt, be far from imputing the Actions of a few Men to a whole Sect or whole Province; and while your Zeal for the good of our Country animates your Council, you will have due Regard to the advantage and Duty of Cultivating a good Correspondence with you Neighbours, and Universal Charity with all Men.

These Principals will lead you to all just and Reasonable Measures for Quieting the Minus and Securing the Property of the Inhabitants, that Industry may be Encouraged and Trade Flourish.

If I can contribute to any of these good Purposes, I shall think my self Happy. And as I shall imploy my utmost Endeavours to promote Unanimity in your Proceedings, I shall be always ready to concur with you to the utmost of my Power in every Thing that may Advance the good of the Publick.

You have the greatest Inducement to Support the Government Cheerfully, and expect Success, in serving the Province, when you Reflect on the Glories of His Majesty's Reign, whose Wise Conduct and Shinning Ventures have Endeared Him to his Subjects at Home, and made Him the refuge of the Distrest, and the Terror of Oppression Abroad.
William Burnet.

PERTH-AMBOY May 31. To his Excellency William Burnet, Esq; Capt. General and Governour in Chief of the Province of New-Jersey, New-York, and Territories thereon Depending, in America, and Vice Admiral of the same &c.

The Humble Address of the House of Representatives for the Province of New-Jersey.

May it please your Excellency,
Since the true Interest of the Governour and the Govern'd are undoubtedly Inseperable, it would have been Reasonable to suppose the punctual Payments this Year made, by those who borrowed Money out of the several Loan Offices, was as Satisfactory to your Excellency as it has been to us; But those you have been pleased to put beyond dispute, in kindly Congratulating Us on that Performance, for which We return You our Hearty Thanks, and assure you, That nothing on our part shall be wanting that may contribute to Strengthen our former Engagement.

The Foundation of which the Bills of Credit were raised, the great Care used for sinking them, and the exact Complyance there-with hitherto, gave us just ground to hope, would have induc'd its Currency in New-York as well as Pennsylvania and other Neighbouring Provinces; but we, Unhappily, find it otherwise, and a considerable Discount insisted between Their Money and Ours: Whence this had its Rise, and what Expedients may be fallen upon to prevent it, must be the Subject of future Inquiry and Deliberating in which we promise our Selves Your Excellency's ready Concurrence from the

Declaration of your generously made of coming into. "All just and Reasonable Measures for Quieting the Minds and Securing the Properties of the Inhabitants, That Industry may be Encouraged and Trade Flourishing."

Our Behaviour for the time to come will best demonstrate the Resentment and Party Dispute are laid aside; and we shall not be so unjust to attribute the Actions of particular Men to a whole Province, nor shall over Zeal for our own Country occasion Us to forget that we and the Neighbouring Provinces are Children of one Common Parent. But we hope Your Excellency will be of Our Opinion, That there is no Inconsistency between "Cultivating a good Correspondence with our Neighbours, and taking all possible Care to prevent Injustice to our Selves."

The Service of our King and Country in the End of our Constitution, and the Business of every Convention, and as We are under the highest Obbligation to discharge this Trust, it shall be Our particular Care this Session to demonstrate the just Sense We have of it, as well by making Honourable Provisions for Supporting of Government, and the Officers thereof, as by perfering such Bills which we conceive necessary for the Benefit of Those we Represent. In Pursuit of which good Purpose, besides the Assurance Your Excellency is pleased to give Us of Contributing your utmost Endeavours, We have all the Inducements that proceed from the Mild and Gentle Reign of a Gracious Prince, who se Conduct at Home and Abroad renders Him Remarkably Conspicuous.

PHILADELPHIA June 3. To be Sold by William Cornwallis of Mulbury-Street in Philadelphia, the present Owner, 6 Tracts of Land, in Dorset, and Baltimore County's; containing 5500 Acres call'd by the name of Planter's Paradise, Painters Range, the Grove, and Willshires Kindness, near Shoptank, also several other Tracts of Land, lying in Queen Anns, Talbut, Cecil County's in the Province of Maryland, containing 2500 Acres, being late Estate of the Honourable Tho. Cornwallis, and Nicho. Painter Esq; Deceased, and Purchased from the Honourable

Dame Penelope Cornvallis, and of Henry Bray, of Alchurch Lane London, Gent. and other Legacies of the said Tho. Cornwallis, and Nicho. Painter afore said; which said Lands are old Surveys, and Lyes on Navigable Rivers, and on Chesapeake Bay, some having large Improvements, yet nevertheless, will be sold as Ruff-lands by reason that the said Cornwallis after such Sale, designs for England.

As whereas there has been an Evil report Industriously spread by some designing Persons, who endeavours to invalidate the Titles of said Lands Alleging they were never conveyed to the said William Cornwallis, these are therefore to satisfy such Persons that are willing to purchase any of the said Lands, that the said Cornwallis, is willing after such Purchase to take only security for the moneys and give reasonable time for the Payment thereof, in Order that the Purchasers may have Opportunity to be satisfyed in the Title by sending to England, to know the Validity thereof.

PHILADELPHIA June 10. Run away from his Master George Riscarrick at Cambray Brook, on the 24th of May, a Servant Man named Thomas Schowthrip, of a middle Stature, thick set, and hath short Sandy coloured Hair, a light coloured Fashionable Coat and Wastcoat, an old pair of Leather Breeches with Brass Buttons, good Shoes, and Yarn Stockings. Whoever takes up the said Servant and secure him, (or bring him to his Master,) so that he may have him again, shall have three Pounds as a Reward, besides reasonable Charges.

Run away the 26th of last May, from Gabriel Steele of Shewsbury, in the County of Monmouth, and Province of New-Jersey, a Negro named Jack, aged about 40 Years; he is a short Negro, and a Mallagasco, he had on an ole Hone-spun Coat, old Shoes and Stockings.

Whoever takes up the said Negro, so that his said Master may have him again, shall have a Pistole as a Reward, besides reasonable charges. PHILADELPHIA June 17. Run away from Andrew Fresnean and Mr. Cornelius Van Horne the 30th of May last, a New Negroe Man pretty well set of a middle Stature, aged about 30 Years, his upper teeth ground sharp like unto the Ebo Negroes Teeth, he speaks no English, has on a pair of Oxenbrigs Trousers and Breeches.

Whoever can take up said Negroe and bring him to the said Fresnean or Van Horne or Give Notice thereof so that he may be had again shall be well Rewarded for their Trouble.

PHILADELPHIA June 24. Run away the 13th of this Instant, June, from Samuel Carpenter, Sr. Three Negroes, the one is a Negroe man named Jack, a Tall slender Fellow, about 50 Years of Age; he has pretty good Cloaths, and bad Teeth: the other is a lusty Negroe Woman, call'd Rachel, aged about 40 Years, and is of a Tawney Complexion; having on a suit of Calico very Gay; and a Negroe Boy about 7 Years of Age, of a Tawney Complexion, being the Negroe Woman's Son. Whoever takes up the said Run aways and secures them so that their said Master may have them again, shall have 40 Shillings as a Reward paid by me,   Samuel Carpenter Sr.

Ran away the 20th Instant June, from William Chancellor of Philadelphia a Servant Lad, named James Prouse, Aged about 16 Years, of a fair Complexion white Hair cut short, his Hands coloured with Tar, he is a Sail-Maker by Trade, having on a corded Drugget Coat, Lined Jacket and Breeches, and Speckled Shirt, Whoever shall take up the said Servant, or secure him so that his Master may have him again, shall have 40 Shillings Reward and reasonable Charges.

PHILADELPHIA July 1. This is to give Notice to all Shoemakers, Sadlers and others, that they may have Hides curry'd Waxt or Black grain for 3 Shillings and 6 Pence by the single Hide, ready Money down, 3 Pounds by the Score; and Calf Skins for 10 Shillings per Dozen, one shilling the single Skin by Abraham Spicer Currier living in Chestnut-Street Philadelphia.

PHILADELPHIA July 8. Yesterday in the Afternoon Mr. James Parnel an Attorney at Law (which came in from Hanover from London this Spring) as he was washing himself in the River, went beyond his Depth and was unfortunately Drowned.

On the Second Instant Capt. Derias Picks

arrived here in a Ship in about seven Weeks from Bristol, but having the Small-Pox on Board, they were ordered to lie below the Town, we hear they have, since obtained liberty to bring their sick on Shore to a house about half a mile from Town.

PHILADELPHIA July 15. Reading, writing, Arithmetick Vulgar Decimals and Longarithmical, Trigonomitry plain and Oblique, Surveying, Gauging, Dialing and Navigation, carefully thought at the Sign of the Tun, in Water-Street by

John Shields.

Whereas some time past encouragement was given for the Printer to make Proposals for Re-Printing the Book entitled. The History of the Rise, Progress and Increase of the Christian People called Quakers. The Proposal made, they were approved of, and such a Number Subscribed for, as gave the Printer encouragement to undertake the Work. Which being now complete, these are to give Notice. That the said Book is now Reprinted, the second edition Corrected, on fine Paper in fair Character, and well bound in Calf Leather, ready to be delivered to the Subscribers, and others, by William Bradford in New-York, and Andrew Bradford in Philadelphia.

Run away from their Master William Bissel of the Ciry of Philadelphia, Blacksmith, and John Coats of the same place, Brickmaker, two Carolina Indians, a Man and a Woman, the Man's name Peter, of short Stature, about 26 Years of Age, he has a stripped homespun Tickin Jacket and Breeches, also a Kersey Jacket, two sorts one fine and the other Ozenbrigs, two pair of Shoes, and a Felt Hat. The Woman's name is Maria, of a middle Stature, well set, about 40 Years of Age, she hath with her four Pettycotes and several Jackets and other Cloaths, a new pair of Shoes, she has also a Blanket with her. They both speak good English.

Whoever shall take up the said Indians, or either of them, and secure them, and give Notice to their Masters so that they may have them again, shall have 40 Shillings for each as a reward, besides reasonable Charges.

NEW-YORK July 19. Last Wednesday a Barn full of Corn was set on Fire by Lightning and burnt to the ground.

On Thursday last Thomas Byng, a Felt-maker who was a soldier in the Garrison here, was committed to the Common Goal of this City, for beating his Wife (who was very big with Child) so unmercifully that she dyed immediately.

PHILADELPHIA July 22. Deserted from the ship called the Stanhope, William Braggington Commander now laying at Philadelphia, 2 Sailors, the one named Edward Rese, a middle siz'd Man of a fair Complexion, he has black Curled Hair; the other named Nicholis Hopkins, a tall Young Man of a fair Complexion, and hath Brown Curl'd Hair, if any Person brings the said Sailors to the said ship shall have Twenty Shillings as a Reward; also a Passenger or Servant, Deserted from the same Ship, named George Stevens, he is a Brick-Layer by Trade, he is a tall Man very much Pockfretten, and wears a Wigg. Whoever brings him to the said Captain, shall have 20 Shillings and reasonable Charges.

Run away on the 6th of 1st May, from John Gibbin of York Town in Virginia a Servant Man named Lewis Davis of middle sized, red Hair and Beard, much Freckled, by Trade a Brick-Layer. Whoever takes up said Servant and secures him or brings him to his said Master shall have three Pounds Reward.

PHILADELPHIA July 29. Whereas divers Persons, stand indebted to the Estate of William Tayler. late of the City of New-York, Brazier, they are hereby desired to Pay in the same within the space of three Months to prevent farther troubles, also any Person or Persons have any Demands on the said Estate, they are desired to give Notice thereof, within the said time to Thomas Grant, Ironmanger, or Joseph Leddel, Pewterer of the said City Executors.

New-York July 19, 1725.

PHILADELPHIA Aug. 3. All Persons concerned are hereby informed, That a Council of Proprietors of the Eastern Division of New-Jersey, are to meet at the House of Phineas Mackintosh at Perth-Amboy, on Tuesday the 10th of this Instant.   Lewis Morris.

Philadelphia Aug. 5. These are to give Notice

to all Persons, that on the 4th Instant August, arrived here on the Snow Elizabeth and Lydia, Edward Willcocks, Commander from Dublin, with Men and Woman Servants, several of the Men Being Trades-men, as Smiths, Taylors, Malsters, &c. Whoever are desirous to Purchase any said Servants may apply to said Commander, or Thomas Broughton, Super Cargo, on Board the said Snow, Lying opposite to Mr. Robert Ellis's Wharfe, to agree on reasonable Terms.

PHILADELPHIA Aug. 12. The Speech of Sir William Keith, Bart. Governour of the Province of Pennsylvania, and the Counties of New-Castle, Kent and Sussex upon Delaware.

To the Representatives of the Free-men of the said Province of Pennsylvania, in General Assembly.

Mr. Speaker and Gentlemen of the Assembly, I am Heartily glad of the opportunity to congratulate with you, upon his Majesty's most Gracious Condescension and great goodness to the People of this Province, by Ratifying, in so ample a Manner, the late Act of our Assembly, for the further ease to Persons of Scrupulous and tender Consciences; and I cannot on this occasion but exhort you to use your best endeavours in the several Counties amongst the People whom you Represent, in order to make them truly Sensible of the singular Favours, and happy Repose which they securely Enjoy under the Influence of his present Majesty's most Auspicious Reign.

Surely so great an Example from the Throne must Contribute very much to raise & conform in our Minds, That universal Charity, Forebearance and Brotherly Love, which we always ought to be Exercising towards one another; and this leads me to put you in mind of a Bill which now Lye before you in behalf of some Protestants from the Paladines, and other parts of Germany, who having great desire to Enjoy equally with us the Inestimable Benefits of an English Government under the Reign of so good and Gracious a Prince, have transported themselves and their Families from Europe, at a considerable Charge in order to Settle in this Province, and has besought me in the humblest Manner to procure for them, by your Assistance, the common Privilege of Naturalization on the same Terms, upon which it has been usually Granted in England, and other of his Majesty's Colonies to Foreign Protestants.

I should be very glad if the Season of the Year would permit you at a Juncture to bestow a little Time in Considering of some proper Method effectually to maintain and support the credit of your Paper Currency, by encouraging the Exportation of the Country Product to proper Markets abroad, and favouring our own Manufactures, and the most Beneficial Returns for Remittance to England; which could they be rendered more frequent and easy, the present Exorbitant Exchange would be thereby Reduce to the old Equal Standard of one Third, and Consequently the now Extravagant Price which is demanded in the Stores for European Goods would also abate in proportion to the Exchange.

I observe some Ingenious Disinterested Person bearing an Apparent good Will to Prosperity of this Province has lately published some very useful Thoughts relating to the further Improvement of our Product and Commerce: I am of Opinion that such generous Views deserve to be Encouraged, and will become a very proper Subject for the Deliberation of this and future Assemblies, and if by any decent Representation to the Court of Parliament of Great-Britain, we can reasonably propose to Advance the Trade of this and other Neighbouring Provinces, by such means as shall appear to be perfectly consistent with the true Interest of our Mother Country: I shall not only be ready to give all the Assistance that is in my Power, but also to use my best Endeavours to Engage our good Neighbours to Concur with us in such Things, as evidently tend to our Mutual Advantage, and the Prosperity of the British Trade in General.

William Keith.

PHILADELPHIA Aug. 19. Strayed away the 11th of this Instant, August, from James Donaldson of Annapolis, Merchant, at the Plantation of William Moon's on the Branch of Schuykill, a large Surrel Horse; with a Star in his Forehead, his mane thin, the one half cut, the other hanging down, branded on the right Buttock, with a pentagon, has a switch Tail, Paces fast, he formerly belonged to Isaac Wortel, nigh German Town.

Also a thick short dark Bay Hourse, bob Tail, a thick Mane, Buttock with RD. Whoever secures the said Horses, and sends them to Nicholas Scull Innkeeper, at the further End of Second-Street Philadelphia, shall have 40 Shillings reward and Reasonable Charges.

All Persons who are Indebted to Henry Sutton, Glasier now living in the Front-Street, are desired to come and pay the same forthwith, he designs to leave this Province in a short Time: He has several sorts of very good Household Goods to sell, and a Servant Maids time very Reasonable.

PHILADELPHIA Aug. 26. Broke out of the Goal of Dorchester County in Maryland, about the 23d of February last, James Smith Alias Spurling, a tall proper Person, aged about 40 Years, much Pock-fretten, speaks very Hoarse, he hath a large cut on one of his Thighs supposed to be with a Sword, which occasions him to Limp in or againg bad weather; he hath been a manifest utterer of Counterfeit Gold Bars, commonly Styling himself Capt. Smith.

Whoever takes up and secures the said Person so that he may be brought to Justice shall have Twenty Pounds Reward, paid by Charles Ugle Esq; High Sheriff of said County. When taken and secured, Notice is desired to be sent to the said Ugle in Maryland, or to Owen Roberts Esq; High Sheriff of the City and County of Philadelphia, or William Bradford in New-York.

PHILADELPHIA Sept. 2. Run away the 18th of this Instant, from George Carter of the County of Chester, and the Township of Bradford, near the Forks of the Brandywine, a Servant Man named John Double, of middle Stature, and about 24 Years, he has Short Hair, the end of his Nose flatish; he is in a Saylor habit, his Jacket with Red and White strips, he has a pair of grey Stockings, and round Toe'd Shoes, with Brass Buckles. Whoever takes up and secures the said Servant, to his said Master aforementioned shall have 40 Shillings as a reward.

NEW-YORK Sept. 15. The Speech of his Excellency William Burnet, Esq; To the General Assembly of the Province of New-York.

Gentlemen,
I cannot but look back with Pleasure on your Conduct ever since I have had the Happiness to be among you: Your readiness to Support the Government in an honourable manner; Your repeated Endeavours to prevent Growth of the French Power, and strengthen the British Interest among the Indians, and your Seasonable Supplies for the Repairs of his Majesty's Forts, will always be remembered to the Honour of the Assembly. If you have sometimes met with Opposition it has had little or no effect than to justify your Proceedings. A late Instance of this kind has appeared in unwearied, and I wish I could not say, Indirect Methods taken by the Merchants to defeat your Acts against the trade with Canada, which by Diligence and Ability of your Agents, the Justice of your Laws has been so well Represented, that the success has been in your Favour.

It is more and more evident every Year, of how great Advantages these Laws have been to the Trade and Security of this Province, the Quantity of Peltry brought from the Country of the Five Nations, during the Summer, has far exceeded our Expectation, and is more than what used to come from Canada; and the far Indians from the Lakes, have, as I am informed, all stopped at our Trading Place, and none of them proceed to Montreal, as they use to do. I am Confident, that the Surprizing Success and good Effects of this new Trade, and the Applause it has met with in Great-Britain, will engage you to the effectual Measures to Encourage it by Renewing and Enforcing the Prohibition of what pernicious Trade of the Indian Goods to Canada, and by providing Amply for the Charges necessary to keep the Indians Faithful to Us. To this End it will be requisite that some fit Person be appointed, Completely to Reside among the Onandagas, as with the Senecas, who may be always ready to defeat the Arts which the French industriously Employ to Seduce those Indians. I have begun with this Subject, and dwelt the longer upon it, because it highly concerns your Safety.

The Revenue for the Support of the Government is near less Expectation. I depend on your own Observation and Experience to plead with you for as Ample and extensive a Provision for the Time to come; where Actions ought to speak, Words should not be offered to their room.

I shall only Recommend the Officers of the Government to your Care, who are doing their Duty are often liable to Private Resentment, and are on that account entitled to Protection as well as Subsistence from the Legislature, and without sufficient Number of Officers the Administration cannot be carried on, and the Laws must loose their Force.

The Provisions you have already made by renewing the Decay'd Buildings of the Fort will, I believe, appear to have been frugally and Effectually employ'd; and I depend on your dealing to a Resolution, that so good a Design shall not fail of what is still wanting to complete it.

I can Acquaint you with a further Instance, besides what I have mentioned of the Diligence of your Agents in the Service of the Province, and particularly for the Benefit of this City, and that in their Soliciting by My Directions and obtaining the East-End of Long-Island to be restored to the District of the Collector of New-York. You cannot desire more convincing Proof of the usefulness of having such Agents, and therefore I relie on your making good your former Engagements to them, and on your giving them Marks of your Esteem and Consistence, in Continuing their Appointment for a long Term than you have hitherto done, and providing suitably for their Payments.

I have gone through the several Particulars which I had to lay before you, and I shall only add this general Consideration, to enforce them all, That at this time the happy agreement that has always fulfilled between his

Majesty and his Parliament, ever since the Accession to the crown, in the Administration of all Europe, and the Glory of the British Nation, I am perswaded you will do your part in following so great an Example, and that you will Reward what I Propose to you as it tends to His Majesty's Service.   W. Burnet.

NEW-YORK Sept. 15. This is to certify all Persons concerned as Proprietors of the Eastern Division of New-Jersey, That the next general Slated Meeting of the Proprietors of the said Division is to begin on Wednesday the 29th of this Instant September, and to Continue until Tuesday Night the following, of which all said Proprietors are desired to take Notice, and be present, either Personally or by their Agent or Attorneys, in order to consult and Advise upon such Matters and Things as shall at that time be proposed for the Interest of the said Proprietors.   Lewis Morris.

PHILADELPHIA Sept. 23. Run away the 16th of this Instant September from Joseph Sprinyard, of the County of Baltimore, two Servant Men, the one being a short well set Man named Elijah Westwood, with dark Hair, and of a swarthy Complexion, with a great Scar on his Nose which has been cut with some Weapon; he wears a Pea Jacket, and a Dowlas Shirt, Cloath Breeches somewhat patched, and he has been a Boatswain to some Vessel, and now passes as supposed a Sailor. The other Man a Lusty well made strong Fellow with Redish Hair, with a large Nose, Bluff Countenance, with a pair of new Leather Breeches and a Pea Jacket, his name is Thomas Burns, speaks broken English, he is thought to be an Irishman, he took several things with him. Whoever takes up the said Servant or Servants so that they may be brought to Justice, or to their said Master so that he may have him or them, shall have Two Pounds Ten Shillings for each of them paid by   John Sprinyard.

PHILADELPHIA Sept. 30. Made his Escape out of the Prison-Yard last Night, in Philadelphia, one William Billet, of a middle Stature, fresh colour, about 24 Years of Age, he looks very slie with his Eyes, having gray Breeches and

Stockings, his Head is shaven all over only a small Lock on the top of his Head and has a scar over his left Eye, he is a Cooper by Trade, it is supposed he has also a Blew shag Coat, and some other Cloaths. Whoever shall take up said William Billet, and bring him to Owen Roberts, Esq; High Sheriff, or secure him so he may be had again shall have Five Pounds as a Reward and Reasonable Charges.

PHILADELPHIA Oct. 7. To be sold, (very Reasonable) by William Vilant, Gold Smith, in Philadelphia, a half Lot, of Land in the Township of Freehold in East New-Jersey containing about 250 Acres some good Meadows belonging to it; Whoever pleases to view it may apply to Mr. John Hepburn, in Freehold, and he'll shew the said Land, the which joyns with his and the Widow Vanhook.

PHILADELPHIA Oct. 14. The Green York of Bristol of abour 400 Tons, from Holland, with about 300 Palatines, was lost in our Bay, but the People all Saved, and some of the Cargo. She went on the Bank the fourth of this Instant.

A very likely Bristol Woman (fitted for either Town or Country Business,) to be Sold for four Years and a half: Enquire of Andrew Bradford, in Philadelphia.

PHILADELPHIA Oct. 15. The Speech of Sir William Keith, Bart. Governour of the Province of Pennsylvania, and the Counties of New-Castle, Kent, and Sussex upon Delaware.

To the Representatives of the Freemen of the said Province of Pennsylvania, in General Assembly met October 15, 1725.

Mr. Speaker, and Gentlemen of the Assembly, If my Services, for some Years have been acceptable to the Country, no doubt, but you will think it jusr Reasonable at this Juncture, to give some Effectual and convincing Proof your Satisfaction with my Conduct; then perhaps some People will have their pleasure to know, that I never did, noe even will use any Means to hold the Administration of this Government, longer that will be acceptable and agreeable unto you, and the Body of the People who you Represent.

As to other Business, I am so much Interested

in, and Heartily concerned for the Publick good, and Welfare of the Province, That I think I ought to loose no Time in laying before you such Matters as seem to call upon Attention, whenever you think fit to consider them.

In the first Place, then it is necessary you should know, that I have late a certain Advises from London, which assure me, that very restless Endeavours are used by one or two Bosie Persons now there, to have the two Acts of our Assembly for emitting Paper Currency repealed, and what Confusion and Distraction such an unhappy Event would, at this Time of Day, bring upon the Country, you are best able to Judge; However, I Conceive it to be my Duty on this Occasion to Represent unto you, the absolute Necessity that there is for some Person to take care of your Interests at the Court of Britain, and that this Province cannot any otherways be Defended from the Malicious Craft of some underhand Projector, but by the Assembly's supporting a Skillful and Active Agent at Home. Under their own proper Directions, from whom they may by all Times be truly Inform'd of the State of Affairs and by whom they may expect to be Defended against such Attacks upon the General Interest of the People whom they Represent; and this I Judge will be most Effectually done by an Act of the Assembly, wherein the Money Yearly to be Paid by the Publick Treasurer, for the Encouragement and Support of such an useful Officer, ought to be preferr'd to all other Charges of Government whatsoever.

The Next thing I shall Mention for the Benefit of the Province, is to provide a suitable Encouragement by Law, for promoting a Fishery, for when we consider the great Variety and vast Quantity of valuable Fish which may so easily be caught at Sea, about the Capes and in the Bay and River Delaware; It is Evident that an Improvement of that Kind would Advance Navigation, force a New and Profitable Market abroad, and enlarge our Commerce every Way; to Accomplish which it will be very Helpful, that we Endeavour to obtain the Concurrence of the Neighbouring Provinces with us, in an Humble

Application to the Crown, that the Act of Parliament which allow the Importation of European Salt in New-England, may be equally and more fully explain'd in our Favour, as in all Probability, it was at first intended, for These Parts at that Time were certainly Comprehended under the General Title or Name of New-England.

You will find upon the Journals of the last Sessions of the Assembly, that I then laid several things before the House, which they not having Time to enter upon, were pleased to refer some of them as matters of Importance, to your Consideration, amongst which I cannot but mention again, the Ease and Advantage which would Accure to our Trading People at this very Juncture of Time by making the Paper Bills of the Lower Part of the Government equally Current, with those of the Province.

Gentlemen,
A Course of above Eight Years Experience, must have Convinced us all of the Advantages, wherewith Unanimity and Concord in the Legislative Power is attended, and as there never seemed to be more need of it than at this Time, I shall Conclude with Observing to you, That on Humble Patient and Peaceable Deportment, without suffering the good Order of Publick Business to be Disturbed by any Passionate Heats and Animosities, will be the most decent and secure Method of preserving our Liberties and Defeating the Design of Your, and the Province's Enemies.

W. Keith.

PHILADELPHIA Oct. 16. To Sir William Keith Baronet Governour of the Province of Pennsylvania, &c.

The Address of the Representatives of the said Province in General Assembly met, in answer to the Governour's Speech of the 15th Instant.

May it please the Governour,
The sense we have of the Governour's prudent Administration Obligeth us to acknowledge the benefit this Province has Enjoyed from the same; especially in his ready Concurrence to such Laws, as have been (under Providence) conducive to the Encrease of Trade, and the Peace and Plenty of our Country; which we cannot Reflect

on, without Satisfaction: and as a Demonstration of our sincere Acknowledgement, We beg leave to assure the Governour, We shall not be wanting to provide him an Honourable Support.

Among the many Instances of the Governour's Signal Regard to our Welfare, those Matters of Importance which he has been pleased at this Time to lay before the house, We cannot but look upon as further Proof of his Good-will towards us; Which We have deliberated upon, and beg leave to acquaint the Governour, that the House is so far of the Opinion, with him, That it is Necessary to have an Agent in Great-Britain for Negotiating the Passing of our Laws; And that we have Resolved, so soon as Time will allow to Consider of such proper Ways and Means as may Accomplish the same.

And as to the second Thing proposed, for promoting a Fishery, and obtaining Liberty to Import Salt from Europe; as there is great plenty of Shadd, Herring, and Sturgeon, Yearly catch'd in this River; as well as great Quantities of Codd and other valuable Fish, which we are creditably inform'd are to be taken, not far from our Capes: We doubt not but a regular Management far greater Quantities may be Catch'd than ever been done; which cannot fail, very much to enlarge our commerce, advance our Navigation, and Force a new profitable Trade abroad: But till some more certain way can be found to procure Salt, which very often is so scarce with us, as to render the Profit of Curing Fish, not worth the undertakers pains; especially in the Spring Season, which is the Time the River Fish are to be Catched, Salt is sometimes not to be had, which obliges us to send to Boston and other distant Places, to supply our selves at a large Expence: Therefore we earnestly desire the Governour would be pleased to move the Neighbouring Governments, Joyn with us in an Humble Application to Great-Britain to obtain the Liberty of New-England, for some Time have done; And we doubt not, with the Governour's Assistance; and regular Application, this Affair which evidently tend to enlarge the Trade of the British Empire in America, will reduce the Crown to redress us.

As what the Governour has been pleased to recommend to our serious Consideration for rendering the New-Castle Bills, Current amongst us; We are of Opinion that by passing an Act for Encouraging the same, may Subject us to many Inconveniences which ought to be Avoided: And the Bills would be rendered more Current, If the Persons concerned in the Trade of the Government, would unanimously resolve to take them at Value, at which they first past amongst us.

We are so far of Opinion with the Governour the Unanimity and Concord of the Legislative Power, and an Orderly and Peaceable Deportment in the Dispatch of Business, is so absolutely necessary, that we shall make it our Constant Study to maintain and promote the same, Signed by Order of the House.   David Lloyd, Speaker.

PHILADELPHIA Oct. 21. Run away the 18th of September last, from Lawrence Reynolds of the City of Philadelphia, a Servant Man named George Rogers, Aged about 30 Years, by Trade a Nailer, he is af a middle Stature, thin Visage, short Hair, and a lump on his Throat, and also one of his Hands, like a Wen, about as big as a small Apple, he hath on a Check Shirt, an old gray Coat trim'd with black and a pair of old Leather Breeches, Course Stockings, and used Round Toe'd Shoes, and an old Hat. Whoever takes up the said Servant snd secure him so as his Master may have him again, shall have forty Shillings Reward, paid by me.   Lawrence Reynolds.

PHILADELPHIA Oct. 28. Four Servants time to be sold, two Men for 4 Years and two Boys for 6, one of the Men is a Frenchman and a Plaisterer by Trade. to be agreed for, with Capt. Thomas Colvill or Patrick Baird in Philadelphia.

NEW-YORK Nov. 1. The Speech of his Excellency William Burnet, Esq; to the General Assembly of New-York, October 27, 1725.

Gentlemen,

I have put an end to the last Session, that I might have a fresh Opportunity to Recommending to you to provide as honourable and Ample Supply for Support of the Government, and for as for as long Terms as was established, upon my

Arrival.

It has not been pretended, that any Inconveniency has arisen from the Consequence, you there expressed, in the Administration; and therefore I cannot, in Duty to his Majesty and in Justice to my own Conduct, agree to a less sufficient Provision, or to a Shorter Term.

The Administration of Justice will Require the same Encouragement, and the Collection of the Revenue the same Officers: Without such necessary Protection there will be great Deficiencies, and the Burden must, at last, fall upon the Land.

If there are any Laws formerly passed in this Province, which you are desirous to have now conferred by his Majesty, The Agent only want your Instructions to Solicit them, and I shall very readily joyn my hearty Endeavours to Obtain whatever will be to your Satisfaction.

I have expressed my Self fully, as to all other Matters, in the last Speech, to which I Refer; and desire you to take it again into your Consideration, and to proceed with that Dispatch with the Season of the Year Requires.

W. Burnet.

PHILADELPHIA Nov. 4. Pennsylvania Court of Vice-Admiralty.

Whereas on the 4th of October last, the Ship York Frigate of Bristol, was Bilged and Stranded in Delaware Bay; and whereas several Informations have been given to the Judge of the Court of Vice-Admiralty, that divers Goods, as especially certain Parcels belonging to the Palatines, who came in the said Ship Passengers have Illegally taken out from the said Ship, and brought into the City of Philadelphia and other Places in this Province, and are there concealed by evil disposed Persons, and privately Sold for their unlawful Gains. These are therefore to give publick Notice, that by an Act of Parliament made the 4th Year of his present Majesties Reign, any Person or Persons concealing Goods so taken as aforesaid are rendered Lyable to the Forfeiture of treble the Value of such Goods and other Penalties. And all Persons who are or shall be possessed of any Goods whatsoever taken from the said Ship the York are required to give just and true Accounts thereof into the Office of Vice-Admiralty, (where in due Time they will be intitled to the Lawful Reward of Salvage) that Justice maybe done to the true Owners thereof: And all Persons concealing any such Goods are afore-said will be prosecuted for the same as Law directs.

PHILADELPHIA Nov. Pennsylvania Court of Vice-Admiralty.

By Order of the Judge of the Court of Admiralty Publick Notice is hereby given, That an information is exhibited by John Moore, Collector for the Port of Philadelphia, viz. Seven Barrels of Gun Powder, supposed to be illegally Imported; and now in the Possession of William Chancellor, that any Person Interested therein may attend the Court the 10th Day of December next, and make good their Claim; otherwise the said parcel of Powder will be condemned to be Forfeitured as the Law Directs,

Pat. Baird Regr.

PHILADELPHIA Nov. 11. Last Night broke out of Common Goal of Chester, between the Hours of Twelve and Four; Two Prisoners, one named William Bennet (an Irish-Man) of large Stature and well set, with short thick Brown Hair, has on a Brown Cloath Coat, Oxenbrig Shirt, dirty leather Breeches, Brown Yarn Stockings, Old round Toe'd Shoes and no Hat unless he has got one since he broke Prison. The other named John Bull, (an English-Man,) Thick and of a short Stature, with short Brown Hair, has on a felt Hat, Copper Coloured Jacket, Exenbrig Shirt, Leather Breeches, Cotton Stockings and old round Toe'd Shoes. Any Person that will take up the said William Bennet and John Bull, (they are two Notorious Rogues) and secure them in the next goal so as they may be had or bring them to the Common Goal at Chester aforesaid shall have as a Reward Four Pounds Pounds or for each of them taken Forty Shillings, paid by, William Weldon.

PHILADELPHIA Nov. 25. On Monday last at White Marsh, two Stables with about 30 Loads of English Hay was burnt; it was done by a Traveller, who set a Candle burning in the Stable.

Samuel Hackney of Philadelphia, Disteller, intending to begin a Voyage in two Weeks time, from this Port for Great-Britain, desires all Persons Indebted to him forthwith to come and Settle their Accounts, to prevent the trouble and Charge of legal Prosecutions against them. Also any Person who would buy a valuable Piece of Ground for a Pasture, Quantity three Acres and three Quarters at Wicaco on Minceasing Road, let them repair to said Samuel Hackney's House in High-Street, where they may know of the Terms and Title.

PHILADELPHIA Dec. 2. These are to give Notice to all Persons, that are indebted to David Evans at the Sign of the Crown, that they come forthwith and Pay the same or else they may expect to be sued and those that have not settled their Accounts are desired forthwith to come and settle the same, and all Persons to whom said Evans is indebted, are desired to come and receive the same, for he designs for Great-Britain, early in the Spring.

All Persons who are indebted to George Forrington of the City of Philadelphia, inn-holder now living at the Crooked Billet, are desired to come and pay the same for he designs to depart this Province in about two Months Time and all Persons that he is indebted to come and receive the same.

A choice Parcel of Men and Women to be sold, on Board the Ship Lovely, now lying at the Wharf of the Widow Allen, at Twelve to Fourteen Pounds per Head, also very good Cheese at Eight Pence per Pound.

Philadelphia Dec. 9. Run away from his Master Henry Enocks of the County of Bucks, Blacksmith, a Servant Lad named James Smart, of middle Stature round Visage Brown color'd Hair, about 17 Years of Age, having on a strip'd Jacket a Leather pair of Breeches, a new Hat, and several other Cloaths, he has stolen or taken away his Indenture from his Master. Whoever shall take up said Servant and bring him to his Master, or give Notice thereof so that his Master may have him again, shall have Twenty Shillings and reasonable Charges by   Henry Enocks.

A very Likely Negro Girl, about Twelve or Thirteen Years of Age to be sold, Enquire Andrew Bradford.

Run away the 2d of November last, from the Ship Betty, Capt. Stollard, at Lads-Cove, a Negroe Man belonging to said Thomas Lawrence, he has an Ozenbrig Shirt, a black Cloath pair of Breeches, a Cinnamon colour'd Pea Jacket, and Worsted knit Cap, he speaks very good English, and lost his foremost two upper Teeth, he Formerly belonged to John Weldon, Black-Smith near Christeen in New-Castle County. Whoever secures the said Negroe so that his Master may have him again, shall have Twenty Shillings Reward.

A new Brick House near Mulbery Street (commonly called Arch Street) also a new Cart and Team of Horses, and a Negro Man to be sold by John Orron, Gun-Smith, in the Front-Street Philadelphia.

PHILADELPHIA Dec. 21. There is to be sold, by George Campion at the Plum of Feathers, in Front Street, in Philadelphia, a Servant man about 26 Years, of middle Stature, he has served in these Parts of America 5 Years to Plantation Work. He can Ditch, Chop, Plow, Mow, and do all kind of Husbandry to the utmost perfection his time being Seven Years, will be reasonably sold by

George Campion.

PHILADELPHIA Dec. 28. This is to give Notice, that at the Prince Eugene in Front-Street, there is to be sold a good Billiard Table with all Necessaries fitted, also a Servant Woman by

Matthew Gariguts.

To be sold at the Prince Eugene, over against Mr. Carpenter's Wharf, Excellent Red-Wine, Bristol Beer, Loaf Sugar, Raisins, also a Parcel of Neat Iron Weights Half Hundred, Quarters &c. And other British Goods, at Reasonable Rates by William Cole, lately from Bristol.

1726

PHILADELPHIA Jan. 4. Whereas there hath been lately Published and Spread abroad in this Province and elsewhere, a lying Pamphlet called an Almanack, set out and Printed by Samuel Heiner, to reproach and ridicule, to rob an Honest Man of his Reputation, and strengthening his Adversaries, and not only so hath Notoriously Branded the Gospel Minister of the Church of England, with ignominious Names, for Maintaining a Gospel Truth, and reprocheth all Professors of the Christ and Christianity as may be seen in the Almanack in the Month of December, now all Judicious Readers may fairly see what the Man's Religion Consisteth in, only his Beard and his Sham keeping of the Seventh Day Sabbath, Following Christ only for Loafs and Fishes. This may give Notice to the Author of this Mischief, that if he do not readily Condemn what he hath done, and satisfy the Abused, he may expect to be Prosecuted as the Law shall Direct.

         Arron Goforth, Senior.

PHILADELPHIA Jan. 11. At the Court of Record held for the City of Philadelphia the 4th Day of this Instant January before William Hudson Esq; Mayor, and Robert Ashenton, Esq; Recorder and several of the Aldermen of the said City.

Edward Mullun jun., Joseph Smith, and Thomas Morrill were indicted for Forging an Obligation, with intent to Recover Four Hundred Pounds Sterl. from James Cooper and Mary his Wife, Administratrix of John Burrow, deceas'd. Joseph Smith and Thomas Morrill pleaded Guilty, and Edward Mullun not Guilty, but the Jury found the said Edward Guilty and they they received the following Sentences, That they should stand in the Pillory in the Market Place of this City one Hour, and each of them have an Ear cut off, and should pay the Party Griev'd Double Damages and suffer one Year Imprisonment.

Richard Kinner at the Court of Records, held here July Last, was convicted of Counterfeiting and Uttering a Bill of Credit of 25 Pounds and pursuant to a Law of this Province received the following Sentence. That he should be set on the Pillory in the Market Place of the City; and thereto have both of his Ears cut off and be publickly Whipt on his bare Back with Thirty Lashes and forfeit the Sum of One Hundred Pounds, and Pay to the Party Grieved double Damages.

William Van Reddlesden alias William Cornwallis, was Convicted of Forging a Release in the order to acquaint and Discharge himself from an Obligation come into to Francis Gaedouit, for the Payment of Fifty two Pounds, and being asked by the court if he had any thing to offer, wherefore Judgement should not be given against him, he desired Time till next Day, to file some reason he had an Arrest of Judgement. Which was Granted him, the next Day his Reason were argued and Considered by the Court but as the said Cornwallis complained that he was Streightened in Time, and was in a Book and Authority's to support his Reasons, the Court so far indulged him as to put the said Reasons under Advisement till the next Court.

NEW-YORK Jan. 17. At the Supreme Court held in this City in November last, one Thomas Bing received Sentence of Death for Murdering his Wife, and on Wednesday last was Executed accordingly.

PHILADELPHIA Jan. 18. These are to desire all Persons inhabiting with the Eastern Division of New-Jersey, and the County of Hunterdon in the Western, who have any Demands on the Estate of Jeremiah Bass Esq; late of Burlington deceased, and those indebted to the said Estate in the Place aforesaid, That they Apply forthwith to Mrs. Fredrick Lyall of Middletown, in the County of Monmouth, in Order to adjust the same, and pay their Debts; and all those Inhabitants elsewhere are desired to apply to the Widow and Executrix of the said Deceased, in Burlington, to the above end mentioned. Also those who are

Indebted to the Estate of Mr. Robert Talbot, late of Burlington, aforesaid Deceased, or have any Accounts or Demands, on the same, are desired to Settle the same with Mrs. Catherine Talbot Widow of the said Deceased in Burlington as soon as may be.

PHILADELPHIA Feb. 1. Spirit of Wine, Cinnamon Water, and several other Cordials, and Rum, Sold by George Brownell, at the Corner of the Market, against the Court-House Stairs.

Very good Chocolate and also good Behea Tea, to be sold by Andrew Bradford.

An Indian Woman fit for all Manners of House Work, to be Sold. Enquire Andrew Bradford.

PHILADELPHIA Feb. 8. Capt. Allen is arrived at Cape-May from London, who left it the 9th of November, about 300 Leagues off the Coast she lost her Masts, and had 3 foot of Water in Her Hold, they have one Hundred & odd Servants on Board, & they were very much put to it for Water.

PHILADELPHIA Feb. 8. On Wednesday the 16th of February 1726. Will be sold by vendue by Daniel Hall of Philadelphia, about half a Mile from the Market, at the North-End of this City, a Lot of ground, containing about 3 Acres and a half, with a good Brick House, the Lot very well Planted with English Fruit-Trees, as Cherries, Plumbs, Apprecots, Pears, with one Acre of good Grafted Apple Trees, and a Nursery with English Trees.

NEW-York Feb. 14. No Vessels Entered Inward or Outward this Week, abundance of Ice Standing in the bay and people have gone over the ice from this City to Long-Island.

PHILADELPHIA Feb. 22. There is to be dosposed of, by Sale, at the Parsonage House in this City, the Goods of Dr. Richard Welton, who is call'd Home.

And especially a Collection of Excellent and useful Books, Chiefly in English; of Practical Divinity, and of the best Edition. Which the Dr. Himself had Collected, and which are adapted (and without Controversie, or any Thing Polemical) to Instructions, and fit to be made use of, in all Families, of every Peswasion whatever.

PHILADELPHIA March 1. Very good New-Castle Grind Stones of several Sizes to be Sold by Joseph Trotter, Cutler, in the Second-Street.

PHILADELPHIA March 12. Ran away about the 8th of February last, from Patrick Creagh of Baltimore County, on Patapsco River in Maryland; a Servant Man named Edward Jones, aged about 30 Years, by Trade a Glasier and Plummer, he can work at plain Painting, and is a Convicted Person, he is a Welsh-man, but talks very good English, he is a tall Slender Man, with short Red Hair and Beard, he wears a Cap or Wigg, he is full of Pockholes, and had on an old Blue Coat, and white Fustain tite Bodied short Coat, a pair of Leather Breeches; but may have changed his Cloaths and Name and may have a false Pass. Whoever takes up the said Servant and secures him, so that his Master may have him again, shall if found in Maryland, have Five Pounds Reward, if taken in Pennsylvania, and brought to Owen Humprie, at the Sign of the White-Horse in Philadelphia, shall have the same, if in any other Province, he or they shall have Five Pounds, and reasonable Charges by me,
Patrick Creagh.

Philadelphia March 24. Run away March 3d 1726. From the Ship John Galler, John Ball Master, two Men named Joseph Newell and James Ensworth, the former is a Man of middle Stature, and a brown Complexion full favoured, grey Eyes short brown Hair, has Cheeks spotted with little black specks like Gun-Powder. James Ensworth, is a tall Space youg Man full favoured with short Hair, sometimes he wears a Wigg with a short brown Jacket. Whoever can secure the said Runaways, so as they may be had again shall have five Pounds Reward with Reasonable Charges.
John Ball.

PHILADELPHIA March 24. Whereas Francis Gambie, late of the Island of Barbadoes, by Virtue of sundry mesne Conveyances under William Penn, late Proprietor of the Province; was seized of sundry contiguous Tracts of Land, situated on the River Delaware, between two Navigable Creeks, in the County of Kent; containing upward of Eleven Thousand Acres, And whereas it is Reported that one William Van Reddlesden, otherwise called William Cornwallis gives out that he is entitled to the said Land, by Conveyance derived from the said Francis Gamble, and hath Sold some part thereof and offers the residue to Sale.

Now these are to certify the Inhabitants of the said County of Kent, and all the others who it may concern, that the said William Cornwallis is a Person of very suspicious Character, and is suppos'd to be guilty of some vile Practices in Relation to the premises aforesaid, it being highly unprobable he has any genuine Title thereupon; since the same Land by regular Conveyances from the said Francis Gamble is now vested in one John Haidon and Benjamin Curtis, or their Heirs or Assigns, in Trust for certain Persons, known by the name of the Pennsylvania Land-Company; and the Original grant from the Proprietors and Mesne Conveyances, down to the said Company; are new at the Hands of Henry Hodge of this City, and ready to be shewn to those who may doubt the Truth hereof. Wherefore all Persons are desired to be cautious how they Purchase to said William Cornwallis's pretended Titles; and on this Occasion are desired to remember the well know proverb, Buyer Beware, Philadelphia the 16th of the first Month 1726.

Henry Hodge.

NEW-YORK April 6. The Speech of his Excellency William Burnet Esq; To the General Assembly of his Majesty's Province of New-York.

Gentlemen,
I never begin with a Subject more worthy of your Attention, than the admirable effects of the uninterrupted Harmony that Subsist between our Most Gracious Sovereign, and His Parliament. Our Enemies had no other hopes, but from their unwearied Artifices, &c. even Popular Pretences to weaken this Mutual Confidence, but without effect; and this happy Union it is, that renders Great-Britain a Pattern to all Europe in time of Peace, and lodges the Balance of Power in its Head, in case of War.

Tho' you cannot equal His Majesty's Subjects at Home in Abilities to serve him, Yet I am persuaded that you will not Yield to any Loyalty and Inclination. The great and constant Charge at which Great-Britain Maintains Forces for the Defence of this Province in a more eminent nanner than any of the Neighbouring Provinces partake of, as it is a very distinguishing Mark of his Majesty's Royal Care, so it calls upon you to make the most natural Return for so singular a favour, by providing honourable and amply to the Support of his Government here. And since the Sums you have usually raised for the purpose have not amounted any near to so much as those issued from Great-Britain for your Security, it should induce you rather to think if increasing than lessoning your Supply, and rather of Extending than of shortning the time of its continuance; and as no occasion has been given to alter your former good Opinion of the Administration, I have reason to depend on your providing in the most hearty and effectual manner for the Support of it in all its Branches.

I wish I could say, the Laws for promoting a Trade with the far Indians and prohibiting it with Canada, has been as duly executed as they were intended, and I leave it to your Consideration in better a method less severe, may not be more effectual.

The great Success we have already had in the Trade upon the River of Onondaga, and the noble Spirit that Animated the People to go on with it, gives us Encouragement to leave no Measures untried to establish and increase it; the only danger we have to apprehend, is from the unwearied Artifices of the Inhabitants of Canada among our Indians, to alienate their Affection; and particularly to interrupt this Trade, which has put them unto great Consternation because it is so sure a means to strengthen our interest and to weaken theirs, with all the Nations of North-America. I am sorry to inform you, That they have taken great Advantage this Winter of the want of proper Persons from this Government residing among the Onondagas and Senecas, & have inflicted groundless Scars into their minds of the Five Nations, of dangers that may arise to them by this open Trade with the far Indians, which I have done my utmost Endeavours to remove, But I am convinced that the most effectual means to keep them steady will be your enabling me to maintain a sufficient Number of fit Persons constantly among them, as I have formerly done with good Success; if I am earnest with you on the head, it is your own Safety, and that our Posterity, that make me so. All that I desire of you is, Not to be wanting to your selves.

Your Agent who is ever watchful in what relates to your Interest has acquainted me by the first opportunity he had, that some Apprehension had been made at come to your Disadvantage which I will Communicate to you, This with many other instances of his ability and diligence will, I doubt not, confirm you in the Resolution taken in your last Session upon the Head.

I have received a Letter from the Government of Connecticut, about finishing the Partition Line, which I will lay before you, that you may make provisions for so necessary Work.

I need now only Remind you, That the Repair of the Buildings in the Fort stand in immediate Care, That the Season proper to Finish them may not be lost.

I have no greater Pleasure than in Contributing to the Publick Service, and if there are any more Laws wanting to that end, or any former Laws that you are desirous to have Recommended for His Majesty's Conformation, you may depend on my readiness & Zeal to joyn with you in that, or any thing else, that can make this Province Happy and Flourishing,   W. Burnet.

The Humble Address of the General Assembly of the Colony of New-York, to his Excellency the Governour, &c.

May it Please your Excellencu;
We his Majesty's Loyal & Dutiful Subjects, the General Assembly of this Colony of New-York, return your Excellency our hearty Thanks for your kind & obliging Speech to us.

We observe, with Pleasure that constant Harmony which Subsists between His Majesty and his British Parliament, and hope, all endeavours to lessen that exact Confidence, will always prove ineffectual and all Attempts of the Enemies to the Publick Peace, Vain.

Our Inclination to serve and promote the Interest of His Majesty(the best of Princes) are as strong as those of any of His Subjects, tho' our Abilities are not equally Sufficient, but these shall be exerted to the utmost of our Power, by providing an honourable Support for His Government here, in such a manner as shall be most suitable to the Circumstances of this Colony.

The other Matter recommended by your Excellency, shall in course of our Proceeding, have their due Wright; and our endeavours shall not be wanting for the Publick Service.

His Excellency's Answer.

Gentlemen,
I Thank you for this Affectionate Address, I will not neglect this Opportunity to acquaint you, That a Report has been spread about the Country, that the Money to be raised for the support of Government, is to be apply'd to private Use, &c. in case of my Death or Removal and to go to my Executors, which if it should happen soon, would put the Government to a double Expence. As you know that this is entirely False & Groundless, I depend on you joyning with me on all proper occasions, to underceive those who may be deluded by it.

PHILADELPHIA April 14. There is a Plantation on Neshaminy Creek, in the County of Bucks, in the Province of Pennsylvania; Joyning to the Ferry, within two Miles of the River Delaware; it contains Four hundred and Forty six Acres level Land, near one Hundred Acres clear within Fence, an Orchard of about Three Hundred bearing Trees, and winter Fruit; a Log House with two lower Rooms, two Chambers, four Fire places, a Barn, a Out-House of Sixty Foot Long, and Twenty Foot wide not yet finished, a Stonequarry close to the water. A large Swamp of Oak Timber, a large quantity of Meadow Ground not improv'd, and Navigable for a loaded Shallop to the Landing; it is within three Miles of the Town of Bristol, five Miles from Burlington, and seventeen Miles from Philadelphia, also 3 Negroes, and Stock, Household Goods, &c. to be

Sold the first Day of May by   Mordyiac Howell.

To be Sold by Michael Royal at the lower End of the Front-Street a new sloop upon the stocks, 44 foot Keel 18foot 4 inches Beam, 9 Foot Hold, if any Persons have a mind to Purchase the said sloop, may apply at said Royal.

These are to give Notice unto all Millers and Exporters of Merchantable Wheat, Flour, fit to be exported from the port of Philadelphia.

That in Order to it's being branded, without any contest of Difficulty, They take due Care of its Quality and Goodness, for the future; otherwise such as of late seem industriously to contrive to mix their Flour, after such a manner to create a Dispute whether it be truly fit to be branded or not, will be disappointed in the Contrivance: The Law must be executed by

Jam. Carpenter.

PHILADELPHIA April 21. A Servant Maids time to be disposed of, for 3 Years, she is a good Cook, can Wash very well, and do all manner of Household Business, she is an excellent Spinner both Linnen and Wooling, and perfectly well understands the Bleaching, and managing of Cloath, Enquire the Printer for terms and conditions.

PHILADELPHIA April 28. Lately Imported from London, a Choice Parcel of London Cut Tobacco, to be sold at the Widow Gardner shop, opposite to Andrew Symes in the Front-Street, at Ten Shillings and Six-pence a Pound.

At the Corner shop. over against Nicholas Scull's at the George Inn in the Second-Street, Philadelphia, are to be sold, all sorts of useful Medicines and Druggs: where also all Masters of Trading Vessels may be furnish'd with Boxes of Medicines, fitted for their Voyages, with ample Directions for their Use, at reasonable Rates by   Patrick Baird Surgeon.

PHILADELPHIA May 5. Run away from his Master Robert Shephard, of the County of Philadelphia, Carter, a Servant Man, named Joseph Knight, he is 28 Years of Age, of a short Stature, black bushy Hair, and is of a Rudy Complexion, having on a gray homespun Jacket, Ozenbrig shirt and Trousers, Wooden Heel'd Shoes, stitch'd on the Quarters, he had on a narrow brim'd Hat.

PHILADELPHIA May 12. All retailers of Liquors in this Province, are hereby required to return their Permits to the Collector of the Excise, and to enter into Recognizance with Surities in the sum of Twenty Pounds, for keeping good Orders and due observance of the Act of Excise, passed the Tenth Year of His Majesty's Reign. Also those retailers, who are in arrear are required to pay what is from them respectively due, to the 24th Day of this Instant May, or they will be prosecuted.   Charles Read Clerk.

NEW-YORK May 12. Extract from the Votes of the General Assembly of New-York.

The House (according to Order) resolved into a Committee of the whole House to consider further of his Excellency's Speech. After some time spent therein, Mr. Mayor of the City of New-York reported from the said Committee, That they had come to a further Resolution therein. Which being read was agreed into by the House, and is as follows, viz.

Resolved That the Monies to arise by virtue of the Bill ordered the Tenth Instant to be brought in for the Support of His Majesty's Government of this Colony, shall be issued and imployed, during the Three Years therein Mentioned, to and for the several salaries and other Services following, That is to say, To his Excellency the Governour, for his Salary, 1560 Pounds per Annum during the said Three Years.

For Fire-wood and Candles, for the Garrison at New-York 400 Pounds per Annum, during said Three Years.

For Repairing Fortifications, 200 Pounds per Annum, during the said Three Years.

For Presents to the indiand, 400 Pounds per Annum, during the said Three Years.

For the Governour's Voyage to Albany, 150 Pounds Annum, during the said Three Years.

For Fire-wood and Candles for the Garrison in the City and County of Albany, 200 Pounds per Annum, during the said Three Years.

To the chief Justice for his Salary, of 250 Pounds per Annum, during the said Three Years.

For the Commissioners of the Indian Affairs at Albany, 200 Pounds Annum, during the said

Three Years.

To the Indian Interpreter, 60 Pounds per Annum, during the said Three Years.

To the Secretary, for enrolling & engrossing the Acts of the General Assembly, 30 Pounds per Annum, during the said Three Years.

To the Clerk of Council 30 Pounds per Annum. during the said Three Years.

To the Printer, for Printing the Acts, Votes, Proclamations, and what shall be ordered more for Government, 50 Pounds per Annum, during the said Three Years.

To a Searcher of the Colony's Duties 40 Pounds per Annum, during the said Three Years.

To Land and Tide Waiter dotto, 30 Pounds per Annum, during the said Three Years.

To a Gauger, 30 Pounds per Annum, during the said Three Years.

To the Door Keeper of the Council, 20 Pounds per Annum, during the said Three Years.

To the Door Keeper of the General Assembly 20 Pounds per Annum, during the said Three Years.

To the Clerk of the General Assembly, for his Service as Clerk, for engrossing all Publick Acts, and for all other Incidents of his Office, Twelve Shillings per diem, upon Certificate from the House, for the number of days he served each Session.

PHILAdelphia May 19. Deserted from the Ship Betty, Samuel Manthrope, Master at Philadelphia, the following Persons, May 3d. Edward Willson a slender Man, aged about 20 Years, with his own curled dark brown Hair, of a fresh Complexion. Robert Collet middle Stature Man, with his own dark brown Hair, very much Pock-fretten, and aged about 20 Years. May the 10th James Twhaits a Boy, about 15 Years of Age, with his own light coloured sleek Hair, of a Pale Complexion, small and slender in Stature, they have all Sailors Habit. Whoever takes up and secures them so they may be had again shall have 40 Shillings as a Reward for each and reasonable Charges.

PHILADELPHIA May 26. Two Sailors Deserted from the Ship Betty, Timothy Williamson, on Monday the 16th at 6 in the Evening, both scotch

Men, the one named John Hall a short black Man, his own black short Hair, wearing a light coloured Pea Jacket, a pair of large Silver buckles on his Shoes. the other named Archibald Hall, his own brown Hair, a thin Complexion, and aged about 28 Years. Whoever takes up and secures them so that they may be had again, shall have 40 Shillings as a Reward for each, and reasonable Charges.

PHILADELPHIA June 2. The Speech of Sir William Keith, Bart. Governour of the Province of Pennsylvania, and the Counties of New-Castle. Kent and Sussex upon Delaware.

To the Representatives of the Freemen of the said Province of Pennsylvania in General Assembly met, May 31st 1726.

Mr. Speaker and Gentlemen of the Assembly, I herewith lay before you an Abstract of the Contents of some Letters which I lately received from the Corespondents at London, so far as they relate to the Publick Business of the Province: and the present situation of Affairs: I think it will best become me to submit this Subject into your own prudent Deliberation, without any commentary whatsoever.

It is this very Day, nine Years Compleat since I arrived at Philadelphia, and took upon me the Government of this Province, by Virtue of such Legal Powers as were Satisfactory to all Parties concern'd and by the blessing of God upon my Honest Endeavours, it is Universally known that the Province of Pennsylvania, has during my Time Enjoyed Tranquility at Home, acquired Reputation Abroad, and is now in a more Flourishing Condition than ever it was at any time before.

The Kings Majesty's Royal Subjects, has indeed been Asserted and Maintained on all Occasions, but at the same Time the Peoples Liberties and Privileges has also been Inviolably preserved, and the Proprietors just Rights supported.

It is well known to many of the present Members of your House, in what a miserable lame Condition the Executive Powers of Government were in at my Arrival, and how Diligently I have all along Supported the Authority of the Magistracy with Repeated and Distinguishing marks of favours to the People called Quakers.

You cannot therefore but be of Opinion, That to Charge me with being an Enemy to that People in a Monstrous Composition of Falsehoods and Black Ingratitude, Nay, I do have it to be a Duty Incumbent to you. To justify the Body of the People here, from being suspected to have any share in Abetting such a Calumnious Forgery against their Constant Friend, Benefactor and Governour.

Gentlemen,
The Integrity and good Harmony that has ever subsisted between, Me and the Assemblies of this Province, urged me to think it a Part of my Duty, as well as a piece of good Manners to call you together on this Occasion to Thank you, as I do most Heartily for many Favours, and General Benefactions which I have from Time to Time Received at the Hands of the good People of Pennsylvania, and if there be any thing wanting which is yet in my Power to do for the future Service of this People and Country, I have now the pleasure to assure you that you shall Command all the Faculties which belong to a most grateful and willing Heart in your Service; And as long as the Remembrance of things which have been Publickly Transacted during my Administration here can be faithfully preserved. I doubt not but the Example will be both useful and Acceptable hereafter unto those amongst us, who truly hate Oppression, and Love the things that is just.

PHILADELPHIA June 9. To the Honourable the House of Representatives of the Freemen of the Province of Pennsylvania in General Assembly, met May 31st 1726.

The Petition of the Free-holders, Merchants and others, the Inhabitants of the City and County of Philadelphia.

By Humble manner Showeth,
That whereas it is more than probable that our present Worthy Governour Sir William Keith, will speedily be removed from this Government, and as the People of the Province in General, cannot but have sensibly Felt the Happy Effects of his Prudent, Mild and just Administration.

And as there is but too much cause to believe, that his Removal is owing, Partly to having steadily Affected and Vindicated the Rights and Privileges of the People, (which has unhappily been Misrepresented,) and partly to Misrepresentation of his Conduct, to the Honourable Proprirtors Family. We therefore humbly Pray, that the Honourable House will prevent all Imputations of Ingratitude in the People by giving, while Opportunity serve some sensible Mark of those Esteem befitting the said Sir William Keith to receive, and a grateful People to give, which we humbly conceive, it not only due to the Merit of the said Sir William Keith but will also Prove an Encouragement to succeeding Governours of the Province always to have at Heart and Maintain the Interest and Welfare of the People and your Petitioners as in Duty Bound, &c.

Signed by 238 Hands amongst whom were divers of the Magistrate, and a great Number of the most considerable Merchants and Free-holders.

Having in our last given Readers, Sir William Keith our Governours Speech to the Assembly of Pennsylvania, at the opening of their late Session: We have now an Opportunity of incerting their Addresses in answer thereto: which is as follows.

To Sir William Keith Bart. Governour of the Province of Pennsylvania, &c.

The Humble Address of the Representatives of the Freemen of the said Province in General Assembly met, this Second Day of the Month called June 1726.

May it please the Governour,
This Colony by the good Providence of the Almighty God, hath been favoured with many inestimable Blessings ever since it was first Settled, and the Trading People for the most Part being careful to preserve their Credit, abroad and at Home, acquir'd a good Reputation before as well as since thy accession to this Government; But of late, the Gold and Silver Currency falling short to support the Administration, and to carry on Trade and Answer other Occasions, the Governour was pleased to relieve the

Province by Joyning with the Peoples Representatives to Strike a Paper Currency, and if the Governours Character has in any respect suffered for his apparent Good will to the People, in that part of his Conduct, We are heartily Sorry.

It is most agreeable to the desire and Concern of the House, that the Kings Majesty's Royal and most just Authority here over his Subjects, has been Affected and Maintained, and the Proprietors Just Rights supposed, and this House by Address to the Descendents of our late Proprietor in December last, as well as the other Times, have acknowledge the Governours good Offices to this Colony, in the Course of his Administration, and the great Services he performed to the People in General, by his care and diligence in supporting the Magistracy, whereby the People called Quakers were restored to a Right, which they ought to have enjoyed, at their first Settlement of this Country, but were laid aside, because they could not take nor Administer Oaths, so that the Executive Powers of Government, with respect to Magistracy, were in a lame Condition at the Governours Arrival, as he is pleased to observe.

From whence we conclude that the Body of People called Quakers here, are far from charging the Governour with being an Enemy to them, having repeated Instances of his good Wishes to them by his prudent Care over them, equal to the rest of the Kings Subjects.

Signed by Order of the House this 3d Day of the Month called June 1726.

David Lloyd Speaker.

PHILADELPHIA June 6. Publick Notice is hereby Given, That the four Wheel Chase belonging to David Evans, is now intended to be continually kept in Order by Thomas Shelton, Living near the Three Tuns in Chestnut-Street, who will duly attend Persons at the following Rates, viz.

From Philadelphia to German-Town, for four Persons together Twelve Shillings and Six-pence. And for any other further Journeys as far as New-Castle, Amboy, or elsewhere either with two or four Horses, at as reasonable Rates as to be agreed for from Time to Time.

PHILADELPHIA June 23. Yesterday Arrived here the Honourable Patrick Gordon Wsq; Lieut. Governour of the Province of Pennsylvania, and the Counties of New-Castle, Kent and Sussex upon Delaware, in the Ship London-Hope, Tho. Annis, Commander: And his Commission was Published at the Court-House about 6 a-Clock in the Evening.

We have Advice by Captain Samuel Harris from New-London, (who in his Passage from thence, was taken by a Pirate Snow, Commanded by William Fly, as he calls himself) about 5 Leagues to the Eastward from Cape-May; she had Four Carriage and Two Swivel Guns mounted, and about Twenty three Men; the Pirate had on board about 50 Buts of Rum, some Sugar, Indian Corn, Beans, and a large Quantity of small Arms; the took from said Harris all their Wearing Apparel, and other goods to the Value of about One Hundred Pounds; they detained the said Harris about Twenty-four Hours; But before they parted with him, they forced one of his Men named James Benbrook. They left him in Lat. 38.20. then stood to N. E. They also told said Harris, that there were Two more Sloops comming on the Coast, commanded by Sprigg and Low, and they said, they had parted with one of them, off the Capes of Virginia, four Days before they took them.

PHILADELPHIA June 30. On Monday last the Honourable Patrick Gordon, Esq; our Lieut. Governour, set out for his Government of the Three lower Counties, in order to Publish his Commission there, who was accompanied from this City, with his Council, the Mayor, Aldermen and Chief Magistrate; and a Number of other Gentlemen.

Run away June 23, from the Township of Richmond, in Bucks County, an Irish Man, named William Bannet, of large Stature, Palish Complexion light colour'd Hair, having homespun Wastcoat and Trousers, dark colour'd Coat, old Leather Breeches, gray Yarn Stockings, a pair of Pumps and Shoes, an old Felt Hat, he formerly belonged to Mr. Hunter of Chester County, Tanner, and having Committed several Villainies, was committed to Chester Goal, from whence he broke loose some time ago, and he also has taken with him a Dark colour'd pacing Mare, having a Star on her Forehead, and branded with S. B.; also a Gun about Five foot long. Whoever takes up the said runaway, and secure him in the next common Goal shall have seven Pounds Ten Shillings as a Reward paid by William Moore of the Great Swamp, in the County of Bucks aforesaid.

N. B. It is supposed he has a Counterfeit Pass with him.

PHILADELPHIA July 7. The General Proprietors of the Soil of the Eastern Division of New-Jersey, are desired to meet and assist in a Council of Proprietors, to be held in the City of Perth-Amboy, on Tuesday the Twelth Day of this Instant July, 1726.   Lewis Morris, Presdt.

Strayed or Stolen from Christopher Cox, about the 12th of June last, a large Bay Horse Natural Pacer Branded IH on the near Shoulder, a Star on his forehead, one of his Hind Feet White, Switch Tail. Whoever takes up said Horse, and brings him to said Cox, in High-Street in Philadelphia, shall have a Reward of Ten Shillings and all reasonable Charges, paid them be me.

MARYLAND July 12. The Speech of his Excellency Charles Calvert, Esq; Lieutenant Governor of Maryland to both Houses of Assembly.

Gentlemen of the upper and Lower House of Assembly.
Several Petitions having been delivered to Me, from the Inhabitants of divers Parts of this Province, complaining of the low State Tobacco is reduc'd to. and humbly desiring that the Assembly might be conven'd in order to call upon some Method to relieve Ourselves in these Melancholy Circunstances: I (having nothing more at Heart than the Good of the Province) have Thought fit, with the Advice of his Lordship's Council, to Convene You, that you may have an Opportunity to make the Staple a real benefit to Us:

In Order to which it will be proper to Consider, to what causes the present low Price of Tobacco is owing, which I take to be chiefly These, The sending Home trash Tobacco, and Uncertainty of Shipping our Crops: To prevent the first, it would undoubtedly be, the Interest of the Country to destroy the trash here; for no body but a Mad man would ship bad Tobacco, to bring himself in Debt: This would, in a great measure, lessen the Quantity, especially in Tending of Seconds were prohibited.

And if the good Tobacco was shipp'd at a Time certain, the Merchants might regulate the Market at Home, very much to our Advantage.

This Gentlemen, is what accurs to Me; And I leave it to your Consideration.

Charles Calvert.

Maryland July 13. To his Honourable Charles Calvert Esq; Governour of Maryland.

The Humble Address of the House of Delegates,
May it Please your Honour,

We Return you our most hearty Thanks for your kind Speech at the opening of the Session: And beg leave to assure we observe You to be contantly exerting Yourself to advance the Interest of this Province.

It is with no small concern We find Tobacco our Staple, reduced to so low a State as it now is, and are fully convinced that the lessening the Value of the Commodity, is chiefly owing to those Causes Your Honour is pleased to attribute it to. And though Tobacco Laws within the Province have seldom had any other Effects than the utter ruin of some of the Inhabitants thereof. We shall endeavour to do every thing that may contribute to the Relief of the People we represent, in their present melancholy Condition, with the greatest Dispatch We possibly can.

R. Ungle Speaker.

MARYLAND July 14. The Speech of the Right Honourable c. Baltimore Lord Proprietor of Maryland, to both Houses of Assembly.

I Thank you for Your late dutiful Addresses; and notwithstanding so Difference among you, I persuade Myself you severally pursue the same End; and aim in general at the good and Welfare of the Province: And as it is our mutual Happiness, that the Province has with Justice, Equity and Prudence, been hitherto governed; for the best means to continue these inestimable Blessings among us, is to preserve in the same Method of Rule and Obedience: And I think I cannot better manifest My Steadiness, in Making the

Publick Good the Rule of my Government, than by Preserving to you His Majesty's Subjects in this Part of the World under my Care, such Laws, Rights, Customs & Usages, as are undoubted, certain, constantly adhered to, and practiced among You.

Gentlemen of the Lower House,
In Your Address, You agree the Council of the State deserve their Reward, tho' you are unwilling They should find it out of the same Levies they received it long before, at the same Time, & ever since the making of the Act, which (among other Things) raises the Making of Twelve Pence per Hogshead, in the Absence of the Lord Proprietory towards the better Maintaining the Dignity and Station of his Lieutenant Governour, actually inhabiting & residing within this Province; and to such other necessary Uses towards the Support and Defence of the Lord Proprietory's Government of this Province, as in His Lordship's Wisdom to Him shall seem meet: But on the contrary allege, that ample Provisions was made, and annually raised by the Act, and therefore it ought not to be annually levied by a Poll-tax against the People.

Whereas it was never mentioned, or intended, or even imagined till of late by some, that their Allowance should come out of any Part of the Duty raised by Virtue of that Act, whereby I give up so great a Part of my Property as all my Quit-Rents and Alienation Fines are: And I hope none of my good Tenants will persist in thinking any longer that it ought: but rether choose to shew their Duty in their Actions, as well as Expressions, by consenting that the Council of State should have their Recompence in the same Manner They have long since found it, & not put me upon unwilling Task of Shewing the People of Maryland the true Value of the said Rents and Fines, and the necessary consequence of Advantage attending Me in a Just & legal Collection of them, above the Composition I consented to take Lieu of them, by the temporary Continuance of that Act.

C. Baltimore.

PHILADELPHIA July 21. From Wright Town in Bucks County, we have the following lamentable Account, of a Tragical Accident which happened there on Sunday Night last, being the 17th instant, at the House of one Cephas Child, which was burnt to the Ground in the following manner. His Wife being the last up in the family, at her going to Bed putting out the Candle (she snuff of it as is supposed) catched some straw, which was under the Bed instead of a Matt, she endeavoured to extinguish it that Time, which proving ineffectual she awake her Husband, who immediately Endeavoured to save the Bed, but in Vain the Fire increasing to Prodigiously, and then securing his writings which were inclosed in a Trunk in the Room, and going in haste to relieve his poor Children which lay in the Room above, being 6 Boys, but the Flames increasing so violently he could not come at them no ways, but by pulling the Clapboards off the Gable end, which being also by the time he could come to them were a Flame, he could not do any thing to purchase his Eldest Son, about 14 Years of Age endeavering to get out, was struck back by the Flames, to that all the six Children perrished miserably in the Fire; the Woman had an infant at her Breast, which thro' God's Mercy was preserv'd.

Such Tragical Instances as there ought to stir up diligence in every Person, of what Station soever to do their utmost Endeavours in their respective Places, to prevent such terrible calamitys as these poor miserable Objects are plung'd into.

PHILADELPHIA July 28. Notice is hereby given, That there is come to the House of John Leonard at South River Bridge, near Amboy, in the Eastern Division of the Province of New-Jersey, a Negro Man, who was forced to the said House, for want of Sustenance: he is a middle size man, talks no English, or signs that he cannot, he calls himself Popow, his Teeth seems to be fil'd or whet sharp; he will not tell his Masters name. Whoever Owned the said Negro, may have him from the said Leonard, on coming or sending for, paying according to Reward, (if any be) Or if not according to the Laws of the Province, and also reasonable his Diet 'till fetched.

The Sun Inn in Burlington is to be let, there is to be had with it a sufficient quantity of Oats and Hay for the Winter, ready laid in, and several sorts of Furniture to be Sold at reasonable Rates fitting for said Inn, if wanted; the Pasture and Meadow will be let with the same, under the Rents and Covenant now held and enjoyed. Any Person inclined to take, may Enquire of Samuel Bustill, and no further.

PHILADELPHIA Aug. 2. The Speech of the Honourable Patrick Gordon Esq; Lieutenant Governour of the Province of Pennsylvania, and the counties of New-Castle, Kent and Sussex upon Delaware.

To the Representatives of the Freemen of the said Province of Pennsylvania.

Mr. Speaker and Gentlemen of the Assembly, After my arrival here with my Family, I earnestly wished for the Opportunity your own adjournment has now given me, of seeing and Speaking to the Representatives of the good People of this Province; whose general Character for Sobriety, and Industry, above many other of his Majesties Subjects added much to the Pleasure I received from our Honourable Proprietors Nomination of me to serve them, and you, in this Station.

And I question not, Gentlemen, but all those who have due sense of Gratitude for the Merits of the worthy Founder of this Colony under the Crown, will be very well pleased, to find by my Accession, that no Dispute amongst his Descendents could disable them, for pursuing the common Measures, according to their undoubted Rights, in substituting their Deputy for the Administration of this Government, nor prove any Obstructions to the Kings gracious Approbation of the Appointment.

His Majesty's concurrence, is what may be rationally expect from a Sovereign, whose goodness, impartial Justice, and unwearing Vigilance, not only for the Security and Liberties of His Subjects, but for the general Benefit and Freedom of Mankind, have made him the object of the Love and Terror of the Nations round him: and the Proprietors Family, I assure you Gentlemen, express so sincere a Zeal, and so tender a Concern for your Happiness, that principally on this Foundation, I hope to Recommend my self to their Regard. For their Interest and yours they esteem inseparable, and consider those as Friends to neither, who would attempt to divide them.

From hence it it, that I, in a great Measure, account to My Self for their choice of me before divers others, who Solicited their Favour; For knowing that I had been bred to the Camp, remote from the refined Politicks which often serve to perplex Mankind; and that an honest Plainness, free from Art or Disguise, made up the main of my Character, amongst my Friends and Acquaintances, the Honourable the Proprietors rightly Judged, that such a Person could form no Views, but what would be openly showed, and therefore be understood by every Man they could affect.

This notwithstanding may lay me under some Discouragement, left on nicer Occurrences, I might fail in the Discharge of so important a Trust, but I have ever been persuaded, that to do right is not so difficult a Task, as some would render it, In Emergencies of Weight and Moment, I shall Endeavour to fortify my self with the Advice of the Representatives of the People, when it may be had, and at all Times with the Judgement of such only, & I can be assured have the most Interest of the Publick, so seriously at Heart, that nothing private can interfere with it.

The discountenace Parties, Divisions, and Factions in Government, to maintain Rights and Justice, to promote Virtue, to suppress Vice, Immorality, and Prophaness, to assist and protect the Magistrates in the Discharge of their Duty herein, to encourage legal Trade, and to use the Indians well; as they are plain, so they are the principal matters I have in Charge, in all which I shall depend on the Concurrence of

the Assemblys of this Province where any further Provisions by Laws, to be Enacted so any of the said Purposes may be necessary, and on my Part, nothing in my Power shall be wanting to enforce their Execution.
To transmit our Laws, duely to His Majesty's Privy Council pursuant to an Injunction in the Royal Charter, and to have a proper Agent appointed, in another Article. Gentlemen, I am to recommend it and you will easily perceive this to be of such Importance that I promise my self, it cannot fail of your Serious Thoughts and Consideration.

These Heads Gentlemen I Judge necessary to maintain together at the most proper Season, but duly considered, to which I shall only add, that to secure the Peace, and advance the Prosperity of the People of this Province, and to concur with the Representatives in such Measures as may be best obtain those Ends being equally my Duty and Inclination, for what relates more immediately to my self. I shall so far depend on their Goodness and Justice, as to hope I shall never Occasion to put them otherways in mind of it, but that we may on both sides rest secure of the Homourable Discharge of what is incumbent on us, reciprocally to each other. 	P. Gordon.

Philadelphia Aug. 4. To the Honourable Patrick Gordon Esq; Lieut. Governour of the Province of Pennsylvania &c.

The Address of the Representatives of the free men of the said Privince in General Assembly. In Answer to the Governours Speech of the 2d Instant.

May it Please the Governour;
With great Thankfulness, to Almighty God for preserving Thee and thy Family, in your Voyage hither: We hold to our Incumbent Duty to Congratulate thy Accession to this Government, and Acknowledge thy Condescension in not requiring our Attendance before the Time of Adjournment.

We are Heartily glad, that the Heir at Law and Executrix of the later worthy Proprietor, has such regard to their own Honour, and good to this Colony, as to appoint thee to represent them in Government, according to their undoubted Right. And it is Obvious that his Majesties wonted Care and Justice rewards his Subjects, induced him to favour their Appointment; so that no Dispute amongst themselves could Obstruct his Royal Apprehension thereof.

We are exceedingly pleased to understand that the Proprietors Family esteem their Interest and our's Inseparable, and that they consider those as no friends to either, who would Attempt to divide them: And we are of Opinion, That those who Act with an Honest plainness free from Art or Disguise, though they are remote from the Governour is pleased to give us an Expectation, that, in Emergencies of Weigh and Moment, he will Endeavour to Fortify himself with an Advice of the Proples Representatives: We hope it will prove the most Effectual means to Support the Interest of the Publick, as well as discover the Private and Sinister End of Designing Men.

The Governour may depend that this House (and we hope all succeeding Assemblies) will Heartily join with him, to Discountenance all Parties, Divisions, and Factions (whereby the Established Government of the Province is or may be opposed) as shall delight to see Right and Justice maintained, Virtue promoted, Vice Immorality and Prophaness Suppressed, and the Magistrates assisted and protected in the Discharge of their Duty: And it will be no less pleasing to us and the good People's we represent, that Legal Trade be encouraged and the Indians well used, and as these particulars are plain and become the principal Matter which the Governour has in Charge (as he is pleased to initiate) so we have no reason to Doubt but he will exert his Authority in Discharging that part of his Trust, and Concur with the Assemblies of the Province in what may think necessary and requisite on their part to be proposed for any of these good purposes.

This House has had it under Consideration to pitch upon an Agent at Home: But it does not seem Clear that the Royal Charter Enjoyns the People Delegates, to Transmit our Laws to His

Majestties Privie Council; therefore we desire the same may be further Considered, at the next Assembly.

And inasmuch as the Governour is pleased, so generously to acknowledge, That to secure the Peace and advance the Prosperity of the People of this Province, and to concur with their Representatives in such a Measure as they may best obtain those Ends, are Equally his Duty and Inclination. We can do no less than assure him, That nothing shall be wanting on our part to make suitable Provisions for his Support, and We hope that such as Succeed us in this great Trust, will come under the like Care, Honourably to Discharge what may be Incumbent upon them in that respect. Signed by Order of the House, by

Davis Lloyd, Speaker.

PHILADELPHIA Aug. 18. Run away from Mr. Taylor of Baltimore County in Maryland, a Servant Man, named Patrick Malloney, middle Stature well set, round Visage, a little Pock-fretten and brown Hair, he wears a Coat of Irish Frize, lined with black, brown half-thick Breeches, with Mettle Buttons, and has sundry Holland and other type Shirts; he may have cut off his Hair and changed his Name, the better to make his Escape; he is an Imprudent prating Ill looked Thievish Fellow, he has seduced and stolen a lusty likely Negro Woman, about 30 Years of Age, she speaks good English, and has besides common Apparel, a Gown and pettycoat of printed Callico, lined with red and white plad.

Whoever secures the said People and bring them into Baltimore County aforesaid, so that they may be had again shall have Five Pistoles as a Reward, and reasonable Charges, paid by their said Master.

PHILADELPHIA Aug. 25. Whereas Samuel Keimer of this City printer, hath Scandalously and Maliciously reported about this City, (and also by his Printed Advertisements in the Country) That he is the sole Printer of Leeds Almanack for the Ensuing Year, 1727, and all the others are Counterfeits: These are to give Notice, That the next Week will be Published F. Leeds Almanack, for the Ensuing Year, in the same

Plain and Easy Method, as Leeds used heretofore, by usual Printer thereof; where Country Chapmen and others may be supplyed with any Quantity of them, at reasonable Rates.   Andrew Bradford.

PHILADELPHIA Sept. 1. Run away on the 29th of August last, from Doctor John Browne in York Road West-Jersey, a servanr Woman named Sarah Parier or Sartin, supposed to be Inveigled or Conveyed away by one Richard Sartin, who served his time at French Creek in Pennsylvania, at the Iron Works, who pretends that he is her Husband but is not; she is a little thin Person, having on a Callico Gown strip'd with Blue, or a black and white one of wool or worsted, a new Bonnet, and other tolerable Cloaths. Whoever takes up said Servant Woman and secures her to her said Master, shall have Forty Shillings as a Reward and all Lawful Charges, paid by me,

John Browne.

Run away the 28th of August last, from Rockey-hill in East-Jersey, Two servant men belonging to Richard Wright of Burlington: The one named John Lewis, Aged about 25 Years, middle Stature, with short brown Hair, Ledden colour'd double Breasted Pea Jacket, Home-spun blue and white strip'd Linnen Jacket and Breeches, an Ozenbrig Jacket and Breeches and Shirt, an old Felt Hat, good Shoes and grey Stockings. He can speak Welch. The other named John Edwards, a Welch Man, about 21 Years of Age, middle Stature, speaks good English, has short black Hair wears a brown coat with Brass Buttons, Home-spun blue and white Strip'd Linnen Jacket and Breeches, an Ozenbrig Jacket and Trousers and Shirt, a new Felt Hat, dark Grey Stockings, new Wooden Heel'd Shoes. Whoever takes up said Servants or either of them and secures them so that their said Master or Owen Owen Esq; High Sheriff of Philadelphia, shall have 20 Shillings Reward for each and reasonable Charges.

PHILADELPHIA Sept. 8. That there is in Custody of William Battell Sheriff of the County of New-Castle on Delaware; a very likely Negro Man, who was taken up and committed as a runaway, he calls himself Toby, and says his Master's name is Captain Bond, but he has not English enough to describe where his Master Lives. Whoever can make a legal Claim to the said Negroe and will pay the Lawful Charges, may have him delivered by the above Sheriff.

That the 31st Day of August ran away from Samuel Atkinson of Burlington County in West-New-Jersey, a Servant Man named William Day, of a middle Stature, aged one or two and Twenty Years much Pock fretten Cleare Skin'd light Sandy Hair a large Scar on the back of his left Hand he came out of West England, his Apparel if not changed is a felt Hatt, a brown Homespun Coat with large Brass Buttons, an old Course Striped Vest and old Oxenbrigs Breeches. Reddish Yarn Stockings, also he took with him a Leather Jacket and Breeches, and a pair of light coloured Worsted Stockings. Whoever shall take up and secure the said Servant, so that his Master may have him again, shall have Forty Shillings Reward and Reasonable Charges paid by

          Samuel Atkinson.

NEW-YORK Sept. 12. Yesterday Four Vessels arrived here viz. Two Ships from Rotherdam, with 300 Palatines, a Brig and a Sloop from Jamaica and Bermuda. Two Ships more were to sail from Rotherdam, in 4 or 5 Days after these came away with Palatines, one of them for New-York, and the other for Pennsylvania.

Philadelphia Sept. 15. Run away on the 11th of this Instant September, from John Throckmorton of Shewsbury, in East Jersey, a Servant Man named John Prichard, about 24 Years of Age, a Watch-Maker by Trade, he is a short thick Man, with a round blush Face, dark Skin, short black Hair very much curled, if he has not shaved it off, as he used at time to do, he has some Impediment in his Speech; he had on when he went away, a Liver coloured Homspun Vest, a Felt Hat and Ozenbrig Shirt and Breeches, gray Stockings and round Toed Shoes. Whoever shall take up the said Servant and secure him, and give Notice to the Printer hereof, or to Nataniel Leonard, Esq; of Trent Town so his Master may have him again, shall have Forty Shillings if taken in Jersey, but if out of the Jerseys Three Pounds Reward and reasonable Charges, paid by me,

John Throckmorton.

Run away the 2d of August last, from Thomas Ashton, of the City of Philadelphia, Ship-wright, a Servant Man named James Riley, about 25 Years of Age of middle Stature fresh Colour'd and Pock-fretted; he has no Hair on his Head, but wears a white Cap; he took with him a common coloured Doroy Coat, a pair of new Shoes. Whoever secures said Servant to his said Master shall have Twenty Shillings Reward and reasonable Charges.

Philadelphia Sept. 24. Whereas a Written Paper was some Days ago put into the Coffee-House at Philadelphia, containing some bitter invectives against the People call'd Quakers with a no less sensible than Malicious Insinuations concerning a supposed Author. These are to certify all such Persons as have any regard to Truth, that the underwritten has no manner or Knowledge of the writing or Publishing the whole or any Part of the said Paper.   W. Keith.

NEW-YORK Oct. 3. The Speech of his Excellency William Burnet Esq; to the Representatives in General Assembly, on the 27th of September.

Gentlemen,

The Choice which the People of this Province have so lately made you to represent them, gives Me a fresh Opportunity of knowing their Sentiments and Inclinations. I have always endeavoured to promote their Interest to the utmost of my Ability, and it will add to my Pleasure to do it in the manner which they themselves desire.

When you enquired into the State of the present Revenue, I believe you will find it insufficient to answer the usual Expence for the support of the Government. And considering the Flourishing and Increasing Conditions of the Colony, it would be to its Dishonour, as well as Disadvantage, to lessen the Encouragement that has been given the necessary Officers of the Government. I depend on your Readiness to the best of Kings, who has so, shown, during the whole course of his Reign, That the constant Employment of his Thoughts and the most earnest Wishes of his Heart, tend wholly to the Securing to his Subjects their just Rights and Advantages. You need not fear that any of his Servants will dare to abuse the Confidence reposed in them, when they must expect that their Neglect of Duty are abuse of Trust will draw upon them His Just Displeasure.

You will find, that the supply last provided for finishing the new Apartments in the Fort, has been imployed with the utmost Frugality; and I hope, that by the same Management, the Repairs of the Roof of the Chappel at the Barracks, which are in a Condition entirely Ruinous, will require no very large Sum, tho' it is plain, that the charge of doing it will encrease considerably, if it is delay'd any longer than the next Spring, which Obliges Me to recommend it to your Care at present, that Provisions may be made for so pressing and so necessary a Work.

I must Remind you, that your Agent continues his Diligence in watching over the Interest of the Province, that he has remain'd a long time without any Allowances so generous a Conduct on his part, will not fail of engaging you to take Care about his past Services may not go unrewarded, and that so useful a Person may be fixed in your Service, and a Settled provision made for his Encouragement.

I shall lay before you my late Conference, with the Six Nations, in which I flatter myself that I have contributed not a little to fix them in their Duty to his Majesty, their Affection to this Government, and their just apprehensions of the ill Designs of the People of Canada, in Fortifying so near to them at Fagara. I have sent a fit Person to reside among the Sennaka's this Winter, who is not permitted to Trade, and will therefore have the more weight and credit with them. I doubt not your Joyning with me in taking such further Measures, as are necessary, to make the Six Nations remain as effectual Security to our Frontier. The Indefatigable Endeavours of the French, to employ all possible Methods, whether of Art or Force, to make themselves Masters of these Neighbours, shew what Opinion they have of their Importance. And their Diligence calls Us to lose no Time and spare no

Cost, in Disappointing such dangerous Attempts, and in doing every thing that may conduce to our Safety on that side.

The Trade on the Anondagas River has now encreased considerably by the best Enquiry I could make, more of the far Nations of Indians have been there this Summer than ever before. But I must express to you my Concern at the Disorderly and Fraudulent Conduct of some of the People at the Trading Places, who have used many of the Indians in an Unjust, and sometimes in a Violent manner. These abuses, if not Remedied and prevented in Time, may give much a Disgust to the Indians as to Discourage them from continuing to come Thither on account of Trade, and thereby loose the good Effect of what has been so happily begun, and carried on with so much Success. I hope you will think of proper Expeditions to Cure this growing Evil; and among other things I am of Opinion, that if the Trade be confined to one certain Place, and a fit Person Appointed to Reside there during the Season, with the Power to receive Complaints from the Indians and Redress their Grievances, and the Traders Obliged to be Determined by his Judgement, on pain of being Fined in Case of refusal, it might go a great way to answer the End Proposed. I shall very gladly Joyn with you in this or any other proper Measures to preserve and increase our Interest with the far Nations, which this Trade will undoubtedly do, when duly Regulated.

You may depend on my Concurrence, to the utmost of my Power, in any Laws that you shall frame for the publick Good, and in my hearty Endeavours to obtain His Majesty's Confirmation of them, and of as many of the Laws formerly enacted, as you shall desire, which will, at the same time require the continued Solicitation of your Agent at home.

And now Gentlemen, That I have mentioned to you what particulars I had to Recommend for the Publick Service, I have only to add in general That I hope your present Meeting will be an eminent, Instance of good Effects of an entire Confidence between the several Branches of the

Legislature; it will then appear in the clearest Light, that our Administration is never so strong and well supported as by the general Voice of the People ever so well secured in their Liberty and Property as by the Government being enable to see the Laws duly Executed. W. Burnet.

The General Assembly's Address to his Excellency.

May it please your Excellency,
We his Majesty's Dutiful & Loyal Subjects, the General Assembly of this Colony of New-York, do in the most respectful Manner, return our hearty Thanks to your Excellency for your kind and Obliging speech; and take leave to assure you, that the several Matters therein Recommended to us, shall now maturely be Considered, & in the Course of our Deliberations, have their due Weight.

We likewise take leave in behalf of the Freeholders, and Freemen of this Colony whom we have the Honour to represent, to return your excellency their & our sincere Thanks for your giving them the Opportunity of a new Choice of Members to serve in General Assembly. which we do acknowledge was highly agreeable to the People; and its own'd by most, that the several Elections, have been performed with as great Freedom, Ease & Impartiality as any within their Remembrance.

We also gratefully acknowledge the kind Assurances your Excellency is pleased to give us, of your ready Concurrance in any Laws which we may be for the Publick Welfare of the Colony & using your hearty Endeavours to obtain His Majesty's Conformation of them. And we take leave to assure you on our part, That in Framing Bills, it shall be our constant Care to do the same of such Manner as may give no Just Cause for your Disapprobation.

We took upon our Selves, bound in Duty, to have equally at heart, the Service of his Majesty's & the Interest of our Country, so we take leave to assure your Excellency, That we met together with a sincere Disposition to make these good Ends to Rule & View of the Proceedings; and that all Business to come before us shall meet with such Dispatch as the Nature & Weight thereof will reasonably allow to the End the Country may not be put to the Expence of longer Sessions than what are absolutely necessary for the Publick Service.

We are sensible, that a Mutual Confidence between the several Branches of the Legislature, tend very much to the Benefit of the Publick, and we shall therefore use our utmost endeavours to promote & preserve the same, by all reasonable Measures on our part.

Signed by order of the General Assembly,
Adolph Philipse, Speaker.

To which his Excellency was pleased to answer, Gentlemen;

I Am very glad to find this Affectionate Address, that what, I have done has been so agreeable to you, and the People who you Represent.

I perfectly agree with you, in having equally at heart his Majesty's Service and the Interest of the Country, which are inseparable, and in making these good Ends and Rules & Views of all my Actions. W. Burnet.

PHILADELPHIA Oct. 13. Run away from this City, a Servant Man belonging to Richard Moore of Maryland, named James Watmore, of middle size, brown Complexion, has a light coloured Fulstain Coat without any Cuffs, but buttons on the upper side of the Sleeves, with Linnen Breeches. Whoever apprehends the said Servant, and brings him to Sam. Preston of the City of Philadelphia shall have Forty Shillings as a Reward and reasonable Charges.

Run away the 17th of last September, from Gabriel Steele of Shrewsbury, in the County of Monmouth, and the Province of New-Jersey, a Negroe Man named Jack, aged about 40 Years; he is a short Negroe, and a Malagasca, he had on Homespun Cloaths. Whoever takes up the said Negroe so that his Master may have him again, shall have a Pistole as a Reward, besides reasonable Charges.

PHILADELPHIA Oct. 20. Ran away from the Ship Constintine, Edward Foe, Commander; Three Sailors, One named William Fortune, Aged about 21 Years, about 5 foot 4 Inches high, with his own

Hair; he is of dark Complexion, well Proportioned and well Cloathed. The other named Phillip Gammon, Aged about 24, about 5 Foot 3 Inches high, with his own Hair; he is a dark Complexion sometimes Square set than the other: These above two Sailors are comrades and supposed to be together.

The other named John Fenning, a Servant to Captain Edward Foe, Aged about 45 Years, well set about 5 Foot 8 Inches high, his Hair is cut off, and had when he went away a Pea-Jacket and Swanikin Wastcoat. Whoever takes up the abovesaid Sailors, or either of them, and bring them to the said Commander, shall be very well Rewarded: These are likewise to forwarn all Persons from Entertaining any of the above Sailors, as they will answer to contrary at their Peril.

PHILADELPHIA Oct. 27. Stollen or Strayed away out of the Incloser, or Pasture, of Mr. Freeland, at Brunswick, (Commonly called Ingenes Ferry,) a Bay horse about Fourteen Hands and a half high, a Yorkshire make, having a Felm on his near Eye, and a Snip on his Nose. Whoever can secure the said Horse, and give Notice to James Gold at trent Town, William Bradford at New-York, or Andrew Bradford in Philadelphia shall have fifty Shillings Reward.

NEW-YORK Nov. 7. We have Advice from Albany, that there is a New Government arrived at Canada from France, who stirs up the Indians to make war on New-England to commit Hostilities.

PHILADELPHIA Nov. 3. Whereas Caterine the Wife of Joseph Word of Philadelphia, Carpenter having for some Years obstinately refused to Cohabit with her said Husband, and not behaving Commendably in other respects towards him, did lately, in his absence make sale of his Goods removed into another Province, to her said Husbands great Loss and Dissatisfaction; Therefore the said Joseph Word is Constrained to give Publick Notice to said Wives irregular Course, and to forewarn all Persons not to deal with the said Catherine his Wife or Trust up on his Credit.

PHILADELPHIA Nov. 17. These are to give Notice, to all Persons, that there is lately set up at the House of Andrew Duche, living in the Front-Street, near the Coffee-House a Dyer lately from Europe, who Dyeth all sorts of Woolens, Linnens, Silks, and Sattins, New and Old, and of all Colours, according to Persons Desire that is to say Dying and Pressing and Watering of Tabies, Tamies, Silk, and much the like things, and also Dying of Yarn Blew, all at reasonable Rates.

PHILADELPHIA Nov. 22. The Speech of the Honourable Patrick Gordon, Esq; Lieut. Governour of the Province of Pennsylvania, and the Counties of New-Castle, Kent and Sussex upon Delaware.

To the Representatives of the Freemen of the said Province of Pennsylvania.

Mr. Speaker and Gentlemen of the House of Representatives,

Having fully declared to the last Assembly what I take to be incombent on me, in the Discharge of my Trust; I shall now recommend to you such matters relating to the Publick, as may be proper for your Consideration.

As in the first Place our Bills of Credit will claim your Regard: at your first Meeting in October, I acquainted you with a Letter I had received but two Days before, from the Secretary to the Right Honourable the Lord Commissioners for Trade and Plantations, on the Subjects of our Paper Currency, which I now lay before you by the Letter you will observe what Impression the Product of some of these American Colonies had made on that Board, to the Disadvantage of such Bills: Yet Notwithstanding their Dislike to them in General, They have express'd so much Tenderness for the People of this Province, who have now the Currency in their Hands, that we may, I hope justly conclude the former Acts for establishing it, are happily out of Danger to a Repeal. But as the Act past last Year for the re-emitting part of the same Bill out of the Loan-Office, may be thought to interfere with their Lordships Directions, it will require our serious Application, to find out proper Measures for the securing this Equally with the other Acts, which 'tis hoped may be successfully effected, when their Lordships are duly apprized that the Trade between Britain and this Province has been so far from Suffering, that it has been manifestly encreased since the Establishment of the Currency here, and that more British Goods have been Imported, more Ships Built in this Place for their Merchants, that had been for many Years before, But more especially that the Currency instead of Sinking in Value which has been the great and chief Objection to it in some other Colonies, now actually rises with us being at this Time at less than half the Discount, that as I have been assured, it bore with the Gold and Silver but a few Months before my arrival: When this is Duly Represented to their Lordships, I hope we shall have no Room to doubt but they will abate in their Opinion of the ill Consequences of that Currency, especially in this Colony; And therefore seeing Ten Thousand Pounds of the Bills now in the Peoples Hands subsist on the Foundation of the last Act which was past before their Lordships Sentiments were made known to us, we may hope for their Indulgence to that also. To obtain which, I shall very Heartily join with you Gentlemen in whatever shall be reasonably proposed.

I cannot but with great Pleasure take Notice on this Occasion happy prospect that this Province now affords, of supplying by the Industry of its Inhabitants, the want of those natural Advantages, that has attended divers of the American Colonies, (in making Returns with their own Product directly for Britain) which in all Probability must in due Time, introduce real Wealth, and a Currency of Intrinsic Value amomg us. Several Companies are already engaged in carrying on Iron-Works, Hemp, from the Encouragement given, I am told, is raised in much greater Quantities. But the first of these requiring a large Stock, and the very fertile or enriched Land, which may disable poorer Family's for partaking of their Benefits, Providence seems now to have pointed out one Method more for employing even the Mean and Weak as well as others of both Sexes to considerable Advantage; by raising Silk, which (I am credibly informed) is produced here as Fine and Good as most the World affords, and with as much Ease: These three are commodities, for which Britain Pays dear to other Countries and with which they can be no Danger of Overstocking the Market, therefore as nothing can be more Acceptable to Britain, than to receive from its own Colonies what it Purchases more Disadvantageously from Foreigners; nothing perhaps may better deserve the Notice and Encouragement of the Legislature.

These gentlemen, are the Heads, I shall at present mention, what further occurs may be sent to you by Message. I shall only here observe that from the View I have yet had of this Province, it appears very plain, that we are, or may be a very happy People if we can but act worthy of those Blessings, which seem to have attended the Pious and Sincere Intentions of the late Honourable Proprietor, and those sober People who have joyned their Endeavour's in the Settlement of this Colony. A Grateful and Humble sense of the Mercies from the Bountiful Hand of Divine Providence, under the mild Influence of a most benign and Gracious Sovereign, and the Favour of Indulgent Proprirtors, are the only Method of Securing their Continuance. And a steady Resolution in you Gentlemen, to advance the True and Solid Interest of the Country, and Reputation of the Government, by establishing Justice and Sobriety will be the most effectual Means of Disappointing those, who by fomenting Vain and Idle Jealousies might seek to disturb our Repose in all which and whatever may tend to the Honour and Benefit of the Publick, you shall always have my ready Concurrence.

P. Gordon.

PHILADELPHIA Nov. 23. To the Honourable Patrick Gordon Esq; Lieut. Governour of the Province of Pennsylvania, &c.

The Address of the House of Representatives of the Freemen of the said Province in the General Assembly met at Philadelphia, the 23d November, 1726. In Answer to the Governours Speech of Yesterday.

May it please the Governour,
We thankfully acknowledge the Governours, most

favourable Disposition, towards promoting the Happiness and Prosperity of this Province, by first laying before this House, what seems to be Essentially Necessary for that good End, and then promising heartily to concur with us, in whatever can be reasonably proposed to Effect the same.

We unanimously concur, in Opinion with the Governour, that considering the Impressions, which seem to have been made with the Lords Commissioners of Trade, concerning our serious Application to find our proper Measures for securing their Lordships Favour, in Supporting the Act pass'd last Year, for re-Emitting a part of our present Bills, and in order thereto, we have appointed a Committee to draw up an Humble Representation from this House, unto the Honourable Board.

And as the Governour is pleased justly to observe when their Lordships come to be Apprised. That the Trade between Great-Britain and this Province has been Manifestly Increased since the Establishment of our Paper-Currency, That there has been more Goods Imported, and more Ships built in this Place, for a British Account, than ever known at any Time before; But more especially that this Currency, instead of sinking has actually rose especially in Value, since the passing of the said re-Emitting Act. We humbly hope, and have no room to Doubt, but that their Lordships will abate in their Opinion of Ill consequences of the Currency, especially in in this Colony.

It is with great Pleasure, that we observe the Attention which the Governour has been pleased to give to the Improvements which may be made of the Produce of Iron, Hemp, and Silk, in this Province, and from the Justness of the Governours Expressions, and way of thinking, on those Subjects, with respect to Britain; He cannot but promise to our selves on all proper Occasions, very happy Effects.

We do in a Dutiful manner acknowledge the sense, which all People of this Province ought to have, and Constantly express of those Blessings which seem to have attended the pious and sincere Intentions of the late Honorouble Proprietor, and those sober good People who joyned their Endeavours with him, in the Settlement of this Colony, and we Hope that our humble endeavours shall never be wanting, to secure a Continuance of those Mercies from the Divine Hands of Providence, by a conduct which may unable us to preserve that reasonable happiness, We enjoy under the Mild influence of our most benign and Gratious Sovereign King George, and Indulgent favours we hope still to receive from the Honourable Proprietors Family.

We very heartily thank the governour, for the Assurance he gives us to cuncur with this House in promoting the more solid Interest and Reputation of the Province; and in Establishing Justice and Sobriety, as the proper means to disappoint those who shall appear to the Enemies to the Publick Repose and Tranquility; and in Return we lay hold of this opportunity to assure the Governour, That we shall be mindfully of his Interest, by providing in due Time a just and Honourable support for his Government.

Signed by Order of the House this 23d Day of the 9th Month 1726.   David Lloyd Speaker.

PHILADELPHIA Nov. 24. Run away the Eighteenth of this Instant November, from Thomas Spicer of the County of Gloucester, in the Province of West-New-Jersey, a Servant Lad, about 18 Years of Age: he had on when he left his said Master a Home-spun Cinnamon colour'd Coat lined with the same, with Horn or Huff Buttons five or six on the Breast, a Jacket of light colour'd Kersey, with Pewter Buttons, and lined with the same as the Coat, Leather Breeches, with gray Worsted Stockings, Wooden Heel'd Shoes; He is a pretty stocky well set Irish Lad, not tall, pockbroken, lightish thin Hair, a large Nose. Whoever takes up said Lad and secures him so his said Master may have him again, shall have Three Pounds reward and reasonable Charges paid by me,
                                    Thomas Spicer.

All Persons who have fail to pay in their annual Payments due in the Loan-Office, upon both the Acts for Emitting Bills of Credit, may depend that they will be Prosecuted in a few Days, in case of further Delays.

PHILADELPHIA Dec. 1. To be sold or let. The Plantation near Bristol in Bucks County, late in Possession of Joseph Bond Deceased, Containing about 140 Acres of Land, a good Dwelling House with new Barn and Stable, and a Young Orchard and other good Conveniency the cleared Land well growing with Clover, and some Horses, Cattle, and Husbandry Utensils. Also another Tract of Land, about 150 Acres, near the same with a good Meadow, and large Quantity of Suitable criple for making more. Also a Lot in Bristol, to be sold a little Island about 100 Acres of well Improved Meadow in good English and Clover Grass, well fenced with Quickset Hedges and Bank't round: with part of three Grist Mills, Granery's, and, one Saw Mill, and large House. A Fulling Mill, Dye House, hot and cold Presses, Tentor Yard, with suitable Utensils and Conveniences together with part of a considerable Quantity of Upland, Town Lots, Tenantable Houses and Orchards in Bristol aforesaid. Also several Dwelling Houses and Lots (one in the Tenure of William Horne) and Ground Rent in Philadelphia.

The whole abovementioned, or part there of is to be sold by William Fishbourn of Philadelphia on any Reasonable Terms, of whom may be better informed of the Premises.

Runaway from Charles Read, the 19th of November last, an Irish Servant Man, belonging to the Iron-Works, named James Crowder, of a middle Stature about 22 Years of Age, long dark brown Hair curling on his Shoulders, of a pale sickly Complexion and sore Leggs, he wore away with him, an Old Felt Hat a Dark colour'd Kersey Jacket, with a Striped under Vest, a new Ozenbrig Shirt, an Old pair of dark Colour's Drogget Breeches, a new pair of Yarn Stockings, and a New pair of Shoes. Whoever takes him up and brings him to the said Charles Read or Robert Ellis of Philadelphia, shall be well Rewarded. And all Persons are forbid to Entertain him at their Peril.

To be Sold or Let. By Joseph Arthur, laying in the Township of Percian; the Land Adjoyning to Samuel Preston Esq; Containing 178 Acres of Upland and Meadow, with a good House, Barns, and other Houses, with two good Orchards, there is a good Quantity of the Meadow cleared, and the Land well Wooded, Yhose who are a mind to Purchase the same may apply to Joseph Arthur at the Plantation and agree on Reasonable Terms.

PHILADELPHIA Dec. 13. Run away from the Ship Appbia, George Smith Commander on Hendrick a Passenger in said Ship, he is about 60 Years of Age, short white Hair he wears generally a Blew Coat, when he looks any Person in the Face he commonly shuts one of his Eyes. Whoever shall apprehend said runaway, and bring him to said Commander, or to Andrew Bradford in Philadelphia, shall have Fifty Shillings Reward and all reasonable Charges.

These are to give Publick Notice to all Persons, that are Indebted to Robert Bolton, of the City of Philadelphia, Merchant, that they come forthwith and Pay the same, or they may expect Trouble, and those that have not settled their Accounts, are desired to come and settle the same, and all Persons to whom said Bolton is Indebted, are desired to come and receive the same, He designing for Great Britain the Beginning of March next.

Several Negroe Men and Women to be sold by Capt. Spafford in Front-Street very Reasonable.

New-York Dec. 19. Saturday Last Capt. Ratsey arrived here from Jamaica, with whom Capt. Abbot of Philadelphia came Passenger, having lost his Sloop at Jamaica. They gave an account, that on the 21st of October last, there was a violent Storm at said Island of Jamaica, which continued that Day and all Night: That about Sun rise next Morning it came on more violent at E. N. E. till about ten a Clock during which time most of the Ships in the Harbour of Port Royal either broke or had their Masts cut down; Then the wind Shifted to the South, and blew Violently all the vessels in the Harbour (except two Snows belonging to the Assiento Company, and a Sloop belonging to Port Royal drove ashore,) being betwixt 40 or 50 sail in all; among which they were four of them belonging to

Philadelphia, to wit, the Ship George, Brigt. Joseph, Sloop Mount Joy and Sloop Dolphin. The Ship Mercury, Capt. Prichard, Master, which was built at Philadelphia and belonging to Bristol, was also lost.

The Vessels belonging to New-York arrived there safe some Days after the Storm, but 10 or 12 Vessels from other parts of the Storm, lost Masts, and came in with Jury Masts.

N. B. This Paper which is No. 365 begins the first Quarter of the eight Year, these are therefore to desire the Subscribers, who are indebted, to pay in their Subscriptions to the Printer hereof, or to place where they have entered for this Paper, in order to enable to continue the same.

PHILADELPHIA Dec. 27. From the Weekly Jamaica Courant, Nov. 9. An exact List of the ships and Vessels, &c. lost, stranded, got off, or rid out with the Commanders, ships and Vessels Names, and Places belonging to in the Hurricane Oct 20, 1726.

The Ship Luxemburg, from London, William Kellaway Master, 320 Tuns, 40 Men, 34 Guns, got off Nine Days after the Storm

Ship Phoenix, from London, Benjamin Carwell 300 Tuns, 30 Men, 16 Guns, got off 14 Days after the Storm.

Real Gally, from London, Samuel Towers, 120 Tuns, 14 Men, 10 Guns, stranded and Cargo sav'd in hopes to get off.

Ship Nicholson, from London, John Smyter, 200 Tuns 25 Men, 12 Guns, overset, and the Master with 18 Men drowned.

John and Sarah Snow, from London, Alexander Morray, 12 Men, 6 Guns, sank with some Bale Goods.

St. James Snow, from London, Edmund Bedford, 150 Tuns, 40 Men, 40 Men, 18 Guns, put-a-Ground and in hopes to get off.

Ship Prince of Wales, from Bristol, Moses Lilly, 320 Tuns, 30 Men, 6 Guns, stranded and condemned.

Ship Abington, from Bristol, John Smith, 200 Tuns, 30 Men, 10 Guns, Cargo saved, and hopes to get off.

Ship Colstum, from Bristol, Thomas Roe, 100

Tuns, 19 Men, 2 Guns, stranded and condemned.

Ship Nightingale, from Bristol, James Crichton 100 Tuns, 20 Men 2 Guns, stranded and condemned. Ship Hector from Bristol, Benjamin Phipps, 150 Tuns, 25 Men, 4 Guns, stranded and condemend.

Delight, Snow, from Bristol, Peregrine Stockdale, 80 Tuns, 12 Men, 2 Guns, standed and condemned.

Ship Battle, from Liverpool, Edward Trafford, 90 Tuns, 16 Men, 5 Guns, stranded and condemned. Eaglebright, Sloop from Bermuda, Thomas Handy, 70 Tuns, 10 Men, 10 Guns, got off 5 Days after.

Mary Brigantine, from Virginia, Edward Pugh, 80 Tuns, 8 Men, got off 14 Days after the Storm.

Forlix Brigantine, from Rhode Island, Samuel Cries, 90 Tuns, 9 Men, 2 Guns, stranded and condemned.

Mary Flower from Rhode Island, John Brewer, 81 Tuns, 8 Men, stranded and condemned.

Ship Mercury, from Philadelphia, Joseph Prichard, 140 Tuns, 24 Men 2 Guns.

Ship George from Philadelphia, Samuel Farra, 130 Tuns, 12 Men, 2 guns stranded.

Joseph Brigantine from Philadelphia, William Hill, 70 Tuns, 8 Men, 4 Guns.

Dolphin Sloop from Philadelphia Robert Abbot, 60 Tuns, 6 Men, —— Guns stranded, Cargo sav'd.

Monjoy Sloop from Philadelphia, George Slifield 50 Tuns, 6 Men —— Guns stranded.

Brown Betty Sloop, Kingston Jamaica, Peter Bedlow, 60 Tuns, 24 Men, 14 Guns, beat to pieces at Kingston.

Princess Caroline Sloop, Kingston Jamaica, William Smee, 60 Tons, 30 Men, 12 Guns, beat to Pieces.

Love Sloop, Kingston Jamaica, Andrew Newhouse 60 Tuns 20 Men, 6 Guns, Lost.

William Sloop, from Bermuda, Daniel Burch, 30 Tuns, 6 Men, —— Guns, stove to pieces at Kingston, at Ramsey Wharff.

William Sloop, from Barbadoes, Stephen Charnock, 60 Tuns, 8 Men, drove ashore lost.

Warwick Sloop, from Bermuda, John Versey, 50 Tuns, 6 Men, run an Ground, and Sold in hopes to get off, got off, run ashore at the tan House.

1727

PHILADELPHIA Jan. 17. Notice is hereby given, That there is a Plantation Laying on the River Delaware New-Castle, of about 400 Acres, fine upland and Marshes, good House, Orchard and Garden: To be sold by Col. Birmingham, at the said Plantation

There is a Track of good rough Land containing about 356 Acres in Buckinham Township in the County of Bucks in Pennsylvania; likewise there is a Tract of good Land, containing 500 Acres, at Quohawkin near Salem, and several Lots of Marsh in the town of Salem in West New-Jersey: To be sold very reasonable by Edward Shipping of Philadelphia.

This is to give Notice, That the Court-House in Freehold, on the first Monday of March next, will be exposed to Sale at a publick Vendue to the highest Bidder, the Farm Plantation belonging to John Read, situated lying and being at Squankum in the County of Monmouth; containing about one Hundred and seventy Acres, with the Appurtenances, by Gabriel Steele.

At Edward Horne's in Philadelphia, Shoemaker may be furnished with choice Cock soled for Shoes, and Fishermen with Cock to float their Nets, where also Cock for Clogs, and good English Saffron.

PHILADELPHIA Jan. 24. To be sold by Vendue at the Plantation hereafter mentioned, on the 25th Day of April next, (being the Day after the General Meeting at Salem) by Joshua Grainger of Philadelphia, a Plantation in Penn's Neck in the County of Salem in West-Jersey, joyning the Delaware River, about two Miles in breath, (with the Stock thereon) is commonly called Sloeby's Point, over against Christeen Creek, and Lyes between two large Creeks, and on the upper side thereof about 200 Acres of good Meadow, 90 Acres of which is drained and cut into 7 or 8 Acres Fields by Ditches, and on the lower side thereof joyning to one of the lower Creeks, about 300 of good hard Marsh Ground, that the Hay may be fetched at any Time and bears very good Hay. The Upper land is said Plantation being very good, lyes between the two Meadows aforesaid; and about a Mile from the said River there may be kept by hanging only a Gate; on which Plantation there may be kept 3 or 400 Head of Cattle within Fence, with Winter and Summer Food sufficient, besides a very good Outlet; and by the 9th or 10th of March there is most commonly Grass for creatures in the Meadows aforesaid, being they lye so warm; which said Plantation and Stock is now let to a very good Tenant, for 32 Pounds per Anno. and as to what Buildings thereon are as follows viz. A House where the Tenant lives, and a Barn almost new, and a large new House 36 Foot by 28 Foot, not yet Finished, stands on a good Stone Cellar by a new Orchard, Planted about Ten years ago, with 500 Trees of very good Fruit, and two old Orchards more filled up with Young Trees; and for Payment there will be Time given, with Security if required. And if any Person has mind to Treat Concerning the same before the Time aforesaid, they may meet with the sais Joshua Granger in Philadelphia.

PHILADELPHIA Jan. 31. There is now in the Press, and will be Publish'd with all convenient Speed.

Fruit of a Fathers Love, being the Advice of William Penn (late Proprietor and Governour of the Province of Pennsylvania,) to his Children, relating to their Civil and Religious Conduct. Written Occasionally many Years ago, and now made Publick for a General good: By a Love of his Memory.

Note: This Treatise was Deposited in Manuscript; by the late Proprietor, in the Hands of Sir John Rodes, to be Published after the Authors decease but was delay'd till the whole Works were lately Published together.

The Second Edition, reprinted and Sold by A. Bradford.

PHILADELPHIA Feb. 7. Stolen from Andrew Perse of East-New-Jersey, near Crambury Brook, on the Post-Road to New-York, a Dark Brown Stallion about Thirteen Hands and a half high, he has no White about him, he is about Three Years old this Spring, and Branded on the Thigh with the letters A P he is trimed a little between the Ears, and a natural Pacer. Whoever shall take up said Horse and bring him to his said Master, or to David Beffet the Post-Rider or to Thomas Bullock in Black-Horse Alley, shall have Forty Shillings as a Reward and Reasonable Charges.

Whoever has any Demands against the Estate of Thomas Peters deceas'd, are desired to bring in their Accounts to Rice Peters of Abington, or to Thomas Peters of the City of Philadelphia, Executors, in order to a Settlement; and those who owe to the said Estate are required to pay what is due, or they must expect further Trouble: There is also to be Sold, a House, Orchard and two other Lots Adjoining, about a Mile from Philadelphia, in the Road to the upper Ferry. Those that are inclined to buy, may treat with the said Rice Peters at Abington or to Thomas Peters of the City aforesaid.

We have advice by Capt. Ball, who is arrived in Maryland from Liverpool, but touch'd at Dublin for Servants, and left that Place the 1st of December, who says, That there was much talk of War.

We have also an Account from Maryland, That there is a Ship arrived in North Carolina with Convicts, she came from England, bound for South Carolina, but the Convicts Rose at Sea and kill'd the Master and Doctor.

PHILADELPHIA Feb. 14. On Wednesday Night last, a Fire broke out in a Joyners Shop in Combs Alley, which was burnt down without any damage to the other Houses.

We have very Cold weather for these four Days Past which has fill'd our River full of Ice, a Ship and Snow who went down the Night before are now forc'd back again with the Ice.

Province of Pennsylvania

All Persons who are Indebted to the Proprietary Trustees of the said Province, on Act under Quit-Rent, for the Lands they hold, or any other Accounts whasoever, are required to pay the same in the next Month (March) for Collecting whereof James Steel, the present Receiver, hath Appointed to attend at his Office in Second Street of the City of Philadelphia, from the first day of the said first Month to the 20th, inclusive, for Receiving these of the County of Philadelphia. At Chester from the 23d to the 24th Inclusive, for those of that County, and at Pennsbury in the County of Bucks, from the 29th to the 31st (Inclusive) of the same Month, at which respective Time and Place all Persons who are Indebted as aforesaid, are required to bring their several Payments in Money, or Receipts, from the Bills for such Lands whose Rent are to be paid in Wheat. John Steel.

Several Ground Rents to be Sold, issuing out on certain Lots and Tenements on the Bank of Delaware, in Philadelphia, amounting to near eleven Pounds per ann. being part of the Estate of Samuel Richardson deceased: Enquire of William Hudson of Philadelphia, for further Satisfaction.

PHILADELPHIA Feb. 21. From Shrewsbury in East-Jersey on Saturday the last Day of December 1726 Theophilus Longstreat of Shrewsbury in the County of Monmouth, aged Sixty Years, he met with Seven Swans flying over a Meadow who shot down Six of them at one Shot, such a Shot was never known amongst us.

PHILADELPHIA Feb. 28. On Saturday the fourth of March next, will be exposed to sale by Publick Vendue under the Court-House of the City of Philadelphia, the King's Share of a Seizure lately Condemn'd by Decree of the Court of Vice-Admiralty, consisting of Cherry Derry's, Callico's, Hollands, Linning, Ozenbrigs, Kentings, Pepper and sundry other Goods, which may be view'd any Time before Sale at the Vendue Masters House. John Leech V. D. Master.

Run away from the Ship Shadwell on Saturday last, one Henry Pearson a Saylor; He is a tall Hearty Man, aged about 35 Years, having on a brown Jacket, wearing a Cap, and sometimes a a Wigg. Whoever bring the said Henry Pearson to

John Jones Master of the said Ship, shall have 30 Shillings as a reward and reasonable Charges.

On Saturday last Died here Hannah Hill, the Wife of Richard Hill Esq; A Gentle-woman eminent for her Piety and extensive Charity, which makes her Death to be as Universally lamented, especially by the Poor, as her life time she was beloved by all.

PHILADELPHIA March 7. Run away on Sunday the Fifth of March, from Richard Berry and Nathaniel Gubb of Willistown in Chester County, two Servant Men, one named John MacNayley, Aged about 20 Years of a middle Stature, short black Hair, he has a good felt Hat, grey Kearsey Jacket, an old pair of Leather Breeches, with Linned Leggins upon the Stockings: The other named Arthur Mulbelland, younger than the first, of a brown Complexion, with long Hair of a brown Colour; having on a dark Cinnamon Colour'd Suit. Whoever takes up the said Servants, so that their said Master may have them again, shall have five Pounds Reward and reasonable Charges paid by me,
Richard Berry.

Several likely young Negroe Men and Boys: To be Sold by Thomas Sebor.

A very likely Negroe Man, who is fit for all manner of Country Work, to be Sold: inquire of Andrew Bradford.

JAMAICA, LONG-ISLAND March 10. This Day Died Samuel Mills of this Place, Yeoman, (who was born in America) Aged Ninety Years. He was always a very Laborious, honest Man, of a very Temperate Life, and was able to do a good Days work but a few days before he died. He lived Sixty eight Years with one Wife, who is still alive, by whom he had Sixteen Children. He has left behind him Nine Children, Eighty Grand Children, and several of his Great Grand Children are Marriageable. His Wife was Deliver'd of a Child when she was one and Fifty Years of Age.

Philadelphia March 15. Friend Andrew Bradford
The following Order accidentally omitted, in revising the Minutes of the proceedings of the House of Representatives of this Province, thou art desired to Publish in the next Weekly Paper.

Revised by an Order of the House of the 10th of the Month last by   Edward Horne.

Dec. 10th, Post Meridiem,
Ordered. That Job Goodson, Thomas Tresse, Richard Hays and Abraham Chapman, be a committee to audit the Accounts of the General Loan-Office, and that they or any Three of them sink and Destroy the Bills of Credit received by the Trustees of the said Office, according to the directions of Re-Emitting Act; and that the said Committee settle and adjust the Publick Accounts with the Provincial Treasurer and Collector of Excise and Duty upon the Negroes, in order to lay before the house at their next meeting, and that they have Power to send for Persons and Papers.   Thomas Leech, Cler.

PHILADELPHIA March 16. Whereas Reports from Time to Time have been rais'd and spread in the City lately renew'd. That I intend shortly to leave off the Employ I now follow. These may certify all into who's Hands this may come that have heard the same, That as the said Report is False, Groundless and Prejudicial, so being lately remov'd from my Dwelling House back of Letitia Court, (which said House is to be let) to a more Convenient House for my Business in the Market-Street, joyning to Daniel Harrison's, is the Occasion of my giving publick Notice; That Children may not only be thought Writing and Arithmetick there at School Hours as Usual, and Young Boarders by any Children that goes to Grammar School, that have not the Opportunity to Improve themselves there is Writing and Arithmatick, may be taught from Eleven to twelve in the Morning, and from four to Five in the Afternoon. Also, any Young Man or Woman, or others of Young Years that want to Improve themselves therein may be Taught from Five precisely, to Seven in the Evening during the Summer Season, from the 29th of the first Month called March, till the 29th of September, at the House aforesaid; where due Care will be taken and Attendance given, (sickness or other common Casualties excepted) for Information of the Prices for Boarding and Schooling at the set Time aforesaid: Those that are so dispos'd at the said House, may apply themselves to

Richard Wader.

NEW-YORK March 20. In order to prevent as much as possible, the Province and Adjacent ones from being Imposed upon by Counterfeit Bills; we think it will not be Improper to insert the following Account:

On the 14th Instant in the Morning. One David Willson, and one David Wallace, were Apprehended and Committed to the Common Goal of this City for uttering Counterfeit Bills of Credit, made Current by Act of Assembly of this Province, and of the Province of New-Jersey. Upon their Examination before the Mayor and other Magistrates, they confess they brought about Eight Hundred Pounds of that Money from Maryland. David Willson denyed that he knew it to be Counterfeit, but David Wallace ingeniously confessed That about four Months ago, he brought a Thousand Pounds of the Counterfeit Money, over the Ship Richmond to Philadelphia from Dublin. That he had the said Money from Thomas Morough (who lately lived at Elk River, in Maryland) but was then in Dublin, and that the said Thomas Morough told him they were Counterfeit Bills, but that he knows not who Printed and Signed them. That he was to have a Third of the said Counterfeit Money for passing it off. That he said Thomas Morough, designs into North America (to Maryland as he believes) with more of the Counterfeit Money, not thinking it prudent to venture the whole in one Vessel. The whole Counterfeit Money, that was made being Three Thousand Pounds or upward. That the aforesaid David Willson was employ'd by the said David Wallace to Exchange and put off the said Counterfeit Bills for which he was to have Four or Five Shillings in the Pound. That there was from Pennsylvania Counterfeit Five Shilling Bills, among the Counterfeit Bills, he brought from Dublin, some of which he burnt in Maryland, they not being well Signed. That he and the said David Willson had not fully Resolved how to steer their Course, but had some thought going towards New-England. That he paid to the said Thomas Morough in Dublin, about Ten Pounds for his share of the

Printing and Signing the Counterfeit Bills, and was to pay him something more when he came over.

When the said David Willson and David Wallace were taken they had 184 Counterdeit Jersey Bills, at 3 Pounds each, 93 ditto at Twelve Shillings, 244 ditto Six Shillings, 43 ditto at one Shilling each, and had 23 Counterfeit New-York Bills at 4 Shillings each, and 3 ditto at Fifteen Pence each, which were sign'd D. Provost, Jacobus Kip, G. Beckman, John Cruger. Besides upward of 100 Pounds of Jersey Bills, which were pass'd here the day before they were apprehended, and one 4 Shilling York Bill.

The Counterfeit Bills may be known from the True, by taking Notice, that in the counterfeit Three Pound Jersey Bills, the Letter b is left out of the word Publick. That in the Twelve Shilling Jersey Bills, the Flourishing at the Top is handsomer and finer and the Letter T is Blacker. That in the Counterfeit Six Shilling Jersey Bills, the word Six Shillings, at Top, are Larger, and the figure 4 in 1724 is larger, and the down stroke of the great T narrowed. That in the 18d. Jersey, and the Four Shilling, the 15d. New-York Counterfeit Bills, the figure 4 in 1724 is much larger and the Names of the Signers to all Jersey Bills, are sullied and Rub'd, and writ with Ink inclineable to a red Purple, and the Paper Courser and Thinner than the true Bills.

WOODBRIDGE, NEW-JERSEY March 28. On the 26th instant, Jonathan Walker, a good liver among us, being sick and only one Woman in the House to look after him, in the height of his fever, he attempted to go out of the House, which the Woman endeavouring to hinder, he threw her down, then run out and cast himself into a deep Well, and there perished. He has left eight Children behind him, their Mother being dead 3 Months before.

PHILADELPHIA March 30. The Speech of the Honourable Patrick Gordon Esq; Lieut. Governour of the Province of Pennsylvania, and Counties of New-Castle, Kent and Sussex upon Delaware.

To the Representatives of the House of Representatives,

The Weather and Floods having prevented Your Meeting on the 27th Instant pursuant to your Adjournment, I thought fit notwithstanding, as soon as a Sufficient Numbers to make a House were in Town, to unable you, as I now do, to Act again: and altho' I understand you will still, for the Reason that have been mentioned much short being full, yet I cannot decline laying before you a Matter of vast Importance of the whole Country, which requires all our Attention and your serious Application.

This Gentlemen, is the Horrid Attempt of some of the Wickedness of Men, to adulterate the Bills of Credit to our and Neighbouring Provinces, first discovered by me at New-Castle and since more fully by his Excellency the Governour of New-York, who has advised me of his success in Apprehending two of the Criminals there.

The design appears to have been laid so deep, and of such extent, that it may not unjustly be compared to the Poisoning the Waters of the Country; the blackest, and most detestable Practice that is known, and which the Laws of Nations, and those of War condemn even in declared Enemies; for as they destroy the Lives of the innocent in taking their Natural Food, this would as effectually overthrow all Credit, Commerce and Traffick, and the mutual Confidence that must subsist in Society, to unable the Members of it to procure themselves and Families their necessary Bread.

We have seen large Quantities of Counterfeit Bills of our Neighbouring Colony disbursed in this Province to great loss of it's Inhabitants, and I am credibly informed, the design has been laid to pour it upon us a flood of our own Bills Counterfeited from Ireland, where they have so artfully imitated most of those of Jersey, that it requires more skill to distinguish them, than is expected amongst the common, and especially amongst the Country People.

Therefore to prevent the Importation, and of Spreading these Bills, if possible, and to provide for the Apprehending and Punishing of the Importers, or Counterfeiters, and such as shall knowingly utter the same, in a manner more adequate to the Crime, than is yet provided by Law, is what I must earnestly recommend to your most serious Consideration, lest such Provisions should be too late, and the Credit of our Bills should sink, which, for the fatal Consequences that you are sensible must attend the unhappy Event, should be guarded against with utmost Care.   P. Gordon.

PHILADELPHIA March 31. To the Honourable Patrick Gordon Esq; Governour of the Province of Pennsylvania, &c.

The Address of the House of Representatives of Free-Men of the said Province, in General Assembly, in Answer to the Governours Written Message Tuesday.

May it Please the Governour,
We thankfully acknowledge the Governours prudent Condescension to concur with the Peoples Representives in the necessary Act of Legislations, notwithstanding that their Adjournment was elapsed by unforeseen and providential Events: And altho' the Rageing Sickness which in some degree affects every one of our Families, does in truth disable us at present for such an Attendance on the Publick Service, as otherways both the Governourr and the Country might justly expect from us, yet the importance of the Matter which the Governour has been pleased to lay before us is such, that we could not in Duty neglect to make some immediate Progress therein.

We have the pleasure to assure the Governour, that we so far agree with his Sentiments, as to Order a Bill to be prepared for making the detestable Crime of Falsifying or Counterfeiting our Bills of Credit more Penal than it was by former Acts.

And if the Governour pleases, since he is informed that some of the first Impression of our Bills are intended to be brought in Counterfeited from Ireland, we now propose to call in the remainder of those Bills to be Exchanged in the Loan-Office for others of the same Value, which we hope will be an Effectual Method to prevent Counterfeits, and support the solid and Just Credit of our Paper Currency.

But that the People of the Province may not suffer by their Neighbourly good Will in giving a Voluntary Credit to the Paper Bills of New-Jersey; we earnestly request, That the Governour would be pleased to use his Interest and best Offices with the Governour and Assembly of that Province, to take some Effectual Care to prevent the pernicious Consequences of having their Bills of Credit Counterfeited and Uttered among us; and also in case any Persons are apprehended in any part of their Government, for having uttered Counterfeit or Falsefying Bills of New-Jersey, that the Governour would please to give directions to the proper Officers to deliver over such Criminals into the Hands of the Magistrate of the Province, with such Evidence as can be found in Order to their being Punished according to Law.

We hope the Governour will favourably Contruct and Accept this part of out Duty, and indulge us with a more convenient Time to finish the Business of the Current Year; Signed by Order of the House, David Lloyd, Speaker.

PHILADELPHIA April 6. Run away on the 20th Instant March, from Martha Rawle (Widow of Francis Rawle deceas'd) near Philadelphia, a Servant Man named Charles Mugglews an Irishman, of a middle Stature, having round Shoulders, a thin sharp Face, carry'd away with him, one Shirt of Irish Linnen, another Ozenbrig, one pair of gray Stockings, one pair of gray Duroy Breeches, and another pair of Home-spun, one light Cinnamon colour Duroy Wastcoat, and another of Black and white Home-spun, 1 Cinnamon colour Cloath Coat, and one Felt Hat. Whoever shall take him up and bring him to William Rawle in Philadelphia, or secure him so that the Owner may have him again shall have Forty Shillings Reward.

PHILADELPHIA April 13, Run away from William Bantoft of the City of Philadelphia, Baker, a Servant Man, named John Collins, he is a short Fellow, with a down look; he has on a dark colour'd Coat, with Brass Buttons, a check Shirt, good Shoes and Stockings, Whoever takes up said Servant and secures him so that his Master may have him again, shall have Forty Shillings as a

Reward and reasonable Charges.

Run away on the 9th Instant from Thomas Pryer of this City of Philadelphia, Baker, a Servant Man, named Nicholas Park, he is of a middle Stature, he has on a Kersey Coat, a short Wigg, long Breeches, a striped Flannel Jacket, he is a staring Fellow with a broken Nose, and is very fluent in Speech as Latin and French.

Run away on the 9th Instant April from John Bryant, Baker, a Servant Man, named Samuel bond, a likely young fellow, of a middle Stature, with his own Hair very Bushy and long, had a good Broad-cloth Coat, a good Felt Hat, Ozenbriggs Wastcoat and Breeches, with good Shoes and Stockings; he had with him also a strip'd Flannel Wastcoat, a pair of Leather Breeches, a pair of Trowzers, a brown Holland Wastcoat.

Run away at the same time from Charles West, Ship-Carpenter, a Servant Man named John Elford, a likely Fellow, with a remarkable Scar on his left Arm or Hand; he has on a new Duroy Coat, strip'd Holland Wastcoat and Breeches, with new Shoes and Stockings. They are about 22 Years of Age each, and suppos'd to be gone together. Whoever secures the above said Runaways so that their said Masters may have them again, shall have Forty Shillings Reward for each, and reasonable Charges paid by their Masters.

N. B. It is supposed the above four Servants are all together, they stole a small Boat, which was found about Nine Miles up the River towards Burlington.

PHILADELPHIA April 20. There is in Custody of William Nichols Esq; High Sheriff of the county of Monmouth, a likely Negroe Man, about 24 Years, he calls himself James, speaks little English, and can give no Account where he came from, or who he belongs to. Any Person that owns said Negroe paying Charges may have him.

These are to give Notice, That there will be exposed to sale at a publick Vendue, on Wednesday the 17th of May next, in the City of Perth-Amboy, a Plantation within the said City, fronting upon the Raritan River, with a good Brick House, a good large Barn with Leantoes, and a Grainery, which formerly belonged to Mr. John

Rudyard, late of Perth-Amboy, Gelt. deceas's; containing above Three Hundred Acres of upland, and Forty Acres of Salt Meadow. Any that has a mind to buy the same, may apply themselves to John Barclay, in said Perth-Amboy, one of the Executors of the said John Rudyard; where they may be informed of the Title to the said Land, and with the Terms of sale.

PHILADELPHIA April 27. A Lottery opened at the next Door by two to Three Tuns in Chestnut Street, in Philadelphia, consisting of Seven Hundred Tickets; where all Persons willing to try their Chance, may be furnished with Tickets at Two Shillings each Ticket, and may (if they please) see the Goods; it is to be drawn in the 17th Day of May next (if full) and the Prizes delivered the next Day; which consist of Plate and other Goods. It is designed, that the Lottery be full as soon as possible; therefore in Order to be speedy filling and drawing of the same, it is hoped that all Persons willing to be concerned in this trial of their Chance, will be as speedy as possible they can in taking out the Tickets, because the sooner it is full the sooner it may be drawn, to the general Satisfaction of those concerned; and when full Publick Notice will be given by Advertisements, and Publick Proclamation made several Days of the precise Day of Drawing; which will be performed fairly in very good Order and in Publick View.

Two Grey Stallions suitable for a Coach, to be sold, One is four and the other one is Five years Old; they are 13 Hands high. Enquire of the Printer hereof.

To be Sold by Thomas Sober, four very likely young Negroe Men, and a boy about thirteen Years lately arrived from Barbadoes.

PHILADELPHIA May 4. Run away the 17th of this Instant April, from John Justin of Cecil County in Maryland, a Servant Man named Thomas Collins who is a short well set Fellow, full fac'd short black Hair, a brown Beard; he had on an old dark gray Kersey Coat, with large Patches on each side of the Breast darker than the Coat, Old Leather Breeches, he had also with him a Gun about five or six Foot in the Barrel, as also a Powder Horne and shot Bag. Whoever shall take up said servant and bring him to his said Master at the Head of North East, or secure him and give Notice thereof, so that he may be had Again, shall have Two Pitoles Reward and reasonable Charges.

Run away in December last a Servant Woman named Elizabeth Cyphers alias Willson, about 23 Years of Age, a middle Stature full Bodied Woman, round Shouldered, Pockfretten, she had on a dark coloured Shallow Gown. Whoever shall bring her to Samuel Holt of Philadelphia, shall have Forty Shillings Reward and reasonable Charges paid them by Samuel Holy. There is something now come for her, from her Mother.

PHILADELPHIA May 11. To be let or Rent, the Plantation of Francis Rawle, deceas'd, Distant from the City of Philadelphia, two Miles and a half, whereon is a large Brick Dwelling House and Kitchen, a large Barn, Sheep-house and Stable, two good large bearing Orchards, 25 Acres of Summer and Winter grain on the Ground, well stor'd with good Meadow Cultivated and fit for the Seyeth, also a good Quanty of upland Pasturage. Likewise Accommodated with a Creek Navigable to the Dwelling House. Where is to be sold, a Stock of Divers kinds as Horses, Horned Cattle, Sheep and Hoggs. Inquire of Martha Rawle Widow, of the said Francis Rawle, at the said Plantation, or William Rawle in Philadelphia.

PHILADELPHIA May 18. Run away the 3d Instant May, from Jacob Matdaniel of New-Castle County near Christeen, a Servant Man named Timothy Murry, Aged 40 Years, with a gray Homespun Cloath Coat, trim'd with the same, the Ratts has eaten the lower part of one of the Cuffs, a pair of Linnen Drawers patch'd, he has dark thin Hair and Bald on the Crown, he is very Hairy in his Body. Whoever secures said Servant so that his Master may have him again, shall have Forty Shillings Reward and reasonable Charges.

PHILADELPHIA May 22. The Honourable Colonel Gordon our Governour having made a Progress thro' the three lower Counties of New-Castle, Kent and Sussex upon Delaware, where he was met by the Magistracy and great Numbers of the Gentry and Freemen, and entertain'd with the greatest Marks of Esteem and Affection is returned safe here this Evening; the Mayor, Common Council, and a great Number of the Gentry of both Sexes and of the best Fashions, met his Honour some Miles from this City, and Conducted him to his House.

PHILADELPHIA June 1. Sunday last being the Anniversary of His Majesty's Birth, the Mayor, Recorder, and divers other Gentlemen went to our Governours House at Noon; where His Majesty's the Prince and Princess of Wales Healths were drank, and several Guns fired: On Monday Evening there was a great Appearance of Gentlemen and Ladies at his Honours House, where all Royal Healths were again Drank, Prosperity to the Proprietors and People, and to this City, and after a great Entertainment the Night was Concluded with a Ball.

Ran away the 25th of May last, from Principio Iron Works, in Cecil County Maryland, a Servant Man named John Prat, aged about 22 Years and by Trade a Taylor, he is of a Tall Stature and fair Complexion, with a large sharp Nose, is well dressed having on a Chocolate coloured Serge Coat, full Buttoned with open sleeves, wears a Wigg or Cap, hath also with him a bright coloured Finstain Frock. Whoever secures the said Servant and Gives Notice to his Master at Principo Iron Works, or to Mr. Israel Penberton in Philadelphia shall have forty Shillings Reward and all Reasonable Charges paid by

Stephen Orion.

PHILADELPHIA June 8. Run away the 21st Day of May last, from James Leonard, of Sumerset in New-Jersey, a Negroe Man named Will aged about Twenty six Years, and has with him an old lightish colour'd Great Coat and Leather Breeches, and two Shirts, an old pair of black and white Stockings, and 'tis supposed that he has a Gun with him, he speaks good English. Whoever takes up the said Negroe and secures him so that his Master may have him shall be well Rewarded, by said James Leonard.

All Persons Indebted to the Estate of David Biffet, the late Philadelphia Post-Rider, deceas'd are desired forthwith to come and pay the same to Thomas Boore and Magarete Biffet, Executors of the deceas'd; and all such who have demands to said Estate are desired to bring in their Accounts to said Executors, in order to have them adjusted. There is to be sold on the 28th of June next at Vendue, a like Negroe Woman, Horses, Cattle, Hogs, a new Cart, and Household Goods; they that buy less than 20 Shillings worth pay ready Money, above 20 Shillings in Six Months Credit if Required, by

                  Thomas Boore and Margaret Biffet.

  Run away from his Master Stephen Jackson near Schuylkill Ferry, a Servant Lad about 17 Years old, named John Humphrey, having short white Hair, he took with him two dark Wiggs, two vests one of cloth a Cinnamon colour, the other gray Drugget Home made but without Sleeves, a Pair of Leather Breeches, a pair of new strong Shoes, a pair of old black Worsted Stockings an old light colour riding Coat with a Cape. Whoever takes up and secures the said Servant so that his master may have him again, shall be payes Thirty Shillings if found Twenty Miles and Twenty shillings more for every Twenty Miles further from Philadelphia, which shall be paid by me

                              Stephen Jackson.

  PHILADELPHIA June 15. To be Sold, two Plantations, one containing 200, the other 150 Acres on the other side of Schuylkill, situated between Roach's and Maltsby's Ferrys: Those that are inclined to Purchase, may be further Informed by Charles Sober,

  Wery good Wine and Rum to be Sold at a reasonable rate at Ralph Sandiford's over against the Court-House in Philadelphia.

  PHILADELPHIA June 22. Broke loose from Peter Vantilburg, the Post-Rider about South River Bridge, a bright Bay Horse, he has a Rope about his Neck some white Saddle Spots on his Back, a small strake on his near Shoulder, a Bushy tail. Whoever shall take up said Horse and bring him to Peter Vantilburg, or Isaac Stelle at Mount Woodern near Allen-Town, or Col. Tho' Hunlock in Burlington, or Zich. Hutchins, Butcher in Philadelphia, shall be very well Rewarded for their Pain.

Run away the 12th of this Instant June, from Joseph Jackson of London Grove, in Chester county, a Servant Man named Richard Prat, Aged about 18 Years, of a small Stature, Sandy coloured short Hair and curled, with a grey Linsey Coat, a good Felt Hat. Whoever takes up the said Servant, or secures him so that his Master may have him again, shall have Twenty five Shillings as a Reward and reasonable Charges.

Joseph Jackson.

PERTH-AMBOY June 23. This Day was held a Special Court for Trying of Wequalia, an Indian King, he was found Guilty of the Murder of John Leonard, late of this Place, and accordingly received Sentence of Death in the presence of a great Number of Christians, and about 20 Indians, the latter of which were all well pleased at the justness of his Sentence, and says, That he had his Deserts he should have received a Reward like this long ago for murdering several of them. And the Interpreter being (two days before the Trial) in Company with three other Indian Kings, who were attended by 50 other of their most principal Men; The said Interpreter to know of them, what they intended to do for said Wequalia, or whether they had any Message to send by him or not, to whom after they had by themselves considered the Affair, they said, We thought of this matter, and desire you will tell Wequalia, That we neither have nor intend to do any thing in this affair it is he that has wronged the English, and not us and therefore he must himself make them Satisfaction without expecting any Assistance of hearing any more of Us; which Message the Interpreter did faithfully deliver unto the said Wequalia, at his Tryal not having the Oppertunity to do it sooner, and on Friday next he is to be Executed at this Place, whose wretched Example we hope will deter all his Indian Spectators from committing any acts of the like kind.

PHILADELPHIA June. 29. Whereas there has been a Report spread abroad, That John Jones of Cunslago was in the Goal of Philadelphia, and there did offer to commit Fornication to the body of

Jane Smith, these are therefore to certify whom it may concern, that the Report is notoriously False. Given under my Hand this 8th Day of May, Anno. 1727. Test, Bryant Steald.   Jane Smith.

Ran away the 9th of this Instant June, from the Widow Sheppard of Philadelphia, a Servant man, named John Blanchet, about 24 Years of Age, Pockfretten and Freckled, red Hair, very thick Legs; wears a short Wigg of a light Colour, an old fine Cloath Vest, a pair of Ozenbrig Trowsers and Shirt, a Felt Hatt, speaks broar West-Country. Whoever takes said Servant and secure him so that he may be had again shall have Five Pounds as a Reward and reasonable Charges by
                                                Aemy Sheppard.
PERTH-AMBOY July 4. On Friday last Wequalia, (the Indian King) was Executed here according to Sentence passed against him, for the Murder of Capt. John Leonard. And whereas the said Wequalia had lived a base inhumane Life, and Murdered his own Brother and other Indians formerly, so he Dyed a hardened and Impenitent Wretch not showing the least Remorse for any of the Actions of his Vile Life, nor would he own the Murder of Capt. Leonard, of which he was so notoriously Convicted. He saved us the labour of writing his Confession, having made none; he only bid Adue to a few Indians that attended him to the Gallows, which were only his Relatives, all the other Indians refused to shew him the least Regard. When the Sheriff asked him, if any of the Ministers should pray with him before he Dyed? he indifferently Answered, they might if they would, and being asked, which of them? he named Mr. Morgan a Presbyterian Minister, and that because he was his Neighbour, which he implied was all the reason for his Choice. There was a great concourse of People at the Execution, together with two Companies of the Militia in Arms, in order to protect the Sheriff & Officers from any Insult of the Mob or Indians.

PHILADELPHIA July 6. Strayed from Mr. Samuel Blunston of Aequehana, near Conostogoe, about the middle of May last, a Red Roan Horse, with a black Mane and Tail, and some white on his hind Feet, he is Branded on the Thigh with E or such a like Mark, and went away with a small Bell on, in Company with a Roan Mare of near same Colour but something Lighter, with a grey short Mane and Tail, she is an indifferent Pacer, has sharp Peaking Ears, and a lowish Neck, and a little taller than the Horse. Whoever shall bring both or either of them to the aforesaid Owner, or to Peter Lloyd Mercht. in Philadelphia, or give certain Intelligence of them, that they may be had, shall have a sufficient Reward.

PHILADELPHIA July 20. From Annapolis in Maryland we are advised, That on Saturday the first Instant, arrived there the Ship Baltimore, Clement Brooke, Commander, The Honourable Benedict Leonard Calvert Esq; Brother to the Right Honourable the Lord of Baltimore, whom His Lordship has been pleased to appoint, with his Majesty's Royal Approbation Governour of Maryland: He was received with the usual Ceremony &c. and his Commission was published the third Instant.

PHILADELPHIA July 20. This is to give Notice to all Travellers, that the House where ———— Bagley lived at the Town of Bristol, is now kept by Simon Nightingal, where all Persons may have very good Entertainment, both Man and Horse.

To be Sold a good Plantation situated lying and being upon Bohemia River in Maryland (called Rick Neck) about 3 Miles below Bohemia Landing, between Mrs. Bryard and Mr. Herman V. Biverklo's containing about 130 Acres, about 40 Clear and in good Repair, the Clear Land as well as Wood Land being Rich, lying very near Commodious for Trade, and Choice Place for Fishing; having a River and a Creek at the side, which spares a great deal of Fencing. Whoever will buy said Plantation may Treat on Reasonable Terms with James V. Bobber.

To be Sold by Capt. Spafford, several likely young Negroes lately Imported from Jamaica.

There is to be exposed to Sale at the Sign of the Rose and Crown in Chester, in the said county, between the Hours of Twelve and Two in the Afternoon of the Fifth day of August next after the date thereof, by John Taylor Sheriff of the

County aforesaid, by virtue od a writ of Venditicui expoat, issued out of the Court of Common Pleas of Chester County aforesaid, at the Suit of Edward Hoene, a certain Messuage or Tenement and Tract or Parcel of Land thereunto belonging; containing by Estimation 225 Acres, situated lying and being on the North Branch of Brandywine Creek, in the Township of Caln in the said County of Chester, lately taken in Execution by him the said Sheriff, at the suit of the said Edward Horne, against Joseph Cloud late of Chester County aforesaid, Yeoman.

PHILADELPHIA July 27. The Corn Mills, Saw Mills, Fulling Mill, Dye House, Yards and Utensils, and conveniences thereto belonging together with some Houses and Lots, in the Burrough of Bristol; also a considerable Tract of Land adjacent all in Bristol Township, in Bucks County, in the said Province of Pennsylvania, are to be Sold at Reasonable Rates, either in Parcels or together, as may best suit the Buyer: Enquire of Joseph Peace of Bristol aforesaid, or William Fishbourn & Joseph Buckley at Philadelphia, dated 25 day of July, 1727.

The George Inn, in Philadelphia, accommodated with good Stables, and Brew-House, &c. to be let by   James Steel.

PHILADELPHIA Aug. 3. Joseph Antrobus, Sworn Appraiser Vendues Constable and Cryer, is removed next Door to the Coffee-House, where are done Writings and Accounts.

On the 3d of November next the Time of Fair at New-Castle, will be exposed to sale by Publick Vendue, the Plantation lying at the Head of Apoquinomie Creek, in the County of New-Castle, belonging to the Estate of Sylvester Garland deceas'd, and which formerly belong'd to Capt. Haily, containing between the two places nearly 700 Acres; there is an Orchard upon each Plantation, a House and Barn upon one of them, there is good Conveniency for building either Fulling or Grist Mill; there is on the Land a landing Place from the Creek, to which a small Sloop may be brought from Delaware Bay &c. there is a pretty deal of clear Land on it, the Land is good, and the Title indisputable. The two

Places may be sold either Joyntly and seperately: If any want to Enquire further into the Premises they may be informed by James Anderson Minister, late of New-York, now at Donnigall, in the County of Chester Pennsylvania, who has the Power of Disposing of said Plantations either publickly or privately, as he shall see Cause.

NEW-YORK Aug. 7. Last Saturday the Governour of Canada arrived here: We hear that he is come to demand the Demolition of the Fort, which we have built in the Sennaca's Country, to cover our Indians, and the far Indians that come to Trade with us. He expects an answer in 14 Days, and if his demands be not Complyed with, he says he had 12 Hundred Men ready, and he will go with them and Demolish said Fort.

PHILADELPHIA Aug. 14. We have Account fron New-Jersey, That a great Number of Indians are come to the Plantation of the late Wequalia, (who was Executed for the Murder of Capt. John Leonard) in Order to Crown a new King in the room of the said Wequalia; which has put several of the Inhabitants in a Fright, and made them remove to New-York & Long Island, but the said Indians design no Harm, only to Crown their new King.

Run away the 12th of this Instant from John Bryan senr. living near New-Castle, a Servant Woman named Magarete Murphy, She is of low Stature, wears a black and white Gown, has very red Hair, and much Freckled and goes in Company with a young Man, named John Bryan a Freeman. Whoever apprehends the said Servant Woman, and returns her to her said Master, shall have 30 Shillings paid as a Reward by me

                                          John Bryan senr.

All Persons who are Indebted to the Estate of Nicholas Gatau (commonly known as the French Cook) deceas'd are forthwith desired to come and pay the same to his Widow the Executrix to the said Nicholas Gatau, or else they may expect further Trouble. And all Persons who have any Claims to the said Estate are desired to bring in their Accounts, and receive all their just Demands.

There is also to be let by said Widow, a good House, Kitchen, with about Eleven Acres of good Land most of it has English Grass and been Moved, about a Mile from the City of Philadelphia: There is also to be Sold a good Cart and two Horses, with the Gears thereupon belonging; also a Negroe Man to be hired out by the Year.

PHILADELPHIA Aug. 24. Run away two Servant Men, one from Ruth Hoskins of Chester, named Gregory Cook, a lusty well set Man, with thick curl'd black Hair, of a swarthy Complexion, has lost some of his fore Teeth, and much show's the rest; he has several Suits of linning Jackets and Breeches Ozenbrigs, a snuff colour'd Pea Jacket, a Felt Hat, and a pair of new Shoes. The other from Edward Smout of the same Place, named David Gibbens of a small Stature, without Hair, excepting some behind, which is not long: he is of a fair rudy Complexion, long Visage, Peeked Chin with a Scar about an Inch long across it, may have with him a black Wigg, took with him a dark brown Broad-Cloth Coat full Fashion and Breeches of the same, his Wastcoat without Lining of Homespun, and sow'd with Yellow, a good Beaver Hat, shoes stitch'd round the Quarters, Silver Buckles; has in pocket a silver Needle-Case, with two letters AA on the top, a pair of Roll-up Stockings of a Mixt Colour Cinnamin and White. Whoever takes the said Servants and bring them as aforesaid, shall have Two Pounds for Each with reasonable Charges, by us
                    Ruth Hoskins, Edward Smout.

NEW-YORK Aug. 28. On Monday the one and twentieth of this Instant Month of August, His Majesty King George the Second was proclaimed at the City of New-York with the usual Ceremony. And the 25th He was in like manner Proclaimed at the City of Pert-Amboy in New-Jersey.

PHILADELPHIA Aug. 31. This Day at Noon, the Honourable Colonel Gordon our Governour, attended by his Council, the Mayor, Recorder, and Commonalty of the City, and divers other Gentlemen, Proclaimed here His Majesty King George the Second, with the usual Ceremony of Firing of Guns and other Demonstrations of Loyalty and Affection.

The Lyon King of Beast is designed to be carried from this Place the 20th of September next, and is to be seen at Abraham Biekly's new Store in Water-Street, till that Time, for one Shilling each Person.

Run away August the 15th, 1727, from Alexander Lockart of Trenton, in the County of Hunterdon & Province of New-Jersey, a Servant Man named Thomas Griffe, a Welch man, aged about 40 Years; he hath on a brown colour'd Coat of Homespun Drugget, a Homespun course Shirt, a pair of homespun striped Breeches, blue and white, a pair of black Stockings, with old Shoes, a flat Hat & of low Stature, a black Beard and Hair, grey Hairs mixt among his Hair, If any Person takes up said Servant and secures him so that his said Master may have him again, shall have Twenty Shillings for his or their Pain and other reasonable Charges. paid by the said

        Alexander Lockart.

TRENTON, WEST-NEW-JERSEY Sept. 1. Notice is hereby given, That one Thomas Wright, a Weaver by Trade, who used to go by the name of Thomas Smith, and how many other names we know not, he says he was born in Maryland, but hath Lived on Long-Island and New-England, and hath Traded from one end of the Country to the other: if any Person has any Business with the said Thomas, they may find him in Prison in this Place, on suspicions of stealing a Bay Stallion, five Years old, a white spot on his Nose: if any Person have said Stallion in Custody, they are desired forthwith to discover him to Andrew Bradford, or if found afterward, he shall be counted as stole by the Possessor.

PHILADELPHIA Sept. 7. Stray'd or Stolen away out of the Pasture of William Trebern in Chester, on the 27th of August last, a Middle Size Bay Horse, branded on the Shoulder with the Letters ED joyn'd in one another, with a grey Scar on the Top of his Fore-Head, the fore-top is cliped, and one lock of his Mane cut off close behind his Ears, and has a switch Tail. Whoever brings the aforesaid Horse to the Printer hereof, shall have Ten Shillings as a reward and reasonable Charges, by me Joseph Johnson.

This is to give Notice, That at the Lyon and Glove in Water-Street, in philadelphia, all Gentlemen and Ladies may be furnished with all sorts of Gloves, Kid and Lamb, hard Gumed and Glazed after the best London Manner, and likewise all sorts of riding Gloves: Sold at reasonable Rates, either Wholesale or Retail, by the maker.   Edward Morris.

PHILADELPHIA Sept. 14. Run away the 4th of this Month September from V. Van Cox and John Copson, of North-East in Maryland, a Covananted Servant, named Edward Mattock, a Hereforshire Man, by Trade a Smith; he is a tall slender fellow, black long Visage, short Hair, commonly wears a Speckled Cap, and dark coloured Cloaths: he is supposed to be at some of the Iron-works. Whoever takes him up & secures him in the County Goal, and give Notice thereof, shall have Five Pounds Reward and reasonable Charges paid by,   John Copson.

To be Sold by John Connor, a parcel of Young Negroe Men, Boys and Girls, at Reasonable Rates, are to be seen at William Coopers in the Jersey and Joseph Huggs at Gloucester: for further intelligence Enquire of said Connor at his House in Water-Street, near Benjamin Morgan in Philadelphia.

To be Sold by Mary Owen, Relict of Evan Owen late of this City of Philadelphia deceas'd, 300 Acres of good Land, near Colebrook-dale Iron-Works, called Little Oley, 10 Acres whereof is Fenc'd, and part clear'd, and a considerable quantity of Meadow; and 400 Acres more of good Land well Timber'd, lying near People Forge, togrther also with a Sixteenth part of Colebrook Furnace, leased for a Term, whereof 25 Years are unexpired and an eight part of a Forge. The Price and Conditions of Sales whereof, are to be Enquired after from the said Mary Owen.

ANNAPOLIS MARYLAND Sept. 16. On Thursday Morning King George the Second was Proclaimed here, with extraordinary Solemnity.

Early in the Morning, his Excellency Benedict Leonard Calvert (Brother of the Right Honourable the Lord Calvert) and the Council met and Signed the Proclamation; and the decease of our late most Gracious Sovereign, was made known to the People by the tolling of the Church-Bell, and the Discharge of 67 Minute Guns, the Number of Years his late Majesty lived: Whereupon the Worshipful Mayor, Recorder, Aldermen, Common-Council, and several other Principal Inhabitants of this City, proceeded in order on Horseback, to wait upon the Governour, where they severally Subscribed their Names to the Proclamation for proclaiming his present Majesty; during which time, the Hon. Charles Calvert, our late Governour, in Quality of Major-General of the Western Shore, rode out of the City-Gates, to the Place where the Militia were appointed to rendezvous; there he found 5 Troops of Horse, and 5 Companies of Foot, which the Hon. Col. Holland at their Head: the Foot, he ordered to march to the Stadt-House-Hill, and there make a Line for the Procession to pass Thro', Col. Holland marching the Horses to the Governour's House, Then the Procession began in the following Manner: First, Major-General Calvert and Col. Holland, at the Head of the First Troop of Horse, then the High-Sheriff of the County, followed by 4 Under Sheriffs: Then went his Excellency the Governour, attended by the Hon. Gentlemen of the Council, with several other Gentlemen of the City and County; the whole Company on Horseback, in a very handsome manner; and the other 4 Troops of Horses following, and closing up the Procession.

Being arriv'd at the Stadt-House, the Proclamation was read by the High-Sheriff, being followed with loud Acclamations of Long Live King George the Second, with Discharges of the great Guns and small Arms. Then the whole Company proceeded (as they came) to a Neighbouring Plain, where the Militia, both Horse and Foot, were handsomely drawn up, and review'd by his Excellency the Governour, attended by the rest of the Gentlemen, after which, the Company went to a large Tent, erected on a rising Ground, where His Excellency, and the Gentlemen present drank to the Health of the King and Queen, The Royal Family and the Lord Proprietory of this Province, under a triple Discharge of the great

Guns and small Arms. After which the Militia was discharged, to fall on an Ox, and some sheep roasted Whole on the Plain, several Barrels of Biscuit, 120 Gallons of Rum made into Punch, in several Vessels for that Purpose, and 6 Hogsheads of Cyder; the Appetites made short Work with the Meat as the Inclinations to drink Loyal Healths did with the Drink. Whilst they were thus employed, the Governour and the other Gentlemen, sat down to dine in the Tent, where there was a Table 60 Feet Long, spread with fine Entertainment, in the Handsomest and Plentitulest Manner; there they spent the whole afternoon drinking to most Loyal Healths. In the Evening they went to the Stadt-House, and the same Loyal Healths and Declarations of Joy went round, while the Long Fires and Illuminations, blazed in Distinction of the Solemn Day. And in short it may without Vanity be concluded, there was the finest Appearance of the Gentry and Militia, the noblest Entertainment for them, and the greatest Unanimity of Joy (as appear'd by the Countenances of all) that ever was seen in Maryland.

PHILADELPHIA Sept. 14. The Ship Fame from Holland is now in the River with about 500 Palatines on Board, who give an Account of two more Ships to Sail from thence with more Palatines on Board. There is also another Ship in the River suppos'd from London.

PHILADELPHIA Sept. 21. Proposal for re-printing the Laws of the Province of Pennsylvania.

Whereas a Currect and perfect Book of the Laws was much wanting, the Necessity of which appearing to the Honourable House of Assembly, they were pleased to appoint the Honourable David Lloyd Esq; to collect what Acts are now in force, and after careful Examination to Order the same to be Printed. Now as only a small Number is Order'd for the use of the said Province; those private Persons who are willing to have the same are desired to bring in their Superscriptions by the First of November, the Printer designing to print no more than what are Subscribed and agreed for. The Price to Subscribers is 15 s. the Book. The whole shall be well Bound in

Leather, and ready to be delivered to Subscribers the 25th of May next, by Andrew Bradford.

Taken away by Force on the High-Rode between Trent-Town and Bristol, the 16th of this Instant Sept. by a short Fellow with a Pea-Jacket, from a young Lad, named James Sanders, belonging to William Bantoff, Baker, a small Bay Horse about Thirteen Hands high, Branded on the near bottock with the Letter H, there was on the Horse a black Saddle with a blue Housing. Whoever shall take up said Person or Horse, and give Notice thereof to William Bantoff, shall be very well Rewarded.

PHILADELPHIA Oct. 5. A Smith's Shop with all manner of Necessaries belonging to it situated in Maryland, upon the Road between the Head of Sassafrass and Head of Bohemia, near a Place call the Cross-paths, and by a Plantation belonging to James Heath; there will be Coales ready Burned and Iron and Steel may be had, with Conveniencies on said Plantation by

James Heath.

THis Morning Capt. Phenix, Master of a Sloop belonging to Woodbridge in East-Jersey, came here by Land from Virginia, who gives an Account, that on the 10th Day of September last he was taken off of the Capes of Virginia, by a Spanish Sloop from the Havanas, of eight Carriage, and six swivel Guns; where he and several others were put ashore. He also adds, that this Privateer had taken several other Vessels Viz. Capt. Joseph Allen bound from Virginia to London, Capt. Letherhand, from Maryland for Liverpool, Capt. Grayham, from James River in Virginia for London.

There are to be sold at Publick Outcry the 20th of this Instant October by Edward Horne, six several Yearly Rents, in the Alley called Jone's Alley amounting in all to 9 pounds 3 shillings and 4 pence per Annum. Also two Lots with Tenements on them in the same Alley. Pursuant to a Deed of Trust from Joseph Jones, for the use of Creditors.

And there is also sold by the said Edward Horne for the same Use, 2000 Acres of Land near Shipback. And this may inform the Tenents of

Joseph Jones in and about Walnut Street, that their Yearly Rents are to be Paid, as they become due to Edward Jones, for the aforesaid.

All Persons that are Indebted to the Estate of James Jones, late of Lower-Merion Gent. Deceased, are hereby desired to come and pay the same to his Widdow and Joseph Jones his Son, Administrators to the said Estate, or else they may expect further Trouble; And those who have any demands on the said Estate, are also desired to bring in their Accounts to the said Administrators, in order to adjust the same.

PHILADELPHIA Oct. 12. Run away the 2d of October from John Coure at New-Castle, a Servant Man named Vallentine Dempsey Aged about 18 Years a Rope maker by Trade, he is a well set fresh coloured Young Lad with fair Hair, when he left his Master he wore a light coloured Coat Jacket and Breeches, blew Stockings and new Shoes, He was lately Imported with Capt. King from Ireland. Whoever takes up the said Servant and bring him to James Sykes in New-Castle, or to Alexander Frame in Philadelphia, shall have Forty Shillings Reward & Reasonable Charges, paid by   John Goure.

Whereas several lands laying in Dorset County in the Province of Maryland, near Choptank River, late of Nicholas Painter Deceased, were Advertised to be sold by William Cornwallis, as part thereof by him are sold and other part lay until the People were satisfied of the Title, and whereas the Title to the said Land are now confirmed to the said Cornwallis, These are therefore to give Notice that about 5000 Acres by the said Cornwallis, will be disposed of, to such who desire to buy at very reasonable Rates, with General Warrants for the said Lands by the Owner.   William Cornwallis.
Who lives in Broadkill Sussex upon Delaware.

PHILADELPHIA Oct. 19. Run away the 2d of the 8th Month called October. 1727. From Samuel Jones of Cadbury in the County of Chester, a Welch Servanr Man, named William Williams, 21 Years of age, of a middle Stature, round shoulder'd, thin Visage, brown Coloured Hair; having a striped Jacket, a gree Plush Cap, or a Felt

Hat, grey Yarn Stockings, round Toe'd Shoes: Whoever shall take up the said Runaway and secure him shall have Forty Shillings Rewars, or bring him home, shall have the sum of Four Pounds paid by me   Samuel Jones.

Run away October 10 from Robert Miller of Cain, a Servant Man named John Sitch, about 24 Years of Age, a small Stature, swarthy Complexion, brown Hair; when he went off, he took with him a new Felt Hat, and another old one, an old Jacket, grey Kearsey Coat, Linnen Drawers, an old pair of Trowsers, brown Yarn Stockings, and a new pair of Shoes; he also took with him a Hemp Halter. Whoever secures the said Servant, so that his said Master may have him, shall have 20 Shillings Reward, by   Robert Miller.

Stolen or Strey'd from Robert Gardner of Blockly in the County of Philadelphia, a large Sorrel Horse with a large Blaze in his Face, branded with the Letter H on his near Shoulder and Buttock, a light Grizle Main, a swelling on one Leg, occasioned by a Rope. Whoever shall take up said Horse, and bring him to Peter Gardner, shall have 40 Shillings Reward. There was also a Servant Man Run away from Nathaniel Gibson, named John Evans, of a middle Stature, short black Hair. Whoever takes him up shall have 30 Shillings Reward and Reasonable Charges.

PHILADELPHIA Oct. 26. All Persons who have any Demands, against Roger Owen of the City of Philadelphia, Perriwigg-maker, they are desired to bring their Accounts to him at David Evans, at the sign of the Crown, and receive their Money, for he Designs for Great-Britain, in about three Weeks.

To be let: A Brick Dwelling-House, out-House, and Tann-Yard about half a Mile from the Town near Wm. Masters Mill: enquire of
      Joseph Richards.

NEW-YORK Nov. 2.   To Your Excellency

William Barnet, Esq; Captain General and Governour in Chief of the Province of New-York, New-Jersey, and the Territories thereon depending in America, and Vive-Admiral of the same &c.

The Humble Address of his Majesty's Council of the Province of New-York.

May it Please Your Excellency;
Whilst we are Congratulating his Majesty from whose Reign we are assured we shall reap all Benefits naturally arising to his People, from the good Effects of a wise, a good and just Government, we cannot be so ungrateful as to forget the great Advantaged which this Province has during your Administration, received from your Prudent and wise Directions. You truly representing the Prince of glorious Memory, who was graciously pleased to assign you to the Honourable Station. We have, under you enjoy'd all our Rights, Privileges and Liberties in their full Extent, and you have upon every occasion shown a Love to Mankind in general, in all your Conduct, a strict Regard to Honour, Equity and Justice.

We owe to your Excellency's Care Diligent and Foresight the Settlement of that Important Frontier of Oswego, by much the most rational method for the Security of this Province, against the Neighbouring French, and for encouraging the Six Nations and other remote Indians in the English Interest, that ever was attempted.

We behold among us, with a particular Pleasure, the Son of the good Prelate, to whom the Protestant World are so much obliged for the part he bore in bringing to an happy issue the Establishment of the British Crown, and fixing it upon the heads of that Illustrious Family who now enjoy it, and would esteem your Continuance among us in your present Session, one of the greatest Marks of the Royal Favour to us.

PHILADELPHIA Nov. 2. Monday last being the Anniversary of our most Gracious Sovereign King George the Second, there were very Rejoicing, with other Demonstrations of Loyalty and Affection, over all the City: A handsome Entertainment was provided by the Commanders of Ships and others, at the House of Mr. William Chancellor, Sail-maker, in whose Garden 21 Pieces of Cannon were commodiously Placed, where (His Honour our Governour being then at New-Castle, at the General Assembly of Counties) were present, the Mayor, and Recorder of this City, and divers other Gentlemen; The Healths of his

Majesty, the Queen Consort, the Prince of Wales and all the Royal Issue, with these of the Honourable Proprietory Family, and his Honour the Governour, were drunk, under the Discharge of a great number of Cannon, and the Entertainment concluded with a Ball.

About Seven a-Clock in the Evening, the Mayor, Recorder and a great many other Gentlemen went to the Governour's House to pay their Complements of this Occasion to his Lady, where was a handsome Appearance of Ladies of the best Note and Fashion, and after a splendid Entertainment there was a Ball which lasted till three next Morning.

At New-Castle His Honour our Governour, together with the Honourable House of Representatives, His Majesty's Justices of the Peace, and several other Gentlemen met, and after Dinner drank all Royal Healths, Prosperity to the Proprietory Family, and to the Counties upon the Delaware, then His Honour the Governour's Health under the Discharge of the Cannon belonging to that Place, and in the Evening all Houses in the Town were Illuminated, and the Governour with the same Company met at a Bonfire, where the Royal Healths &c. were again repeated and the Guns Fired, amongst the loud Acclamations of Numbers of People, striving to outdue one another in Expressions of Loyalty on that happy Day.

On Tuesday following all the Royal Healths with several other Loyal ones were again drank at a Feast made by Charles Read Esq; the late Mayor of this City, as it is usual by Mayors at the Expiration of their Mayoralty.

And Yesterday the same were again repeated at the Entertainment made at the expence of the Grand-Jury of this City, where his Honour the Governour was Present.

NEW-YORK Nov. 6. Mrs. Mary Burnet, the Wife of his Excellency Wm. Burnet Esq; Governour of New-York expired on Saturday Morning last, and was to be interred in the Chappel in Fort George on Tuesday following.

ANNAPOLIS Nov. 11. We have Advice from Virginia, that the Ship belonging to Capt. Cockram, homeward bound with Tobacco, from this Province, which was taken by the Spanish Privateers off this Coast, is retaken from the Spaniards by the Crew who went in Her, and carried into the York River. It seems the Spaniards had taken to many Prizes, that they were obliged to return one Sloop, which carried off many of the Prisoners as they thought proper, least in their Passage to the Havana, where they were allotted, they should rise, if they were too numerous: But the Spaniards, being loath to part with too many Prisoners, kept Four Englishmen, one Frenchman and one Dutchman in the Ship of Capt. Cockram's (of which Number one was his Mate,) against an equal Number of Spaniards. The 4 Englishmen had not been long Prisoners, before they fathom'd the Inclination of their French and Dutch Comrades who readily falling into their Measures, it was resolv'd that they should take the first Opportunity to revolt, which soon Happened; for Three of the Spaniards, having Occasion to go down into the Hold, Two Englishmen kept them down while the other 4 secured the Three Spaniards above, of which Number was their Captain, upon whom Hogan Morgan laid such violent Hands, that he killed him, and all the rest readily submitted; and brought in Prisoners of War to Virginia.

PHILADELPHIA Nov. 16. This is to give Notice, to all such Palatines as come over Passengers in the Ship Molly, John Hudson, Master, that if they do not in Eight Days from hereof, come and make due Payment of their Respective Passage Monies according to agreement, they will be Prosecuted for the same at Law.   John Hudson.

NEW-YORK Nov. 13. Yesterday Captain Thomas Smith in the Ship Beaver arrived here, in five Weeks from the Lands End; he left London the 12th of September, by whom we have Advice that the Honourable John Montgomery, Esq; who is Appointed Governour of New-York, was to come away in a Man of War about three weeks after Capt. Smith left London.

PHILADELPHIA Nov. 23. This is to inform those who it may concern, That Sarah Pattison, the now Wife of James Nesbitt of Perth Amboy, Taylor, has made an Elopement from her aforesaid Husband and Clandestinely and Faloniously carried away several of the aforesaid James Nesbitts Goods: Whoever therefore Trusts the aforesaid Sarah Pattison alias Nesbitt, upon her husbands Credit, be it to him or their Peril; for this is to Certify the World that he the said James Nesbitt will not pay any of her Debts Contracted since the 12th of November 1727, the Day that she Elop'd from her aforesaid Husband.

James Nesbitt.

PHILADELPHIA Nov. 30. Whereas Dennis Ryley late of Acrington in Lancestershire in Great-Britain, but now of the Township of New-Hanover in the County of Burlington, and the Western Division of New-Jersey, has had Information of an Uncle of his named John Conliff, said to reside on or near Christeen in New-Castle County upon Delaware, these are to request any Person or Persons that know the said John Cunliff, to give Information to John Eiley of New-Hanover County and Division afore said.

To the Palatines brought over by Capt. William Lea, in the Ship William and Sarah, who have not paid their Passage Monies, or given security for it: That they do not Forthwith from the date hereof make their Payments to Thomas Sober Merchant, in Philadelphia, they will be Prosecuted for the same by Law.

All Persons Indebted to James Conway of the City of Philadelphia, School-Master, are desired to pay the same with all Speed, the better to enable him to pay his, or expect Trouble.

NEW-YORK Dec. 4. At the Superior Court of Judicature held at the City Hall of New-York.

David Wallace and David Willson having last Court been Convicted of Cheat, in passing some Bills, which were Counterfeit of Credit of the Credit of the Province of New-Jersey, were brought to the Bar, and received the following Sentence, viz.

The said David Wallace and David Willson to stand in the Pillory (On the twelfth of this Instant) between the Hours of Ten and Eleven in the Forenoon of the same day, and after being places in a Cart, so as to be publickly seen, with Halters about their Necks, and carried thro' the most Public Streets in the City, and then brought to the Publick Whipping-Post, and there David Wallace on his bare Back to receive Thirty Nine Stripes, and Willson Twenty Eight Stripes and within some convenient time after the Sheriff shall deliver said Prisoners at the Ferry-House in King's County, and on the 3d Tuesday in January next they shall stand on the Pillory and then Wallace to receive at Flatbush 29 Stripes and Willson 28. Then they shall be conveyed to Westchester, and there on the 4th Tuesday of March to stand on the Pillory, and then at the Whipping-Post, Wallace to receive Twenty Stripes on the bare Back and Willson Ten, after which at the End of King's Bridge, they shall be delivered to the High Sheriff of the City of New-York, and from that time Wallace to remain in Prison Six Months, and Willson Three Months and then be discharged paying their Fees.

PHILADELPHIA Dec. 7. To be Sold. Two likely White Servants, a Woman and a Boy, enquire of
            Andrew Bradford.

Two very likely Negro Men to be Sold (they are at William Cooper in New-Jersey,) Enquire
            Andrew Bradford.

Run away on Tuesday the 21st of November, from George King, Mast-Maker of the City of Philadelphia, a Servant Man, named Thomas Whatkins, aged about 40 Years, of a middle Stature, long visage, having a large Tooth in his upper Jaw, he had on an old Felt Hat and Worsted cap, and an old Great Coat, and a Pea Jacket lined with Red, Ozenbrig Breeches, old Stockings and Shoes. Whoever takes up and secures sain Servant to his said Master, so that he may be had again, shall have 50 Shillings as a Reward and reasonable Charges paid by me   George King.

If he returns to his said Master he shall be kindly Receiv'd.

Stolen the 19th Instant, from Christopher Eaton of the County of New-Castle near the Red-Lyon, a Chestnut Sorrel Horse, about 15 Hands high, a large Star in his Fore head and a slip, Two white feet one before and one behind; and branded with the Letters IE Joyned on one, on the Shoulder and Buttock, a short switch Tail, and a natural Mane being trim'd. Whoever shall apprehend said Man and Horse, shall have Five Pounds reward: or, whoever brings said Horse to William Tidmarsh shall have Fifty Shilling Reward.

PERTH-AMBOY Dec. 9 His Excellency Governour Burnet's Speech to the General Assembly of the Province of New-Jersey.

Gentlemen,
I have called you together at this time. to give you as early an opportunity as I could, of Expressing the Universal Loyalty and Fidelity, of the People whom you Represent, to his present Majesty, and their deep concern for the loss of the late King, of ever blessed Memory.

I have one great Uneasiness to find my self hindered from Meeting you at Burlington the last Spring, as I had designed, but the late Emergencies of the French in Canada to make themselves Masters of our Six Nations, by building a Fort among them, made it necessary for me to use my utmost Application to fix those Indians effectually in the British Interest, and cover our Frontiers on that side, by building a Stone Fort in the middle of their Country, and placing a sufficient Garrison in it. As this evidently a Protection to this Province, from the Insults of the French and their Indians and the most to the Province of New-York. I am persuaded that you are not ill pleased with my diligence in that Affair, and that you are convinced of the necessity of my remaining where I could, from time to time give the necessary Orders required by the Plan.

I should now have got you at Burlington as the course I ought to do, if the daily expectation of my Successor's Arrived did not lay an indispensable Obligation upon me to be near at hand and ready to receive him.

I must inform you that the applying the unrest arising from the Loan Office, at the last Meeting of the Assembly, to another use than the sinking of the Bills, according to the Directions of the Act for which they were made, met with Objections from the Lord Commissioners of

Trade and Plantations which however were at last removed, as to that Act, by the repealed and earnest Representation of your Agent. But at the same time, the remainder of the Interest Moneys be destroyed according to the first Act, as the only sure Method to preserve the Credit of the Bills, which I therefore earnestly exhort you to Joyn with me in doing, without delay.

  I Hope you will agree with me, in thinking, that so so considerable a Province as this is, ought at least to have one convenient House Provided for Reception of the Governour, especially in this city, where the business of this Province and the convenient Distance from the occasions his most frequent Residence. I thought it a Difficulty upon me, at any fault coming, to be obliged to make an expensive Purchase upon that account: and I should take a particular Pleasure in preventing the like Inconveniency from falling upon my Successor, who in all respects deserves your highest Esteem.

  I make no Doubt of your providing amply for the incidental Charges of the Government, and of this Meeting, and for the encouragement and continuance of your Agent, who has served you with the utmost Diligence and Ability. You may depend on my Heartily concurring with you in any Law that are wanted for the good of the Province, since nothing can give me greater Satisfaction and Joy than contributing as much as lies in my Power to leave this Province in a happy and Flourishing Condition.   W. Bernet.

  PHILADELPHIA Dec. 12. Whereas those who have publick Demands, also private Persons are very pressing to have Money out of the said Office for payment of Publick Debts, and to borrow upon Loan, which demands cannot be Answered unless those Persons who are Deficient and Neglect, will pay in the Office their annual Quotas of Principal and Interest, therefore all those may hereby take Notice, that Prosecution shall not be any longer delay'd. but Execution taken out against the Estate of those which are upon Judgement, and a proper Process shall issue against others who are Deficient, which will not only be Chargeable but perhaps Ruinous.

PHILADELPHIA Dec. 19. From London Oct. 7. Yesterday Morning early, before Day-Light about 70 Convicts in Newgate, under Sentence of Transportation, with nearly 30 others brought there from Country Goals, were shipped off to America.

To be Sold. A Tract of Land, containing about Five Hundred Acres, lying on the Main Road to Conestogoe; near the Entrance of the Great Valley, and distant about Twenty Miles from Philadelphia. Inquire of Peter Lloyd.

Run away on the 3d of this Instant December, from James Steward, Taylor in the City of Philadelphia, a Servant Man, named John Jones, aged about 20 Years, of a middle Stature and slender, fair Complexion, large Eyes sorish, lame and crumpled on his left Foot, he has a fine Beaver Hat, a dark brown Natural Wigg, a light colour'd Duroy Coat and Jacket, with new Fashion cut Sleeves; also a Linnen striped Jacket and Breeches, with two Holland Shirts, a pair of brown Holland Trousers, brown Worsted Stockings and new Shoes. Whoever takes up said Servant and secures him so that his said Master may have him again, shall have Three Pounds as a Reward and all reasonable Charges.

He pretends to make Leather Breeches and also Gloves, but was willing to serve the said Steward to learn the Taylor Trade; this is the third time of his running away from the said Steward.

To be Let. Two Dwelling Houses, (late the Estate of Richard Anthony, deceas'd) either with or without the Wharfs and Stores thereto belonging at a reasonable Rent, by

William Fishbourn.

PHILADELPHIA Dec. 26. At Mr. Robert Ellis or Mr. John Danby's in Water-Street, to be Sold at Resonable Prices the following Goods, Viz. Broad Cloaths, sundry Colours, Kersey, Penetons and Duffils, ready made Cloaths, great Coats, best Steel Whip Saws, Cross cut Saws, Hand Saws, Scale beams Large and Small, Stilliards Large and Snall, Small Beams and Scales, best Croley's Steel Nails, Sundry Sorts of Iron Shovels, Steel Spades, a Steel Malt-mill and neat Fowling Pieces, Sundry Sizes filed and rasps, most sorts Locks, Sundry sort of Hinges, several sorts of Coopers Axes, and Add's Iron Weights, Glovers, Sheers, Buttons, Buckles, Razors, and Knives, with several sorts of Cutlery and Shoemakers Wares & Iron ware, Cheshire and Gloucester Cheese by William Cole.

PHILADELPHIA Dec. 26. We have Advise (By way of New-York) That the Cape Sable Indians have taken a Vessel and murdered every Soul on board and were seen Dancing on the shore round the Scalps and 'tis said carried some of the Scalps to Louisbourg.

1728

PHILADELPHIA Jan. 2. John Marshall, Son of Alexander Marshall, of Over-Stowey, near Taunton in the County of Sumerset, on whose Life depends a good Estate, having been absent, at or beyond the Sea, some considerable Time, whoever shall discover the said John Marshall to be alive, and where he is, (so as his Friends may hear from him,) to Mr. James Ruscombe, Sail-Maker in Bristol, shall receive of him Ten pounds Reward, and said John Marshall himself, if living will write his Friends where he is, well attested, or repair to Andrew Bradford, Printer hereof, may be further Advised, he shall have the like Reward of Ten Pounds to be paid by the said Mr. Ruscombe: And if beyond the Sea, his Charges born home; with further Gratuity.

Lately arrived the Snow Alice and Elizabeth, Peregrine Stockdale, Master, from Bristol, a parcel of Choice English Servants, (Trades-men and Husband-men) to be disposed of on Board the said Vessel, laying at William Fishbourn's Wharfe, by Captan or Thomas Sober: Philadelphia.

PHILADELPHIA Jan. 16. Whereas Conrad Kann and his Wife Mariana two Palatines, (the former a Tall black grain'd Man, with his own long Hair, commonly wears a Blue Coat with Brass Buttons; the latter a middle siz'd Young Woman, of round Face, brown Complexion) who arrived here the 30th of October last from London, in the Ship John Galley, have now absented themselves for seven Weeks, with intent to screen themselves from paying their Passage: If any one will bring the said Man & Woman, (or the Man alone) or give Notice so as they may be had, shall have 30 Shillings Reward and reasonable Charges: paid by John Ball, Master of the aforesaid Ship, in Philadelphia.

To be Sold by Andrew Bradford, a very likely Negroe Woman (with or without a child) fit for all Manner of House-work, and a good Cook.

PHILADELPHIA Jan. 23. We have had very hard Weather here, for near this two weeks past, so that it froze our River up to such a Degree that the People go over daily, and they have set up two Booths on the Ice, about the middle of the River.

PHILADELPHIA Jan. 23. The Speech of the Honourable Patrick Gordon Esq; Lieutenant Governour of the Province of Pennsylvania, and Counties of New-Castle, Kent and Sussex upon Delaware.

To the Representatives of the Freemen of said Province.

Mr. Speaker and Gentlemen of the house of Representatives,

At your first Meeting after the Election, you had the Opportunity of expressing your Zeal and Affection, in the Name of the Inhabitants of this Province, to His most Excellent Majesty George the Second, upon his happy accession to the Throne of his Royal Ancestors. And now being met on your Adjournment from that Time to proceed on the Business of the Country, I must in the first Place give both my self and you the Pleasure of observing the Harmony and Unanimity, which have appeared amongst People of all Ranks on that great occasion, where the early-contention is who shall be the most forward in expressing an entire Satisfaction in that happy Establishment, to which they owe every thing that's dear to a free People, with a full Dependence of his Majesty's Care for supporting them in their highest and greatest Concerns; and as this certainly procures Peace at home, and will best secure the British Interest abroad, it may justly be look'd upon as the Happy Presage of a Reign equally Glorious to his Majesty, and the beneficial to all Subjects.

And therefore Gentlemen, I shall not in the least doubt of our following this great Example of our Fellow Subjects at home, in pursuing the ways of Peace, Concord and Amity, as the only sure Means of procuring, and continuing to our selves and Posterity, a solid & lasting Blessing of our honest Endeavours.

My Conduct hitherto, I am perswaded, will witness for me, that I have no private Views of my own Ends to gain, and that I have nothing more at Heart, than the real Interest of the Colony: Were not this my indispensable Duty as well as Inclination, I am strictly enjoyned by our Worthy Proprietors, to do every thing that lies in me to promote the true Interest of the Province. And I take this Opportunity again to assure You I shall always (while I have the Honour to be the Head of the Administration) find a most sensible Pleasure in concurring with you, in every Thing that may conduce to the true Benefit and Advantage of the Good People you represent.

What the Service of the Publick requires will naturally fall under your Notice. I shall only here recommend to you Unanimity and Dispatch in all your Affairs, and what further may occur shall be communicated to your House by Message.
P. Gordon.

PHILADELPHIA Jan. 24. The Honourable Patrick Gordon Esq; Lieutenant Governour of the Province of Pennsylvania, &c.

The Address if the Representatives of the Freemen of the said Province in General Assembly met, this 24th Day of the Month called January, 1727-28. in Answer to the Governour's Speech of Yesterday.

May it please the Governour,
It is with the greatest Chearfullness that we do embrace every Opportunity to express, in the best Manner we can, our Loyalty and most Dutiful Obedience to George the Second, our rightful Prince and Liege Sovereign, and it is a great Satisfaction to this House, that the Governour does approve of our Sincere and Honest Endeavours to demonstrate the Zeal and Affection which the People whom we represent have for the King, and all the Branches of his Royal and most Illustrious Family.

The Governour most justly observe that the Harmony and Unanimity which appears amongst people of all Ranks, to express an entire Satisfaction in the present most happy Establishment of the Royal Family, with full Dependence on the

King's paternal Care for the supporting all his Subjects in their highest and greatest Concerns, is under God, the best Means to secure Peace at home, and to establish the British Interest abroad and we hope that we & our Successors from Time to Time will never be wanting in our little Sphere to intimate as near as, we can, that great Example which the Government has been pleased to let before us.

At the same Time, That we declare our selves perfectly Satisfied with the Governour's Conduct hitherto, we beg leave to hope, that as he is strictly Enjoyned by the Honourable Family to do every Thing that lies in his Power to promote the true Interest of this Province, we may firmly depend on the Favourable Assurances which the Governour is pleased to give us, That he will concur with this House in every Thing which may conduct to the true Benefit and Advantage of the good People whom we Represent; and under that Dependance we do assure the Governour, that we shall not be wanting to provide an Honourable Support for his Government, Signed by Order of the House.   David Lloyd, Speaker.

To which the Governour returned the following Answer.

Gentlemen;
I Heartily thank you for this obliging and kind Address, and in Return I promise You, That on all Occasions, no Endeavours of mine that may contribute to the Prosperity of the good People of this Province, shall ever be wanting.

PHILADELPHIA Feb. 6. Whereas there is a Letter Directed to Arthur Oliver in Pennsylvania, Dated Tollard-Royal September 29th, 1727. And Signed Mary Derryman, expressing the meaning of the Superscription to be according to her Sons Direction to who she Writes but does no time Name his otherwise than calling him Dear Son, and neither she nor the Son being known to Arthur Oliver, He therefore Publishes this Advertisement that the Person may know of such a Letter and have it, and thereby be inform'd of the Circumstances of divers of his Relation living, and of Money left him, by an Uncle that is deceas'd &c.

To be sold, a very good Engine, Screw and twenty four new Boxes with all the Necessaries convenient and fit for Cutting, Working and Spinning Tobacco. Also a very good Copper Still of near ninety Gallons, with Worm and all Materials fitting for the same; Note, the Owner thereof hath convenient Stores fit for setting up said Engine, &c. Also a very good and Convenient Still-House which he will let for Years, at a reasonable Rent. Enquire of John Danby at his House, on the Old Tunn Wharf, near Robert Ellis's Wharf in the Ware-Street.

Very good Barbadoes Rum to be Sold by William Bancroft, Baker in Wallnut Street Philadelphia.

Choice New-England Rum, preferable to any of this Country Spirits, to be sold at 2 s. 8 d. per Gallon, by the Hogshead, by Peter Bayton who will if desired allow reasonable Time for Payment.

PHILADELPHIA Feb. 13. We have Account from Maryland, That a large Ship laden with Tobacco, was drove on shore there with the Ice, and her Cargo all Spoil'd.

To be sold by Publick Vendue, at Nottingham in Chester County, on the 8th Day of March next, the Plantation of Stephen Stapler, late deceased, containing 340 Acres, with a Dwelling House and Barn, whereof is cleared, and within Fence about 45 Acres, ten of that being good Meadow, sowed with English Grass Seed, accommodated with a good Orchard well Planted, and of the Compass of about three Acres, distant half a Mile from Merchant Mill, and 12 Miles from Navigable Water, the Condition of Sale are as follow. viz. The highest Bidder the Byer, one half the Price to be paid down, and the other half in 9 Months after Sale, good Security to be given if required: The vendue is to be kept at the same Place.

PHILADELPHIA Feb. 19. Whereas several Persons have Applyed to the Loan-Office to borrow upon Mortgage of the Lands &c. whose Titles being Inspected many of which Trustees cannot approve of as the Law directs, and some Money being now in the Office, and more may be daily Expected to be Paid in as usual. Therefore all Persons concerned, are desired to get their Titles made good, according to the Direction of the several Acts, in Order that the several Sums allow'd may be paid them and also those who took up money last Year, may take this Notice that their annual Payments were due the 17th of January last and all Defaulters will be Prosecuted for Non Payment according to Law.

PHILADELPHIA Feb. 27. To be Sold, on Board a Ship now laying at William Fishbourn's Wharf, a Parcel of likely Servants, very reasonable for ready Money.

To be Sold by Mary Owen, Executrix of Evan Owen. Late of Philadelphia, deceased, Four Hundred Acres of good Land well Timber'd and Water'd lying near Poole Forge; also Two Hundred and Fifty Acres of good unimproved Land, whitin a Mile of Coldbrook-deal Furnace: The Price and Condition of Sale whereon, are to be Enquired after from the said   Mary Owem.

PHILADELPHIA March 5. To be Sold by William Dobbs in the Front Street, opposite the Pewter Platter in the City of Philadelphia, very good Turpentine, by Wholesale or Retail as reasonable as you can agree.

All Persons who are Indebted to Roger Edmonds of the City of Philadelphia, are desired forthwith to come and pay the same or they may be expected further Trouble: And also all Persons that he is indebted to are desired to come and receive the same, for he designs in a short time to leave the City. These are likewise to forewarn all Persons from Trusting his Wife Deborah on his Account, (she being Eloped from him) for he will pay none of her Debts.

On the 26th of this Instant March, will be Exposed on Sale by Publick Vendue, at the Oil Mill in Kriesheim, in German Township a certain piece or parcel of Land, containing about fifty Acres where of fourteen are Cleared, together with Oil Mill and Appurtenances: Whoever has a mind to buy is desired to be there on the Day above said, by   Henry Sellen.

The Drops known by the Name of Mary Baristers Drops, (or the Goulden Spirit of Right Venice Treacle) are to be had at Henry Hodge's. in in Market street Philadelphia.

Friday last being the Anniversary of the birth of Her present Majesty, our most Gracious Queen, the same was observed here with the usual Solemnity: In the Evening there was a handsome Entertainment at his Hounour's House, where were present a great many Ladies and Gentlemen, and concluded with a Ball, which lasted till 2 a-Clock in the morning.

PHILADELPHIA March 14. On Sunday last about 3 a-Clock in the Afternoon, the following unhappy Accident happen'd, to six Boys who went from the City in an open Boat Pleasuring; They design'd to cross the River over to Gloucester, and in their way one of them lost his Hat over-board, the wind being very high at N. W. and they not understanding how to manage the Boat, Tack'd about all on a sudden and endeavour'd to take up the Hat, with their Sails haul'd taught a blast, which occasion'd the Boat to overset and, three were drown, and the other three were saved from perishing in the Waves, (thro' the Divine Providence of the most Merciful God) by some Persons who went in Boats from the City to their Assistance.

ANNAPOLIS March 16. Last Thursday Night, Mr. Amos Garrett was inter'd in a Vault built for him near the Door of our Parish Church, with more Solemnity then ever was known in the Province.

The Manner of the Procession need not be inserted here, because so many Hundred Persons that were invited from all the Counties in the Province, were Eye-Witnesses to it. His Funeral Sermon, suitable to the Occasion, was preach'd by Rev. Mr. Humphreys; but the Church was so through'd thar some Hundreds could not get in. The Expense of the Funeral, 'tis said amounts to 6 or 700 Pounds ——— He was a Batchelour, between 50 and 60 Years of Age, and hath left a very plentiful Estate among the Relations, which he acquired by his extraordirnary Diligence. He was the first, Mayor of this City, and the only Survivor of all the Gentlemen nam'd in the Charter; was a punctual and exact Dealer, a useful man of Trade, and 'tis believed will be much missed by many.

PHILADELPHIA March 19. Run away fron the Iron Works on the French-Creek, in the County of Chester, a Servant Man named Richard Snaggs, of a very short Stature, about 26 Years of Age, of a Swarthy Complection, and has a Scar over one of his Eyes, and goes a little lane with his feet, his Hair is cut off, and sometimes wears a little short light colour'd Wigg: He has a grey Kersey Jacket, and Breeches, with small Pewter Buttons, Whoever secures said Servant so that his Master may have him again, shall have Fifty Shillings Reward, and Reasonable Charges paid by us,   William Branson, Samuel Ness.

PHILADELPHIA March 21. Two Miles above Amboy Ferry, upon the Rariton River, there is a Plantation to be Sold, which is well accommodated with Meadow, convenient for raising and keeping Stock Cattle. Upon which Plantation there is a Saw Mill, and Land well stored with Trees suitable for Timber and Boards. There is also two Negroe Men to be Sold, and Cattle, Horses, an Ox Team, and all Utensils for Husbandry. Whoever is inclined to buy the same or any Part thereof, may apply to the Widow Gordon, living upon said Plantation, who will dispose of the Plantation upon reasonable Terms.

Run away from Isaac Norris, 2 Weeks past, a Negroe Man named Peter, this Country born, about 30 Years of Age (having Variety of Cloaths 'tis uncertain which he may be found of) but went away in a new Leather Jacket and Breeches, a brown Kersey loose Coat, Shoes and Stockings. Whoever shall bring him to me or secure him in the Work-House of Philadelphia, shall be duly rewarded for doing, by   Isaac Norris.

A Boarding School, also reading, writing, Cyphering, Dancing, and several sorts of Needle work, at the Home of George Brownwell in second Street Philadelphia.

PHILADELPHIA March 28. To be sold by Mrs. Magerete Ryley, Widow and Executrix of Dr. Patrick Ryley, deceased, a House, Wharf, and Water-lot in New-Castle, at present in the Tenure and Possession of Mr. Henry Newton, the House is two Stories high, contains eight large Rooms, six whereof have Chimneys, and two Kitchens, well built with Stone, and also Cellars needful and dry; and is scituated in the Front-street; As also an other House and large Lot, at present in the Possession of George Graham, Hatter being the corner Lot and House next to the Great Road which leads to Maryland, and Chrstiana Bridge: As also 150 Acres of Land scituated in the County of New-Castle, in George's Hundred, and adjoyning to the Land of Mr. Andrew Peterson. Whoever inclines to purchase may repair to New-Castle on the third Day of May next, at which Time the aforesaid Houses, Lots, and Land will be exposed to sale, by way of publick Vendue.

PHILADELPHIA April 4. For the Benefit of Trade and Correspondence.

This is to give Notice, that on Friday the third Day of May next, a Post will set out from this City Philadelphia, to proceed by the Way of Chester, New-Castle, &c. down the Western Shore of Chesapeak-Bay, to the City of Annapolis in Maryland. To return from there on the Eastern Shore to Philadelphia. The Stage to be perform'd evry fortnight except the Three Winter Months, then only once each Month, For the conveniency of Merchants, &c. proper Persons will be appointed at Chester, New-Castle, and the several Counties of Maryland to receive Letters and Pacquets which shall be delivered with Judicial Care.

The said Post-Office will be kept at the House of Andrew Bradford in Philadelphia, and William Parks in Annapolis; Notice shall be hereafter given of all the other Places on the Road that shall be fix'd on for Reception of Delivery of Letters.

These are to give Notice that the House and Land in Gloucester, formerly belonging to Richard Bull, Deceased and by him sold to Nathaniel Tylee deceased, is to be Sold to the highest Bidder, at Gloucester, on the 25th Day of April 1728, by Sarah Bull, to whom the same is conveyed by the said Nathaniel Tylee, by Order of the Court of Chancery of New-Jersey, in order to the sale thereof for the Payment of the said Richard Bull's Debts.

The term of Sales are to be seen in the hands of said Sarah Bull.

Whereas Mary Horfman an Indented Servant Woman of Mr. Samuel Ferguson's of New-Castle, was by him legally Sold, on the 27th of July last, to John Copson of North-East in Cecil County Maryland, which Servant Woman hath hitherto absconded from Master's Service, this is therefore to forewarn all Persons from Entertaining or Imploying her. And if any Person will give an Account where she may be secured to the Printer hereof, they shall be Satisfied. Joseph Copson.

FREEHOLD NEW-JERSEY April 5. Run away from Joseph Forman, a Servant Man named William Conally, an Irishman, a Weaver by Trade of a middle Stature, about 25 Years of Age, thin Face, long Nose, something Pockfrotten, dark brown Hair sometimes Curling his Eyes a little inclined to be sore, he has on an old Felt Hat, Brown Coat and Wastcoat something ragged. Whoever secures said servant so his Master may have him again shall have Forty Shillings Reward, and all other reasonable Charges paid by   Joseph Forman.

ANNAPOLIS April 6. Corn in this Province is so very scarce that the Justices of the several County Courts have made Melancholy Representation to his Excellency the Governour, That the People are greatly apprehensive of a common want of the Substance. Whereupon his Excellency has Published a Proclamation so prohibiting the Exportation of Corn out of this Province till October next.

At the Assizes held here for Anne-Arundel County, the 8th Instant, Robert Martin and Henry Templeman receiv'd Sentence of Death for Felony and Burglary.

PHILADELPHIA April 11. Upon seeing an Advertisement Publish'd in the Mercury, the 4th of this Instant April, That a certain House and Land in Gloucester, is to be sold to the highest Bidder the 25th Instant. It is conceived Proper further to Advertise, that Isaac Norris of Fairfield in the Province of Pennsylvania, hath a true and Absolute Conveyance without any covin made to him about Four Years ago, by Nathaniel

Tylee, on a Valuable Consideration, then truly paid for a certain Messuage Commonly call'd the Malt-House, wherein the said Tylee then dwelt, together with Twenty Lots in the said Town of Gloucester, with other Lands adjacent. And all it may concern, are desired to take Notice, that the said Norris hath never alinated his Property therein and hopes it may in Time appear, that he is not legally diverted thereof.

NEW-YORK April 15. This Day his Excellency John Montgomerie, Esq; Governour of this Province, arrived here in his Majesty's Ship ——— Capt. Long Commander: He was received at the Water side by his Excellency Governour Burnet, attended by the Gentlemen of his Majesty's Council, the Corporation, and a great number of the Gentlemen and Merchants of this City; from there he walked to the Fort (a Company of Haltertiers and a Troop of Horse marching before, and the Council, Corporation, Gentlemen and Merchants following, the Streets being lin'd on each side with the Militia) where on his entering he was saluted by the discharge of the Cannon; and after publishing his Commission he walked (attended as before) to the City Hall, where it was also published amidst a vast Concourse of People, and then returned to the Fort. The Militia then drew up on the Parade, and saluted him with three Vollies. The same day his Excellency was pleased to publish the following Proclamation.

Whereas his Majesty by his most gracious Letters present, bearing date at Westminster the fourth day of October, in the first Year of his Majesty's Reign, has thought fit to constitute and Appoint me Captain General and Governour in Chief of his Majesty's Province of New-York and Territories thereon depending in America. I therefore for his Majesty's Service thought fit, with the Advice of his Majesty Council of the said Province, to order and direct, and I do, by virtue of the Powers and Authorities unto me granted by his said Majesty's Letters Patent, hereby order and direct to all Officers, Civil and Military, within the said Province do continue in their several respective Offices and imployments until further Orders. Of which all his Majesty's Subjects in the said Province are to take Notice, and govern themselves accordingly.

   Given under My Hand and Seal at Fort George in New-York, the fifteenth Day of April, in the first year of the Reign of our Sovereign Lord George the Second by the Grace of God of Great-Britain, France and Ireland, King, Defender of the Faith &c.
Annoq; Domini, 1728   John Montgomerie.
   By his Excellency's Command M. Bobin, D. Sec.

   To his Excellency John Montgomerie, Esq; Captain General and Governour in Chief of his Majesty's Province of New-York, New-Jersey, and Territories depending thereon in America, and Vice Admeral of the same &c.

   The Humble Address of the Mayor, Recorder, Aldermen & Commonlity of this His Majesty's most ancient City & Corporation of New-York in America.

   May it please your Excellency,
Your Excellency's safe Arrival gives us a most welcome Testimony of the Divine Protection over your Excellency's Person and this Province, and at the same time, the desirable Assurance of His Majesty's early Goodness to this, so Distant a part of his Dominions.

   Sir, behold, with inexpressible Joy that delightful Prospect which naturally arises to the People whom you Govern, from those conspicious Qualities which compose your Excellency's Character: Your excellency's long and near Access to the best of Princes, your Seat in the British Parliament, and your Military Accomplishments, are so many Garantys to the Colony, for the Enlargement of our Trade, and Security of our Frontiers, and the Preservation of our Liberties and Prosperities.

   As this Corporation is a considerable part of our Excellency'd Government, we desire leave, in the name of this City, to assure your Excellency of our Loyalty, Fidelity and Obedience to his most Excellent Majesty, King George, and that we will always Zealously and Affectionately do our utmost to render your Excellency's

Administration safe, Happy and Prosperous.

Sir, we humbly Recommend our Antient Rights and Privileges to your Patronage and Protection.

We are may it please your Excellecy, Sir, Your Excellency's most Obedient and most humble Servants.

PHILADELPHIA April 18. Whereas they may some Scruple arise, in Persons that may have occasion to purchase Servants by reason there has lately arrived to the Port a Ship from Bristol, hence by Authority by reason of some indisposition amongst the People, this is to inform those that may have Occasion to Purchase, that there is several very likely Servant Men, and Lads Times, Tradesmen and Husbandmen to be disposed of, on Board the Brig. Faro, Thomas New, Master, who arrived here about Six Days since, all in perfect Health, you may agree with said Commander on said Brig, or at the sign of the Scale.

Philadelphia April 28. Ran away the 4th of this Instant April, from Joseph Brittain of Crosswicks in New-Jersey, a Servant Man (lately belonging to Isaac Watson near Trenton-Town) named John Henry a lusty Man, fresh Complexion and I.H. prict with Gunpowder on one of his Hands, when he went away he had on a light Colour'd Bob Wigg, a good Felt Hat a new Kersey Coat of a Snuff colour, a Blew and white striped Linnen Jacket, a Pair of old Leather Breeches, a pair of gray Stockings, old Shoes, he has three Scars on his Head, suppos'd to be cut with a Sword. Whoever takes up the said Servant and give Notice to his Master, or to Joseph Peace in Bristol, so that he may have him again shall have twenty Shillings and Reasonable Charges paid by, Joseph Brittain, Joseph Peace.

A Lusty Negroe Man to be sold inquire Anthony Duebe, (Commonly called the French Glover) in the Front-street.

BURLINGTON May 7. To his Excellency John Montgomerie, Esq; Captain General and Governour of New-Jersey, New-York, and the Territories there on depending in America, and Vice Admiral of the same, &c.

The humble Address of the Chief Justice, second Judge, High Sheriff, Practitioners of the

Law, and Clerk of the Peace, at the Supreme Court held at Burlington, for the Western-Division, of the Province of New-Jersey, on the Seventh Day of May, in the First Year of his Majesty's Reign, Annoq. Domini, 1728.

May it Please your Excellency,
Your safe and Happy Arrival in your Government, has diffused an universal Joy through this Province, and we heartily embrace this first Opportunity to assure your Excellency of our most Dutiful and willing Obedience to the Authority vested in you by the best of Kings, and we shall as far in us lies, influence all that are within our compass to preserve in the same, and likewise study the most suitable method to render your Government prosperous and Happy, not doubting of our share in the many Blessings of your Excellency's most prudent Administration, which we heartily desire may be long over us.

We humbly beg, that your Excellency will be pleased (when you think most convenient and proper) Transmit our Humble Address to his Majesty to whose Person and Government (according to our Duty) we promise unseigned Fidelity and true Allegience.

May your Excellency enjoy a confin'd Health, and all other Happiness imaginable, and that your name and Honour May be transmitted unstain'd to succeeding Ages, is the Hearty wish of, May it Please your Excellency, Your Excellency's most Obedient and most Humble Servants.

We the Grand Jury being the People called Quakers, agree to the Matter and Substance of this Address, but make some objections to the Stile.

Which Address his Excellency received very Favourable, and was please to say, that he would Transmit the Address (directed to his Majesty) by the very first Opportunity.

PHILADELPHIA May 14. Last Friday, two Persons arrived here, sent from the back Settlements of this Country, to acquaint the Governour, That a Party of strange Indians had committed several Insults upon the Inhabitants, whereupon a Skirmish ensued which very much alarm'd the Neighbours.

The Governour immediately called such, of his Council as we were near, to advise what was necessary to be done, and some resolved to go in Person, to be truly informed of the Matter; accordingly by Noon the same Day, he mounted, accompanied by the Mayor, Recorder, and several other Gentlemen of the Ciry, and reach'd Parkeawning that Night being about 25 Miles N. W. from Philadelphia. The next Morning very early the Governour set forward, and about Noon came to Colebrook Dale Iron-Works, being joyned on the Road by a considerable Number of the Inhabitants, here he found several Persons that were Present in the Skirmish, who gave the following Account of what happened: That for 8 or 10 Days past, a Party of about 11 Indian Men (Strangers to the Inhabitants) arm'd with Guns, Pistols and Swords had liv'd at Free-quarters on the People, and taken from them by force their Provisions, and threatened them if they refused; they also compelled Persons to go with them, from one Plantation to another, making their Demands as they went, which increased the Fears of the People for that they resorted together, to consult what was best to be done, imagining that a greater Body of Indiams might be near at Hand, whereupon about 20 Persons with some Fire-Arms, went after them, and coming up with them, sent 2 of their Company without any other Arms but Hand or Walking-Sticks, to demand of the Indians from whence they came, and what was their Business there: The Chief of them Approached, with his Drawn Sword or Cutlass in one Hand, and a Gun in the other, and made several Attempts on the Head of one of the Men, but he being pretty well acquainted with the use of a Stick, defended himself, and sunk the Indian, who recovering himself, let go of his Gun, and ordered the rest of the Indians to fire on our People, which they did, & wounded three Men; whereupon our People returned the Fire, and shot down the Indian Captain, who rising again was carried off by 2 of his Company, who together retired into the Wood, where our People did not incline to follow them.

The Governour having taken several Informations

and given Directions to the Chief of the Inhabitants of those Parts, how to behave for the Future, he returned late in the Evening to Parkeawning, where he had lodged the Night before. About Midnight a Messenger came with a disagreeable News of the Murder of one Indian Man, and two Indian Women, who liv'd in the Neighbourhood, which induced the Governour to repair to a Place called Monotonsy, about 12 Miles higher up the River Schuylkil, where three of the Murderers are brought before himself and two Justices of the Peace, and examined accordingly.

The Examination of the Malefactors publickly taken and signed by themselves, 'tis presum'd, will give the best Account of the Barbarous Action: The Murderers were committed to the Custody of the Sheriff of Philadelphia County to be Convey'd to Chester Goal, in order for tryal.

After which the Governour dispatch'd the Coroner with some other Persons to take care that the Dead Indians should be buried, which as yet lay exposed to the wild Beast, and to assure the Indians in those Parts, that this Murder was Committed without his Knowledge of Approbation, and that the Murderers were sent to Prison, and to be laid in Irons till they should be Tryed in such a Manner, as if they had kill'd so many English.

The Governour also sent Messages to the Indians on the French Creek who accordingly came; he gave them the Assurance of his Friendship, and inform'd them of what had happened, they expressed themselves Satisfied therewith, and took their leave with great Respect. After the Governour had given the People his further Advice and Directions he returned to this City (still accompanied with several of the Gentlemen who he set out with him) the 14th Instant.

The Governour Intends to set out for Conestogoe the next Week, in order to meet and Treat with the several Nations of Indians.

PHILADELPHIA May 15. The Speech of the Honourable Patrick Gordon, Esq; Lieutenant Governour of the Province of Pennsylvania, &c. to the House of Representatives the 15th of this Instant May.

Mr. Speaker and Gentlemen of the House of Representatives.

Tho' I have resolved never to interfere with Proceedings of the House of Representatives, in what concerns their Privileges, of which you are most usually the Judges; yet the last Breaking up of the House has given me no small uneasyness, I shall notwithstanding on your present coming together again, by Summons, recommending it to your all to fall on the most pacifick Measures that may be thought of for making up this Breach, with a due Regard to the Rights and Privileges of the House, which I hope you will all be equally careful to support and Maintain.

But you will find it absolutely necessary from some late unhappy Occurrence in the Province, that all needless Disputes, which might reward your Consultation, should now be laid aside.

On Friday Last, the 10th Instant in the Morning I received an Account from the Iron-Works Mahanatawney, That some Strange Indians very well armed had fallen in amongst his Majesty's Subjects in the Neighbourhood, and had been guilty of such Violence, That some of the People believed it incumbemt on them to know who they were and what their business. They endeavoured to treat with those Indiand in the Civilest Manner, upon which they were attack'd, and Hostilities immediately passed between them, to the wounding of divers of our People, and not without some Execution, as 'tis believed, on the others.

On the first Account I immediately prepared to visit those Parts, and with divers Gentlemen who kindly accompanied me, some of whom have proved herein very serviceable to the Publick, I sett out in a few Hours, and found the Country under very great Terror and Surprized, but this was gradually dissipated, and the People hearing no more Enemies (those first being gone off) began to be appeased; when we were again alarmed by a fatal Accident in the Murder of Three harmless Indians, a young Man and two Women, of our own friendly Nations, who were most inhumanly knock'd in the Head, by three or Four of our People, and this without any Manner of Provocation from the sufferers that I could Possibly learn; of all which you may have a more particular Narrative if Desired.

On this last information, I immediately cased a Hire and Cry to be issued for Apprehending the Mutherers, Three of whom were taken, and are now in Chester Goal, but another, no less deep in the Guilt, when I left the place was not found.

Hearing that some other of our Indians, who were not far from that Neighbourhood, I called them in to acquaint them, in the most proper Manner, with the unhappy Accident: Care is also taken to give Deceased, good decent Burial. But as I am informed, to some of our Indian Chiefs, we cannot expect but that so barbarous a Fact must be resented. I have taken all the measures in my Power, that on the best Advice could be thought proper to prevent the worst Impressions on them, or to remove them if made, and as I am enabled shall proceed in whatever shall then be thought rationally practicable for that End. I have already desired as many of those Indians as I could find Messengers to reach, that they would meet me next Week at Conestogoe, where I have appointed as General a Treaty as can be compassed in that Time, for you will agree (I believe) That in the Cases, Delays ought by all Means to be avoided.

But there is farther absolute necessity that Messages with some small presents should be forthwith dispatched to divers other Parts of the Country especially up the River Delaware, who ought by all means to be seasonably informed of the real Truth of the Matters, to prevent all Mis-understandings from these Quarters.

I am also further to acquaint you Gentlemen, Thar last Night I received Advice from Conestogoe, bu return of the Express, I had sent from hence thither, on Friday last, That some of the Chiefs of the Five Nations, are to be here with us in Philadelphia, on a friendly Visit of which good Use may be made: Seeing all our Indians of these Parts, have an entire Dependence on those Nations.

That these Proceedings, Gentlemen, must necessarily Occasion an Expence you cannot be unsensible: But these People, and the due Effects of such Quarrels are considered, you will undoubtedly allow it to be the highest Prudence to prevent, by an early and seasonable Application of proper Remedy, the Calamities that other of his Majesty's Subjects have been distressed with, in some of the American Colonies: I therefore most seriously recommend it to you Gentlemen, That without Delay on any Pretence whatsoever, you would in behalf of the Country by whom you are intrusted, assist me with your Advice, and make such Provisions as may enable me effectually to put Practice those Necessary Measures I have already mentioned for Establishing the Publick Peace; and thus you may assure your Selves, that I shall decline no toil or Fatigue on my Part that may contribute to so good an End.

P. Gordon.

PHILADELPHIA May 17. To the honourable Patrick Gordon, Esq; Lieutenant Governour of this Province of Pennsylvania.

The address of the Representatives of the Free Men of the Province of Pennsylvania, in the General Assembly met, the 17th day of May, 1728. In answere to the Governour's Speech of the 15th Instant.

May it please the Governour,

We are most sensibly affected with the uneasiness given the Governour, by the late conduct of some of the Members of our house, and the more so because of the unhappy Delay it has given to the Publick Business, the Dispatch of which is so Necessary, and has been so Heartily recommended to us by the Governour, with repeated Assurance of his ready Concurrence is whatever may be for the good of the People of this Province.

We do with Gratitude acknowledge the Governour's Justice in declining to Interfere with the proceedings of the House of Representatives in what concerns their Privileges, and Hope such a Conduct will always meet with Acknowledgement due to a Resolution so just and Honourable, in not taking the Advantage of the Weakness or

Willfulness of such of the said Members, as would rather give up our most valuable Privileges to their own Resentments, that suffer themselves to be governed by the most just and well known Rules of Law and Reason, in being concluded by a Majority or Double their Number; but being now met in Obedience to the Governour's Summons, upon Consideration of what he has been pleased to communicate to us, we think it our indispensable Duty to do every Thing in our Power, to prevent the fatal Consequences that may attend any Mis-understandings with the Indians.

And herein we beg Leave to say, we have not proceeded rashly, for notwithstanding the great Slight shewed to all the friendly Invitations, we made to these Members to return to their Duty, when the left the House of the 20th Day of April last, we have since our present Meeting, in most pressing and civil Manner again requested and required them to give their Attendances in the House, for the Service of the Country, which they did not think fit to do: And that nothing might be wanting on our Part, and to convince them if Possible how much we were disposed to give them an Opportunity of returning to their Duty; we duly acquaint them that the Governour had been pleased to lay before us, an Account of some unhappy Occurrences lately fallen out in this Province, which called for the serious and speedy Consideration of this House; and require their Attendance in Assembly for that Purpose. But this, as all other Attempts of the Kind have proved uneffectual, and they still continue to absent themselves, which, as we continue, shew plainly how much their private Resentments, for no having every Thing accorded to which they desire, are dearer to them than even Peace and Safety of the Province itself: For were it otherwise, they would undoubtedly have extended to us (who are now above double their Number) some small Part of the Charity they claim themselves, and allow us, at least (supposing we had been mistaken in our Judgement) to act from the Principal of Conscience, the only reason they Assign for what they do themselves.

It would have been very agreeable to us, to have had the Assistance of the said Members, but as they cannot be had, we should hold our selves accountable for the Evils that may attend any Neglect on our Part, if we did not apply our selves, with all Care and Zeal we are capable of, to have such measures as may restore the Province to it's former Peace and Security. It is therefore of Necessity, That we now enter upon Business, and we conceive our selves well warranted, by the Royal Charter granted to the Proprietor and People of this Province as well as by our Laws, in proceeding with so great a Majority of the Representatives of the Freemen of Pennsylvania, so we hope the Governour will be of the same Opinion; and that the Law of Majority which takes Place, both in the common and Civil Law, will fully justify the Proceedings of the House, who have no other View but to preserve a peaceable People from the Invasion of a Cruel and unreasonable Enemy, and to support a Government preferable, as we believe, for the great Privileges enjoyed under it, to any other in America.

We are very thankful for the early Care and Pains taken by the Governour and the Gentlemen that assisted him, to apply the most proper Remedies then Practicable, to remove the fears of our Inhabitants, and the Prejudices and bad Impressions which the Indians might receive from so unhappy an Accident, as the Murther of Three of those People, who were in perfect Friendship with us: And as that, with the journey to Conestogoe, and the other Measures, proposed by the Governour to be taken in order to prevent the ill Consequences that may happen upon the People of this Province, and to continue and cultivate the Friendship which has always subsisted between us, will occasion an Expence: We therefore, in Pursuance of the Resolution of the House of the 27th of January last, proceeded to vote the Sum of One Hundred Pounds towards defraying the Charge of Meeting the Indians at Conestogoe; and the Governour may be assured, That this House will take care that provisions be made for defraying all the necessary Charges to have arisen, or that may arise by Reason of the other Negotiations. And as the Charge of visiting the Indians and renewing of Treaties of Peace and Friendship with them, from Time to Time, is advanced out of the publick Money, we conceive, That the said Treaties be laid before the House of Assembly. Signed by Order of the House, D. Lloyd Speaker.

PHILADELPHIA May 23. Some Mistakes having accidentally Happened in the Proclamation published in our last Weekly Paper, which the printer hopes, the Publick will pardon; it's thought proper to insert the same in this Paper, and is as follows:

By the Honourable Patrick Gordon, Esq; Lieutenant Governour of the Province of Pennsylvania and the Counties of New-Castle, Kent and Sussex upon Delaware.

A PROCLAMATION

Whereas by the Special Favours of the Divine Providence, and it's Blessing on the Endeavours of out late Honourable Proprietor, and the first Adventurers with Him, in the Settlement of this Colony; The inhabitants thereof have hitherto enjoy'd a continual Course of Peace and Tranquility, secured from all Hostilities, either by Invasion or Insurrection: To which nothing under the Divine hand, has more effectually contributed, than the prudent care that was then taken by the Proprietor to enter into a firm Alliance, and sincere Friendship with all the Indian Natives, at that time a numerous people, and whereas by several Treaties then made, it was especially Provided and agreed, That said Natives should be considered in all Dealings, and Converse with them, as our Friends and Brethren without Distinction: And by the like Care in this Government, the same Treaties have from Time to Time, been continued and confirmed, and by the sober and prudent Conduct of the ancient Settlers and their Successors, the first established Friendship has been hitherto without any interruption supported and maintained, to the great Benefit as well as Honour and reputation of this Government and it's European Inhabitants, as also of the said Natives, who

have not to this Time been Guilty of any failure
or Breach on their Part of the said Treaties.
But whereas by Persons of some rude insults from
a few Strangers Indians, who had ranged amongst
our Inhabitants, some Action tending to Hostilities ensued: Whereupon the People assembled
themselves in Companies, under an Apprehension
that those Robbers might be followed by much
greater Numbers: And since these Motions, a most
barbarous Murder has been committed, by some
furious Men, to the Bodies of Three harmless
and quiet Natives, our Friends: for which the
Malefactors have been happily seized, and are
in Custody, in Order to be tried and suffer Condign Punishment. Now for Prevention of all further and other Breaches of the established Peace
and Friendship, between Us and the said Natives:
I do by Virtue of the Power and Authority to me
derived, from the Kings Sacred Majesty, and the
Honourable Proprietors and Governour and Chief
of this Province, and adjacent Counties: Hereby
strictly Charge and Command all singular His
Majesty's Subjects the Europeans of whatsoever
Nation they be, who reside in this Province or
Counties, that on no pretence they abuse any
Indian Natives of the Nations around us, viz.
The Delaware, Conestogoe, Genesseo, Shawnee,
Mingoes, or those of the Five-Nations, or any
other coming and demeaning them selves peace-
fully amongst us; but that on all Occasions,
they treat all the said Indians, with the same
civil Regard that they would an English Subject:
And that by all means they avoid that unbecom-
ing Practice of expressing or shewing their
weak unhandsome Fears, by which they greatly
expose themselves to Remarks that are dishon-
ourable, but because on the last Alarm, Apprehensions have been raised of Insults from the
Foreign Indians. To the End that the inhabitants
may not in any such case (should it unfortunately happen) be unprovided. I do hereby Direct
and Require all his Majesty's Subjects within
the said Province and Counties, That they be at
all Times duly furnished with suitable Arms and
Ammunition for their Defence, to be used in case
of real Necessities, by Order and Directions of

Proper Officers, who shall be duly Appointed for that Purpose, And that they fail not to appear with them in proper Time and Place, if there should be Occasion to use them, in Defence of themselves, their Families and Country.

Given in Council at Philadelphia. under my Hand and great Seal of the said Province, the Seventeenth Day of May, in the first Year of the Reign of our Sovereign Lord George the Second by the Grace of God over Great Britain, France and Ireland, King Defender of the Faith, &c.

P. Gordon.

ANNAPOLIS May 28. By His Excellency Benedict Leonard Calvert, Governour and Chief, in and over the Province of Maryland.

A PROCLAMATION

Whereas the present great scarcity of Corn, our necessary Subsistence, the many late loses of Hogs, Cattle, and other Stock, and the numerous destroying Caterpillars which have infested our Woods, are such Signal grievous Distresses to the People of this Province, that they may be justly deem'd a visitation upon us from the Almighty, for our manifold Sins against him; The sense whereof, should induce us to a publick and sincere Humiliation of our selves before the Great God, to whom Vengence belongeth, that we may not suffer his whole Displeasure to arise against us. To the End therefore, that so timely and necessary a Duty may be the more unanimously performed throughout this Province, I have thought fit, by and with the Advice of his Lordships Council of State, to issue this my Proclamation. and I do hereby strictly Charge and Command that the Third Friday in June next, be observed as a Day of General Publick Fast and Humiliation, throughout this Province: And I do earnestly invite and require the Inhabitants of this Province to be religiously and strictly observant to the same, as they render the Favours of Almighty God, and on Pain of suffering such Punishment as may be justly inflicted for the Contempt or Neglect of so necessary and religious Duty. And for the more Solemn Performance of the same, I do hereby require the Ministers in their respective Parishes, to read Divine Service, and to Preach Sermons in their respective Churches on that Day, suitable to the Occasion. And I do further Charge and Command the several Sheriffs of the Province to cause this Proclamation to be Publish'd and read in the several Parish Churches, and other the most publick Places in their respective Counties, as they will answer the contrary at their Peril.

Given at Annapolis this 28th Day of May, in the Lord Proprietor's Dominion, &c. Anooq. Dom. 1728.

PHILADELPHIA May 30. Yesterday the Honourable Patrick Gordon, Esq; our Governour returned from Conestogoe, having finish'd the Treaty with the Indians of those Parts, to the entire Satisfaction of all that were present: This timely and prudent Management of the Governour's have made every Thing quiet and easy, and the Indians were so pleased, that they said, they never had such a Satisfactory Speech made to them, since the great William Penn spoke to them himself: His Honour was met some Miles from this City by Richard Hill, Esq; and divers Gentlemen, and Welcomed back with a very Handsome Collation in the Woods which that worthy Gentleman had provided: At the City Bounds his Honour was receiv'd in a genteel Manner, by Thomas Lawrence, Esq; our Mayor, and a very great Number of Gentlemen, as well Strangers as City Inhabitants, who with several Ladies in Coaches accompanied his Honour to his House: It's reckoned, the Calvalcade consisted of near 200 People, which is a far greater Number than has ever been known to meet together on such an Occasion at any Time before in this Province. We are told, that the Country People in and about Conestogoe, were so highly Satisfied with the Governours in every Part of his Conduct, that notwithstanding the Scarcity occasion'd by the late hard Winter, they brought in their own good will, large quantities of Provisions of all sort, and would take no pay for them. About 250 Men on Horse-back accompanied his Honour to the Indian Town, where the Treaty was held, and great Numbers flocked in from all Parts to pay their Complements to him, so that it is said there was never seen amongst the Inhabitants, a greater Harmony and a more Chearful Readiness to assist with what was in their Power than appeared on this Occasion, which is chiefly owing to the affable courteous Behaviour of our Governour.

PHILADELPHIA June 3. At the Court of General Quarter-Sessions of the Peace, held here this Day for the County of Philadelphia, a Charge was delivered from the Bench to the Grand-Jury of which the following is the close.

Gentlemen,
You, with all others the Inhabitants, must have observ'd the Emotion and unreasonable Panick, which lately poss'd great Numbers of People. It is true, something has happened which rais'd the Notice and Concern, not only of the Government, but of every good Man; but it is really surprising to hear of the many idle, groundless and Lying Stories, which have been bruited and thrown out, to alarm and disturb the People, some of which may have arisen from Ignorance and Fear; but we wish it were less obvious, that much more have proceeded from a wicked Design against the Peace and Safety of the Country; We need not be more Particular, but hope every true Man will, in his Mind, mark such Incendiaries.

You will see published the Governour's Treaty with the Indians on the Susquahanna and some of Delawares about Brandy-wine: The Chiefs with other of the remaining Delawares, are now here at the Governour's request. You will find by the said Treaty, That there never was a more Amicable, open and hearty Freedom between us than at this Time; which appear'd as well in the Countenances and behaviours as in Words; and we doubt not the same now with these.

This is noted to you, That as you are dispers'd to several Parts of the Country, you may, as occasions offer, in all conversations, Endeavour to quit the Minds of the People, and perswade them, for the future not to hearken to, much less assist in spreading, Lyes and rediculous Tales. —— And we heartily wish it may not hereafter be observed. That the Indians are more calm and prudent than some of our People.

This in their Councils have discreet and just Ways of thinking, and Altho' they cannot but be touch'd with Grief, as in every honest Man among us, at such as the late unhappy Accident; yet they wisely make all give way to the strict League of Friendship, which hath from our first Settlements, subsisted between the Christians and them, and impute Crimes (especially when they perceive the Care of the Government) to the Madness, Folly and Wickedness of the Actors.

We shall close with this reasonable Hope of Assurance, That if we do not prove Almighty God by our Forgetfulness of Ham, and by the Immoralities, Animosities and Follies to scourge us that Way; there appears no Danger from the Indians. ——— We intreat you therefore to exite all the People to use them well, and give no Offence, as the Governour, by his Proclamation, has advertised and commanded; and let not that be done indiscreetly, either by tipling with them, foolish talking, or asking childish and impertinent Questions; expressing either a ridiculous Bravery one the one Hand, or foolish Fears on the other; but let it be with Manliness, Gravity, and Sobriety, as well as strict Justice: This will honour our Profession as Christians, and draw their Regards and Love to us as Englishmen.

PHILADELPHIA June 13. Run away from Archibald Craige of Freehold in East-New-Jersey, a Servant man named Joshua Nichols. he is a Man of Middle Stature of a fair Complection with his Hair off, it is of a light colour, he has on or with him, a homespun Coat and Vest the Coat is of a gray Colour trim'd with the same, the Vest Brown, with two pair of Shoes and two pair of Stockings one pair gray worsted Stockings, the other of moss Coulored, and a pair of Leather Breeches and a small Felt Hat, a double worster Cap, he has with him a large Wallet, he has two or three small Scars under his Chin, and says he was born in London, speaks very plain, a Stocking-Weaver by Trade. Whoever takes up the said Servant and secures him, so as his Master may have him again shall have Forty Shillings Reward and reasonable Charges paid by me   Archibald Craige.

Whereas Mary Horfman and Indented Servant Woman of Mr. Samuel Perguson's of New-Castle, was by him legally Sold, on the 27th of July last, to John Copson of North-East in Cecil County Maryland, which Servant Woman hath hitherto absconded from her Master's Service, this is therefore to forwarn all Persons from Entertaining or employing her. And if any Person will give an Account where she may be found to the Printer hereof, they shall be Satisfied.   John Capson.

N. B. If she returns to her Master's Service she shall be well received.

Men and Women Servants lately arrived from Bristol are to be sold by Tho. Willing at his Store on Carpenters Wharf.

PHILADELPHIA June 20. Run away the 10th of this Instant June from Andrew Bradford, of the City of Philadelphia, a Servant Man named Nicholas Classen a Printer by Trade, and a sprightly young Fellow about 21 Years of Age, fresh Complection much Pockfretten, and has on a grey Drugget Coat hem'd and trim'd with Black, a white Demity Jacket, also a white Fustian Coat with mettle Buttons, faced in the Neck with red velvit, a pair of Leather Breeches, and a pair of striped Linnen homespun Breeches, he wears a short Wigg, he has several other Cloaths with him, and good Shoes and Stockings (he formerly lived with William Parks Printer in Annapolis). Whoever takes up said Servant and brings him to William Bradford in New-York, or William Parks in Annapolis, shall have three Pounds Reward, and reasonable Charges paid by me
                                                    Andrew Bradford.

Run away the 4th of this Instant June, from Thomas Wilcox, a Servant Man, named Thomas Ryan, an Irish Man, of a short Stature, well set, short black Hair, somewhat curl'd (or he may have on a dark colour'd Wigg, which he had in his Pocket) of a fresh Complexion, he had on a Linsey Wolsey Coat with large Pewter Buttons, a brown Jacket, an Ozenbrig Shirt and Breeches, a good Raccoon Hat, grey Yarn Stockings, and a pair of new single Sole Shoes. Whoever secures the said Servant or brings him to the Work-House in Philadelphia, or to his Master in Concord

Chester County, shall have Forty Shillings as a Reward, and reasonable Charges. Thomas Wilcox.

PHILADELPHIA June 27. Run away the 19th Instant June, from Samuel Peele, William Chapman, and Richard Hill of London Town in Maryland, two Servants, one a middle siz'd young Man, named John Maynard, he has a pretty large black Beard, wears a dark Frize Coat, a Felt Hat, good Shoes and Yarn Stockings, and is an Irish Man. The other a short well set smooth faced young Man, named George Williams, he wears of brown Cloth or Drugget Coat, Ticken Breeches, a new Felt Hat, fine grey Worsted Stockings, has a white Shirt and several, check'd ones, he pretends to be a Gardener and is an English Man. They Travel'd on foot from the Head of South River towards Patapsco, and were then seen near Thomas Linthbicomes, on the 14th Instant, when they pretended to be Sailors discharged from some Ship in the South River. Whoever takes up and secures the said Servants shall have three Pounds Reward and reasonable Charges allow'd by the Owners.

CHESTER July 3. The Confession of Walter Winter, at the Place of Execution in Chester. on the Third Day of July 1728.

Gentlemen, and you Fellow-Creatures who are Spectators of the most unhappy and untimely End of two of your fellow-Mortals. Our Time as you see, is but very short before we suffer Death, which is justly due to me. and being an offender against the Laws of God and Man. You may expect me to say something (as now it will be the last that I shall speak you will hear from me) in relation to the Fact I have committed, which is the Occasion of my untimely End: You are sensible, I suppose, that it was the Killing some of the Neighbouring Indians back in the Woods. I shall by very short, not insisting to tire your Patience, my Brother John being very large in his Confession, which relates to both of us. It is most certain that John Roberts (who were a false Evidence against me in several Respects) sent for me to come and assist him, for he was afraid of some Strange Indians that he said was about his House, and that he was afraid they would kill him. When I went from home, I had no Ill-will towards the Indians nor did I design to kill any, if they were peaceable, and made no Assault upon us, I do here in Presence of you all confess that I kill'd an Indian Man, and shot a blunt Arrow at the Indian Girl, but she did not receive any Hurt. I declare, as God is my Judge, we had a strong Report among us, that there were Wars between the English and Indians, and that was the only Means that brought me to commit the wicked Murder upon the Innocent Indian. As for my Part, I thought at the Time that I did my Country, my Neighbours and Family Service; for I sincerely protest I did it with no other Intent, than to defend my self, and save Lives. It has been said by some, that I was accessory to my Mother's Death, but in the face of you, and before God, I utterly deny it, for I was wholly innocent of it in any manner Way or means whatsoever. Gentlemen, assist me with your Prayers to almighty God to receive my Soul.

JOHN WINTERS CONFESSION

Gentlemen I will here relate to you the Occasion of my untimely End. on Saturday two Weeks before the death of the Indian Woman I shot, I was at Manhatony, and Robert Stackers told me, that he did see a Man and talk'd with him, and the Man told him, that the Indians had kill'd his Wife and eight Children, and that they all lay dead at his House; and that Tulpehoken was cut off by the Indians, and that he saw fires in several Places. This occasioned me to make all speed Haste home I could that Day; and when I came home I heard to the contrary of what I was told at Manhatony; but I went that Night with my Wife and Child to Brother Walter's House, to secure our selves; for the Report of the Inhabitants that were among us, was, that there was an Indian War: And one Corweitus, an Indian, told my Father-in-Law, that the Indians would come and destroy the white People, and his Corn: This put us into a strong Fear of the Indians. About two weeks after this, my Brother Walter's Wife came and told me, that there was eleven Indians in a Swamp, and that there was Men in

Arms gone after them, and that the Indians had killed two white Men, and wounded three and Israel Robinson had sent them the News in a Letter, which he himself owned since to me and my Brother Walter. This caused me to be under more Fear of all the Indians than I was before; and I made what Haste I could from my Brother's House to my Father-in Law's to fetch a girl from thence that was related to me. Going along to Father's, I went by John Robert's House, and saw some Indians, but could not tell how many there was; and coming back with the Girl, I came by John Robert's House and told him I wondered he did not go to my Brother's House, because there we had appointed to meet, to secure our selves from the Indians, if they should make an Assault upon us. And as I was going home I meet my Brother Walter, and my Father-in-Law. Brother Walter desired me to go along with them; and Father told me, that Robert Stackers saw two of the white Men that were wounded by the Indians. so we concluded, if we saw any Indians, we would not kill them, but bind them, and carry them to Justice Boon's House, to know the Reason why they carried such Arrows and Weapons with them as they did. We all went to John Robert's House, and we saw an Indian Man sitting down on a Pile of Wood; and when he saw my Brother Walter come over the Bridge towards him, he took up his Bow, and fixed an Arrow to it, look'd streadfastly and earnestly to him; and he seeing him in that Posture, immediately shot him, and he fell to the Ground: With that he cryed out to me, Shoot, Shoot, and then I shot in among the Indians and killed an old Indian Woman named Hannah, but did not know it was she, until we had subdued the rest of them, which I thought were enemies to us. I struck another Woman two Blows with the Butt-end of my Gun, and knock'd her down; and then I struck down an Indian Girl, and pursued after more that were in the Swamp, but did no more. Then coming back from Pursuing them I saw John Roberts with an Axe stricking the Woman I knock'd down on the Head, and such a Place in her Scull that I could had laid my fist in it. At Night we went to Walter's House, and kept

Guard that Night for Fear of the Indians; and the next Day we went to John Roberts's House again, and that Woman which John Roberts struck with the Axe, was not dead, but groaned; and then John Roberts went to her with the same Axe and struck the edge of it in her Forehead, that she instantly died. John Roberts was false Evidence against me in several Respects, But I forgive him. Gentlemen I have neither flattered you nor my self in the Confession of mine: I thought all along they were the Enemy Indians, and that we killed them in Defence of our own selves, our Neighbours and Country. I am sorry for the Indians Deaths, that they were Barbarously put to Death by us when in we had known at the Time, we would not have been guilty of their Blood. I was no way or Means whatsoever guilty of my Mother's death, god, who is my judge, knows that I am innocent of it. I pray God to forgive all my Enemies, Persecutors, and them that owe me any Ill-will. And here I come to an End, praying God to forgive me my Sins, which are great and Many, and the great Sin, for which cause I die. I pray God, and I hope you will pray to God, to receive my Soul.

NEW-YORK July 8. On Saturday last his Excellency William Burnet Esq; late Governour of this Province, embark'd with his Family on board his own Schooner for Rhode Island, from thence to proceed by Land to Boston, to execute his Commissoin for the Government of the Massachusetts Bay in New-England.

MONMOUTH County New-Jersey July 9. Run away from Joseph Forman of Freehold, in the County aforesaid, a Servant Man named William Conally, an Irish Man, thin Faced, long Nose, something Pock-broken, dark brown Hair a little Curling, wore a new Oxenbrigs Shirt, an old Homespun Jacket an old Wool Hat, took with him a new pair of Leather heel'd round toe'd Shoes, and a pair of grey Yarn Stockings, any person that shall secure said Servant so that his Master may have him again, shall have Forty Shillings Reward and reasonable Charges paid by me   Joseph Forman.

PHILADELPHIA July 18. Run away the 8th day of July, from William Reed of Great Egg Harbour, a

Servant Man named Lawrence Conor, am Irish Man of a short Stature, aged about 26 Years of a Homely Complection and down Look, his Hair cut off a black beaver Hat, a Brown Duroy Coat Jacket and Breeches, one of the Puffs being out, muss coloured yarn Stockings, a Pair of Wooden heel'd Shoes, a pair of double barr'd Silver Shoe Buckles, a pair of Womens Silver Buckles, took away with him a large Dark brown Mare, with a Star in her Forehead Branded on the Buttock with OB the Mens Buckles mark't with AR and the Women's Buckles mark't with AA. Whoever takes up and secures the said Servant so as his said Master may have him again, shall have Three Pounds Reward and Reasonable Charges, paid by
Charles Crosley.

Several very likely young Negroes of both Sex, just arrived to be sold by George M'Call, Merchant, in Philadelphia, very reasonable.

NEW-YORK July 23. The Representatives chosen and elected to serve in General Assembly by the Province of New-York being this Day met, His Excellency our Governour made a Speech to them, which is the following, viz.

Gentlemen,
When His Majesty did me the Honour to appoint me Governour of this Province, I was very sensible of my Insufficiency for so great a trust: Yet I willingly undertook it, thinking it my Duty to serve my King & Country in whatever Station His Majesty was pleased to imploy me. It was no small Encouragement to me, to hear, before I left England, a general good Character of the Inhabitants of this Province, and I hope, after being some time long with you, I shall be able to Vouch it by Experience.

You are the free Choice & Representatives of the People, who I have so much reason to believe are well Principled, I hope are met together determin'd to support His Majesty's Government, by settling upon them a Revenue in as ample a manner, and at least for as long a time, as former Assemblies have given it to his Predecessors, by so doing you will Express your Loyalty & Gratitude to the best of Kings, who is able and willing to secure to you your religion Laws,

Liberties & Prosperity; Is ready to protect the Trade you are at present possess'd of, and is graciously resolved to encourage the Encrease of your Commerce & flourishing of your Manufactures.

I am fully Instructed to concur with you in every thing that is for the real Good and Interest of the Province, and to take particularly Care that you enjoy your Rights & Privileges in their full extent. At the same time I am Commanded to Support his Majesty's Royal Prerogatives, which I will do with the greatest Zeal, and if any Factions and Presumptuous Attempts be made against so Essential a part of the Constitution, I expect that you will Oppose it.

Gentlemen;
I confide so much in the good Intentions of this Assembly that I shall not propose to you any particular Method of Supporting the Government, or Securing the Province and its Frontier, where all Garrisons are in Ruinous Conditions. The Things I Recommend to you are for your Honour and Safety, and your doing them effectually will confirm his Majesty in the good Opinion he has of his Subjects here.   J. Montgomerie.

To his Excellency John Montgomerie, Esq; Captain General and Governour in Chief of the Province of New-York, New-jersey and Territories thereon depending in America, and Vice Admiral of the same &c.

We his Majesty's Dutiful and Loyal Subjects, the General Assembly of this Colony, do in the first place, humbly beg leave, in behalf of your selves, and those we Represent, sincerely and Heartily to congratulate your Excellency's safe Arrival among us, which, we assure you, was to general Satisfaction of the People, as it had been their ardent Whishes long before.

And in the next place, to return our hearty Thanks to your Excellency for the Favourable and Obliging Speech; and to assure you, that the several Matters therein Recommended to us, shall be maturely Considered, and in the course of our Proceeding, have their Weight, so far as the Circumstances of the Colony will reasonably allow; for we are met together with a Disposition to have equally at heart the Service of his Majesty and the Interest of the Country.

As we had from your long Seat in the British Parliament, from your long and near Attendance of His Majesty and from the Publick Declaration you have been pleased to make upon several Occasions Promis'd our selves under your Administration, the full Enjoyment of Liberties and Properties; so it was the highest Satisfaction to us, that your Excellency has assured the House, That these inestimable Blessings (the peculiar Rights of British Subjects) shall be secured and preserved to the People of this Colony.

And as among the many eminent Virtues of his sacred Majesty, he is known to be equally Tender of the Prerogative of the Crown, and the just Rights and Liberties of the People, so we assure your Excellency, That we shall not presume to encourage upon the One, and we conceive in our Indispensable Duty to preserve the Other. Signed by Order of the House.

Adolph Philipse, Speaker.

To which His Excellency was pleased to make the following answer,

Gentlemen,

I Thank you for your Address in which you express great Loyalty to the King, a dutiful regard to his Prerogative, and laudable Zeal for the Interest of your Country.

I take this Opportunity of telling you again, That his Majesty has Ordered me to preserve to you your just Rights and Liberties; in a grateful return, I expect you will Comply with what I have demanded for the Support of His Majesty's Government, Your own Honour and Safety.

J. Montgomerie.

PHILADELPHIA July 25. To be sold by William Bickley, the 16th Day of September next at Publick Vendue at Burlington, a Dwelling House, with a Brew-House, Malt-House, and Mill-House, ready fitted with utensils, proper for each Vocation: also to be sold a large Lot in High Street, in Burlington. Another good Tract lying between Burlington and the Ferry. A large Stone House adjoining to George Sattwerwalts. Any

Person inclined to buy any of the said Land or Houses may treat with the said Bickley at the Hemlock in Burlington and be further informed concerning the Price and Payments.

These are to give Notice, that there is to be sold in Whiteland Township, in the Great-Valley, a Plantation containing 250 Acres of Land, a Dwelling House Part Stone, and a good Barn, a young Orchard mostly Winter Fruit, Six Acres of English Grass near the House, Ten Acres of meadow within Fence, about a Quarter of a Mile from the Dwelling House and about Thirty more may be made; four Fields within Fence, containing about Sixty Acres in all the four: If any want to buy, they may enquire of David Worthington at Frankford, or George Clapoole in Philadelphia, and know further.

Run away the 16th of this Instant from John Pasmore of Kennet in Chester County, a Servant Man named Roger Burn, an Irishman aged about 27 Years, of a low Stature, something Freckl'd his hair cut off, he had a dark Wigg a dark Cloath Coat with Eight Brass Buttons, Ozenbrig Shirt, Course Linnen Breeches, a pair of grey Stockings and a Felt Hat. Whoever should take up said Servant and bring him to his Master, ot to the Wook-house in Philadelphia, shall have Forty Shillings, as a Reward and Reasonable Charges.

PHILADELPHIA Aug. 1. On the Nineteenth of September will be Exposed to Sale by Publick Vendue, one Hundred and Fifty Acres of Land within half a Mile from Bristol, in Bucks County, (Thirty Acres of which may be made good Meadow,) and some small Improvements nade thereon. Whoever hath a mind to be further inform'd concerning said Land, may apply themselves to Henry Hodge, or Francis Knowles in Philadelphia, or George Clough or John Hall in Bristol aforesaid.

To be sold, By Robert Ellis, a parcel of very likely Servants lately arrived, and most of them Tradsmen, at reasonable Rates for ready Money or Country Produce.

A Servant Woman a good Quilter and seamster, to be sold by Thomas Polgreen, next door to the sign of the Hat in Market-Street, note she has four Years to serve.

PERTH-AMBOY Aug. 3. On Tuesday last, a Special Court of Oyer and Terminer, held at this Place, on David Simes, Carprnter of the Brigantine Rachel and Betty of Whitehaven, was Tryed for the Murder of one John Grines, a Sailor on Board the said Vessel, on the 15th of July last. But it appearing to have been on a Sudden Quarrel between them, and the Vessels Crew giving the Prisoner a good Character, as being a Peaceable Inoffensive Man, the Jury found hin guilty of Manslaughter only & he was the same day burnt in the Hand.

BURLINGTON Aug. 3. Whereas at about Twelve a-Clock last Night, one James Carver and John Brightwell, being in the Custody of the Sheriff of the County of Burlington, and in the Goal of the said County, broke out the said Goal, and escaped from the said Sheriff; the said Carver being a tall Statur'd Man, bushy Hair, is by Trade a Mill-wright, aged about Forty Years; and the said Brightwell is a short thick squart Man, brown Complexion and about Twenty eight Years, has his own Hair cut off, is mean in Habit, by Trade a Taylor and Stay-maker. Whoever shall apprehend the said Escapers and give Notice thereof to John Allen, Samuel Eustist, Richard Allen Esq; or Thomas Hunloke, shr. of Burlington, so that they may be had again, shall have Ten pounds for said John Carver, and Five Pounds for John Brightwell, as a reward and reasonable Charges.

PHILADELPHIA Aug. 8. Run away the 31st of July last from his Master, Christopher Tomson of the City of Philadelphia, a Negro Man named Dick aged about 35 Years, he had on when he went away, a Kersey Double Breasted Jacket, with Brass Buttons, an Ozenbrig Shirt, and a fine Linnen one, a pair of course Linnen Breeches with a Brass Button on the Wastband he had several other Cloaths and has a Scar on his under Jaw. Whoever shall take up said Negro and bring him to his Master shall have Twenty Shillings Reward and Reasonable Charges.

PHILADELPHIA Aug. 15. Run away the 24th of June from Thomas Teatman of New-Castle County near Ellis Lewis Mill. A Servant Man named James Gobbs, he is a very short Stature, with short dark Curl'd Hair, a large mould on his Right side of his Chin, a tow, Shirt and Draws old leggins and Shoes. Whoever takes up said Servant and secure him, so that his Master may have him again, shall have reasonable Satisfaction paid by me   Thomas Teatman.

PHILADELPHIA Aug. 19. Run away the 15th of Instant August from Stephen Orion, and Company of Pricipio Iron-Works in Cecil County in the Province of Maryland, two Servant Men, one named Thomas Cheney, by birth a Welshman, but speaks good English, ages about 21 Years, of middle Stature round Visage small Eyes, he wears a black or white Wigg, sometimes a Linnen Cap, he has with him a white Fustain Frock, a good Suit of Duroy Cloaths, a Beaver Hat, a light Pair of grey Worsted Stockings, a new Pair of Wooden heel'd Shoes, and a pair of Leather heels, a fine Holland Shirt one Course hath also with him Ozenbrig Shirts, Jacket and Trousers.

The other Servant is an Irishman named David Gileons, aged about 25 Years, of a middle Stature, fair Complection he had on a Double Breasted brown Pea Jacket, lined with blew, a pair of Leather Breeches, white Cotton Stockings good Shoes and a Beaver Hat, an Ozenbrig Jacket and Trousers, it is supposed they will change some Cloaths with each other, and that they have made Passes, both can write tolerable well. Whoever takes up the said Servants and gives Intelligence to Stephen Orion in that they may be had again, shall have Five Pounds as a Reward for both, or Fifty Shillings for each paid by
                                        Stephen Orion.

PHILADELPHIA Aug. 22. Whereas many Counterfiets have been made of the Bills of Credit of New-Jersey, bearing Date the 24th Day of March 1724. which has'd made it necessary to strike new Bills sufficient to exchange the former, These are therefore to give Notice, that by a Law of New-Jersey the Currency of the Bills of that Province dated as aforesaid between Man and Man, doth expire on the first Monday of November 1728. And that all who have any of the same Bills, are to have new Bills in exchange for them at all Times, when the Treasurers are in their Offices, until the First of November, One Thousand, Seven Hundres and Twenty Nine. For which Purpose the Treasurers of the Province are at least to give Attendance at their Respective Offices in Perth-Amboy, and in Burlington, on the Monday of every Week between the First Day of June, and the First Day of December, One Thousand, seven Hundred and Twenty Eight, and afterward on the First Monday of every Month until the First Day of November; but not after.

Rees Williams of the City of Philadelphia, Inn-keeper, being about to remove into the country doth hereby give Notice to all Persons who are indebted to him, to come and Discharge the same by the 29th of August next, by which they will prevent Charges, which otherwise they may expect. Also all Persons who have any Demands on him, are desired to come and receive the same.

MOUNMOUTH County New-Jersey Sept. 2. Ran away from Thomas Boels of Freehold, and the County aforesaid a Servant Man named Morgan Jones, Aged about 30 Years, is a Welch-man of midddle Stature, his Hair cut off or shaved, he commonly wears a white Linnen Cap under his Hat, is Sopposed he had two Hats, viz. a new Hat and an old one, he has a grey Homespun Coat and Vest, lined with Shallon, and Buttons covered with the same Cloaths; he has two pair of Ozenbrig Breeches and one pair of Trousers (as I suppose) Three Shirts one speckled, one Ozenbrig, and one Garlick, a pair of brown Worsted and grey Yarn Stockings, and some other working Cloaths with him; he is but indifferent fresh coloured Face, his Nose something flat by a knock he got on it, Lipse or Stutters when he speaks earnestly, especially when he is in Liquor, as he is very apt to be, on one of his Feet next to his Great Toe, he had toes grown together, he has a Scar on his chin, by a cut, occasioned by a fall on the edge of a Board, and has a sort of a Proud Rambling Gate, pretends to be a mighty Plower, Sower and Ditcher. Also one John James being missed ever since. Whoever takes up the said Servant and bring him to Thomas Boels in Freehold, or to Robert Ellis, and Andrew Bradford in Philadelphia, or William Bradford in New-York, shall receive Forty Shillings as Reward and reasonable Charges.   Thomas Boels.

PHILADELPHIA Sept. 5. Run away the 1st of this Instant September from Henry Pugh of Merion in the County of Philadelphia, a Servant Man named Peter Mack Cellick an Irishman of a middle Stature, about Twenty Years of Age, he had on a bob Wigg and sometimes wears a Cap, a dark Cloath Coat and Wastcoat lined, a pair of Leather Breeches, he took with him a white Horse, and an old Rosset Saddle Branded with the Letters BH Whoever shall take up the said Servant and bring him to his said Master, or to the Workhouse, or give Notice thereof, so that he may be had again, shall have Twenty Shillings Reward and Reasonable Charges.

Rees Williams late of the Sign of the Bear in Philadelphia, being now removed to the Country hath left his Book and Accounts with Mirick Davis, of Philadelphia, where he desires all Persons Indebted to him to repair and pay the same, whose receipt shall be sufficient Discharged to all Persons so paying and may prevent Trouble and oblige their Friends,   Rees Williams.

NEW-YORK Sept. 9. On Wednesday last an express came to his Excellency our Governour, the Pirates were landed of Gardner's Island, and were plundering of it. The next Day Capt. Magne in his Majesty's Ship Biddeford (the Station Ship of Virginia) being here sailed in quest of them, and on Friday Morning at Day-break sailed out of Sandy-Hook: We hope either he or two Sloops fitted out from Rhode Island after them, will meet with them. The Sloops sailed from Rhode Island on Wednesday last in the Evening; the Pirates staid on Gardner's Island till Thursday last at ten in the forenoon, and the stood directly out to sea, they say, they want three or four Vessels laden with Flour and Provisions: They are in a Schooner belonging to New-York which they took bound hither from Jamaica supposed to belong to Mr. Paul Richard: they are about 70 or 80 Men, and it it's said, that a

Brigantine and a Sloop are in consort, and that they are in all 300 Men; a Sloop laid two Days off South-Hampton, supposed to belong to them, the Pirates are Spaniards, French and Malattos, and have taken from Mr. Gardner about 500 Pounds in Money, and about 700 Pounds in Goods.

PHILADELPHIA Sept. 12. Run away on the 8th of this Instant September, from Joseph Taylor jun. of Kennet Township in Chester County, a Servant Man, named Joseph Hodges aged about 19 Years, a tall Slender Man, long Visage, pockfretten, with short light colour'd Hair, a Felt Hat, a grey Colour'd Kersey Coat and Jacket with Brass Buttons, a pair of Ozenbrig Breeches nad Trowsers, a pair of Worsted Ash Stockings, and old Shoes, he had also with him when he went away one Ozenbrig Shirt and a fine one. Whoever takes up the said Servant and bring him to his said Master, shall have Fifty Shillings Reward and reasonable Charges, paid by me, Joseph Taylor.

NEW-YORK Sept. 16. We hear the Rhode Island Sloops came up with the Pirates or Privateers off the East end of Long-Island, and one of them engages her, but the other would not fight, by means whereof the Pirate escaped. We have not heard from Capt. Magne, since he sailed.

PHILADELPHIA Sept. 26. All Persons indebted to the Estate of Robert Renalds of the City of Philadelphia, Merchant deceas'd, are desired forthwith to settle the same with Mr. Ralph Ashenton and Andrew Bradford, Executors of the said Robert Renalds: And all Persons who have any Demands on the said Estate, are also desired to bring in their Accounts to the said Executors, in order to have the same settled and adjusted.

PHILADELPHIA Oct. 3 To be sold on the 19th of this Instant October, by the Sheriff of Chester County, at the House of Ruth Hopkin, in the Borough of Chester, in the said County, one House of the Plantation on Chester Creek (formerly Celeb Puley's) together with 15 two and thirty Parts of a Grist-Mill, and some Mills adjoining; also some other Lands near the same, being Part of the Estate of said Lands, and Terms of sale may be seen at the Place.

A very likely Negroe boy about 13 Years of Age to be sold by John Connor, in Chestnut-Street in Philadelphia.

PHILADELPHIA Oct. 17. The Speech of His Excellency Benedict Bernard Calvert, Governour and Commander in Chief over the Province of Maryland.

Gentlemen of the Upper and Lower House of Assembly.

The Prosperity of the Province of Maryland, is the Subject of my daily Wishes; and it ever shall be, of my constant Endeavours: And I Embrace, with Pleasure every Opportunity to advance it. Hence arises the Satisfaction with which I meet you at this Time. The Choice of Representatives which the Country seem to have made gives me the agreeable Prospect of an happy Issue to our Constitution; whereby the Sovereign Interest of the Crown, the Government of the Lord Proprietary; and the Welfare of the People, may be happily improved, to Mutual Satisfaction.

I have it in Command, for his Lorship. To assure you, That nothing could ever be more disagreeable to Him; than the least Appearance of Difference between Him and His Tenants. Some Votes in the House of Burgeses, did first alarm his Lordship, and put him on his Guard, lest Joyning therein, of in some Consequences of treat, he should be led, Insensibly, into Resolutions of the Nature of the Sovereign Rights of the Crown of England, to this Province; an Inquisition equally nice and dangerous; from hence arose a caution Regard to every thing that might seem any way to interfere with a Title so far above his Conusance.

'Tis from a like wary Concern, that he has found himself obliged to Dis-assent to the late Act, prescribing, the Oath of Justice; for as much as the Words thereof, not only seem to reflect on the Crown, but may also be genuinely Construed, as intended to affect his Majesty's Royal Prerogative, in several of its Branches as well in those reserved, peculiarly to his Sovereign Person, as in those Delegated to, or rather deposited and trusted by the Charter to the Lord Proprietary; for the safe Guarding of which, from Diminution, his Lordship is as strictly accountable, as for any ill Use he could make of them: His Lordship in Duty to his Title and Justice to himself and you, has hitherto, and will ever, preserve the Royal Charter inviolable, on his Part. And whatever is the Contitution of this Province by the said Charter, as well as all consequential Rights, Customs and Usage, his Lordship is most willing to secure to you, and has therefore order'd me to lay before you the Forms of an Oath; whereby the same Measures of Laws and Rights, will be preserved to you and your Posterity, which your Ancesters and your selves have ever enjoyed.

I am also to acquaint you, from his Lordship, That the General Address of the last Session of Assembly to his Majesty, has been presented by his Lordship, and by his Majesty most Graciously received:

I am desired by the Government of Virginia to lay before you, the Draught of an Act passed the last Session of Assembly for Erecting a Light-House on Cape-Henry; to which they desire the Concurrence of this Province, by a like, to be made here: It has been a Matter long talk'd of, that you must be apprized of the Usefulness of it.

I think I need not recommend to you, the careful Pursuit of our Common Interest; in Advancing the Staple of Tobacco; but as you best know the Evils that at present debase it, you can best advise the way to relief.

I shall now leave you, with a Word or two concerning My self. As nothing can be more shocking, to an ingenuous Mind; than a Distrust of a profess'd Sincerity; so I hope you will exert that peculiar Characteristick of Englishmen, call'd good Nature, and not be mistrustful of me, because I your Governour; and some Persons void of all Principles of Honour, would without Doors suggest; but rather believe, that (as I have the Honour to Descend from those who were the Nursing Fathers of this Colony, when I may say it was yet at the Breast) Their Affection for this Province, with their Blood descending, is equally infused in Me: And I want nothing so much, to aliken My self yet more to them, but such a

Confidence from you, as They from your Ancestors enjoyed: To be then assured, That as far as the engaged Duty of my Station will admit, I will readily Cooperate with you in any thing you desire: And I hope you will never press me to any thing that a Negative must attend, since I cannot deny you, without the most sensible Regret.

My frequent Indisposition threaten me with a short Continuance among you. Wherever it may be, (if on Earth) every Faculty of my Mind, and Body, will ever be devoted to the Service of the Province of Maryland.

PHILADELPHIA Oct. 17. To his Excellency Benedict Leonard Calvert, Governour and Commander in Chief, in and over the Province of Maryland.

The Humble Address of the Upper House of the Assembly.

May it please Your Excellency,
The many Instances we have already had, of your Excellency's tender Regard, for the Prosperity of this His Lordship's Province of Maryland, increased by the preset Assurance You have been pleased to give us, in your most favourable speech to both Houses of Assembly, at the Opening of the Session, justly merits our unfeigned Thanks; and inspires us with firm Resolutions, to use our utmost Endeavours, for preserving the Sovereignty of the Crown, the Government of the Lord Proprietary, and the Common Welfare of the People, so as to promote Your Excellency's further Satisfaction, and general Tranquility.

The Assurance, His Lordship hath been pleased to direct Your Excellency to give us, of his Aversion to any Difference with his Tenants, we gracefully accept: And, in Reward to such a good sounding Declaration, think our selves obliged to a strict Conformity of our Duty; and in all Respects to demean our selves so to His Lordship, as not to give any just Occasion to Disccmpose so obliging a Disposition.

And as by the Act, prescribing the Oath of Justice, (to which His Lordship has been pleased to Dis-assent) we never intended any Thing that should reflect on the Crown, or effect his Majesty's Royal Prerogative, either in respect to his Soverign Person, or the Charter to the Lord

Proprietary; both which we think our selves obliged inviolably to preserve: So, if we have so unhappy, as to use any Expressions in that Act, which will bear a Construction so contrary to our Intentions, upon being made sensible thereof, we shall readily retract, alter and amend them, in such a Manner, as shall be satisfactory to his Lordship, and your Excellency, and suitable to the Royal Charter, and the Rights, Customs and Usage of this Province, which his Lordship, is so obliging a Manner, has express'd his good Inclinations to preserve to us and our Posterity.

His Lordship's Goodness, in Preserving the General Address of this last Session of Assembly, to his most Sacred Majesty, requires our grateful Acknowledgement.

We shall carefully and maturely consider the Virginia Act, for Erecting a Light-House upon Cape-Henry, when your Excellency shall be pleased to lay it before us; together with what you have been pleased to observe, relating to the Staple of Tobacco, and therein, and in every Matters or Things (else) which shall come under our Consideration, endeavour to act in such a Manner, as may be most Conductive to the Preservation of his Lordship's Interest and Prerogative, the Constitution, Laws and Customs of this Province, and the Common Good and Welfare of the Inhabitants therein.

It is with good Concern we observe, what your Excellency has been pleased to say, relating to your own Person: but hope nothing of that Distrust of your professed Sincerity, which you are pleased to mention can be imputed to our House, or any one Member thereof: On the contrary, we unanimously take leave to assure Your Excellency, that it is with Pleasure we constantly observe your acting with great Concern for the common Good. And we do sincerely believe, that You really intend the Publick Welfare, with a great Affection as any of your Noble Ancestors.

We will, at all Times, carefully avoid offering any Thing to Your Excellency, which we have Reason to believe may justly merit a Denial, But, if at any Time a Difference of Opinion happens, between Your Excellency and our House, or any of the Menber of it, about controverted Points; we so entreat that you will not impute it to sinister Designs, or any Dissidence, in us, or Your Sincerity for the Publick Good; but rather to the infallible Nature of Mankind, which is not always capable of infallibly disconcerning Truth; from whence often arises Contentions, and a Pursuit of the same good End, by different Methods.

We are very sorry for youe Excellency's indisposition, but hope it will not long continue; and that you may enjoy such a State of Health, as will induce You to long remain amongst us and,, by a continued impartial Administration of Government, convince distrustful Minds (if there be) of your sincere Intention to promote the Common Good; for which may receive a general Applause, and the grateful Acknowledgement of all the good People of the Province of Maryland.

To which His Excellency was pleas'd to make the following Answer.

Gentlemen,

My sincerest Thanks attend your very affectionate Address Your Resolution to Support the mutual Rights of Government and People by the secure Rules of the Royal Charter, as it is most just, I think cannot fail giving universal Satisfaction: His Lordship's cautious Mistake of the Words in the late Oath, arose, not from my supposed evil Intention in the Persons, Enacting but from a concern, lest any one hereafter might put a Construction on them, injurious either to the Proprietary or People, which he was afraid the unguarded Generalty of them might possibly admit: The Oath, proposed by his Lordship seems to provide an universal Security against all Innovations, and most likely to attain the good End we all contend for, The Peace and prosperity of the Province of Maryland.

PHILADELPHIA Oct. 31. Run away from his Master, Capt. John Manlester, Sumerset County, in Maryland, the 24th of September last, a Servant named Robert West, he is a young Fellow abour Nineteen Years of Age, middle Stature but very thin black curl'd Hair, an old Felt Hat, a black Camlet and Holland Jacket, he is of a Sharp Visage, with a Down look. Whoever shall take up said Servant and bring him to his Master or secure him, and give Notice thereof, so as may be had again, shall have Forty Shillings Reward and Reasonable Charges.

PHILADELPHIA Nov. 7. Those Palatines, who have hitherto neglected to pay for their Passage in the Ship James Goodwill, are to take Notice, that if they do not pay to me on board the said Ship, or to Charles Read of Philadelphia the sum from them respectively due, the 20th Day of this Instant November, they will be proceeded against according to Law, by   David Crokatt.

PHILADELPHIA Nov. 20. Thomas Phipps of this City, Schoolmaster, designing (God willing) to leave off keeping School on the 25th of February Next, and to depart this Province by the last of aforesaid Month, Thinketh it proper to inform all concerned, that they who have demands on him may come, or send and receive the same; they who are indebted to him may Discharge the same, when come for, to prevent further trouble.

N. B. All Children whose Quarters will expire before the time, or whose Quarters, will not expire by that time, may be continued by the Week at the Quarterly rate if it may so please the Parents, or Masters, by Your obliging Humble Servant,   Thomas Phipps.

PHILADELPHIA Nov. 21. This Day Ran away from John Bagley Cordwainer, Two Servant Men Shoemakers, and both Irish, the one named George Newman, short and well set, had on a light colour'd cloth Coat, strip'd Holland Jacket and Breeches, has also a pair of Buckskin-Breeches, good Wood heel Shoes, Yarn Stockings, short brown Hair, and smooth Face about thirty years old; the other Named Michael Starel, short and Dark Complexion'd, has on a Dark Colour'd Frize Coat and Waste-coat, a pair of blew Buckskin Breeches, a black Wigg, good Shoes and Yarn Stockings, about thirty years old. whoever takes up said Servants, so that their Master may have them again, shall have Five Pounds Reward, or Fifty Shilling each, and reasonable Charges paid by me   John Bagley.

   PHILADELPHIA Nov. 21. Ran away on the first of October last, from John Austin of Kent-County Maryland, Gun-Smith, two Servant Men; the one named John Bell, aged about 40 Years, of a middle Stature, short black bushy Hair, a little grey and bald on the Crown, fresh colour'd and full fac'd: Suppose to wear when he went away, an old course Yarn Cap, a red Broad cloth Coat, trim'd with black, and loose Kearsey Coat, two Ozenbrig Shirts, two pair of old Breeches, one linnen, and the other Leather, a pair of old dark colour's Yarn Stockings. He has gone under the Name of a Bricklayer, or Mason, and carried with him a Plum-rule Line, a Trowel, Broad-Ax an Iron Square. The other named Samuel Alison aged 26 Years, a short Fellow, walks as if one leg was shorter than the other, of a sandy Complection, short Hair curl'd a little, a strip'd Yarn Cap of sundry Colours, tho Ozenbrig Shirts, a Country Cloth Jacket, lin'd with English Flannel much tore, and an old Light colour'd Kersey Vest, a pair of old dirty Leather Breeches, a pair of new Shoes: The aforesaid two Servant Men took with them a large Bay colour'd Horse Branded with S. on the near Shoulder, and W. on the near Buttock, and a dark brown Horse, Branded on the near Shoulder with MC. a large star and a snip, and two Briddles and a Breasted Saddle, with Brass Pummel, and two brown Linnen Bags, one of them very large: Whoever takes up the mentioned Servants, and Horses, and secures them so that they may be had again, shall have seven Pounds as a Reward, and reasonable Charges, to be paid by me,   John Austin.

   Philadelphia Nov. 28. Two very likely Negroe Women fit for all manner of House Work, to be sold by Doctor Charles Sober, upper end of Chestnut-street.

   Just arrived from London, in the Ship Borden, William Harbet, Commander, a Parcel of young likely Men Servants, consisting of Husband-men, Joyners, shoe-makers, Weavers, Smiths, Brick-Layers, Sawers, Taylors, Stay-makers, Butchers, Chair-makers, and several other Trades, and are to be sold very reasonable, either for ready

Money, Wheat, Bread or Flour, By Edward Horne in Philadelphia.

ANNAPOLIS Dec. 3. Last Week dy'd in his House in St. Mary's County, Nicholas Lowe, Esq; one of his Lordship's Honourable Council, an Agent, and Receiver-General of all his Lordship's Revenue in Maryland. We hear the Hon. Col. Matthew Tilghman Wars, succeeded him in the said Office.

PHILADELPHIA Dec. 5. On Sunday last, about one a Clock in the Morning a dreadful Fire broke out by the House of Theopolus Spuryors, a Bisket Baker in Chestnut-Street, which consumed the said Dwelling House and all the Household Goods, Bake-House and Brew-House to Ashes, also two of the Houses adjoining, were burnt down, there were several other Houses in the Rowe very much Damnified, there was a great Quantity of Bisket and Flour burnt.

We also have an Account from Kent County, upon Delaware, of the dreadful Fire which happened there at the House of Mr. Benjamin Shermours, which consumed his House and most of his Household Goods.

Whereas Leather Buckets have been very much wanted, as by Experience at the Dreadful Fire, in Chestnut-street, and several Persons not knowing where to be supply'd. These are to give Notice to all Persons who want Buckets, may be supply'd by Abraham Cox, in High-Street in Philadelphia.

PHILADELPHIA Dec. 11. Runaway on the First day of Nov. from Andrew Cornish, of Conestogoe, in Chester County, a Servant Woman named Mary Rawlman, who since has changed her name to Sarah Wood; she has on a brown Gown and Petty-coat, with one under Petty-coat of grey Kersey join'd at the top with Blue: Whoever takes up the said Servant Woman, and bring her to her said Master, shall have Forty Shillings Reward and all reasonable Charges paid by, Andrew Cornish.

BURLINGTON Dec. 13. The Speech of his Excellency, John Montgomerie, Esq; Captain General and Governour in Chief of the Province of New-Jersey, New-York, and Territiries thereon depending in America, and Vice Admiral of the same. &c.

To the General Assembly of the Province of New-Jersey, held at Burlington, the 13th of December, 1728.

Gentlemen,

This being the Season of the Year, in which your Absence from your Country affairs will be attended with the fewest Inconveniencies, I have called you together, that you may have an Opportunity of making such Laws, as will secure and Advance the Interest of the Province.

His Majesty who has the good of all his Subjects at Heart, has Instructed and Commanded me to contribute all I can towards your being happy and flourishing People: and it must be the utmost Satisfaction to you to be assured, that although you have the Misfortune to be at a great distance from your Sovereign Person, and the Seat of his Government, yet that does not hinder his Care and Concern for your Prosperity.

I do not doubt but you will express your Duty and Gratitude to His Majesty on all Occasions, and particularly at present, by Settling upon him a Revenue in an ample a Manner, and at least to, as long a Time, as former Assemblies have given it to his Predecessors: and I confide so much of your Loyalty and good Intentions, that I shall use no other Argument on this Head, but to assure you, that what you give for the Support and Incidental Charges of the Government, will be employed for your own Honour and safety.

Gentlemen,

I am very sensible of my Insufficiency for the Trust repose in me, but I shall endeavour to discharge it faithfully, with a strict Regard for His Majesties Service, and the good of his Subjects, always thinking His Interest and theirs Inseparable.   J. Montgomerie.

PHILADELPHIA Dec. 17. The Speech of the Honourable Patrick Gordon, Esq; Lieutenant Governour of the Province of Pennsylvania, and the Counties of New-Castle, Kent and Sussex, upon Delaware. To the Representatives of the Freemen of the said Province met at Philadelphia December, 17, 1728.

Mr. Speaker and Gentlemen of the House of Representatives,

I am Perswaded you will not think it proceeds from any Disregard to your Message to me, at your last Adjournment, that your present Meeting has not been appointed in some other Place than this City, in which your Members had been indecently treated: For as ever since my Arrival amongst you, it has not only been my Inclination, but fixt Purpose to devote my self to the Service of the Country committed to my Care, I should take a much greater pleasure in attending that Service with the Peoples Representatives, wheresoever their Safety, and best Conveniencies for the Dispatch & Business might call themn than in consulting my own Ease, or that of my Family: But having laid this Matter before the Council, as the Charter enjoyns, they are of Opinion, that considering the Severity of the Season, with the shortness of the Day, and that the Settlement of the Publick Accounts, which is one considerable Article of the House Business, can no where so conveniently done, as where the Offices are kept, it may be more expedient to hold your Session, at least for somw time here, and then, if on further Experience you find Reason to continue in the same Sentiments, that another place will be made suitable, they agree with me, that you should adjourn to Chester, which, next to Philadelphia, seems the most convenient Place for your Meeting.

In the mean Time, Gentlemen, I must put in mind, that a Legislative Assembly in Conformity to the British House of Commons, is Invested with a very great Authority; I hope therefore you will not be wanting, as well in Regard to yourselves, as succeeding Assemblies, to make all such sensible of their Error, who shall dare to treat it with any Indignity, in which you shall have my ready Concurrence, if necessary, as you shall in every thing else that tend to the true Interest, and real Service of the Publick.

If you Zeal for the Service, and our Unanimity, Gentlemen, that will most effectually contribute to extinguish the small Remains of a Faction, raised up by the deepest Ingratitude, and cultivate by means that I hope will be of no long Duration: for when on one Hand I observe, that the ancient Settlers, the most Substatial and Judicious of the Inhabitants, who are most Deeply interested in the Peace and Prosperity of the Country, are generally cast, and the Dissatisfied are made up of some restless Persons amongst our selves, joyned by other turbulent Spirits from abroad, who having been uneasy at home, through the meaness of the conditions, of want of Room to display their busy Horrours, Tho' they have but very little at Stake, and scarce any thing but their noise and Clamour to distinguish them, think fitt to discharge themselves here, to the disquiet of a good and peaceful People; and while even the most uneasy amongst these cannot point out one real Grievance in the Administration, for I am sure these shall be none that is in my Power to prevent our remedy, when those things, I say, are considered. I see no reason to doubt, but that many of those who have been misled, will on due Reflection recover themselves, and see how much Union and Order are preferable to Diversion and Confusion, and thereupon resolve to study the Ways that lead to this our Peace, as well as that of the Publick, for this I conceive, is the only thing wanting, to render the People of Pennsylvania as happy amongst themselves, as any now in the Universe.

The better to effect this, I must earnestly extort you, Gentlemen, in all Proceedings to exert that Courage and steady Resolutions, with a becoming Gravity and Solidity that should ever attend the Powers of Government, and those concerned in dispensing them. Government is Sacred. It is from God himself for the Punishment of Evil doers, and the Praise of them that do well: As you therefore are one part of the Legislature, which in every Government is the supreme, and are the Grand Inquisitors of the whole Province, I now seriously recommend it to you to consider, what Laws already in being require to be re-inforced, and what new ones may be necessary to be enacted for encouraging of Virtue, Sobriety and Industry, the only means by which a Country can flourish, and for suppressing

Disorders of every kind, and more effectual Securing to the People their most momentous Privileges against every Attempt to invade them: And so far as the Execution as any of these shall depend on me, you may assure your selves, that all Vigilance and Care shall be applied on my Part that may contribute to procure to us that Tranquility, which every good Man and Lover of his country must sincerely wish to see Established.

What relate to the necessary Provision for the Exigencies of the Government, with other matters that may require your Attention, I shall leave to your own Consideration, and as any thing further occurs, it shall be communicated to you by Message. Only I must make use of this first Opportunity to acquaint you, that I have now positive Orders from Britain to provide by a proper Law against those Crowds of Foreigners, who are yearly pour'd in upon tis, of which the late Assembly took Notice, in a Message to me the 1st of April last: Nor does this arise, as I conceive, from any Dislike to the People themselves, many of whom we know are peaceable industrious and well affected, but it seems principally intended to prevent an English Plantation from being turned into a Colony of Aliens. It may also require our thoughts to prevent the Importation of Irish Papists and Convicts, of whom some of the most notorious, I am credibly informed, have of late been landed in this River.

I shall now only add Gentlemen, that as we are Bless'd in a Sovereign, who makes the Happiness of all His Proprietors, who I am well assured, have nothing more serious at Heart, than the Prosperity of the People who would under them, I hope for the future there will be no other Contention known amongst us, than who shall be most forward in making suitable Returns, with grateful Acknowledgement to Heaven, for the vast Privilege we enjoy.　　　　　　　　　　P. Gordon.

PHILADELPHIA Dec. 20. To the Honourable Patrick Gordon, Esq; Lieutenant Governour of the Province of Pennsylvania &c.

The Address of the Representatives of the said Province,

May it please the Governour,
We gratefully Acknowledge the Generous Disposition, which, has at all Times appeared in the Governour's Readiness to gratify the Assembly of this Province, as well as his Condescension to the request of this House, made to him at our last Adjournment: And though we now hope, there may be no need to renew that Application, yet if the House should hereafter have reason to think, the meeting of the Assembly might be more convenient at another Place than Philadelphia, We pray the Governour will still be pleased to favour us with his Concurrence to our Request.

We think Our selves highly obliged to the Governour, for the Assurance he has been pleased to give to us, of his ready and favourable Assistance, if necessary, to support the authority which justly belongs to the Legislative Assembly, as also his constant Readiness to concur with us in every thing, which may tend to the true Intent and real Service of the Publick.

And as we are fully perswaded, that a well grounded Zeal for the Service of the Publick, and the Unanimity in the Legislature, are the best Means to promote the Peace and Prosperity of a Country, so we Doubt not, but the Harmony and good Agreement which hitherto has subsisted between the Governour and Assembly of Pennsylvania, and which we shall on all Occasions endeavour to Improve, will most effectually extinguish any small Remains of Discontent, that may yet be left among us.

It is with great Satisfaction that we hear, the Representation of the late Assembly to the Governour, complaining of the great Importation of Foreigners amongst us, countenanced by those in authority over Us; and as the Governour is more immediately Entrusted and Instructed by the Honourable Proprietary Family, we hope he will be pleased to Communicate to the House such Measures, as he thinks may best conduce to the Interest of the Proprietors, and the Security of the People of Pennsylvania: And we do likewise Conceive it to be of the greatest Consequence to the Preservation, both of the Religion and Civil Rights of the People of the Province, to prevent the Importation of Irish Papists and Convicts, in which no Endeavour of ours shall be wanting; and we earnestly Request the Governour to recommend the same to the Consideration of the Assembly of the three lower Counties, to make like Provision against the Growth of so Pernicious an Evil in that Government, which, if not timely prevented, will sensibly affect the People of this Province.

The assurance of the Governour has been pleased to give Us of his ready Concurrence, to re-inforce, and pass such Laws, as may be necessary to Encourage Virtue, Sobriety, and Industry, and such also, as may more Effectually secure to the People their most Momentous Privileges, are such repeated Instances of his Care and Zeal for the Welfare of the People of the Province, that we should be Insensible of our Duty, as well as our Interest, did we not acknowledge his Benevolent and Generous Regard of us, by making an Honourable Provision for a Governour so well Affected to the People and Province of Pennsylvania.

We are sensible if the Invaluable Privileges, the Inhabitants of this Province Enjoy, under the Influence of a Gracious Soverign, who Care for the Welfare of his Subjects, does fill their Hearts with the highest Acknowledgement of Love and Gratitude, as well as Proprietors, who thought we have not of late had the Pleasure of seeing any of the Honourable Family amongst us, yet real Sentiments We Entertain of thier good Inclinations for the Welfare for the People of this Province, will forever render them most Valuable and Dear to us. For which Blessing we gratefully Acknowledge the Bounty and Goodness of the Almighty Giver of all good things.

Signed by Order of the House,

David Lloyd Speaker.

PHILADELPHIA Dec. 24. Sculkil's Ferry on High Street Philadelphia, (which is a place of considerable Custom, most of the Carts and Waggons passing that way from Chester County, and that part of Philadelphia-County on the other side of Sculkil) is to be sold by John Maultby, who has a Lease on the same for about Sixteen years yet to come; any Person inclined to Purchase may be further informed by the said Maultby living at the said Ferry.

ANNAPOLIS Dec. 31. This is to report in Town, that Mr. Aquilla Hall, of Baltimore County, was unfortunately shot to Death on Christman-Day in the Morning, as he was walking in his Orchard, by one of his Negroes, who had been run away some Time before; and lay in Ambush to execute this barbarous Murder; since which he has made his Escape. It seems this was not the first Time this Villain had attempted his Master's Life having struck at him with an Ax, which cut him over the Eye-brow and had certainly split his Skull, if he had not suddenly mov'd his Head.

Several fires have lately happen'd particularly one which burnt down the Dwelling-House of the Hon. Philip Lee Esq; in Prince George's County, and almost all the Furniture and Wearing Apparel, himself and Family narrowly escaping the Flames. Another which burnt down a dwelling-House of Widow Hyat, on the Clifes in Calvert County: and another in New-Town, in Kent County, which burnt down the Store-House of Mr. Wilmer and Mr. Nicholson.

Some time since, one Wilson a Carpenter, being at Work on a new House, building in this City, fell from the Top thereof, & received such hurt thereby, that he dy'd the next Day. About the same time, one Joseph Sutton, of Cecil County being at Work Digging some Gravel to mend his Mill Dam, caev'd and undermin'd the Bank so much, that the Earth fell down upon him, and kill'd him on the spot.

PHILADELPHIA Dec. 31. Our River is full of Ice and all our Ships that were bound out are froze in, they are froze up in our Docks 14 large Ships, 3 Snows, 8 Brigantines, 9 Sloops, in all 36 Vessels, besides small Crafts.

1729

PHILADELPHIA Jan. 7. We have 2 Ships arrived in our Bay from London, with Passengers and Servants, viz. Capt. Pearce and Capt. Ball. Capt. Pearce is run upon the Sands in the Bay, and lies in great Danger, has 2 foot water above his Ballast, has cut down his Masts and thrown part of his Cargo overboard. He sent out his Boat to get help, but Night coming on they lost sight of the Shore, and by mistake were rowing out directly to Sea, but Capt. Ball was coming in took them up, and they were so far spent that it was supposed they could not have lived two Hours longer. Capt. Ball is got up as far as New-Castle, and is hoped will get clear of the Ice.

We hear that Sir William Keith has obtained the grant of a Commission to settle a Stamp Office through North-America, for Stamping all Bills, Bounds, Deeds of Conveyances, Writs, &c. as in England.

BURLINGTON Jan. 14. By His Excellency John Montgomerie, Esq; Captain General and Governour in Chief of the Province of New-Jersey, New-York, and the Territories thereon depending in America, and Vice Admiral of the same, &c.

A PROCLAMATION

Whereas the House of Representatives of the Province of New-Jersey, have presumed to make some Resolves, in order, as they pretend, to obtain a District Governour for the said Province, without taking any proper Measures to know the King's Pleasure as to the Subject Matter of them. This I think highly Disrespectful to His Majesty, who has it solely in His Power to Appoint a Governour of that Province.

Therefore I have thought fit, by and with the Advice and Consent of His Majesty's Council for this Province, and by Virtue of the Powers and

Authority given, unto Me by His Majesty's Letter Pattents under the Broad Seal of Great Britain, to Dissolve this House of Representatives; and they are hereby Dissolved and Discharged to Meet the Act hereafter as the House of Representatives of the Province of New-Jersey.

Given under my Hand and Seal at arms at Burlington, in New-Jersey, this 14th Day of January, the Second Year of the Reign of the Sovereign Lord George the Second, of Great Britain, France and Ireland, King Defender of the Faith &c. Annoq. Dom. 1728-29. By his Excellency's Command, Jo. Smith Secry.   J. Montgomerie.

PHILADELPHIA Jan. 14. At the Free-School in Strawberry-Lane near the Market House, Philadelphia are thought, Writing, Arithmatick, in all the parts, Vulgar Decimals and Duo Decimals; Merchant Accounts, after the Italian Manner through all parts of Commerce; Measuring all Artificers Work, Gauging, Dialling, with some other practical parts of Mathematicks: also English and Latin, by   John Walby.

N. B. He also Teaches a Night Scool at the Place aforesaid.

ANNAPOLIS Feb. 4. Last Wednesday Night, Col. Thomas Lee's House in Virginia, was burnt, his Office, Barns, and Out-Houses: His Plate, cash, (to the sum of 1000 Pounds) Papers, and every Thing entirely lost. His Lady and Child were forc'd to be thrown out of a Window; and he himself hardly escaped the Flames, being much scorched. A White Girl of about 12 Years old (a Servant) perished in the Fire.

"Tis said Lee's Loss is not less than 5000 Pounds.

THe fine House of Col. Carter on Rappahannock, was also burnt lately. The particulars of his Loss we can't give you, but we are inform'd it is very great.

PHILADELPHIA Feb. 4. To be Sold. The Plantation of Mr. Joseph Piggion, deceas'd: situated upon the River Delaware, about three Miles below the Falls, containing five Hundred Acres of wery good Land, with a large convenient new Brick House thereon, a Brick Kitchen, a new Barn, a large Orchard, a considerable Quantity clear'd and improv'd Land, and about thirty Acres of good English-Grass Meadowing; with sundry other Conveniencies. Any Person Inclined to purchase, may apply to Mrs. Piggion on the said Plantation, and be better inform'd.

A very good Fulling-Mill with proper Utensils for Dying &c. situated in a good Neighbourhood, near the Township of Horsham, in the Manner of Maryland, and County of Philadelphia; is to be lett on reasonable Terms, by Thomas Pemington, dwelling near the said place.

Lost, or let some Person have it to look upon; a Piece of Red and White Satten of about Twenty eight Yards, out of the House of Owen Humphrie, at the White Horse in Market Street; This is to desire the Person to bring it to the above-mentioned owner, and they shall be satisfied for the same.

NEW-YORK Feb. 7. Last Thursday Night about 7 a Clock a Violent Fire broke out in the Stable of Derick Cook, in this City, which burnt and Destroyed three Houses and some out Buildings; it was by the carelessness of a boy going into the Stable with a Candle.

Whereas John Diswa, came from Stockholm in Sweden, about Seven Years ago; Publick Notice is hereby given to the said John Diswa (if living) That there is a considerable Estate fallen to him, and if the said John Diswa apply himself to the Reverend Mr. Leadman, Minister of the Viccar Church, or to Charles Springer, Esq; at Christian, he may be further informed as to the Particulars.

ANNAPOLIS Feb. 11. The Honourable Edward Calvert, Esq; Brother to the Right Honourable the Lord Proprietor, (who lately arriv'd here) is by Virtue of a special Commission from his Lordship, Appointed Commissary General of this Province; in which Office he is accordingly sworn; and also President of his Lordship's Honourable Council.

PERTH-AMBOY Feb. 22. Whereas the Quit-Rents, due from Lands and Lots in this Province have of late Years, but especially since the late Proprietor's Decease, run very much into Arrears, by which his Testamentary Heirs have to their very great Loss been long kept out of their Rights, and the said Heirs upon full Confirmation of their Father's Will, by a Decisive Decree obtained of the late in the Kings Court of Exchequer, have thereupon directed the following Trustees of the said Will, viz. Richard Hill, Isaac Norris, Samuel Preston and James Logan, who are thereunto impower'd by the Will, without further Delay, to receive and get all the said Arrears and other Debts due to the late Proprietor in his Life Time, or to themselves since his Decease, in this Province or elsewhere.

These therefore are to give Notice, to all Persons holding Lands or Lots in this Province, for which Quit-Rents are due, that they forthwith make Provisions and pay off the same.

Also all Persons who have obtained Warrants for the Lands by Purchase, from the Commissioners of Property which have been survey'd but are not yet Confirm'd, are hereby Required forthwith to provide the Pay for such Lands: They are desired also without Delay, to take Deeds or Patents of Confirmation for the same to the Land Office held by James Steel, in Philadelphia: for the Commissioners Powers from the Morgagees will in a short Time determine.

Notice is hereby further given, that for Receiving of Quit-Rents in pursuance of the Law for that end provided James Steel will duly attend at his Office in Philadelphia, from the first Day of next Month (March) till the 18th of said Month, for receiving of the Quit-Rents, due from the Freeholders of the City and County of Philadelphia, or any other Sums of Money: And on the 20th 21st and 22d, of the same Month at the Town of Chester for that County, and on the 27th, 28th, and 29th Day at Pennsbury, for the County of Bucks: at which Time and Places respectively, all Persons are hereby required to bring their Quit-Rents: And such as cannot fully discharge all their Arrears at the same time, are required to provide the Remainder without delay, for that the whole must now be speedily be Collected. J. Logan.

ANNAPOLIS Feb. 24. An Idle Servant Man who belonging to Mr. Samuel Hasting, Ship-Carpenter of this Place, being Seiz'd with a fit of Laziness, absented himself from his Business for some Days, but being brought home again, his Master let him to his Sawing-Work as usual, which nor agreeing with his Constitution, he chose rather to disable himself, than be obliged to Work, and accordingly about a fortnight ago, he took a Broad Ax and chopt off one of his Hands.

PHILADELPHIA Feb. 25. Run away the 25th of this Instant: February from his Master Humphry Day of Gloucester County in West-New-Jersey a Servant Man named John Harris aged about 19 Years well set fellow, about 5 foot and a half High, much pockfretten a Bluff Face, short Hair, he wears a Cap and good Felt Hat, silk Handkerchief about his Neck, dark cinnamon colour'd Coat with Brass Buttons, Dark Vest with mohair Buttons, dark grey clouth Searge Breeches with Mettle Buttons, Yarn Stockings, Whoever takes up said Servant and secure him so that his Master can have him again, shall have Twenty Shillings as a Reward and reasonable Charges.

Whereas Joseph Sturgus of the City of Philadelphia, in the Province of Pennsylvania, Saddle-maker by an order of the Court of the City, was adjudged to serve Caleb Ransted in the same place Turner, a certian Term of Years not yet expired, notwithstanding the said Servant has absented himself from his said Masters Service, for the space of Eight Months in Nine Months Time, and is now Absent, he is of middle Stature, thin Visage Squint ey'd ill look't he is supposed to have on Yarn Stockings, Buckskin Breeches, Elkskin Jacket, Cinnamon colour'd Broadcloth Coat, Felt Hat. These are therefore to inform all Persons that if they can take up the said Servant and bring him to his said Master or secure him, that he may be had again, shall have Twenty Shillings as a Reward and Reasonable Charges.   Caleb Ransted.

PHILADELPHIA March 13. The following Letter to me, carrying on air of Sincerity, I permit it to be published, nor knowing but it may be a good Consequence.

My busy Friend,

As I esteem thee a Person of sound Judgement, and willing to relieve People from uneasiness in thy Power to remove, I take the Liberty of sending thee this Remonstrance in hope Thou wilt publish it; the Design is to prevent a Grievance which many are at this time threatened with. I am, thou must know, one of the People called Quakers, and it is not suiting me at present to discover matter so freely with our Elders as I could desire, I have chosen to let them and others know my Sentiments by this Indirect method, which if they do not entirely approve. I doubt not but they will of the Justness of the Complaint. Since I shall have the strictest Regard to Truth to all I allege.

Our Half-year Meeting now approaching, a great many Friends from the adjacent Parts of the Country are expected in Town; but the open Hospitality wherewith Friends in Town entertain all Strangers at such Times, make them liable to many Impositions. There are many indiscreet People, who crowd the Meetings and our Houses with rude Servants and Children, and thereby render these Seasons less comfortable and serviceable, by which Means we are at Times so hurry'd and hard set at home to provide Victuals, and Lodging for them, and to find Seats and the way to them for our selves at the Meeting, that the Benefit we receive is not satisfied. Formaly the head of every worthy Family took some Care to prevent such Trouble and Confusion; and at this Time the Meeting in England have Orders which are observ'd throughout the Kingdom, to regulate the Practice, and hinder sorry Persons, not to Fellowship with us, from foisting themselves among Friends to live well a few Days at their Charge, and perhaps with an Evil-Eye to discover what small Failings they can. Besides that some of the Country Friends, notwithstanding the Trouble and Expence they put us to, are as backward to deal with us, and let us get a Penny by them, an any other People. And Indeed, were I minded to add all that I have heard remarked on this Occasion by several very sensible Friends, I might carry this Complaint a great deal farther.

The Error and Indecency of pressing noisy Children and ill bred Servants into Company of Men and Woman, without Distinction, at Table, at Meetings, and in Beds, has been frequently mentioned. One assured me, that his Opinion of Yearly Meetings was, that they were now become Times of great Liberty and Profusion as any Fair or Festivals; and tho' said he, some Elders and others of our Society that are religious, do still keep view and maintain as much as they can to End and first Establishment of our Annual Congregatings, there are many loose Folks that hide their Vices under plain Clothes and formal Speech, which come to Town at those busy Times to pilfer in their Lodging Room, (as he had known at his Father's) some for good Eating and Drinking, and some to make themselves Father's and Mothers. And they again continu'd he, there's ———— the sober Man, that lives ———— He was well entertained at our House, a Bed provided for him and his Wife, His Horse taken Care of, &c. This ungrateful Person, when he went Home, told his Neighbours how highly he had lived at such a Friend's House, and I'll warrant you, said he to them, he makes Us pay for this: ———— I'll buy no more Goods at his Shop. And this Brings to mind, added my Friend, a silly Woman, who, after drinking plentifull at my Father's, last Meeting, went into our Shop to buy a pair of Scissors, and would have Three-Pence abated in the Price, and a Pennyworth of Pins into the Bargain, in Consideration of her laying her Money out with us; ———— but she was not the only Person that served us in that manner, tho' the same Day no less than Thirty at a Time, Old and Young, eat at our Table. ———— I am Satisfied, concluded he, at the very Meeting we spent in our House, besides Drink, Bread, Butter, Cheese, Sauces, Fowles, and small Meats, no less then Four score Pounds of good fat Beef (which is dear at those Sessions) Fifteen Rice and Plumb Puddings, hald a Score of large Apple Pies and a Bushel of Tarts. ———— I shall trouble thee no longer at this Time, but conclude thy Friend and Welwishers in the Work of Reformation. T.Z.

I am ablig'd to several Gentlemen for their

Considerations which shall be regarded in due Time.

NEW-CASTLE UPON DELAWARE March 20. Run away from Mrs. Aves French and William Battell, Two Servants, on the Fourth of February last; one is a Man born in Staffordshire, named Richard Cook, a Brick-maker by Trade, and a bold pretending Fellow, had on a Felt Hat, Light Wig, short Black Hair, a Homespun Gray Jockey's Coat, with Pewter Buttons, a Blsck Jacket, with other under Apparel necessary; The other an Irish Woman, named Bridget Duncan, who passes with him as his Wife; she is a well set short Woman, down look'd, took with her a Ridding-Hood and Cloak of a Yellowish colour, Fac'd with a Persian suitable; a Silk Gown of an ash colour, with small dark Stripes, a Drugget uper Petty-Coat, &c. Whoever will take up, and secure both, or either of the said Parties, so that they, or either of them may be had again, shall receive Thirty Shillings as a Reward for each, and reasonable Charges from William Battell.

PHILADELPHIA March 27. Run away from Samuel Warne, of the Township of Middle-Town in the County of Monmouth, in the Province of New-Jersey; an Irish Servant Man, nam'd Thomas Lowry, a Shoemaker by Trade, of a short Stature, black Hair, dark Complexion, Cloathed with a gray Coat, a black Vest, a brown Pair of Breeches, Two Pair of Stockings, the one Yarn, and the other Worsted, a Round toe'd Pair of double Sol'd Shoes, a Felt Hat, and commonly wears it all Round, without Cocking; he is Aged about Twenty three Years: Whoever takes up said Servant, or secures him, so that the said Samuel Warne, may have him again, shall have Thirty Shillings Reward, and reasonable Charges, Paid by Samuel Warne.

A very likely Servant Man's Time to be Sold; being about three years, he is a Miller, also very handy at House Carpenters Work or fit for a Farmer. Inquire of Charles Read.

A Likely Negro Man about Twenty years Old, Speaks very good English to be sold by Samuel Hasell in Front-Street Philadelphia.

To be sold very good English Cherry Brandy, and the Right Irish Usquebaugh in Quart Bottles;

Enquire of Andrew Bradford.

A well-strung Virginal to be sold; being in good order Enquire Printer hereof.

PHILADELPHIA April 3. To the Honourable Patrick Gordon, Esq; Governour of the Province of Pennsylvania, &c.

The Humble Address of the Representatives of the Freemen of the said Province, in General Assembly met.

Sheweth,

That whereas the Province of Pennsylvania was at first settled by a Sober and Orderly People, whose Religious Principles was, and still is well known to be, against the use of Arms, and who for a long time lived Peaceably and Quietly under the Protection of the Civil Magistrate, but for as much a greater Nunber of Disolute and Disorderly Persons have of late been Imported, and daily do come from our Neighbouring Colonies into this Province, and knowing we have no Military Forces, either from their own evil Dispositions, or by the Countenance, and Encouragement of some Dissatisfied Persons among our selves, have of late taken the Liberty to Menace, and threaten, not only many private Persons whitin this Province, but likewise some of the Members of this House, to the great Terror of the Inhabitants of the City of Philadelphia in particular, to the Disturbance of the Peace, and in Delay of Publick Service of the Country: And we being highly concern at the restless and unjust Designs and Attempts of the Enemies of the Peace and Prosperity of the Province; We think it our Duty at this time to Express our Abhorrence of all such Riotous Tumultuous Attempts, and our Resentment against all Persons who shall discover to be the Authors or Promoters of such Tumults, which we conceive we cannot better do, than by Declaring, that we on our Part will contribute all that is in Our Power to Support the Administration, and secure the Peace of the Government.

And to that End, we pray that forasmuch as by an Act of General Assembly of this Province, it is Provided and Enacted, That Roits and Rioters shall be Punished according to the Laws of

England. The Governour will be pleased to give Directions to the several Magistrates throughout this Province, that the Laws now in Force in the Kingdom of England, against Riotous and unlawful Assemblies may be speedily be put in Execution, against all such Persons, as shall be found any ways concerned in such Riotous and Tumultuous Practices, their Aiders and Abbettors, and particularly that the Statute made in the first Year of the Reign of the late King George of Blessed memory, and be duly Published at the respective Court of Quarter-Sessions, within the Province of Pennsylvania, according to the Directions of the said Act: And that the Governour would be pleased to Issue forth His Proclamation for the Purposes before-mentioned.

Signed by Order of the House, Philadelphia March the 29th 1729.   David Lloyd, Speaker.

The Governours Answer,

Gentlemen,

I hereby thank the House for the just Concern they shew for the Preservation of the Publick Peace, and am sorry there should be any occasion given for this Address: However the House may be assured, that I will fully exert the Powers of Government against all those, who shall either openly dare to disturb our Peace, or privately formeth Seditious Practices.

ANNAPOLIS April 7. A few Days ago, a Negroe Man belonging to one Aldridge, in Prince George's County, without and Provocation barbarously Murder'd his Master's Mistress, and two of her Children, whilst his Master was absent: After which, he took two Guns out of the House, with all the Powder and shot he coulf find, and made his Escape. He was speedily pursued by his Master and his Neighbours, for several Days, and at last was taken, after an obstinate Resistance of the Negroe, who in the Fray shot his Master through the Hand.

We have accounts from Baltimore Assize, that the Negroe who shot his Master, Mr. Aqualla Hall pleaded Guilty upon Tryal, and received Sentence of Death.

PHILADELPHIA April 10. Run away the 5th of this Instant April, from Zachariah Hutchins,

Butcher of the City of Philadelphia: a Servant Man, named Thomas Chit, a short well set fellow, of a fresh Complexion, about 35 Years of Age, having his Hair cut off, or a light Wig, having on an old Hat, with brim sow'd on to the Crown, Cinnamon colour'd Coat, with bright Metal Buttons upon Wood, a light Sagathie Jacket, a Pair of Buckskin Breeches something Greasey, a New Garlick Shirt, a Butcher by Trade: Any Person that can take up the said Servant, and secure him, so that his Master may have him again, shall have Three Pounds as a reward, besides reasonable Charges, paid by me.

Zachariah Hutchins.

Run away on the 7th Instant April, from the House of Thomas Wilson of New-Hanover, in Burlington County; a Man named James Davis, and took with him, a Horse belonging to William the Son of the said Wilson, the said Horse is White, about six Years old, long Main, long Main, long Switch Tail, Paces midling; the Saddle in of sort called a Hunting Saddle with Ears, and a Brass Cock: The said Davis is of a Middle Stature, about Thirty Years of age, a fresh Colour, something Pockfretten, had on a Caster-Hat, a new Cotton and Linnen Shirt, a Camlet Coat and Vest, old Leather Breeches with Brass Buttons, a Pair of mixt coloured stockings, Black and Blew, New Shoes: Whoever secures the said Davis or give Notice of him, to the said William Wilson, or John Snoden, shall have Twenty Shillings Reward, and reasonable Charges paid by me

William Wilson.

PHILADELPHIA April 17. To be sold by Samuel Hasell, in Front-street Philadelphia, an Indian Woman and her Child, a Girl about Nine Years old, lately imported from Bermudas; she Washes, Irons and Starches very well, and is a good Cook: Any Person Inclin'd to Purchase may have her upon Trial for some time if they desire.

Run away the 25th of January, 1729. from Mr. Thomas John of New-Castle County, Farmer an Malatto Man, named Joseph Williams, about 24 Years of Age, having on a Ozenbrig Jacket and Breeches, and Gray Homespun outside Jacket, Gray Yarn Stockings and New Shoes; a White Woman went away with him, which he calls his Wife, named Bridget: Whoever secures the said Malatto Man, shall have Thirty Shillings Reward Pay'd by Thomas John.

NEW-YORK April 21. By his Excellency John Montgomerie, Esq; Captain General and Governour in Chief of the Province of New-York, New-Jersey, and Territories thereon depending in America, and Vice-Admiral of the same,&c.

A Proclamation.

Whereas the Inhabitants of the said Province of New-York, who hold Lands by Patent from the Crown, or sundry mean Conveyances of the same, have not paid their Quit-Rents, as by their Patent they ought to have done, whereby considerable Sums of Money have been long due and in arrear to his Majesty. And whereas Application has been made to Me for my Orders to the Attorney General to cause Prosecutions to be forthwith commenced against the Persons Indebted, or who shall from this time be Indebted to his Majesty for Quit-Rents, as aforesaid. But that all Perosns concerned may have timely Notice, and prevent Prosecution thereupon, I have thought fit, by with the Advice of His Majesty's Council of the said Province, to issue this Proclamation, Requiring all the Inhabitants of this Province, who are Indebted to his Majesty for Quit-Rents, That they forthwith pay the same to the Receiver-General, at His Majesty's Custom-House in the City of New-York; and that all and every Person or Persons holding Lands by patent, as aforesaid, do from henceforth pay their Quit-Rents, to the Receiver-General, at the Custom-House aforesaid, at such Days and Times as by their Said Patents they are obliged to do, Whereby they will prevent the necessary Prosecutions that otherwise will unavoidably follow, for the Recovery of the same.

Given under my Hand and Seal of Arms at Fort George in New-York, the Twenty-first Day of April, in the Second Year of His Majesty's Reign, annoq. Domini 1729.   J. Montgomerie.

ANNAPOLIS April 21. A Ship from Montrose is lately gone up our Bay, with upward of 60 Indentur'd Scotch Servants.

It being represented, that the Negroe belonging to John Aldridge, who Murder'd his Mistress and 2 Children, was so ill in Prison, that 'twas thought he could not live till the Assizes, and Consequently not receive lawful Punishment for his Horrid Crime; his Excellency was pleased to order a special Commission for trying him, which was accordingly done; he confessed the murdering his Mistress and one Child, but said the youngest was killed by a fall of its Mother upon it; he received Sentence of Death, was Executed at Marlborough last Friday, and on Saturday was hung in Chains in the old Field near Capt. Murdock's.

The negroe who kill'd his Master Mr. Aquilla Hall, is also to hang in Chains. Which Example 'tis hoped will be a means to Terrify such wicked Wretches from the like Practices for the future.

PHILADELPHIA May 6. Just Imported from London, in the Ship Providence, Capt. Jonathan Clarke, a Parcel of very likely Servants, most Tradesmen, to be sold on reasonable Terms; the Ship now lies at Mr. Lawrence's-Wharf, where either the Master or the said Lawrence are to be spoken with.

PHILADELPHIA May 8. These are to give Notice, That on the First day of this Instant May, 1769. was taken up a Negroe Man, about Forty Years of Age, and put in the Goal of Burlington, for Stealing from several Persons, sundry Sorts of Goods; the Negroe Man saith he belongs to one Roger Matthews' being in Baltimore County, in Maryland, Brother-in-Law to one Edward Hall.

N. B. The said Negroe Man formerly belonged to Governour Markham, and was sent down at Maryland, by Mr. Reuch, Attorney at Law.

Just arrived from Barbadoes in the Sloop Rose, Joseph Wilson Master now lying at Mr. Fishbourn's Wharf a Parcel of very likely Young Negroes of both Sexes, to be sold, very reasonable by George M'Call Merchant in Philadelphia, either for Money, Flour, Bisket or Pork.

NEW-YORK May 14. The Speech of his Excellency John Montgomerie Esq; Governour and Commander and Chief of His Majesty's Province of New-York, to the House of Representatives, on Mednesday the 14th of May 1769. Viz.

Gentlemen,
I have called you together, to concert, and concur with you in advancing the Interest and Prosperity of this Province: And I take this Occasion of Acquainting you, that since our Adjournment I met the Six Nations of Indians at Albany, and I do assure you with great Pleasure and Satisfaction, that I find them Thoroughly attached to our Interest: You will see this confirmed by Publick Conferences with me, which if you desire shall be laid before you.

They think the House of Oswego, which has been Builded and hitherto Supported by you, of so great Consequence to themselves and us, that they expect you will keep a Garrison there, and we shall appear very Contemptible in the Eyes of the World, if you do not Seasonably and Amply provide for the Maintenance and Support of it, which I earnestly and heartily recommend to you.

The indians on their part promish to assist us against any Power that dares to attack it.

I am sorry that the Expence of that place has been so Burthensome to the Province, but I believe there will be Methods proposed to you, of doing it at for less Charge, than what it has hitherto cost you: I leave that entirely to your consideration, not doubting but you will provide for it effectually, and the less Expence of the Province is as it will be the more pleasing to me.

I have one thing more to recommend to you, which is appointing an Agent to solicit your Affairs at the Court of Great Britain, and I must take this Occasion of doing Justice to the Gentheman you last employed, by telling you, that to my certain Knowledge, he served you Deligently and Honestly, and very well deserves, the Continuance of the Trust you repose in him.

J. Montgomerie.

PHILADELPHIA May 22. Coach and Chaize-work done after the best and newest Fashions. Made and sold at reasonable Rates, by Thomas Barton, Coach-Maker in Third-street, Philadelphia, next

Door to Widow Priest's.

N. B. He has a new Convenient Two Wheel'd Chaize to Hire and several good ones near finish'd to dispose of.

There is to be Sold by John Cheyney of Thornburg near Concord in Chester-County, Two New Copper Stills, the one containing Twenty Gallons, the other Forty, with good Pewter Worms to them; to be Sold either together or separately, very reasonable, by me.   John Cheyney.

N. B. Also a set of very good English-Ear-Bells for Horses.

PHILADELPHIA May 26. Whereas, it has been industriously Reported and spread abroad, by Alias Hagg of Philadelphia, That I the Subscriber am actually Absconded from the said City for Debt. This is to certify whom it may concern, that the said Report is utterly and notoriously False, Groundless and Malicious, and designed only to do me a prejudice in my Credit and Business; and he will forthwith be prosecuted for it, on an Action of Scandal.   James Davis.

PHILADELPHIA May 29. To be Sold. The Plantation late of George Trechard deceased; situated upon Alloways Creek, about three miles from Salem; containing three hundred and seventy two Acres of excellent good Land; a House, a large Orchard, and a considerable quantity of Clear'd and Improv'd Land, in very good English Grass, and a great quantity of Meadowing, and sundry other Conveniencies; It is a very good place for Stock. Any Person inclined to purchase the same, may apply themselves to Mrs. Mary Trechard, Executeix of George Trechard, deceased, at her House at Salem, and be Better inform'd.

PHILADELPHIA June 5. Lately Imported by James Coutts, from Montrose a Parcel of Choice Scotch Servants, all Young Men and Women: the Men have been mostly bred up to Country Work, and the Women are fit for Service, either in Town or in Country. They are regularly indented, some for the Term of Five, and others for Seven Years, Whoever inclines to Purchase any of these Indentures, may apply at Patrick Baird, in Second Street.

PHILADELPHIA June 17. Run away on Tuesday the

10th of this Instant June from Captain Thomas Colvill of Cecil-County in Maryland; Two Servant Men, one named Thomas Walker, a low well set Man, of a brown Complexion, aged about 25 Years, he is a Northumberland Man, speakd broad, and had on a light Pea-Coat.

The other nam'd William Ryeres, aged 21, of a middle size and pale Complexion he is partly Bald-Headed, and had on a Light colour'd Frock with Brass-Buttons. Whoever takes up the said Runaways, or secures them, so that their Master may have them again, shall have Three Pounds as a Reward, or Thirty Shillings for either of them Paid by Thomas Colvill, or Patrick Baird in Philadelphia besides reasonable Charges.

Run away from James Chalmers out of Philadelphia, the 10th of this Instant June; a Servant Man, named Alex. Sloane, a well set little Fellow, Black Wigg, swarthy Complexion, New Coat of a dark Brown Colour, White Wastcoat, with Brown Breeches and Stockings.

Also Samuel Worthington the same Day out of the same Place.

One William Sergisson, his Servant, a pretty tall and Lusty Fellow, about Twenty Years of Age, a Brownish Coat much worn, has very large Breeches, Brown Worsted Stockings. He took from his Master Five Pair of Silver Sleeve Buttons.

PHILADELPHIA June 26. Run away on the 9th of this Instant June, Two Servant Men belonging to Thomas Arnold of the Township of Bradford, in the County of Chester and is named John Burk, he is about 18 Years of age, of Middle Stature, fresh Colour'd with short Black Hair; he had on when he went away a Felt Hat, Black Coat, White Jacket, Leather Breeches, and Brown Yarn Stockings.

The other belonging to Thomas Thornbury, of the Township aforesaid, is named James Cownden, he is about Twenty five Years of Age, Tall in Stature, thin fac'd, long hock'd Nose, and with straight Light colour'd Hair; he had on when he went away, a Felt Hat, a Gray Double Breasted Pea Jacket with Brass Buttons, a New Pair of Linnen Drawers, Black Stockings, and a Pair of Shoes newly Tap'd. Whoever secures either of the above-mention'd Servant Men, shall have Three Pounds Reward, paid by,

Thomas Arnold, or Thomas Thornbury.

PHILADELPHIA June 26. Went away about 10 Days ago, James Denune, Master of the Free-School, in Prince George's County; a Contracted Servant named Thomas Smith, by Trade a Stocking-Weaver, but was lately employed by the said Mr. Denune, as User of his School. He is a young Man of middle Stature, Long Visage, and Pock-fretten, He sometimes wears a Grey Duroy Coat and Westcoat, and sometimes a Scersucker Suit, and a fair natural Wigg, He had no Certificate, only a Duplicate of his Indenture. He had a young Black Stallion. Whoever secures the said Thomas Smith to Mr. Denune, aforesaid, ot to Mr. Annon, Master of the Grammar-School, in Philadelphia, shall have Two Pistoles Reward, over and above the Allowance by Law.

PHILADELPHIA July 3. We the Commissioners for Receiving and Distributing the Goods saved from on board the Wreck'd Ship Rachel, Labouriously Peace Master from London. Do hereby give Notice, That pursuant to the Directions of the said Commission, a Parcel of Felt Hats; and sundry other Goods remaining in our custody, for which no Claimer does appear will be exposed to Sale by publick Vendue, on Wednesday the Ninth of this Instant July, at two a-Clock in the Afternoon, under the Court-House in Philadelphia.

Samuel Hasell, Charles Read, Peter Lloyd.

On Tuesday the 2d of this Instant July, one John Shennan, a Prisoner of William Read, Sheriff of New-Castle County, upon Delaware, and in Execution for several Debts due to divers Persons; Deserted from the said Sheriff, and made his Escape: The said John Shennan is an Irishman, but speaks good English, he is a Tall proper Man, and well Limb'd, fair Spoken, and about twenty eight years, wearing his own black Hair: Whoever takes up, and secures the said John Shennan, so that the said Sheriff shall have him again, shall have Five Pounds reward, and all reasonable Charges paid by

William Read Sheriff of New-Castle County.

Run away from George Shad, Peruke-maker in

Front-street Philadelphia, the 30th of June; a Servant Man named John Granger, a short fellow hard favoured, long Visage, a Scar under his Chin like the Evil, he waddles in his Gate; and had on a Felt Hat, light Wig, an Ozenbrig Jacket and Breeches, White Garlick Shirt, round Toe's Shoes and no Stockings on when he went away: Whoever takes up said Runaway, and brings him to his said Master, or secures him, so that his Master may have him again, shall have Forty Shillings Reward and all reasonable Charges for Ten Miles from Philadelphia.

ALBANY July 10. Last Night about 12 a Clock a Fire broke out in a Bakers House in this City, and with great Violence burnt down Seven Houses, and destroyed a great part of the Goods Merchandize therein. And there is about 17 or 18 are in a great part destroyed by being pulled down and broke, in order to stop the fury of the Fire.

PHILADELPHIA July 10. An Indented Servant Man, named James Roberts, is run away from William Bradford's Paper-Mill at Elizebethtown in New-Jersey. He is a middle-sized well set young fellow, about twenty years of Age, has dark brown Hair, somewhat curl'd. Round Visage, gray Eyes; one of his Fore-fingers is crooked. He wears a brown Wastcoat with black Buttons, a Homespun Linnen Jacket, a light coloured Drugget Coat, lined with dark Shallon, a pair of Leather Breeches and a pair of New home-spun Linnen ones, a pair of Thread Stockings. Pump-Shoes, a good Beaver Hat, two new home-spun Shirts and an old one: His hat has neither Buttons or Loops. He is a West. Country-Man, has been about one Year in the Country, and a Paper-maker by Trade.

This James Roberts is supposed to be run away in company with John Hill, a strong well set Fellow, who says he came from Boston, and has a home-spun Pea-Jacket with Mettle Buttons, a sort of Kersey, with an old Slouching Hat, and in a poor Habit. Whoever can take up and secure the said James Roberts, and give Notice to William Bradford in New-York, or to Andrew Bradford in Philadelphia, or John Bracley in Perth-Amboy, they shall have Fifty Shillings, and reasonable

Charges.

All Persons indebted to Thomas Adams of Philadelphia, Inn-holder, deceased, are desired to pay the same to John Bringkurd of said City, Administrator. He has a Servant Woman's Time to dispose of, being above four Years to serve; and also a Negro Woman to sell reasonable, and if need be, will give some time for Payment.

Run away on the 15th of June past, from Arthur Wells of this City; a Servant Man named John Blowden, aged about 22 Years, by Trade a Shoemaker; he is a middle Stature, full Faced, of a fair Complection, and Effeminated Voice, with short Brown Hair: He has on a striped Homespun Jacket, and Breeches of the same, without Pockets, and Parched on the Knees, a Garlick Shirt half worn'd an old Beaver Hat, with sides Flopping down, Brown Worsted Stockings, and Wooden Hel'd Shoes cover'd over the Toes.

N. B. He has been Lurking near the Town this Forthnight past, and last Sunday Night, having procured a Duroy Coat, he went further, he often pretends to be worth a great deal of Money, by which he has imposed on several. Whoever shall secure the said Servant so that his Master may have him again, shall have Forty Shillings Reward, and reasonable Charges, paid by

Arthur Wells.

ANNAPOLIS July 15. On Thursday last both Houses of Assembly of the Province met pursuant, to their last Prorogation. We hear, that the Question having been put, in the Lower House whether a Bill for a Paper Currency should be brought in, or not, it was carried in the Affirmative.

PHILADELPHIA July 21. Our Assembly have Pass'd a Law to lay a Duty of 40 s. per Head upon all Aliens that shall be imported into this Province, and 20 s. per Head upon Irish Servants that shall be Imported. About 10 Days ago a Ship arrived from Ireland with 200 Servants, and to avoid paying said Duty they were put on shore at Burlington & Trent Town in New-Jersey. There is now four Vessels more arrived here from Ireland with Passengers; and Yesterday one of the Passengers gave Information that on board the

Sloop Charming sally from Dublin there was a Quantity of Counterfeit New-Jersey Bills, which were found in the Chest of one Eanon a Passenger who died at sea as they were coming over. Where upon the Mayor & Magistrates of the City Immediately gave the Sheriff Orders to make Inquiry into this Affair, who upon search found in the Chest of said Eanon, about 118 Counterfeit Eighteen Penny Jersey Bills, not Signed; (they are of the new Bills that is now Currant) and are in the hands of Thomas Lawrence, Esq; Mayor of the City of Philadelphia. Its supposed there is a greater Quantity of these Bills gone to Burlington in the Ship Woodside Galley, on board of his Goods, but was left behind himself.

ANNAPOLIS July 29. This Day the Bill for Emitting four Thousand Pounds, Paper Currency &c. was read a second time and pass'd in the Lower House; and was sent to the upper House.

Last Saturday a young Woman was killed by Lightning, at the House of Mr. Levin Hill, near this City, and a great part of the said House was much shatter'd. It's remark'd that more Damage of this kind has been done this Year, in these Parts, than has been known in any one Year in memory of Man.

PHILADELPHIA Aug. 7. The Art of Dancing Carefully taught (as is now Practiced at Court) by Samuel Perpoint at his School next door to Mrs. Brindley's Hatter in Front-Street; where for the Recreation of all Gentlemen and Ladies: There will be Country Dances every Thursday Evenings, likewise he Teaches small Sword: Any Gentlemen that has a Desire to learn in Private, he will wait upon them, and always to be spoken with at his School from Eight to Eleven in the Morning, and from Three in the Afternoon to six in the Evening.

NEW-CASTLE Aug. 14. There is come here this last Week about 200 Irish People, and abundance more are daily Expected. In one Ship about 100 of them Dyed in the Passage hither. It is computed that there is about 6000 come into this River since April 1st.

PHILADELPHIA Aug. 14. We have the following Melancholy account from West-Jersey near Manta

Creek, That there was found on the Shore, a Girl of about 8 or 9 Years of Age, she was naked only a Cap on her Head, and it is Supposed she was shot, having seven Shot holes in her Breast and two in her Arm. There was also a Man taken up on the shore, sow'd up in a Blanket.

PHILADELPHIA Aug. 21. Whereas by an Act of Parliament made in the Ninth Year of the Reign of her Majesty Queen Anne, Entitled, an Act for Establishing a General Post-Office for all her Majesty's Dominions &c. It is among other things Enacted, That all Masters of Vessels, Sailors and Passengers, shall immediately upon their arrival in any Port, deliver the Letters and the Pacquets on Board to the Post-Master, or his Deputy, under the Penalty of Five Pounds British Money, for every several Offences.

And wheras by the same Act it is also Enacted, that if any Master, Sailor or Passenger on board any Boat or Vessel, passing or repassing, on any River or Rivers, in any of her Majesty's Dominions, shall or do collect, carry or deliver any Letters or Pacquets, he or they shall forfeit and pay Five Pounds, British Money, for every Week he or they shall continue to carry or Deliver any Letters or Pacquets, as aforesaid.

This is therefore to give Notice to all Masters of Vessels, Sailors, Passengers and others who may be concerned, That they be Careful not to Offence against the Aforesaid Act of Parliament, Upon pain of being Prosecuted for the several Penalties therein mentioned, Pursuent to the Orders of the Post-Master of Philadelphia.

PHILADELPHIA Aug. 28. We have the following Account, of an Accident which happened at the Plantation of Timothy Hanson, in Kent County upon Delaware. On the 7th of July last, as the Reapers were cutting down the remainder of his Wheat, they found a Hens-nest with rotten Eggs; whereupon one of them an Irishman, cast some Eggs at a young Man in the Field, who returning one of the Eggs at the Irishman; he instantly cast his Sickle, and Pierc'd the young Man through the body; the Sickle went into the Body near the Backbone, and the Point came out a little below, and within the Left Breast reckoned about three Inches: The Young Man stood while the Sickle was taken out of his Body, but afterwards got over a high Fence, and walk'd to the House, but so much Blood issuing from the wound, soon occasion'd Faithness and Weakness on him; and no Surgeon being near the Place, except an Hibernian Quack, who pronounce the Young Man Dead in spite of all the Doctors in the World, and in Compassion to him, told the Maid, that was providing some Comfortable Refreshments, that it was of no Purpose, as it might be better let alone; and the good People of the House, used their Endeavours with simple Applications, which had with God's Blessing such Effect on the Young Man, that in less than a Month, he rode six Miles, and is now almost Heal'd, and in good Health.

The above Account was taken in Writing, at the before mention'd Plantation, the 15th Instant.

PHILADELPHIA Sept. 4. Run away from Benjamin Acton, of Salem, Two Servant Men, one White, the other an Indian. The White Man's Name is Henry Stack, short Stature, and has a Scar in his Face, his Hair is newly cut off, and is of a Tawney Complection; had on a brown Duroy Coat full trim'd, Ozenbriggs Trowsers, thin Shoes seam'd round the Quarters, a Felt Hat almost new.

The Indian called Isaac Gamitt, is of middle Size, has very thick Lips, and speaks good English, had on an old Vest and Breeches, old Stockings and Shoes and an old Hat. Whoever secures the said Runaways, so that their Master may have them again shall have Forty Shillings Reward for each, and reasonable Charges by

Benjamin Acton.

Edward Sedgickk, Coach and Harness-Maker from London, who hath been here these Seven Years, and hath now a New-Chaise by him, to be disposed of very Reasonable, he shortly Designs for London; and all Persons who are indebted to him, are desired forthwith to come and Pay him, in order for him to pay his debts.

PHILADELPHIA Sept. 11. On Friday last was decently Inter'd in Philadelphia, the body of Richard Hill, Esq; He had his Birth in Maryland, was brought up to the Sea, and Commanded some good Ships in his Youth; but afterwards settled in Philadelphia on account of his Wife, the Relick of John Delaval, an Eldest Daughter of Thomas Lloyd, Esq; once our Governour of Pennsylvania; he was 25 Years a Member of Council for the Province, had been divers times Speaker of the Assembly, had born several Offices of Trust, and during the last ten Years of his Life, was one of the Provincial Judges. His Intrepidity and Resolution in what he undertook, his found Judgement, his great Esteem for an English Constitution and its Laws, his Tenderness for the Liberty of the Subject, and his Zeal for preserving the order Established in his own Community, with his great Generosity to those he accounted proper Objects of it, Qualified him for the Greatest Service in every Station he was Engaged in, rendered him valuable to those, who more intimately knew him.

Stolen or taken away from Richard Clymer's Wharf the 30th of August last, a Red Cedar Boat Painted Red, she has six Iron Knees. Whoever shall take up the said Boat, and bring her to Richard Clymer, shall have Ten Shillings as a Reward.

To be Sold, by Stephen Brook at Mr. Masters's Mill, Northern Liberties of the City of Philadelphia, a New Shallop well fitted, any Person that hath a Mind to purchase the same, may apply to the said Stephen Brook, at the aforesaid Mill, and agree on very reasonable Terms.

PHILADELPHIA Sept. 17. Run away September the 15th, from John Van Horne of Piscatua; Two Irish Servant Men, one of them named Felix Mack Guier, short young Fellow, about 19 or 20 Years of Age, of swarthy Complection, almost as brown as a Mulatto; he wears a dark Gray Pea-Jacket, Faced with Blew, and a short Blew under Jacket, he has short Hair, and either wears Trowsers, or a pair of Black Breeches, a Pair of New Shoes, and White Stockings, speaks English pretty much with a Broge: The other John Reyley, a Blacksmith by Trade, a well made young Fellow, about the Age of the other, of a Middle Stature, Square Shoulders, of a fair and rudy Complection with long

Brown Hair, wears a dark Pea-Jacket with an under Jacket Olive coloured, and Trowsers, speaks plainer English than the other; the Jackets of both of them, are such as servants generally bring with them from Ireland.

Whoever takes up the said Servants, and bring them to me said John Van Horne, or secure them, and give Notice so that their Master may have them again shall have Thirty Shillings Reward for each Servant, and all reasonable Charges paid by the said   John Van Horne.

AMBOY Sept. 23. On Friday Night last, one William Scot, was Apprehended in Woodbridge, for uttering one of 18 Penny Bills, who on search, own'd he had Five more of the like Bills, he had a Parcel of Ribbons, and said he got them from some of the said Ribbons he sold at Long-Island, but from whom he cou'd not tell. The Justice there sent him to our Goal in this City, being betwext 11 and 12, at which time I went to the Prison and had him Strip'd (the Justice at Woodbridge, having only searched his Pockets) and had thro' search, but could find no more Counterfeits, but found upon his Examination, that there was a great reason to suspect him, next Morning the Mayor and Aldermen, after some search, Examined him; on which we Dispatch'd an Express to Acquaint his Excellency therewith, to know what Bills he had Passed on the Road; and to have his Chest searched, which he suspected was at his Lodging in New-York. Our Governour gave Orders to search his Lodging, and other suspected places, but John Thimin the Express we sent, Braced his Chest and Bedding, to be put on board the George and John, Anthony Adamson Commander; and likewise found sundry of the Counterfeit Bills, pass'd in New-York, and on the Road by the said Scot.

Yesterday the said Thimin returned, on which he went on board of the said Ship, and demanded the said William Scot's Chest and Bedding, which was delivered by the Captain, and on search we found a false Bottom of a small Trunk 476 Counterfeit Bills, Sign'd but not Numbered, and 106 Bills neither Sign'd nor Numbered; on which we went to the said Scot and there acquainted him therewith, who on his examination, did confess, that this Adamson had carried one of the said Bills (he believed) from hence to Dublin, and that the Company of the said Adamson and Thomas Eanon, the said Adamson told them, that if they could get the like Printed, they would get Money enough by them, for that they pass in those Parts, as well as Gold and Silver, that the said Eanon agreed with the Printer, whose name the said Deponent was sworn not to discover, that they paid their Proportion to Eanon for Printing, and that they divided the Bills betwixt them, buy does not own what Number; he assumes they had not a Thousand Each, that the said Eanon, Adamson, and himself, the said Scot, had all the Bills, and there was no other concerned with them on the Affair. The Captain we had Examined as well as all his Men, and his Ship was Searched, but they all deny that they knew any thing of the said Scot, or ever see him but at Salem in New-England, where the Ship Landed her Passengers, and the said Scot came first into these Parts, and when he put those things on board in New-York, as there is great reason to suspect the Captain, he was committed likewise last Night to our Goal, but are in hopes, to fix passing parts of the said Bills on him.

PHILADELPHIA Sept. 25. Run away the 20th of August last from William Parks, of Annapolis in Maryland, Printer; a Servant Man, nam'd Andrew Hanna, born in Scotland, aged about 21, of a small Stature, fresh Complexion, sometimes wears his own Hair, which is black, short curl'd and at other times a Wig over it; and was cloath'd with a red Duffil Coat, trim'd with black wastcoat and Leather Breeches, &c. and hath taken with him a large White Horse branded thus E on the near Shoulder and Buttock, and a pair of Leather Bags, belonging to his said Master, And 'tis suppos'd to be gone towards New-York, or further that Way.

Any Person that will secure the said Servant in Custody, and give Notice of it to Mr. Marshal, Post-Master in Boston, Mr. William Bradford Printer in New-York, Mr. Andrew Bradford Printer in Philadelphia, or to me in Annapolis, shall have Five Pounds Reward; and Forty Shillings for my Horse, Paid by me   Wm. Parks.

Run away from the Subscriber, Minister of St. John's Parish in Baltimore-County, on Sunday Night the 10th of August 1729. Two Servant Men, the one named Albert Barnham of middle Stature, well set, dark Complection, short Blach Hair, having the Jerusalem-Arms on his Right Arm (and if I mistake not) a Woman's Name on his Left: The other called John Heaton about Twenty three Years of Age, somewhat Lower in stature, of a Rudy Countenance, short brown Hair and a little Curl'd, speaks the Yorkshire dialect, and professes Husbandry.

The carried with them One Cloath and Ozenbrig Jacket, two Pair of Trowzers, one Pair of white and one of brown Yarn Stockins, Two Pair of Shoes, two Ozenbrig Shirts, and one of Chequered Linnin, one Hat and one Milled Cap. Whoever secures the said Servants and give Notice thereto to the Subscriber with Convenient speed, shall receive Three Pounds current Money for their Reward, and Proportionable for Either of them paid by   William Cantheen.

N. B. The aforesaid Barnham being a Sailor, Masters of Ships are hereby cautioned against taking him into their Employment.

PHILADELPHIA Oct. 5. Run away from Ralph Smith, of the City of Annapolis, in Maryland, a Servant Man, named John Charlton, a Taylor by Trade; aged about 27, of a middle Stature, or rather tall, full fac'd a swarthy Complexion and a black Beard, which is pretty thin, black Eyes, and black, short, curl'd Hair, but may have cut it off, to disguise himself: His Legs were sore, and are pretty thick. He has a smooth, sort of way of Speaking.

His Wearing Apparel, when he went away, was a white corded Fustian or Thuckset Coat, with the Sleeves cut like Wastcoat Sleeves, with white Metal Buttons wash'd with Silver, and are wrought like Silver Thread Buttons, and in lin'd with ordinary brown Holland, plain behind: his Wastcoat and Breeches were strip'd Holland, the Stripes blue, red, white. He had with him a pair of blue Silk Stockings, and 2 pair of Grey

Worsted Ditto, a pair of good shoes, stitch'd round the Tops, a good Castor Hat, and his shirts were of white Sheeting course Linnen. Any Person that will secure the said Servant in custody, and give Notice of it to Mr. Marshal, in Boston, Mr. William Bradford, Printer in New-York, Mr. Andrew Bradford Printer in Philadelphia, or to me in Annapolis, shall have Four Pounds Reward, if taken up in this Province; and Six Pounds Reward, in any other, paid by   Ralph. Smith.

PHILADELPHIA Oct. 9. Run away from Peter Galloway, in Maryland some time past; a Tall Negro Man, of a Yellowish Complexion, about Thirty five Years of Age, strong and well set, talks pretty good English, Named Corfey, but since has called himself Will, having a scar upon or near one of his Breasts, and it is said that he is gone towards Albany. Whoever takes up said Negro Man and delivers him to William Fishcurn, Merchant in Philadelphia, shall receive Ten Pounds as a reward from me Peter Galloway.

To be Sold. A likely Young Woman's Time to be disposed of, that can Write, Flourish, do plain Work and Marks very well, fit to teach School; by George Brownwell, School-Master in Philadelphia.

PHILADELPHIA Oct. 16. These are to give Notice, That on Monday the Third of November next, the Treasurers of the Province of New-Jersey, will attend at their Respective Offices in Burlington, and Anboy, to Exchange all such Old Bills of New-Jersey, as shall be brought unto them, and that after the fourth Monday of November next the Law does not allow them to Exchange any more of the said old Bills.

NEW-CASTLE Oct. 21. The Governour's Speech to the Assembly of the Three Lower Counties.

Mr. Speaker, and Gentlemen of the House of Representatives;
It give me small uneasiness, that I found my self incapable of attending the Assembly of those Counties, at the time of their last Adjournment: But being then scarce recovered from the severest Fever I have been visited since I came into America, my Physicians were of Opinion I could not, in that condition, undertake the Journey,

without such manifest Danger of a Relapse, as might at least render my Visit to you Altogether fruitless. For this Reason I judged it most advisable for the Ease of the Gentlemen I was to meet, to give them such timely Notice as might prevent their Trouble and Disappointment. Therefore what was then be done, viz. The Revising and compiling a body of your laws, will I hope, by your Application, be this Year perfected; that those digested and Published, the People, by that easier Opportunity of making themselves acquainted therewith, may with more certainty know what is required of them, and accordingly conform themselves to what they enjoyn.

It is a great Pleasure to me, Gentlemen, to observe, that after the small struggle that appeared at my first Entrance on this Government, We are now universally fallen into regular an Administration, that I scarce know any one Thing necessary to be Recommended particularly to your Care, or that requires any immediate or uncommon Provisions. This, next to the Blessing of God on the Sincerity of my Endeavours (whithin any Partial Views) to make every good Man easy in the Station Providence has placed him, must, undoubtedly be owing to the Strength of Reason and good Sense in the People, in Distinguishing rightly between the solid Enjoyment of real privileges, in which it shall ever be my Study to protect them, and the idle Suggestions and Jealousies, by which designing Persons would have endeavoured to put them out of the way of reaping the happier Fruits of a regular Conduct, with inward Peace and Contentment.

I have indeed heard Complaints of the Scarcity of a Currency in these Counties, as we have the same of late in the Province: For a Remedy to the latter, I have ventured to pass an Act of Assembly for emitting a large Sum, which by its Circulation must undoubtedly affect all Parts of this River; but I am anxious to hear the success of the Act in Britain, and Account of which I expect soon. In the mean time, it will be convenient for you to make an exact and thorow Inquiry into the Accounts of the Loan-Office for those Counties, to discover how Payments have been made, and to deduce as exact a Computation as may be of the Sums now abroad on both Emissions: And so soon as our Condition in repect to this Currency can be more perfectly understood, I shall be very ready to join with you in any just and safe Measures that may prove for the true Interest and Honour of those Counties, in This or any other Point, wherein my Concurrence can contribute to the Ease and the Benefit of His Majesty's Subjects committed to my Care; In which I have His own glorious Example set before me, to imitate in our low Sphere: And I doubt not but you will be equally ambitious of Copying after That of His Loyal and Faithful Commons.   P. Gordon.

PHILADELPHIA Oct. 25. We hear that on Monday last a Cart and five Horses, together with their Driver fell from the Top of a Stone Bridge in Derby, which is near fourteen foot high, and came all out unhurt.

On Tuesday last, one Conrad Oldhan, riding in his Cart on the Road to Townenson, in this County (by the Plantation of Daniel Williams) the Horses turning short round a Corner, the Wheel took a Stake in the Fence & mounted so high that the Cart overset and turned Bottom upward, and the Wheel falling upon his Head, killed him instantly. Taken from the Coroners Inquisition Dated Oct. 22.

NEW-YORK Oct. 27. The Ship Jenny Galley of Dublin in Ireland, whereof Richard Murphy is Master, took Passengers and Servants on board, to the Number of 200, bound to New-Castle in Delaware River, and about the 25th of July last, set sail from Londonderry for said Port. In the Passage the Master brought the passengers to short Allowance. And the 14th of September coming up the Coast of America, and having a fair Wind, he lay by, whereupon the Supercargo and first and second Mate, enquired the Reason of it? The Captain told them, He would go into Virginia; the Supercargo opposed it, because he had chartered the Ship to New-Castle, and was oblig'd to carry the Passengers to that Port. And a Difference arising, the Passengers were call'd to know if they were willing to go to Virginia? They all answered No, they would go to New-Castle, the place where the Vessel was to Land them. Upon this the Master said, if they would not let him go to Virginia, they might do what they pleased with the Ship, he would take no further care of her, and betook himself to his Cabbin. Then by consent the Supercargo, the 2d Mate, and Passengers, William Kinley the Chief Mate, took charge of the Ship and made the best of their way for Delaware River; but being a Stranger to the Coast, he came into Sandy Hook, where they were met by His Majesty's Ship the Shoram, and Capt. Long enquiring whence they came, & Richard Murphy the said Commander, cried out; There was Piracy among them, that he was Master, and they had taken his Ship from him. Whereupon Capt. Long confined the two Mates, the Supercargo, and some of the Passengers; and the Ship proceeded and came into the Harbour of New-York: And his Excellency the Governour being Acquainted of this Affair, he sent for the Mates and Supercargo, called a Council, and examined into the same; and his Excellency and Council finding that the Master was not forced to his Cabbin, but that he went voluntarily to it Himself, and it appearing that the said Mates and Supercargo had no Piratical Intentions, but only to avoid going to Virginia, and endeavouring to go to the Port where the Ship and Passengers were bound to go, the said Mates and Supercargo and Passengers were discharged, and the Captain left at Liberty to get Satisfaction at common Law, if he see cause.

The Captain detains the Passengers Goods on board, and they are thereby obliged to stay in New-York upon charge, till they can get them by Law.

PHILADELPHIA Oct. 30. Run away from the Widow Earlington of Rockey-Hill, East New-Jersey the 28th of September last, Two Servant Men the one named James Wilson of a Middle Stature Dark Brown Hair, Fair Complexion, Blew eyes, he had on a dark Brown Vest and Breeches a Pair of Worsted, and a Pair of Yarn Stockings, he is a Weaver by Trade, he has taken with him several

Weavers Tools.

The other named Thomas Breadey, he has dark Brown Hair of a Fair Complexion, a little Taller than the other, and speaks much upon the Broue, he has on a Brown Jacket, and Buckskin Breeches, and small Brass Buttons, a Grey Jacket with Red Lining, a Holland Shirt, a good Hat; They have 2 Black Wigs with them. Whoever shall take up said Servants, or either of them, and secure them, and give Notice to their Mistress, shall have Forty Shillings for Each, and Reasonable Charges.

PERT-Amboy Nov. 1. At a Special Court of Oyer and Terminer, Held at Perth-Amboy on the 29th of October last, were Tryed at the said Court, one Anthony Adamson and William Scot, for Counterfeiting the Bills of Credit of this Province of New-Jersey, and for uttering the same, who were found Guilty of the Crime so Charged upon them, and the Court gave Judgement against them as following, viz.

That you the said Adamson be taken into a Cart at the Prison Door on Friday the last Day of October, and so carried thro' the Streets of Perth-Amboy, with a rope about your Neck; and that you be, about eleven a Clock in the forenoon of the same Day put in the Pillory, and there to continue for an Hour, and from thence Carted aith a Rope about your Nech to Woodbridge, to the Meeting House of said Town, thence to the Square before Mr. Hords Door; and to stand in the Cart a Quarter of an Hour: And that you have a Paper fixed on your Back and Breast declaring your Offence, with one of the Counterfeit Bills fixed thereto; and from thence back to Goal, there to remain until you pay the fees and Charges.

The same Sentence was pass'd on William Scot with this Difference, he was to be carried to Piscataway, and not to be inflicted on him until Saturday the fifteenth of November.

NEW-YORK Nov. 3. We hear that a sore Accident happened on Sunday the 26th of October last, viz. That at Kingston in the County of Ulster, the Malt-House and Brew-House of Mattias Slest, with a great Quantity of Wheat, Barley and Malt, and all Utensils therein burnt and Destroyed.

PHILADELPHIA Nov. 13. Run away from Simon Hadley, Esq; of New-Castle County, the 28th of October 1729, a Servant Boy, named Edmond Kenny, about 18 Years of Age, of a Middle Stature, of a Fair Complexion, light Brown Hair, goes close with his Knees, and out with the Toes; having on when he went away an Old Beaver Hat, a Homespun Shirt, a Brown English Drugget Jacket, a Homespun Coat of dark colour, with Broad Pewter Buttons, he has on a Pair of Linnen Draw's, Old Shoes, and Stockins, he took with him, when he went away, a Spoon Mold, and likely Gray work'd Horse, Branded on the Shoulder, and the rear Buttock eith I. W. Whoever takes up said Servant, and brings him to his Master, or secure him, so that he may be had again, shall have Five Pounds Reward; and if they secure the said Horse, so that he may be had again, shall have Twenty Shillings Reward, paid by me

Simon Hadley.

NEW-CASTLE COUNTY Nov. 13. On the 13th Day of October last, a Strange Negroe Man, was taken up as a Run-away, in Mill-Creek Hundred in this County; He is low sized Slender and nimble Fellow, seems to be about Twenty five Years old, has a Large Head, small Hands and Legs, looks Wild and Staring, wears a Brown Jacket, ragged Black Shirt, short Ozenbriggs Trowsers, with a Pair of Leather Breeches underneath; he seems, as if he cannot Speak, or understand English, or the Language of any of the Negroes of this Place, so that 'Tis not yet known here, to whom, or where, he belongs. Whoever knows the said Negroe, or his Owner; are desired to make the same known to the Sheriff of said County,

Wm. Read.

PHILADELPHIA Nov. 20. Broke out of Newtown Goal the 6th of October last, the following Persons, viz. Thomas Lamb, of a Middle Stature, Black Complexion; had on when he went away, a Light colour'd Broad Cloath Coat without Pocket Holes, or Flaps, Burnt in several Places on one of the fore Skirts, had with him 2 Wigs, one Black, and Ty'd behind, the other a White short Wig, and he has a great Scar over his Right Ear:

At the same Time broke out of the said Goal one Edward Gartage, who pretends himself Mate of a Ship, also a Ship-Carpenter, nigh six Foot high, Pale Visage, and a little Pock-broken; is supposed to have a good fine Hat and Light colour'd Wig, Ty'd with a black Ribbon behind, or else a Double worsted Cap, a good white Shirt, a double Breasted Cinnamon colour'd Broad Cloath Coat trim'd with the same, a gray Broad Cloath Vest, and black Breeches, Light gray Worsted stockings, good Wood-Heel'd Shoes and Brass Buckles; Escaped at the same Time, one George Tesdall, a Labourer, of a Middle Size, Pale Visage, very much Pock-broken; and has a Stuttering, or Impediment in his Speech, also brown Hair, supposed to have on an Old blew gray Broad Cloath Coat, an old Light Gray Kersey Vest, an Ozenbrigs Shirt, and Trowsers, Leather Breeches, gray Yarn Stockings, and old Leather-Heel'd Shoes, but no Buckles.

Whoever takes up the said Men and brings them to John Millnots of Newtown, or secures them, so as they may be had again, shall have Fifty Shillings for each, as a Reward, and reasonable Charges paid by   Timothy Smith, Sheriff.

PERTH-AMBOY Nov. 26. Last Saturday our Ferry-boat coming over from The other side with 7 Men and 7 Horses, a Gust of Wind arose and overset the Boat, and 2 Men and 2 Horses were drowned.

PHILADELPHIA Nov. 27. Captain Wright in a Schooner bound for Boston loaded with Wheat, overset in the Bay not long after the Pilot had left her. It is not yet certain whether any of the People are sav'd or not.

NEW-YORK Dec. 1. On Friday last, at the Court of Admiralty held here, His Honour Patrick Gordon, Esq; being President, John Wells, John Hogg, Peter Bard, and John Moore Esq; Commissioners; Thomas Lawrence, Esq; Samuel Hatel Esq; Capt. John Hopkins, and Capt. Thomas Burns Assistants; on the Tryal of Capt. Mercer for the Murder of Thomas Flory one of the Passengers.

The Commission being read, and the Court Qualified, several Articles were exhibited against the Prisoner, charging him with putting to Death Thomas Flory in a cruel inhumane and barbarous

Manner on the high and open Seas, contrary to the Laws of God and Man, and to the Peace of our Sovereign Lord the King, &c. To all which he pleaded not Guilty: Then Counsel for the Prisoner moved for a Copy of the Articles, which was granted; and the Court adjourned 'till Saturday Morning 10 a-Clock.

The Court being met according to Adjournment, several Witnesses were examined for the King, who deposed that being on board the Ship Degheda Merchant on her Passage from Ireland to Philadelphia, Thomas Flory the Deceas'd was brought upon Deck by the Captain's Order, a Rope put about his Neck, and a Prayer-Book in his Hand; and that he was threatened with immediate Death; but that afterwards had Irons put on his Hands, by which he was hoisted up from the Deck, that Matters dipt in Brimstone were put between his Fingers, and Toes, and being set on Fire they burnt the Flesh to the Bones, leaving some of the Joints bare; that he being in that Manner near half an Hour, making grievous Lamentations; and that Captain being advised to halt such proceedings, answered, That he was King, Judge and Governour aboard his own Vessel, and would do what he Pleased. That the said Flory was afterwards thrown over-board with a Rope round his Middle, and continued to lie above Deck in the open Air, not being admitted into his Birth below; and being in a miserable Condition, unable either to stand or go, or feed himself, and cry-out for Water, a Bucket of Salt Water was thrown upon him; that he languished upon Deck several Weeks and at length died; and that the Night he died all the Passengers were ordered below Deck, and the Hatches nailed down on them.

The several Witnesses were called by the counsel for the Prisoner; who deposed as follow, That some Days after their Departure from Cape-Clear in Ireland, Mr, Steward, one of the Passengers, made a Complaint to the Captain, that he was robbed by the aforesaid Thomas Flory of near 100 Guinias, and Intreated his Assistance in recovering it: that accordingly the said Tho. Flory was examined and Threatened 'till he confessed he had taken the Money: and being asked where it was, he said he had put it in a Place by the side of the Pump: But it not being found there upon Search, the Matches aforementioned were put between his Fingers, in order to certify him to a true Confession. It was likewise deposed, that the Captain neither ordered or approved his lying upon Deck, having several Times directed him to his Birth below, but that Passengers, one and all, refused to admit him among them, he being an odious filty fellow, and having a Distemper, which together with his Laziness rendered him extremely uncleanly. That the Water thrown on him was not by the Captain's Orders, nor was it by his Orders; or with his Knowledge that he was thrown over-board as above. That the Passengers being ordered down, and the Hatches nailed on them the Night Flory died, was no more than usual when they were like to have bad weather, and that Night in particular they expected to come in with it Hard, when it was by no means proper to have the Decks crowded.

It did not appear by any of the Evidence, that Capt. Mercer had ordered the Matches to be lighted; or that what he had done was out of particular Malice to the Deceased, but from a Desire to do Justice to Mr. Steward and his Family, who having, sold their Effects in Ireland and embarked what they had together with Themselves, on board his Vessel for a strange Country, it was apprehended were greatly injured by the said Flory. That what was done to him was with the general Consensus and Assistance of all aboard; he being regarded by each one in the Ship, not even by his Sister, who after he had suffered as above, used frequently to reproach him with the theft, and beat him with her own Hands, and that tho' no one by any means retrained from comforting or ministering to the Deceased in his Weakness, it did not appear that any of them had been at all forward so to do, by which it seems, he was the general Aversion of the whole Company. It appears likewise that there might be some Malice to the Prosecution; One Monogenny, one of the Passengers, who had been very active in the Thing, being called as a Witness for the King, it was deposed in Court that he had attempted to subdue Evidence against the Prisoner, and had undertaken his Death, saying if he were not hanged he would hang for him; and if the Prisoner was not hanged, it should not be for want of Swearing, or Words to that effect, upon when he was put by, and not suffered to give Evidence. Several Persons appeared to the Prisoner's Reputation, and spoke very handsomely of him, declaring that they had known him for many Years; that he always bore a fair Character, and was never accounted to be of a Tyrannical or Cruel Disposition. The Tryal lasted 'till five in the Afternoon, when upon the whole the Court acquitted him, to the general Satisfaction of the People, who before had been greatly exasperated against him.

PHILADELPHIA Dec. 16. These are to give Notice, to all Planters, Husbandmen, and others: That there liveth at the House of Mr. Isaac _____ in Third street opposite to the Quaker Burying Ground, one John Wilkinson, from London, Brush Maker; who makes all Sorts of Brushes, as horse, Weavers, and Scrubbing Brushes &c. He likewise sells strong Russian-Bristles, fit for Shoemakers, very Reasonable: He will give ready Money for good Hogs Bristle.

PHILADELPHIA Dec. 22. Yesterday several Vessels, who attempted to go out of the Harbour last Week, but were forc'd back by reason of driving Ice, proceeded on their respective Voyages.

Last Night died at his House in this City, George Claypoole, Esq; Alderman.

PHILADELPHIA Dec. 23. Last Week at the Court of Oyer and Terminer held in this City, two Servants, James Prouse and James Mitchel (the same who broke Prison some time since, and were retaken at Amboy) were tried for Burglary. It Appears by the King's Evidence, that Prouse entered the House of Mr. Sheed, Barber, in Front Street, (being admitted by a Servant of the Family) and there broke open a Desk, from whence he took Seven Pounds Ten Shillings in Paper Money, and four Copper Half-pence; and that Mitchel in the meantime waited without to watch. It was proved that the Money lost was found upon Prouse when he was taken; who only said in his Defence at the Bar, that it was given him by Mr. Sheed's Man to keep. Mitchel in his Defence said that tho' he had been in Company with Prouse and other Servants Drinking Rum out of Town in the Day Time, being Sunday, yet that he heard nothing of any Contrivance to rob or the like; and that he was in Bed when the Fact was committed, from whence Prouse afterwards called him to go and drink, but did not acquaint with what had been done. The Jury brought them both in Guilty, and Prouse being asked what he had to say why sentence of Death should not pass against him, answered that he had nothing to say in his own Behalf but declared that Mitchel was wholly innocent, and knew nothing of the Fact.

The Court passed Sentence on them both, but directed Mitchel to apply to his Honour the Governour for Mercy.

Mr. Sheed's Servant (who in the above Tryal was Evidence for the King) is hereafter to be tried for Robbery, the Law not making it Burglary in a Servant to open a Door in the night Time, tho' it be to admit Thieves,&c.

PHILADELPHIA Dec. 23. We have an Account from New-Castle, that their Prison is Burnt down to the Ground, and the Prisoners that were in it narrowly Escaped.

PHILADELPHIA Dec. 30. Broke out of the Goal at Burlington on the 17th Day of this Instant December, 1729, about One of the Clock in the Morning, one Man named James Burnside about Twenty six Years of age; Middle Stature, Sanguine Complexion, Short curl'd Red Hair, an Irishman, has a Broage on his Tongue, a Shoemaker by Trade. Whoever takes up the said James Burnsides, and bring him to Burlington, shall have Five Pounds Rewaed, and reasonable Charges by   Thomas Hanlock Sheriff.

Run away from Christian Peters, about four Months ago, of Cecil County in Maryland, a Negroe Man named Peter, about thirty Years of age, a well set fellow, he has a scar or a cut over his Left Eye. Whoever shall take up said Negroe, and secure him, and give Notice (or bring him) to his said Master, in Maryland, or

to Mr. Arron Hasset, living in Front-street in
Philadelphia, shall have forty Shillings Reward
and all reasonable Charges.

1730

PHILADELPHIA Jan. 6. Yesterday was interred here the Body of Mary Bradway formerly a noted Midwife. She was born on New-Years Day 1629-30. and died on the Second of January 1729-30, aged One hundred Years and a Day. Her Constitution wore well to the last, and she could see to read without Spectacles a few Months since.

PHILADELPHIA Jan. 13. On Monday sennight was killed near Shewsbury in Jersey a monstrous Panther, the like never seen before in these Parts. Its Legs thicker than that of a Horse, whith a Body proportionable, and the Nails of its Claws longer than the middle Finger of a Man's Hand. It seems the Indian who killed him was creeping up on the Ground, in order to have a shot at a Buck, but hearing a rustling of Leaves behind him, accidentally saw the Panther a few yards off, just ready to leap upon him, he thereupon instantly fired, and luckily, with about 4 or 5 Swan shot, hit him in the Head, and killed him. The indian received a considerable Reward for the Service, from the Liberality of the Neighbouring People.

About the same Time, another large Panther was killed near Conestogoe. He had got among some of the Swine in the nightime, & the Owner hearing them cry, went out with a couple of Dogs, which drove the Panther up into a Tree. Ignorant what was that went up the Tree, he made a Fire near it, and left two Women to watch while he went to fetch a Neighbour that had a Gun. They fired at it twice broke both his Fore-Legs; upon which, to the great Surprize, he made a desperate Leap and fell to the Ground near the Man who could but get out of the Way. The Dogs immediately seiz'd him, and with another shot in the Head he was dispatched.

On friday last, Charles Calagham, was whipt

round Town at Cart Tail, and received 35 Lashes, pursuant to his Sentence at the Mayor's Court for an Assault with an Intent to ravish a Child under 10 Years of Age. He was accompanied by two Men who had 21 Lashes, one being convicted of stealing a Saddle off a Horses Back; and the other who received the same Number for another Robbery.

PERTH-AMBOY Jan. 14. On Saturday last, a Negro Man was tried here for Murdering a poor Man; one Thomas Cock, who was a Taylor by Trade, and went about working at People's Houses: For the said Murder the Evidence against the Negro being very clear, altho' he denied the Fact at his Trial, he was found guilty of the Murder and condemn'd for the same; and sentence was pronounced against him, viz. That he should be burnt the Monday following, which was then put into Execution, and he was then according to the said Burnt alive, and confest the Fact before he was Burnt.

NEW-YORK Jan. 27. For some Nights past several Houses have been broke open, and Robberies committed in this City.

PHILADELPHIA Jan. 30. The 24th Instant, being the Day appointed for the Execution of James Prouse and James Mitchel for Burglary, about 12 o'Clock a numerous Crowd were gethered to the Prison Door to see these young Men bro't fort to suffer. While their Irons were taken off and their Arms binding, Prouse cry'd immoderately; but Mitchel endeavoured in a friendly Manner to comfort him; Do not cry, Jimmy: (says he) in an Hour or two it will be over with us, and we shall both be easy. They were then placed in a Cart, together with a Coffin for each of them, and led Thro' Town to the Place of Execution: Prouse appear'd extremely dejected, but Mitchel seemed to support himself with a manly Constancy: When they arriv'd at the Place of Execution, they were told it was expected they should make some Confession of their Crime, and say, something by way of Exhortation to the People. Prouse said, his Confession had been taken the Evening before; he acknowledge the Fact for which he was to die, but said, That Greyer who had sworn against him was the Person that persuaded him to it; and declared that he had never wronged any Man besides Mr. Sheed and his Master. Mitchel being desired to speak, reply'd with a sober Countenance. What would you have me to say, I am innocent of the Fact. He was then told, that it did not appear in him to persist in asserting his Innocence; that he had had a fair Trial & was found guilty by the twelve honest and good Men. He only answered, I am Innocent; and it will appear so before God; and far down.

Then they were both bid to stand up, and the Ropes were order'd to be thrown over the Beam; when the Sheriff took a Paper out of his Packet and began to read. The poor wretches were at that Time fill'd with the immediate Terror of approaching Death, and having nothing else before their Eyes, took but little Notice of what was read, till they heard the Words Pity and Mercy. [And whereas, the said James Prouse, and James Mitchel have been recommended to me as proper Objects of Pity and Mercy.] Immediately Mitchel fell into the most violent Agony; and having only said, God Bless the Governour, he swooned away in the Cart. Suitable Means were used to remove him; and when he came a little to himself, he added, I have been a great Sinner, I have been guilty of almost every Crime; Sabbath-Breaking in particular, which led me into ill Company, but theft I never was guilty of. God Bless the Governour; and God almighty's Name be praised; and then swoon'd away again. Prouse likewise seem'd to be overwhelm'd with Joy, but did not Swoon. All the way back to the Prison, Mitchel lean'd on his Coffin, being unable to support himself, and shed Tears in abundance. He then went out with a large share of Resolution & Fortitude, returned in the most dispirited Manner imaginable, being utterly over-power'd by the Force of that sudden Turn of excessive Joy, for which he had been no way prepared.

The following are copies of the Papers delivered out of Prouse and Mitchel the Evening before.

I James Prouse, was born in the Town of Brentford, in Middlesex County in Old England, of Honest Parents, who gave me but little Education. My Father was a Corporal in the Oxford's Regiment of Horse, (then named the Lord's Blues) and I was for some time in the care of an Uncle who lived at Eling near Brentford aforesaid, and who would have given me good Learning; but I being Young would not take good Counsel, and in the 12th Year of my Age came into Philadelphia, where I was recommended to one of the best Masters, who never let me want for any thing; But I minded the evil Insinuation of wicked People, more than the good Dictates of my Master, and not having the fear of God before my eyes, and deservedly brought to this shameful end. I Acknowledge I justly merit Death for the Fact which condemns me; but I never had the least Design or thought of the like, until often press'd, and at length seduced to it by John Greyer, who was the only Person that ruined me. He often solicited me to be guilty of other Crimes of the like Nature, but I was never guilty of any such, neither with him or any one else; neither did I ever wrong any Man before, say my too indulgent Master: from whom I now & then pilfer'd a Yard or the like of Cloth in order to make Money to Spend with the said Greyer. As for James Mitchel, who dies for the same Fact with me, as I hope to receive Mercy at the great Tribunal, be the said James Mitchel is intirely innocent, and knew nothing of the Fact until apprehended and taken. I am about nineteen Years of Age, and Die a Protestant.   James Prouse.

The Speech and Declaration of James Mitchel, written with his own Hand.

I James Mitchel was born at Anthim in Ireland of good and honest Parents, & bro't up by them until the Age of 13 Years, and had a suitable Education given me, such as being taught to read and write English, with some Latin; and might had been further instructed, but at my earnest Request was bound Apprentice to a Book-binder, and served four Years to that Trade; after which I left the Kingdom and went to England, in order to be further improved in my Business; but there had the Misfortune to be press'd on board the Perwick Man-of-War, commanded by the Honourable George Gordon, and having been at several parts abroad, returned to England in October of 1728. where I was by sickness reduced to a very sad Condition, through which I came over to this Country a Servant; here I was it seems unfortunately led into bad Company, and one Evening by James Prouse was raised out of my Bed to go and drink with him and one Greyer, to which was all the Money I saw that Night and till the next Morning, and then James Prouse took out of his Pocket a 15 Shilling Bill, and desired me to get it changed for him, in order to spend some of it; but coming into Town, I was apprehended for the robbing of Mr. George Sheed, and now am to die for the same. I die a Protestant.

James MItchel.

PHILADELPHIA Feb. 10. On Sunday last an unhappy Man, one Sturgis, upon Difference with his Wife, determined to drown himself in the River, and she, (kind Wife) went with him, it seems to see it faithfully performed, and accordingly stood by silent and unconcerned during the whole Transaction: He junp'd in near Carpenter's Wharf. but was timely taken out again before what he came about was thoroughly effected, so that they were obliged to return home as they came, and put up for that time with Disappointment.

Last Week a Brigantine came up which brought Passengers into New-Castle from Ireland; they had been Two and Twenty Weeks at Sea, and had thrown Seventy five People over-board which died on the Way.

An Account of Passengers and Servants landed in Pennsylvania from December 25, 1728 to December 25, 1729. English and Welsh Passengers 199, and Servants 68, makes 276.

Irish Passengers 925, and Servants 230, makes 1155.

Scotch Passengers none, Servants 43.

Palatines Passengers 243, Servants none.

In New-Castle Government have landed 4500 Passengers and Servants, chiefly from Ireland in all 6218.

ANNAPOLIS Feb. 10. We are inform'd, that a

Woman of this City, having by her Industry sav'd a considerable Sum of Money, and not willing to let it be known, put it into an Earthen Pot and hid it under Ground; but a certain Man living near the Place where she hid it, had the good Fortune to find it out, took the Money, and left the Pot for the same Use another Time.

PHILADELPHIA Feb. 10. By Vendue on the Seventeenth Day of March next, at Plymouth Township, in the County of Philadelphia: The Water Corn Mill and Boulton Mill (commonly called Plymouth Mills) with a large Stone Messuage, a new Barn, and two Hundred Acres of the best land in the whole Township; about five and forty Acres whereas are cleared, and the Land is extraordinary well timbered, There is also a good Meadow and a fine young Orchard, consisting of two hundred and fifty Trees, with several other Convenient Improvements, for the completing a good Plantation, The Land is very Pleasantly situated near the River Schuykill.

And on the 19th of the same Month March; will be Sold, the House and Lott in German-Town, formerly belonging to Peter Gaerlin, adjoining to the Quaker Meeting House.

Whoever is inclin'd to Purchase the said Mill or House, may apply themselves to Samuel Powell Jr., Benjamin Godfrey, Merchants, or Catharine Sprogell's Widow in Philadelphia, where they may treat, concerning the same.

PHILADELPHIA Feb. 19. The Assembly have adjourn'd till the 10th of August next, having made the following Acts, which on the 14th Intant were by his Honour the Governour passed into Laws; viz.

An Act for Regulating Pedlars, and Vendue, &c.

An Act for the better enabling divers Inhabitants of the Province of Pennsylvania to hold Land, and to invest them with the Privileges of natural born Subjects, of the said Province.

An Act for lending the sum of 300 Pounds in Bills of Credit, for building a Prison & Government-House in Lancaster County, &c.

A Supplement Act entitled an Act for preventing Clandest Marriages.

A Supplement Act to an Act of Assembly in this

Province, entitled, an Act against buying Land off the Natives.

An Act laying an Ecise on all Wines, Rum, Brandy and other Spirits, retailing in this Province.

An Act imposing a Duty on Persons convicted of serious Crimes and to prevent poor and impotent Persons from being imported into the Province of Pennsylvania.

An Act for continuing the Encouragement for raising good Hemp within this Province, and Imposing certain Penalties on Persons manufacturing or working up tainted and unmerchantable Hemp into Cordage and Cable.

The above Acts were published on Wednesday the 18th Instant.

PHILADELPHIA Feb. 24. The dwelling House and Lott, formerly belonging to Nathan Shanbury, clear of Proprietaries Thirds; and also several Ground-Rents well Secur'd are to be Sold by
William Fishbourn.

This is to give Notice. That the Subscriber hereof, being desirous to be Generally useful as he can in this Country (wherein he is new and a Stranger) do declare his willingness to Teach Logick, Natural Phylosophy, Metaphysicks, &c. to all as are willing to learn. The Place of Teaching, will be the Widow Spangle's, in Second-street Philadelphia; where he will attend, if he has Encouragement, Three Times a Week for the Exercise.

N. B. All Persons that come, either as Learners or Hearers, will be civilly Treated, By G. M. Minister of the Reform Palatine Church.

PHILADELPHIA March 3. Sunday last, being her Majesty's Birthday and St. David's Day, it was kept on Monday following, by the Antient Brittans, and the Sign of the Crown where all Loyal Healths were drank, at the Discharge of several Cannon; and the Night Concluded with a Ball at the House of Capt. Hopkins.

Run away the 23d Instant February, from John Campbell of Bohemia Manner, in Cecil County, in the Province of Maryland; a Servant Man named George Thompson, a Yorkshire Man, he is broad Faced, hath the Small-Pox, aged about Forty, he hath on a Dark colour'd Jacket and Breeches, and Ozenbrig Shirt, a Pair of Yarn Stockings, a Pair of French Fall Shoes, and speaks broud Yorkshire, and is, or professes a Carpenter, but he mostly goes by Name of Wheel-wright.

Also runaway at the same time from John Winterberry of the same County; a Servant Man, named Daniel Maldin, a Short well set Fellow, of a Dark Complexion, aged about Twenty two, or there about, black short colour'd Hair, a large burnt Scar upon his Breast; the Cloaths he wore when he went away, was a Country Cloath Jacket well worn, and a Patch'd pair of Kersey Breeches, an old Chequered Shirt, a Pair of old Shoes and Stockings, a new Felt Hat, and he speaks pretty thick, but not so much of the Yorkshire as the other does; and supposed both to have gone away with a large Poplar Canoe, that goes with Oars, and both imported by Capt. Allen Gile into this Province, from York Goal. Whoever shall take up the foresaid Servants, so their Masters may have them again, shall have Forty Shillings Reward for each, over and above what the Law allows, which shall be paid by

    John Campbell and John Winterberry.

PHILADELPHIA March 5. Run away from Martyn Jarvis Feb. 9th 1730. A Negroe Woman named Jenny about eighteen Years of Age, she had on when she went away a Grey Jacket and Petty-Coat, She is of a Yellowish Complexion and has lost Part of three Fingers of her Right Hand, she speaks good English, and is Country born. Whoever takes up the said Negroe Woman, give Notice to Martyn Jarvis, at the Sign of the Hat and Hand, in Second-street Philadelphia, shall have Twenty Shillings Paid by me,   Martyn Jarvis.

NEW-CASTLE March 9. The following is a Copy of the dying speech of William Kelsey who was executed on Saturday last for Burglary and burning the goal in this County; he would not suffer any Person to write it for him, but penned it himself. I cannot easily conceice how any Man could die with a greater Presence of Mind, than this unfortunate fellow, I am. Sir, Yours, &c.

Copy of Kelsey's Speech and Dying Words.

I hope this will be an Example to all that

behold me this Day, and that they will refrain all evil Ways; for I confess to God and the Congregation, that I have been a great Sinner but especially these four or five Years past. The Sin which I was first guilty of, was breaking the Lord's Day in many Ways, and that led me into other grievous Sins; Then Secondly, disobeying my Mother, who gave me many Counsels, but I refused to take them; for my Father died when I was a Child. Thirdly the first Sin I was guilty of is Stealing, was one Shilling one Penny Silver, which I stole from my Brother and that led me into another of the same kind: I went and broke a Man's Barn, and stole a Sack out of the same, and went and sold it to a Man, and it being found with him, he was taken by a Warrant and put in Prison, and tried for his Life, which is a great Trouble to me, but he was cleared by the Law, having a Man who proved I sold him the sack: That I was Taken for the same Fact, and was committed to Prison and was found guilty of the same, and was to be Whipped for the Crime, but chose to be Transported to this Country than to suffer that Punishment; and being a Servant with one, Edward Mayne of Kent County, stole from him; one Hat and a pair of Gloves, and run away from him; and went and stole a Suit of Cloaths from one William Milliner; and from thence I came to John Garrirson's in Christiana, and broke his House and stole one Wastcoat and a pair of Breeches, a Crock of Honey and a Loaf of Bread; and being Apprehended for the same, was committed to the Prison of New-Castle; and thinking to make my Escape, went and put Fire in the Dormant Window of the upper Part, the which wicked Crime, with all my other Offences, had brought me to this shameful and untimely End. I hereby beg, and desire all young Persons who behold me this Day, may take Warning by me, and that they may not be guilty of Breaking the Lord's Day or Blaspheming his Holy Name, which I was so much guilty of; and that they may not disobey their Parents, nor keep bad Company, or frequent Taverns. I Declare, now as I am a dying Man, William Scott, Who I said was with me at breaking John Garrison's

House. was not, nor any other Person.

William Kelsey.

PHILADELPHIA March. 12. Stolen out of Mr. Heath's Stable at his Plantation, at the Head of Sassafras, in Maryland; a Middle Size Bright Bay Horse, with a pretty large Star on his Forehead, belonging to his Son, James Paul Heath, and is Branded with a Crow Foot. He Paces very fast, and goes very remarkable wide behind, and is shoed all around: There was likewise stol'n a Saddle and Bridle.

Whoever can secure the Horse aforesaid and give Notice to Mr. Charles Read of Philadelphia, or Mr. Richard Grafton of New-Castle, or the to the Subscriber hereof, shall be well Rewarded by me.

James Paul Heath.

PHILADELPHIA March 19. William Dowell Books being lost in his Life's time, and yet missing; all Persons are hereby desired and required, not to pay any pretence whatsoever, any Money due to the said Dowell's Estate, to any Person or Persons posses'd of said Books; and whoever can give any Intelligence of the said Books, so that they may be had again, shall be well rewarded by me, Simon Edgell Executor of the said Dowell.

All Persons who have any Demands on William Dowell, late of Philadelphia, Merchant, Deceased are desired to bring their accounts, and settle with the Executor; and all Persons who are indebted to the said William Dowell, are desired to come forthwith and pay their respective Debts, or expect further Trouble

N. B. There is also a House on Society-Hill (commonly call'd the Stillhouse) to be sold by the said Executor.

All Persons that have any Demands against the Estate of John Knight, late of Philadelphia, deceas'd; and likewise those that are indebted to said Estate, are desired forthwith to come and settle with Hannah Knight, Relict and Administratrix of said John Knight.

N. B. There is to be sold several Tenements with Two large Stills, Cisturns, and other Conveniencies for Distilling.   By Hannah Knight.

NEW-YORK March 23. By his Excellency John

Montgomerie, Esq; Captain General and Governour in Chief of the Province of New-York, New-Jersey, and Territories thereon depending in America, and Vice-Admiral of the same, &c.

A PROCLAMATION

Whereas his Majesty's Fort at Albany, on the Third Instant, was set on Fire in some several Places, by some Malicious and ill designing Persons: To the End therefore that the Actors, Abettors, or Contrivers thereof may be discovered, I have Thought fit, by Virtue of my Powers and Authorities granted to me by His Majesty's Letters, Patents under the Broad Seal of Great Britain, to make an order to be Published this Proclamation, promising a Reward of Twenty Pounds to any Person or Persons who shall discover the Person or persons Guilty of the above recited Crime, so that he or they be convicted of the fatal Offence according to Law. And I do hereby further Promise his Majesty's most Generous Pardon to all Persons who shall make such Discovery except the Person who did actually set the Fire to the said Fort.

Given under my Hand and Seal at arms at Fort George in New-York, this nineteenth Day of March, in the third Year of His Majesty's Reign, Annoq; Dimini, 1729-30.   J. Montgomerie.

ANN-ARUNDEL COUNTY March 29. Run away from the Ship Hume, James Atking Commander, lying in the South River, Two Brothers, Richard and Samuel Goodman, the one a Carpenter, and the other a Sawyer, one a Middle Stature, the other Taller; having on loose Coats, one if not both, a Blew Duffles, their under Coats, the one supposed to be Yellow coloured Drugget, the other Grey, Duroy; both wears either Caps or Wigs, the rest of their Apparel unknown, their Cloaths New, and very little wore, 'tis supposed they have a bundle of spare Shirts, &c.

Whoever secures the said two Men, out of the Province aforesaid so that they may be had again, shall have Five Pounds Reward for both, or Fifty Shillings for one of them, paid by either Thomas Worthington or John Brice.

PHILADELPHIA April 2. At last we have the Pleasure of Publishing the following Advertisement, for promoting the Circulation of the Currency of the Lower Counties which we hope will be an agreeable Piece of News to all Readers.

Whereas divers Acts have been passed, in the Lower Counties upon Delaware; for the Emission of Paper Money; a considerable Part of which (in the ordinary Course of Trade) is daily brought into this Province, and altho' the Credit thereof, subsists on equal Foundation; with that now is current in Pennsylvania, yet it's Circulation here, has been in a great Measure, unhappily stopt, to the Discouragement of Trade; and Breach of that good Agreement which ought naturally to subsist between the Inhabitants of these Counties, and those of the Province; upon Pretence, that the Bills of Credit there used; will now discharge the Requirements in the Loan-Office of Pennsylvania, yet all as much as the receiving a Part of the present Currency of the said Counties, in all payments, will be no inconveniency to the Borrowers here, and to the End that the Value of the said Paper Credit may be kept up, and the true Design and intention thereof (viz. That of being a method of conveying) fully assorted; we whose Notice we under written have agreed, and do hereby promise and oblige our selves every Man for himself, that from and after the 25th Day of January Instant, we will accept and receive in all Payments of Money, now due, or hereafter becoming due to us on any Account whatsoever, one fourth Part thereof in Currency of said Counties, as the same is now Established, and stands limited to the sum of Twelve Thousand Pounds, and what yet remains Circulated by Virtue of the former Act passed in that Government: Promising further to do what in us Lyes, towards abolishing all Distinction between the said Currency, and that of the Province Dated at Philadelphia this First Day of January 1729-30.

PROVINCE OF PENNSYLVANIA

Whereas many Gentlemen Merchants and others, Inhabitants of this Province, has unanimously agree to take, and receive in Payment-Bills of Credit already Emitted, and made Current in the three Lower Counties upon Delaware as the same

Pass there, and in order to facilitate the same, and give said Bills a more free Currency in this Province, without Scruple: The Trustees of the general Loan-Office of Pennsylvania have also agreed to take, and receive the said Lower County Bills of Credit of all the Borrowers for Payment now due in the said Loan-Office not exceeding one fourth Part of the Annual Quota's to be paid in.

Signed in behalf of the said Trustees at Philadelphia the 25th of March 1730.

William Fishbourn.

PHILADELPHIA April 9. At the dwelling-house of the Widow Hoskins, in the Town of Chester, on the 5th of May next, at Three a-Clock in the Afternoon; will be exposed to Sale, by Publick Vendue, a Plantation on Brandy-Wine Creek, formerly taken in Execution by the Sheriff of said County, and Sold for the Payment of said Debt, due from Joseph Cloud, to Edwr. Florne containing 225 Acres, of which about 40 or 50 Acres is Clear'd; whereon is a dwellin House, Barn and Orchard; said Plantation Lyes Contiguous to, and on the North Branch of said Creek 230 perches, which also runs through said land about 100 Perches, whereby it may be Accommodated with a considerable Quantity of good Meadows. For and behalf of Edward Florne. Wm. Rawle.

NEW-YORK April 13. On Saturday Night late, arrived here from the East End of Long-Island, with an Account, that on Wednesday last towards Evening, a Whaling Sloop belonging to Barnstable in New-England, about 160 Miles Southward of the East-End of Long-Island, saw 2 Sloops at Sea, which made towards her, and in short time hailed the Whaling Sloop with a speaking Trumpet, the Whaler answered and then hailed the other from whence, &c. but had no Answer, the other Sloop bid them put out a Boat, and come on board, on which the Whaler suspecting them to be Pyrates, quitted the Sloop, and took to the two Whale Boats, which the other Sloop perceiving, fired a Volley of fire Arms at them, and five great Guns with shot (it is said hoisted a Black Flag) but the Night coming on, and the Whalers Rowing for Life, got on Shore in two Days, at the East

End of Long-Island to their great Joy, tho' with their loss. The supposed Pyrate Sloops, are of about seventy tons.

ANNAPOLIS April 19. Run away from William Parks, Printer, a Servant Man about 21 Years of Age, of a fresh Complexion, long brown Hair, pretty well set, full Ey'd, thick Legs, speaks very broad, and is a House Carpenter by Trade. He had on, when he went away, a good grey Cloth Coat, with close Sleeves a blew and white strip'd Holland Wastcoat and Breeches, grey Stickings, and good Shoes; and took with him Two spare Shirts and a pair of Breeches. Whoever brings him to his said Master at Annapolis, or Andrew Bradford in Philadelphia, or William Bradford in New-York, shall have Three Pounds as a Reward, and reasonable Charges.

AMBOY April 19. On Tuesday last we had a sudden storm of Wind and Rain, in which a Canoe that was going over the Ferry here, was overset and three Persons Drowned; There was likewise several Houses and Barns blown Down.

ANNAPOLIS April 21. Last Tuesday, the Assizes ended here, when the two following Persons received Sentence of Death, viz. William Burridge, for breaking open a Store of Mr. James Donaldson; and Charles Clark a Lad of about 16 Years of Age, for breaking open the House of Mr. Poloks of this City.

PHILADELPHIA April 23. To be Sold a Grist-Mill (having Two pair of Stones) at Salisbury Town, upon the Head of Duck-Creek, in Kent County upon Delaware, distant a Quarter of a Mile from the Navigable Water, accounted 37 Miles from New-Castle; with about forty Acres of Land Adjoined to the said Mill, Part whereof is clear'd whereon is an Orchard, containing about 60 good bearing Apple Trees within Fence: Any Person having a Mind to Purchase, may apply to William Rawle in Philadelphia or Joseph Rawle, at the said Town of Salisbury.

Run away the third of this Instant April, from his Master Thomas Robinson, of the Township of Salisbury, in the County of Bucks; a Servant Man, named Henry Rice, he has black Hair, a swarthy Complexion, Long Stature, a Weaver by

Trade; he had on, when he went away, a Whitish Coloured Coat, with Mettle Buttons, Whoever shall take up said Servant, and secure him. or bring him to his Master, or give notice, shall have thirty Shillings as a Reward, and all reasonable Charges, paid by   Thomas Robinson.

ANNAPOLIS April 28. Thursday last, being the Festival of St. George. Patron of England, the same was observed here as usual, an Excellent Sermon suitable to the Occasion, was preach'd by the Rev. Mr. John Humphrys, after which, His Excellency the Governour, and Hon. Charles Calvert, Esqrs: and the rest of the Gentlemen, went to review the Militia, who were under Arms, from whence they went to the Council-House, where a very splendid Dinner was provided. After all the Royal Healths were Drank, as were also to the Right Hon. the Lord Proprietary's and his Family. And the Evening concluded as usual on the Occasion.

Late Friday between Five and Six o'Clock in the Afternoon died the Hon. Edward Calvert, Esq; President of the Council, Commissary-General of the Province of this Province, in the 28th Year of his Age.

PHILADELPHIA April 30. On the 24th Instant, between Ten and Eleven at Night, the greatest Fire happen'd in this City that ever has been known here. Some say it began in a Store among Rigging, Several Stores under a long Roof on a Wharf (all belonging to Mr. Fishbourn) were so suddenly in Flames 'twas impossible to save much of the Goods in any of them: From these a vast pile of Staves took Fire, which increased the Heat there was noe coming near. Among other Parcels of Staves and Wooden Buildings were so nigh the Flames, that all that End of Town was in eminent Danger; but the Wind was low. Two Coopers Shops on Kingstreet, at the west End of the Stores flamed surprisingly, communicated the Flames to two new Tenements of Mr. Fishbourn's one of which is almost entirely consumed, and flying across the narrow Street to Mr. Fishbourn's House that was Capt. Anthony's: Mr. Plumstead's new House and Mr. Dickinson's large fine Buildings; all which are reduced to Ashes, except the Brick Walls, some of which and the Chimneys except Mr. Plumstead's House, which is not wholly destroy'd. Many Gentlemen have lost considerable Quantities of Goods by the Fire and by Thieves and several other adjacent buildings have suffer'd. But the Vigilance and Industry of great Numbers of well-disposed People saved Abundance of Goods and Valuable Things, and stopt the Flames from Spreading further; on which Emergency the greatest Men in the Town did not disdain to labor very hard with their own Hands, and several of them, with others, have taken this Occasion (for people would not be mov'd at another Time) to make a Collection of Money for a better Engine than what we now have, and good Buckets. The lost sustained by the late Fire, amounts to several Thousand Pounds.

NEW-YORK May 4. Last Thursday Night a Fire broke out in New-Street, in this City, and destroyed three Houses.

AMBOY May 7. His Excellency's Speech to the General Assembly met at Amboy at New-Jersey.

Gentlemen,
I with great Pleasure I meet with this Assembly, because it Gives me an Opportunity of Convincing you and your Constituents, that I have the prosperity of New-Jersey sincerely at Heart, and gives you an Occasion of Expressing your Loyalty, Fidelity and Gratitude to the best of Kings.

His Majesty, who during the whole Course of his Reign, has shewn a constant and unwearied Care to promote the Ease and Happiness of his Subjects, and a tender Concern for the Welfare of his remotest Dominions, have commanded me to have strict Regard for all your Rights and Privileges, and has fully instructed me to concur with you in every thing that is for the real good and Advantage of the Province, particularly the encouraging of your Trade and Manufactures.

He expects on your Part, that you will support his Government by setting upon him a Revenue in an ample a Manner, and for as long a Time as former Assemblies have given it to his Predicessor.

I do earnestly desire you to shew on this

Occasion such Temper and Unanimity as becoming the Representatives of so considerable a People; that will certainly be the most effective Way of Serving your Country, and of recommending your selves to his Majesty's Royal Favour.

J. Montgomerie.

PHILADELPHIA May 7. Whereas Christ-Church in Philadelphia, was broke open Monday or Tuesday Night, the 20th or 21st of April last by some Prophane Wretches, who like Brutes, abused some things belonging to the said Church; and stole from the Reading Desk, one large Bible and one Common-Prayer Book in folio, and another in Octavo. These are to give Notice, That whoever will discover the Authors of such Villainy, so as he or they, may be brought to Justice, shall be amply rewarded, by the Church-Warden and Vestry, of the said Church.

A Very likely Negro Woman to be Sold by Charles Hargrave, Opposite to William Tidmarsh's, in Chestnut Street Philadelphia.

NEW-YORK May 13. On Tuesday last a new born Child was found dead in the cellar of Mr. Inglis of this City, Victualler; it appear'd to be the Child Eleanor Lloyd, Servant of the said Inglis, she pretends it was dead born, but they suppos'd she Murder'd it, accordingly was committed to Prison.

PHILADELPHIA May 14. There will be Exposed to Sale, by way of Vendue, to the highest bidder, the Plantation that Newt Steele now lives on, near Allen-Town within Two hundred Yards of Nathan Allens Mill, in the Jersey's, on the 3d of June Next, containing about Five hundred and Fifty Acres of Land, Two hundred and Fifty whereof clear'd, and in good Fences, well run-over with English Grass. There is on that Place, a large Dwelling-House, Barn, Out-Houses and Stables, an Orchard of about 300 Apple-Trees; there is also good Meadowing on said Place, There will be also sold Cattle, Horses, and dry sorts of Household Goods at said Place, where the Conditions of Vendue may be seen.

PHILADELPHIA May 21. Motherkill Kent-County on Delaware, april 10, 1730, To Mr. Andrew Bradford,

Sir,

I thought fit to let you know, that you, likewise may tell the Publick, of a wonderful Storm of Wind, attended with some Rain, in Kent County on the West Side of the Delaware-Bay, March the 28th about 9 at Night; which lasted about one Minute. I began about 12 Miles from the Bay, and took the Course straight to the Bay, destroying 12 Houses, which were all that were within its Compass; The Breath of this Tempest being about 50 Yards, it broke or rooted up all the large Timber it met with; but was at it seems to be most Violent where it began, forcing a Tree or Log of a Foot over, and 30 long to 20 Foot Distance out of the Bed where it had lain by falling down formerly. Nigh to that Place it took entirely a strong 40 Foot Barn the like Distance of 20 Foot, tearing it to Pieces and scattering the Parts as a handful of Corn. There is also tore up Part of an Orchard, and a Parcel of growing Rye; that the Earth looks as if there had been none in it. The Verge or Wing of the Storm brush'd off the Roof of another 40 Foot House, scattering it in the distant Air, and shattering the Rafters into the Earth, as if they had been Arrows, above Half a Mile from the Building. I shall not take upon me to tell you all the Destruction it had made, nor all the wonderful Marks I have seen; but I shall mention the loss of one poor Man who had newly built a Log-House; the Wind took off the Roof and dash'd it to pieces, then a Tree fell upon the House; THe Storm threw out his Bacon that he never got again, and also his Pewter to the Distance of two or three hundred Yards, totally spoiling the form of it; The Man was from Home, the Woman of the House asleep all the while to it.

I Had my Fencing and a New House tore all to Pieces, tho' several Score Yards from the Stream of the Storm, Sir, I am, &c.   Robert Comings.

ANNAPOLIS May 22. Extract of the votes of the Lower House of Assembly May 22, 1730.

The Question being put, Whether a Bill should be prepared for Amendment of the Staple of Tabacco? Resolv'd in the Affirmative.

The Question being put, whether in the Tobacco

Bill to be prepared, the Restriction shall be to a Number of Plants, or to a Number of Pounds? Resolv'd, that the Restrictions be to a Number of Plants.

The Question being put, whether the Quantity of Plants to be allowed, be 6000, or 5000? Resolv'd that the Quantity be 6000.

The Question being put, Whether that in Tobacco Debts, a Fourth should be deducted, or more? Resolv'd that more should be deducted.

The Question being put, Whether a Bill should be prepared for a Paper-Currency, or not? Resolv'd in the Affirmative.

ANNAPOLIS May 26, On Thursday last, both of the Houses of Assembly of this Province Met, pursuant of their last Prorogation. His Excellency went to the Upper House, and sent for the Members of the Lower House, who immediately attended him, he was pleas'd to open the Session with the following Speech.

Gentlemen of the Upper and Lower House of Assembly,

However Inconvenient, in many Respects, this Time of the Year may be, for our Meeting in Assembly, yet such is the present Condition of our Staple, that a speedy Care for its Amendment is Necessary: It is therefore, you are now convened, that you might have an early Opportunity to consult the Publick good Thereof.

The late Affliction wherewith it hath pleased Divine Providence to visit me, and Indispositions that have attended me, have very much impeded the Application of my thoughts to Publick Business, so that I have little to lay before you at present, as my own Consideration.

Pursuant to the Joint Address of both Houses, I have concerted, as far as possible, since last Session, a Correspondence with Virginia: Some Time before a Scheme had been formed, towards an useful Tobacco-Law, and sent to England for Approbation: and I understand, it is so far Approv'd of, that it is to be now laid before the Virginia Assembly: A Copy of it shall communicate to you, for your Communication. The main scope of it is, I apprehend, to prevent Trash from being Exported from these Parts, and the running of our Tobacco Home, which, by many, is esteemed a more probable Method of advancing the Credit, and thereby the Value of our Tobacco, than a bare Limitation to a Number of Plants; and surely, Trash is the greatest Cancer to our Staple. I hope you will not delay to enter most seriously and calmly on a Subject so important to the Province.

I wish you now to advise on all other Matters relating to the Publick, that the trouble and Expence of another Session this Year may be saved to the Country.

May Wisdom and Moderation direct your Councils, otherwise they will be render'd ineffectual, and the Country possibly may grow daily more and more uneasy in its Circumstances.

Certain you may be of my Inclination, to advance the real Happiness of his Lordship's Tenants; and nothing can ever be more agreeable to me, then to see Blessed Harmony leading us into such Measures, as may fix it on a lasting Foundation.

The next Day, the Address of the Lower House being prepared, (by a Committee Appointed) was agreed to by the House and presented to his Excellency, by Col. Greenfield, and eleven more.

To the Honourable Benedict Leonard Calvert Esq; Governour of Maryland,

The humble Address of the Lower House of Assembly.

May it please your Honour,
We his Majesty's most dutiful and loyal subjects, the Representatives of the Freemen of Maryland, in Assembly convened, return to your Honour our most humble and hearty Thanks; for giving us this Opportunity (however inconvenient it may be to us, with Regard to out private Concerns) of consulting a Matter of such great Importance to our Country, as the Amendment of the Staple.

And we are truly sorry for, and condole with your Honour on the Cause of your Affliction, as well as your own Indisposition.

We acknowledge, with the deepest Sence of Gratitude, your regard to the Welfare of the Province, and the Compliance with the joint Address of both Houses of Assembly, in concerting a

Correspondence with Virginia, the People of which Colony, cannot but be convinced, as we are, that their Welfare, as well as ours, depend on the Amendment of our common Staple, Tobacco. And and that whether we persue the same, or different means, the End ought to be the same.

As to the Scheme your Honour has been pleased to communicate to us, we shall take the same, as well as every Thing else that shall occur, or be proposed to us, into our most serious Consideration, and endeavour to the best of our understanding, to form such a Tobacco Law, as may remove some of the Miseries under which at present our Country groans. And do all we can to dispatch the other Publick Business, with the least Expence to the People we represent.

Your Honour's Wishes, that Wisdom and Moderation, may direct our Council, and the assurances you have been pleasd to give us in your Inclination to advance our Happiness, not only deserves our most thankful Acknowledgement, but ought to excite us, as we hope it will, to Act with the greatest Zeal and Unanimity, in the Service of our Country, under a firm Renance on your Concurrence with us in the Means; which never were more necessary, than at this juncture.

Signed by order of the House, per

John Mackall, Speaker,

PHILADELPHIA May 28. Run away from Samuel Thrramorton of Freehold, in the County of Monmouth, and the Province of New-Jersey, a Servant Man named Edward Holland, of a middle Stature, sandy straight Hair, old Felt Hat, a lightish Grey Kersey Coat with close Sleeves, a Cinnamon coloured Duroy Jacket, an Ozenbrigs Shirt, and Leather Breeches. Whoever shall take up said Servant, and bring him to his said Master, or give Notice thereof, or to the Work-House in Philadelphia, shall have Forty Shillings Reward and reasonable Charges.

N. B. He lived formerly with John Maltsbury at High-street Ferry.

Very large Siz'd well made Leather Buckets, they hold about three Gallons each, made and to be sold by Abraham Cox in High-street, by a large or smaller Quantity, at reasonable Rates:

Where old Buckets may be repaired.

PHILADELPHIA June 3. On Monday was hanged at Gloucester a Negro Man, for an attempt to murder, a White Girl of about Eight Years of age, in the middle of the Night; he entered the House of Mrs. _____ (whose Negro Woman was Wife to the Villain) he endeavoured to murder her, but upon her saying she'd cry out if he defaulted, and went into the next Room, Where the Girl and two small Children were in Bed: It is reported he distinguished between the Children by their Bigness, and would not touch the others, he having found out this Girl, upon whom he intended to commit the cruel Act, he endeavoured with his Knife to cut her Throat, but it proving too dull, he put his knee upon her Neck to keep her down, while he took a Whet-stone out of his Pocket to sharpen the Knife, and then Stabb'd her on one side of her Neck into the Windpipe. The Girl strugling to prevent her being kill'd got from under him, and ran into another Room to the Mistress of the House, who perceived the Child to be in a cruel Freight, Scream'd out and Waken'd some Men who lodg'd in the House, The Negro then made his Escape. Upon Examination he confest he intended to have murder'd his Wife's Mistress; the Reason he gave for committing this Fact, was first, about a Week before, he attempted to ravish the same Girl, but she resisting very strongly prevented him, and told the Woman of the House where she Lodged, the Negro's Design.

PHILADELPHIA June 4. This Morning about Seven a Negroe Man going out of his Master's Entry with a charged Gun upon his Shoulders, in order to go Fowling, it went off, and accidentally shot a Negroe Woman that stood behind him in the Head, so that she died soon after.

Run away from Martyn Jarvice of Philadelphia, the 24th Day of May Last; a Negroe Girl, Daughter to Doctor Justs, the Free Negroe Man, well known by the name of Jenny, she hath last part of three Fingers in her Right Hand, she had on when she went away a Horse Lock about her Neck, a strip'd Blue and White Pettycoat, and Wastcoat, a Greenish Pettycoat, a Cap and White

Apron, Aged about Eighteen Years, she is of a Yellowish Black, large Blubber Lips, she speaks good English. Whoever takes her up, and brings her to her Master, or to the Work-House, shall have Ten Shillings Reward; it is supposed that she lurks about this Town.

PHILADELPHIA June 8. Run away from William Smith of Philadelphia, shoe-maker; a Servant Man named John Norris, aged about 24 Years, of Middle Stature, smooth Fac'd (his Hair cut off) and sharp Skin'd; he had on when he went away, a dark colour'd Coat without Sleeves, Strip'd Homespun Jacket and Breeches, and a Pair of Leather Breeches, and Trouzers, with two White Shirts; supposed to be in Company with one James Curry, a Apprentice to Mrs. Paris of Philadelphia, Brass-Founder, he is about 19 Years of Age, Tall and Slender, with Ash colour Cloathes Whoever secures the said Servant so that his Master may have him again, shall have Five pounds Reward, and reasonable Charges, paid by me,
William Smith.

To be Sold. By Joseph Jackman, a very likely Negroe Man, (barbadoes born) a Wheel Wright by Trade, Enquire at the Widow Coat's in High street opposite to the Butchers Shambles, or at William Rabley's Store in Water-street, near the Crooked Billet.

PHILADELPHIA June 11. From Maryland we have Advice, that their Assembly now sitting, are very intent upon mending the present ubhappy Condition of their Staple. They have also passed a Vote for making Paper Currency, and a Bill for emitting Twenty Thousand Pounds is now in the House, under consideration.

This Week a Man was committed to Prison, being charged with beating and abusing his Wife so that she Died in a few Days. A Woman is committed with him as an Accessory.

PHILADELPHIA June 18. Run away from Joseph England pf Nottingham, in Chester County Pennsylvania, upon the First of this Instant June, a Servant Man, named Alexander Mac'Connel, an Irish Man indifferent Tall, a Lusty well set Man, very Swarthy, thick Lips, his Hair cut off, and having an old Pisburn'd Wigg, a good Felt

Hat, and a strip'd Lincy Jacket, and a pair of Leather Breeches, or Ozenbrig Trousers, and light Grey Stockings, and a pair of new Shoes, too short for him to wear. Whoever shall take up the abovesaid Servant, or secure him, or send him to the Work-House in Philadelphia, and give Notice to his Master, or Andrew Bradford, shall have Five Pounds Reward, paid by me

Joseph England.

To be hired by the Year or Month, a very likely Negroe Man, named Scipio, fit for most sorts of Labouring Business in the House or out of Doors, he is also a good Cook, there is likewise to be hired or Sold, a very likely Negroe Boy about sixteen Years of Age (this Town born) he understands something of the Taylor's Trade, Enquire John MacComb.

There is a Livery Stable kept by John Orton, between Combe's Alley, and Mullbury-street (and commonly called Arch-street) where all Gentlemen and others, may have their Horses fed with good English Hay and Oats, very reasonable.

PHILADELPHIA June 25. Run away from Joseph Britain, of the Township of Nottingham in the County of Burlington, and Province of West New-Jersey, the Fourteenth Day of this Instant June; Two Servant Men (both Irish) the one named David Willings, a lusty fellow with short black Hair, and two Warts on his Nose, a Connamon colour's Linsey Coat, Jacket and Breeches, the Jacket and Breeches not lined.

The other named Constantine Mackmanners, a short fellow (no Hair) a Taylor by Trade, he has a Homespun Drugget Coat, Jacket and Breeches of an Orange Colour, and Buttons of the same, Whoever secures the above mentioned Run aways, and give Notice to their Masters, and bring them to Burlington Goal, shall have Forty Shillings for each, and reasonable Charges. paid by me, Joseph Britain.

PRICIPIO IRON-WORKS June 30. Run away from Stephen Orion and Company, of Pricipio Iron Works in Maryland, a Negroe named James, is of lowish Stature, something bow-leg'd, a high and thin Nose, his Face full of Pockmark Holes, and hath a small Dent in one of his Cheeks, where formerly he was shot, the said Negroe formerly belonged to Sir William Keith; hath a Dove-Coloured Pea-Jacket, lined with Blue, with Leather Breeches and Linnen Trowsers, Shoes, Stockings and Hat, aged about 40 Years.

Whoever takes up the said Negroe, and secure him, so that he may be had again, shall have Fifty Shillings Reward Paid by me,

          Stephen Orion.

PHILADELPHIA July 2. Lately Published and are to be Sold by the Printer Hereof; Fruits of Retirement; or Miscellaneous Poems, Moral and Divine. Being some Contemplations, Letters, &c. written on Variety of Subjects and Occasions, By Mary Melineux, Late of Liverpool. Deceased. To which Prefixed: some accounts of the information and Benefit of Christain Professors in General; recommended more particularly to the Youth of either Sex amongst the People called Quakers.

PHILADELPHIA July 9. Yesterday was apprehended Zeachariah Fields on suspicion of Counterfeiting the current Money, upon an Information from a Person in New-Castle to our Governour's Secretary, of having uttered several pieces in his Progress from Virginia. He was search'd and there was found in his Pockets some Pistoles, pieces of Eight and Dollars, and an unfinish'd Piece, supposed a Pistole, not coloured like Gold, all Counterfeit. Upon his Examination before the Hon. Mayor & Aldermen in Court he would make no Confession. A Person was Dispatch'd to Frankford, where he had left his Horse, as to search his Saddle-Baggs, who found 101 Counterfeit Dollars. He is a New-England Man by Birth, Personable, stout and very active in any manly exercise, and very understanding in any Mettel Work.

PHILADELPHIA July 16. We have advice from New-Castle, that the Brigantine Plain Dealer, John Watts, Master, bound from this Port to Ireland, sprung a Leak and sunk off Bombay Hook, the Water appear'd above the lower Deck before they knew any thing of it, when making all the Sail they could, with an Intent to run her ashore, and they immediately sunk. The Men were all saved, and they are hopes of getting her up again.

To be Sold, Negroe Men, Women, and Girls and Boys, Imported in the Sloop Sarah and Francis, from St. Christophers, lying at Clymers Wharf.

CHESTER July 17. This Day the Coroner's Inquest is to sit on the Body of an Irishman late-killed on the other side of Brandy-wyne in this County. It seems the deceased and one Bourk, his Countryman, both lately out of Servitude, were reaping together all the Morning, and about Noon Bourk Stabb'd his Companion in The Breast with a Knife, of which Wound he languished a few Days and then died, charging the said Bourk with his Death; who is now in Irons in our County Goal. This Affair makes a great Noise in the Country, the rather because some of the more ignorant sort, have been so indiscreet as to give out threatning Words against Authority, of what they would do in case any Irishman should be executed in this Country; and two of them, for saying they would fetch the Prisoner out of the Goal, with some other ill behaviour of the like kind, have been sent to keep him Company.

There are various Reports about the Circumstances of the Murder, so that we are impatient to hear the Verdict of the Inquest.

We hear an unlucky She-Wrestler who has late-thrown a young Weaver, and broke his Leg, so that 'tis thought he will not be able to tread the Treadles these two Months. In the meantime, he may employ himself in winding Quills.

NEW-CASTLE July 20. Whereas Notice was published in the American Weekly Mercury, and the Maryland Gazette, in the Month of November and December last, concerning a strange Negro Man, in the Custody of the Sheriff of New-Castle County, which Negro was taken as a Runaway, in Mill Creek Hundred, in the said County, on the Thirteenth Day of October last; and no Person has since that time, claim'd the said Negro, or brought any Account of him, but, all that can be discovered, from the Account the Negro gave of himself; it seems, his Master is a Practitioner of Physick or Surgery, in some part of Maryland or Virginia. These are therefore to give Notice, That, if there be no further Account of the Master or Owner of the said Negro, before the Twentieth Day of August next, the Negro is to be Sold for Payment of his Prison Charges, &c. He is a short small Limbed nimble Fellow, about twenty five Years of Age, has a great Head, wide Mouth, and large Eyes, looks wild and flaring; seems as if he cannot speak or understand English, nor the Language of any of the Negroes about New-Castle.

    Charles Read Sheriff of New-Castle.

PHILADELPHIA July 23. Lost or Stray'd away from Thomas Hatton in Front-street, Philadelphia, ever since the Night of the late great Fire; a Middle sized Sorrell Mare, a Slit in the farther Ear, and a small nick cut out of the other, a small Star, and a blackish spot about two inches Broad, on the outside of her farther thigh, about a Hands breath above the Gambrell Joint: Whoever brings her to Thomas Hatton, shall have Ten Shillings Reward, and all Charges paid by me,   Thomas Hatten.

PHILADELPHIA July 30. Run away the 21st of this Instant July, from his Master, James Johnson, near White Clay Creek, a Servant Man named Timothy Sullivan, a well set strong Man, had a small Piece cut off his Right Ear, he wears a Dark Coloured Kearsey Coat, a Blue Jacket and Buckskin Breeches, with Buttons of Mother of Pearl. Whoever secures the said Servant, shall have Twenty Shillings, with reasonable Charges paid by said Johnson or by Mr. John Henry at White Clay Creek.

Run away on the 19th Instant July, from her Master Charles Sandiford (Lately form Barbadoes) a Covenanted Servant Woman, named Jane Braiser, She is of a Middle Stature, Pockfretten and Freckled, she has a striped Callamico Gown of Red and White Stripe, a Yellow Quilted Pettycoat, she has taken the following Goods, viz. a White Fustian Gown, the Sleeves turn'd up with an Indian Chintz a Blue Camblet Ridding-Hood, also a Gallon China Bowl, and many other Valuable Goods (if any person will give any Intelligence of any of the above Goods shall be well Rewarded.) Whoever shall take up the said Servant bring her to the Work-House, or give Notice to her Master, shall have Five Pounds reward, and Reasonable Charges.

PHILADELPHIA Aug. 6. These are to give Notice, That any Persons, who have Old New-Jersey Bills of Credit, if they repair to John Allen, Esq; Treasurer, at Burlington, they may have them Exchanged.

PHILADELPHIA Aug. 13. Whereas one William Morally, came over into this Country some time since; If the said Morally, will come to the Printer hereof, he may be inform'd of something to his Advantage.

Run away the 22d of this Instant July, from Jonathan Fisher of Philadelphia, Glover, a Servant Man named Thomas Forrest.

PHILADELPHIA Aug. 20. Lately Imported from Bermuda, in the Brigantine Lancashire Witch, Samuel Spafford Master, four likely Negroe Boys and one Negroe Man, all Burmudas born and speaks good English, which are to be sold by him, very reasonable, at Richard Clymer's Wharf.

Strayed or Stolen away from the Plantation of William Hewes of Chester in Chester County, the 18th of July, a Gray Horse much Flea bitten, Branded with H. B. on the neat Buttock, fourteen Hands high or more, he hath two Shoes on before, he hath been Galled on the Shoulder with the Geers, likewise on his Back with the Saddle, he hath a slow shuffling Pace, carries himself Proudly on the Road.

Whoever shall secure the said Horse, and give Notice to William Hewes, or Joseph Pennils of the Township of Edgemont in the same County, or bring him to Joseph Pennils, shall have Twenty Shillings Reward and reasonable Charges, paid by me,   Joseph Hewes.

BURLINGTON Aug. 21. To be sold by Mahlon Stacy, Jonathan Wright and Thomas Scattergood, of Burlington, Executors of Abraham Porter lately deceas'd; a large Tract of Land in the County of Gloucester, in West-Jersey containing about Three Thousand Acres, well Accommodated with a good Orchard, a Saw-Mill and a great Quantity of Timber and Meadow-Land, bounding on both sides of Gloucester River, commonly call'd

Timber-Creek, within Twelve Miles of Philadelphia, Navigable for a large Boat up to said Mill. Any Person desirous to Purchase the said Land, or any Part thereof, may apply to the Executors as above-mentioned.

PHILADELPHIA Aug. 27. From Woodbury Creek on the other side of the River we hear, that on Lord's Day Night last, a Servant Man belonging to one Tatcham got out of Bed-about Midnight, and telling a Lad who slept with him that he was going on a Long Journey and should never see him more; he went into the Orchard and Hanged himself on a Tree: But it seems the Rope broke in the Opperation, and towards Morning he found himself alive upon the Ground to his no small Surprize. He then went and hid himself in the Barn among the Straw, for several Hours, while his Master and the rest of the Family were searching and inquiring after him to no Effect. At length having procured a better Rope, he hanged himself again in the Barn, and was there accidentally found by the Maid in the Afternoon: When he was cut down there appeared no sign of Life in him, nor were any means used to recover him; but by the Time the Coroner and his Inquest were got together, and come to View his Body, he was upon his Legs again, and now Living.

PHILADELPHIA Aug. 27. Peter Bainton, at the Lower End of Front-street sells the best London Double refined Sugar, at Two and twenty Pence to single Loaf for Cash, New-England Double refined at twenty Pence per Pound; and New-England Midlin Sugar at Eighteen Pence per Pound the single Loaf. And sundry sorts of European dry Goods, Pickle Salmon by the Cag.

To be sold. One Third of Six Hundred Acres of Land, an undivided Tract, lying in Willis-Town, in Chester County, and Bounded by the Lands of Tarnell Mitchel Jobson, Rees Thoman and Peter Jones, and by several Lots of the Valley Town, Inquire of Peter Lloyd, Merchant Philadelphia.

Brought over in the Brigantine Swan, Alex Downing Master, from Bristol, one Cask of Nails, One Box of Iron Ware, No. 32. mark'd ne. whoever has law of Claim upon said Goods let them repair to said Master, and paying they may have them.

NEW-YORK Aug. 31. On the 25th Instant, the General-Assembly of this Colony met, and on the 26th his Excellency made a Speech to them, which is as follows, viz.

Gentlemen,

The Principal Reason of my calling you together at this Time, is to acquaint you, That his Majesty has Disallowed all the Acts you have passed, Prohibiting the selling of Indian Goods to the French, or laying Duties on them, from the year 1720 to the year 1729, which I believe is what you expected, from the late Accounts we have had from England.

By repeal of these Acts, which I shall lay before you, the last Provision you made for the support of the House and Garrison at Oswego, is rendered all together ineffectual.

Every Man knows the Interest and Circunstances of this Province, may be very sensible of the Importance of that Place, on which chiefly defends the Prosperity and Success of our Indian Trade, the fidelity and Obedience of the Six Nations to the Crown of Great Britain, and the Protection and Defence of our Frontier Settlements. The Season of the Year for Transporting Men and Provisions being now far advanced, I earnestly desire, thst you will speedily provide effectual and unexceptionable Supplies for this Service.

I also expect you will take into serious Consideration the Ruinous Condition of all the other Frontier Garrisons, and the Miserable state of the Officers Barracks in the Fort in New-York.

It gives me very great uneasiness to propose any Expence to the Province, but the Things I have mentioned, are so absolutely necessary for His Majesty's Service, and the Safety of his Subjects, that I think my self indispensably Obliged to Recommend them most earnestly to you.

J. Montgomerie.

PHILADELPHIA Sept. 3. Last Week was informed in the Pennsylvania Gazette, an Account of some fruitless Attenpts, made by a Servant Man at Woodbridge Creek to Exchange this World for another; we have since heard, that his Master has

Try'd his Luck that way, but with no better success than the Servant, some busy People being so impertinent as to pull him out of the Creek before he had quite finish'd his Work.

NEW-YORK Sept. 7. On Friday last the Garrison and Malitia of this Place were all under Arms for the Reception of the Honourable Patrick Gordon, Esq; Governour of Pennsylvania, who was then expected here but the weather proving Rainy they were Discharges. The next Day about Noon his Honour arrived, and was received at the Water-side by his Excellency our Governour, attended by the principal Gentlemen of this Place; and was immediately conducted to the Fort, the Garrison being under Arms, where, upon his Entrance the Military Honours were paid him, under the Discharge of the Cannon of the Fortress.

We hear that last Saturday a Violent Rain, Thunder and Lightning happened in Bergen County in New-Jersey, & that two Barns full of Wheat were set on Fire by the Lightning and burnt down.

PHILADELPHIA Sept. 10. To be Sold. By Thomas Hetton, near Walnut Street End, arrived One Smith, a Barber, a Taylor, the rest for Plantation Work. Also six Guns with Carriages, well mounted, above four Hundred weight each: Enquire of Thomas Hetton, aforesaid, or James Bean, on board the Mary Pink, where the Servants and Guns are to be seen.

Two likely Negro Men to be sold on Credit (if requir'd,) by John Connor, in Chestnut street in Philadelphia.

PHILADELPHIA Sept. 17. These are to give Notice to all Persons who it may concern, That I William Hutchinson of this City of Philadelphia, Sawer, do for divers Causes, and Considerations to be known, Direct and Desire, That any Person or Persons, Having any occasion of Dealing with Sarah Hutchinson, Wife of said William Hutchinson may not at their Risque, after the Tenth Day of this Instant September, Trust or Credit the said Sarah Hutchinson, for or on my Account she being Eloped from me. Witness my Hand the 7th of September, 1730.   William Hutchinson.

Strayed or Stolen from William Tuffey of

Brandy-Wine Hundred, in the County of New-Castle, two Brown Horses, one is Branded with I, on the Shoulder, and with the letter F upon the near Buttock; and the other has a half Crop in the near Ear, and a Crop and two Nicks in the far Ear, and shod round. Whoever shall or will take up the said Horses or either of them, shall have fifteen Shillings as a reward for each Horse, paid by me   William Tuffey.

PHILADELPHIA Sept. 24. Taken up by Capt. Ellis Davis, in the Brigantine Peggy from Maryland, on the Thirteenth Day of this Instant September, about Three Miles without Cape Henlopen, a Ferry (as he supposes) with only one Oar in her, and a Piece of Durrow, with Trimming for the same, with some other small things. Whoever own's the said Boat or Goods, let them apply to the said Master, at the sign of the Queen's Head, in Water-Street, paying the Charges, may have the Boat and Goods again.

To be Sold. By Capt. John Ball, on board the Ship John Galley, Lying at the Widow Hun's Wharf; a very likely Negroe Boy, and good Muscovado Sugar.

PHILADELPHIA Sept. 27. This Day Run away from the Ship John Frigate, Thomas Smith, Master, a Servant Lad named John Gibbs, (alias Griffins) aged about 19 Years, Short Stature, round Fac'd and Fresh Colour'd, had on a Tarry Ozenbriggs Frock anf Trousers, a Blew Jacket, Grey Yarn Stockings, thin Double Soled Shoes, an old Hat very narrow in the Brims. Whoever can take up the said Runaway and bring him to the Ship by the 1st of November next, shall have Forty Shillings Reward and reasonable Charges paid by
                              Thomas Sober.

To be sold by Joseph Harrison, a very good Brick House, next door to the Sign of the Indian King.

PHILADELPHIA Oct. 1. Yesterday our Mayor made his Feast according to Custom the Corporation attending. There were present also His Honour the Governour, the Council, and several of the principal Gentlemen of the Town: Where after a very handsome and Plentiful Dinner, His Majesty's Health with the rest of the Royal Family were drank, at the Discharge of the great Guns of the Shipping in the Harbour.

A very likely Servant Woman's Time for about Three Years, she is fit for all manner of House-Work, and works well with the Needle. Enquire of William Rabley in Water street, near the Broken Billet or the Printer hereof.

Run away the 21st of September last a Servant Man, from Robert Chapman of Chesterfield in the County of Burlington; a short thick Man, full Fac'd and fresh Coloured, of a Brown Complexion with short Bushey Hair, with some Grey Hair, and about Forty Years of Age, and had got with him a Light Brown Kersey Coat and Dark Brown Drugget Jacket with Brass Buttons, and a pretty good Felt Hat, a Pair of good Leather Breeches, good Shoes and Grey Stockings, and he walks Crimptin, as tho' he was Lame in his Feet or Toes, named Michael Hambleton, Any Person that can take up said Servant, or secure him so that his Master may have him again, shall have Forty Shillings Reward and reasonable Charges, paid by me   Robert Chapman.

PHILADELPHIA Oct. 8. Run away from Peter Rose, Brewer of Burlington, on the 21st of this Instant September, 1730, a Servant Man named John Smith aged about Twenty one Years, a Weaver by Trade, and understands Country Work, pretty full Fac'd, of Middle Stature and Bushy Hair, with a large Scar down his Forehead, when he went away had a new White Ozenbrigs Shirt, Wast-Coat and Breeshes, White Cotton Stockings and new Felt Hat. Whoever takes up the said Servant and secure hin, so that his said Master may have him again, shall have Forty Shillings Reward, and all reasonable Charges paid by me   Peter Rose.

PHILADELPHIA Oct. 15. The following unfortunate Accident happened lately near Darby. Two Young Men being a Fowling in a Canoe, one of them whose name was Reilings, jumping ashore, took hold of the Barrel of his Gun and it Lean'd towards him over the side of the Canoe and drawing it carefully to him the triger, not having any Guard to it, catch'd the Gun went off and shot him dead on the spot.

PHILADELPHIA Oct. 21. Titan Leed's and William

Bickett's Almanacks, for the Year 1731, both Printed, and Sold by William Bradford in New-York and Andrew Bradford in Philadelphia, where all Shop-keepers, Pedlars and others may be supplyed by Wholesale or Retail, very Reasonable.

Run away from Charles Blakey, at the Sign of the Brigantine in Water Street, an East Indian Man, named Thomas Tamelin, has on a Pea-Jacket, a Leather Pair of Breeches, and an Ozebriggs Pair of Trowsers over them, a good Raccoon Hat, he is of small Stature round Shouldered, speaks and writes good English. Whoever secures the said runaway so that his Master may have him again shall have Thirty Shillings Rewars, and reasonable Charges paid by   Charles Blakey.

NEW-CASTLE Oct. 21. The Speech of the Honourable Patrick Gordon, Esq; Lieutenant Governour of the Counties of New-Castle, Kent and Sussex on Delaware; and Province of Pennsylvania.

To the Representatives of the said Counties in General Assembly met at New-Castle, the 21st of October 1730.

Gentlemen,

My steady endeavours to put in Practice as well his sacred Command to me, which I mentioned at My first Arrival here, as my Instructions from our Honourable Proprietors, together with the happy Concurrence of the People in joining with what they manifestly saw was timed solely at their own Good, have by Divine Providence been blessed with such Success, that now on our annual Meeting, there seems little more Incombent on me, than to express My Satisfaction in the Opportunity given Me of seeing the Representatives of His Majesty's good Subjects under my Care, convened together; and I hope it proves no less agreeable to you, Gentlemen, to have the same on your Part of meeting me; that we may between Us shew that mutual Harmony, which will ever be the happy result of a Disposition in those concerned in the Affairs of our Government, to discharge their respective Duties with Loyalty to His Majesty, Fidelity to our Proprietors, and with Benevolence and Affection in every Individual towards his Neighbour.

The Continuance of this, Gentlemen, I Heartily

recommend to You, and that if Particulars should yet Harbour any Misunderstandings or private Uneasinesses, they should from a View of the Loveliness of Peace and Publick Tranquility, entirely lay them aside, that we may truly appear to all, what I think We really are, as happy a People among Ourselves, as any in His Majesty's Dominions.

Gentlemen,

You will undoubtedly of Course, at this Meeting take into Consideration what yet remains from former Assemblies to be Completed or regulated; and herein I hope, you will shew much Unanimity, and make such Dispatch, as will fully prove We are all sensible of the Blessings we enjoy; and on my Part, nothing shall be wanting to improve them   P. Gordon.

NEW-YORK Oct. 26. His Excellency our Governour has been pleased to give his Assent to the folliwing Acts.

An Act for continuing an Act, entitled, An Act to amend the Practice of the Law, and to regulate the giving of Special Bail.

An Act to continue an Act, entitled, An Act for Regulating Fences for the several Cities and Counties within the Colony of New-York.

An Act to Continue an Act, entitled, An Act to prevent Swine running at large in Dutchess County, and in the Mannor of Livingston, and in the Precinct of the Mannor of Resselaerwyck, called Claverach, in the County of Albany.

An Act to prevent Swine running at large in the City and County of New-York, the County of West-Chester, Queen's County, King's County and Richmond County.

An Act for the further continuing an Act, entitled, an Act to let to Farm the Excise of Strong Liquors retailed in the Colony for the time therein mentioned, and for declaring Shrub liable to the same Duties as Distilled Liquor.

An Act to revive an Act, entitled, An Act, entitled, An Act for the better regulating and further laying out Publick High Roads into the County of Westchester.

An Act to unable the Mayor, Aldermen and Commonalty of the City of New-York to raise Money

for the term of three years, to purchase two
Fire Engines, and for other the purpose therein Mentioned.

An Act for Striking Bills of Credit to the
Value of 3000 Pounds, and putting them into the
Treasury to be exchanged for Shattered, Torn and
defaced Bills struck and issued by several former Acts.

An Act for the better Preservation of Oysters.

An Act to revive and Enforce an Act, entitled,
An Act for Settling and Regulating the Militia
in this Province, and making the same useful for
Security and Defence thereof, and for Repealing
all other Acts relating to the same, during the
Time there-in mentioned.

An Act for the further Continuing the Currency
of Bills of Credit struck and issued in the Year
1720. to the Value of 5000 Ounces of Plate,
during the time therein mentioned.

NEW-YORK Nov. 2. By his Excellency John Montgomerie Esq; Captain General and Governour in
Chief of the Province of New-York, New-Jersey,
and Territories thereon depending in America,
and Vice Admiral of the same &c.

A PROCLAMATION

Whereas the General Assembly of his Majesty's
Province of New-York, did on the Twenty eight
Day of October last, represent to me, That one
Solomon Jennings, hath been a notorious Horse-Stealer for many Years past, in several of the
Counties of this Province, and particularly in
the Counties of Westchester, Dutchess, Orange
and Ulster, and to avoid being brought to Justice, retired to and keeps in Place secret and
remote, and from thence frequently goes to flolow the same Wicked Practice; whereupon the said
Assembly addressed themselves to Me, for my Issuing a Proclamation for the Apprehending of the
said Solomon Jennings. To the End thereof that
the said Solomon Jennings may be apprehended
and brought to condign Punishment, I have thought
fit, by and with the Advice and Consent of His
Majesty's Council for the Province aforesaid to
issue this Proclamation, and to hereby promise
a Reward of Twenty Pounds, current Money of the
Province aforesaid, to any Person or Persons

whatsoever, who shall apprehend the said Solomon Jennings, and produce a Certificate from the High Sheriff of any City, Town or County within the Province aforesaid, of his or their having delivered the Body of the said Solomon Jennings to such Sheriff, as aforesaid, and every such Sheriff to whom or into whose custody the Body of said Solomon Jennings shall be delivered, as aforesaid, is hereby strictly charged and commanded immediately upon receiving the Body of the said Solomon Jennings with Irons, and him so put in Irons to keep in Goal under strict Guards, until he shall be thence delivered by the due Course of Law.

Given under my Hand and Seal of Arms at Fort George in New-York, the Second Day of November, in the fourth Year of the Reign of our Sovereign Lord George the Second, by the Grace of God, of Great Britain, France and Ireland, King, Defender of the Faith, &c. Annoq, Domini, 1730.

           J. Montgomerie.

By his Excellency's Command F. Morris, Secry.

PHILADELPHIA Nov. 5. On Saturday last under our Mayor's-Court here; and the Persons following receiv'd the here-after mentioned Judgements.

William Donne. For Assault and Battery on Frances, Wife of Roger Thomas, to be whipt at the Whipping-Post with 15 Lashes, and give Security for his good Behaviour.

Glascow an Indian. For Assault on Rachel Chivers, with intent to Ravish, to stand in the Pillory one Hour, and receive 39 Lashes at 6 Corners of the Streets of this City, and give Security for his good Behaviour for 7 Years.

Martha. Wife of Leonard Cash, for Stealing Muslin, the Property of ——— to pay 4 Pounds towards Support of the Government and receive 21 Lashes at the Whipping-Post, and immediately to depart this City.

Griffith Jones. For Assault on one Elizabeth Rogers, with Intent to Ravish, fined 10 Pounds to stand in the Pillory one Hour, and receive 39 Lashes at 6 Corners of the Streets of this City, and give Security for his Behaviour for 2 Years.

John Heathcoat, Butcher. For killing and wounding about 3 Years since, several Sheep, the Property of Thomas Lacy of this City, Butcher, fined 25 Pounds to stand in the Pillory one Hour, and give 100 Pounds Security for his good Behaviour for one Year.

And accordingly Yesterday Martha Leonard received 21 Lashes at toe Whipping-Post, Griffith Jones and Galscow the Indian, stood in the Pillory one Hour and had 39 Lashes each at the Cart's tail.

We hear William Donne was so far indulg'd as to receive his 15 Lashes in private.

On the Second of this Instant One Jonathan Bradley was found in a Ditch near Willian Hudson's Orchard in High-street, in this City. The Coroner's Inquest upon View of the Body, brought in their Verdict, Accidental Death.

PHILADELPHIA Nov. 12. This Day ended our Court of Oyer and Terminer and Goal Delivery when,

Thomas Seames, indicted for Berglary and Felony, in entering the House of Capt. George Roach of this City, and guilty there of by his own Confession received sentence of Death.

Zachariah Field, against whom two Bills of Indictments was prefer'd the one for High Treason in Counterfeiting the Coin of another Kingdom, made current by an Act of Parliament in His Majesty's Dominions, of which Indictment he was acquited. The other for Misprison of Treason, in Counterfeiting the coins not made current by any Act of Parliament, of which Indictment he was found Guilty, and adjudged, To Forfeit the Profit of all his Lands during Life, to forfeit all his Goods, and Chattels, and be imprisoned during Life.

Sarah Porter for the Murder of Magaret, the Wife of John Crump, was ordered to be continued in Custody, the Jury being positive enough in their Verdict to enable the Bench to proceed to a Judgement.

John Crump, indicted also with the said Sarah, for the Murder of his Wife aforesaid, was acquitted, it appearing the Evidence that he did was an Act on intended Kindness than otherwise.

William Pemach, indicted for Burglary and

Felony with Thomas Seames, and by said Seames impeached thereof, was by Jury Acquitted, but the Court ordered to gige 90 Pounds Security for his good Behaviour.

On Monday last the Body of a Man was found near Robert Heaton's Mill, in Bucks County; he seemed to have lain there about a Month. He had half his Hankerchief ty'd hard round his Neck, and at some considerable Distance was found the other half round a small Sappling. It is remarkable that when he was search'd he had exactly Thirteen Pence Half-penny in his Pocket.

TRENTON Nov. 12. Run away last Week from Robert Comming of this Place, a Servant Man named James Smith a thick short black Fellow, pretty elderly has a Mark on the side of his Head, a little above the Eye-brow; he was well cloathed, had a Cloth Coat and Vest of a brown Snuff Colour, new Wash-Leather Breeches, a pair of Boots; and also with him a black Mare, and had Three or Four Pounds in his Pocket; he formerly lived at New-Castle and it may be possible he is gone that Way, he formerly used the Sea, but of late has been chiefly employed in Distilling; he is so prodigious a Lyer that if observed he may easily be discovered by it. Whoever secures the said Servant so that his Master may have him again shall have Forty Shillings Reward and reasonable Charges, paid by   Robert Comming.

NEW-YORK Nov. 22. On Wednesday last a sad Accident happened in this City, viz. The Wife of Thomas Gleaves having occasion to go to a Neighbours House, set he Child about 18 Months old, in a Chair by the Fire, she staid a short space, and on her return found that the Childs Cloaths had taken Fire, and the Child burnt almost to Death. They gave it some wine, and it cry'd and Dyed immediately.

PHILADELPHIA Nov. 26. To the Printer of the American-Mercury.

Sir,
It is a real Concern for the Welfare of my Fellow Creatures makes me give you this Trouble. I should think my self very happy could I persuade them from a Custom of the most fatal Consequence. (I mean habitual Tea-Drinking) which universally

prevails among us, were it only the consideration of so much expended on what is altogether superfluous and which in many Families is pinch'd from what is absolutely necessary, it would not give me much Concern, and I should silently lament the unaccountable Follies of Human Kind: But when not only the Fortunes, but their Health and Happiness are in Danger. I think it my Duty openly to forewarn them, and endeavour, as much as in me lies, to prevent Ruins. I am sensible how little it would avail to argue against it from the Folly of Things, Custom have prevented me here, and give an Authority which no such Argument can Destroy. When a few People make themselves in any Thing particular, they are scorn'd and reduc'd; but let the very Thing be followed by a Multitude, by being Fashionable it becomes Praise —— worthy, and will find Advocates, even amongst those, who before were its greatest Enemies; nay, even Things of the utmost Consequence, not Reason but Number so much prevails, as, did not daily Experience put beyond Dispute, would be scarce conceivable. But altho' the Folly of this Custom, which, at its first Appearance, might have been urged with Success, is now of no Force, there is still one argument left me which deserves being considered; and this is, its pernicious Effects on the whole human System: Whoever value Health will listen to me here; and, I doubt not, if I can presuade them to do so without Prejudice, the Truth of this Assertion will so fully appear, that it may in some Degree, decrease the Consumption of this baneful Drug. I appeal to the Experience of those who will give themselves the Trouble of reflecting, whether there does not a strange Disorder follow the drinking of this Liquor, especially if in any Quantity? I am sure my self (tho' it was some Years before I took Notice of it) have constantly found so; and, upon enquiry, find all my Acquaintance disturbed by it after the same Manner, as I am persuaded Thousands are besides, who know not what ails them, nor have, once imagin'd this to Cause their Malady. The continual pouring into the Body such Quantities; of what (if not much worse) is no better than warm Water, dissolve the firmness of its Parts, loosens their Contexture, relaxes all its Fibres, and, by over-charging it with Moisture, puts it in a State of a sure, tho' slow Decay. This is plainly evident from the Inactivity, that weakness and Trembling, which it occasions. Nor does the Body suffer alone, the Soul also is hindered in the free Performance of its Functions, and has its Share of Disorder: Hence that Melancholy, that Heaviness, that Peevishness, those unaccountable Fancies, those groundless Fears and Apprehensions; in short, whatever come under the Name of Spleen, I may very justly charge here; nor will I acquit this Drug from laying the Foundation of many other Distempers. When we compare a Constitution strong and vigorous, with one weak and dispirited; a free and undisturb'd Soul, with one byass'd and confus'd; the simple pleasure of drinking warm Water can never sure be thought an Equivalent for such Exchange. I doubt not many will object there never having been disorder'd in this Manner; but their being insensible of it is no conclusion against its being hurtful, nor makes it at all less fatal to them. It is one particular Effect of this Liquor to cloud the Understanding; Besides, we daily see something like this in a Case where every Body is sensible of its Truth, and that it is, the constant drinking of Spirituous Liquors, where, tho' a person should never at any Time drink so much as to occasion any sensible Disorder in the Body or Mind, yet by frequent Use, it will certainly impair his Constitution, and shorten his Days; and exactly the same, tho' from a quite contrary Cause, will be the Consequence of what I am exclaiming against with so much Justice.

 I have already exceeded the Bounds of a Letter; and therefore will but just hint one Thing more, which is my fear, that the fatal Effects of this Custom are intail'd on our Posterity; and that possibly, should it prevail some Ages, greatest Honours and Estates may not only be possessed by those of effeminate unhealty Constitutions, but by Fools and Madmen.

 Sir by putting thin in a Way of doing Service

to the Publick, you will very much oblige.
                    Your humble Servant.

   PHILADELPHIA Dec. 1. Run away from William Rumsey, on Saturday Night, the 21st of November last, an Indented Servant Man, named Richard English, a native of the County of Cecil in Maryland, aged about 23 Years of Middle Stature and very brown and Swarthy Complexion, having short curled Hair a little Sun-Burnt. He wore a Felt Hat, Ozenbrigs Shirt, Ducroy Coat, a new Jacket and Breeches, made of white Cotton, and an old Camblet Vest, a Pair of New strong Shoes and Yarn Stockings od a deep Cinnamon colour, and a large India Ink Silk Check'd Handkerchief. Whoever apprehends the said Servant and secures him, so that his Master may have him again, shall have Thirty Shillings Reward, and if dwelling near the Head of Bohemia in Cecil County, they shall have Forty Shillings Reward, paid by
                      William Rumsey.

   PHILADELPHIA Dec. 3. Last Sunday one John Long, a Servant to Jonathan Jones of Kingfess attempting to lead a Mare over a small Bridge across Cobb's-Creek, the Mare's Fore-feet slipping, she with a violent spring endeavoured to recover her fall, Struck him on the Stomach with her Head, threw him off of the Bridge and fell upon him; so that he was there immediately drowned. on Tuesday the Coroner's Inquest upon View of the Body, brought in their Verdict, Accidental Death.

   PHILADELPHIA Dec. 8. Whereas a Bill was pass'd in a Session of General-Assembly, held at New-Castle, Kent and Sussex upon Delaware, in the Year 1723, Intitled An Act for the Emission of 5000 pounds in Bills of Credit, which Act will expire the 25th of April, 1731; and whereas another Bill was also pass'd there to said former Year, in a following Session of Assembly for the said Counties, Intitiled, An Act for the Emission of 6000 pounds in Bills of Credit, which will expire also the 2d of November next following: These are to desire all Persons who are possessed of any of the said Bills that they will take care to pay in the same during the Terms above-mentioned, either at the respective

Loan-Office for the said Counties, (where they will be exchanged for Bills of new Currency) or otherwise, at their Discretion, within the said Counties, that the same may be destroy'd in due time, according to the tenor of the Act aforesaid. Published by Order of the Assembly for the said Counties.   Hen. Brooke, Speaker.

PHILADELPHIA Dec. 15. Whereas one Elizabeth Corry of Dunory or Chew Magna in the County of Sumerset, cane here into this Country, supposed to be given Account of by one Edward Cook a Cooper, living with John Stroud, Cooper in Brandywine Hundred, im New-Castle County. Let the said Corry repair to the Printer hereof, and she may be sent home to her Friends, id she is so Inclined.

PHILADELPHIA Dec. 22. Yesterday several Vessels, who attempted to go out of our Harbour last week, but were forc'd back by reason of the driving Ice, proceeded on their respective Voyages.

Run away from George Parker, Butcher, near Philadelphia, about the 4th of the 9th Month, a Servant Man named Andrew Hilton, aged about 30 Years, a short Man with black Hair, a Scar under his Chin, much like the King's Evil, and with crooked Legs, a pair of Leather Breeches new Trowsers, an Ozenbrigs Shirt, a Linnen Jacket a dark colour'd Kersey Coat, and Felt Hat; There is supposed to be with him, a little Woman with black Hair, named Anne Pram, an English Woman, with a black Gown and Petticoat. whoever secures the said Servant, so that his Master may have him again, shall have Thirty Shillings Reward, and reasonable Charges paid by one,
                             George Parker.

Thomas Sharp, intending for Britain, with Capt. Abel Cain, who will sail soon as weather permits; all Persons who have any Accounts with him are desired to settle the same.
                             Thomas Sharp.

PHILADELPHIA Dec. 29. Notice have been given, That whereas, the Inhabitants and Owners of the several Lots in Chester-Town, commonly called New-Town, in Maryland, are obliged to Act of Assembly to build on their respective Lots within

Eighteen Months, Any Carpenters, Joiners, Bricklayers, and other Tradesmen that will repair thither early in the Spring may have good Employment.

N. B. Tanners, Curriers, Hatters and others are much wanted in the said Town, and may have good Encouragement.

Lately Imported from London and to be Sold very Cheap by Andrew Bradford Printer at the sign of th Bible in Second-Street, Philadelphia, A Choice parcel of Blank Books, of Royal, Medium, Demi and Pot Papet. Also a parcel of good Slate. Choice Ink-Powder and Japan Ink, Sealing Wax and Wafers, Folio Letter Cases fit for Merchant Desks or Counting Houses. Likewise a parcel of very good Paper as Royal, Demy, Superfine large Post Fools Cap and pot; Ink-Stands of several sorts and much sorts of Stationary Ware.

N. B. All sorts of Old and New Books neatly Bound and cheap.

1731

PHILADELPHIA Jan. 6. The Speech of the Honourable Patrick Gordon, Esq; Lieutenant Governour of the Province of Pennsylvania, and the Counties of Newcastle, Kent and Sussex upon Delaware.

To the Representatives of the Free-Men of the said Province met in General Assembly.

Gentlemen,
The Tranquility which this Province at present enjoys and the growing Unanimity which has heartily prevailed over the past fueds and dissensions, are now so visible, that I cannot but congratulate the Representative Body of this good People, on a Prospect so delightful in it self, so desirable by every good Man, who has a real and hearty Love for his Country, and which, as it must give the highest Satisfaction to a Governor, cannot fail of being equally agreeable to the Governed.

Amongst the many valuable Privileges derived to this Colony from our late Honourable Proprietor, that of Annual Election is none the least, whereby frequent Opportunities are given to the Legislature of inspecting and regulating our Publick Affairs; and as the Persons chosen to that important Trust are suppose to be Men of Virtue, Wisdom and Ability, so likewise from the Opportunity they have in their respective Counties of knowing the State and Condition of their Country, they cannot but, when convened together, and seriously dispose to promote the Publick Interest, be very good Judges of those Means by which our Happiness and Prosperity may be promoted, and from hence it is, Gentlemen, that I think it unnecessary at this Time to mention to you several Things which, as they equally fall under your Consideration in the Course of your Proceedings, will no Doubt be as seriously attended to, as if they had come particularly recommended from me? I must nevertheless observe that as it hath please God this last Year to bless not only these Parts of America with very plentiful Harvest; but also we hear, most of the Countries of Europe, which of Course has put a Stop to there Demand for produce; it therefore naturally follows, that our Provisions must be low: We ought however, as plenty of fruits of the Earth has ever been held on of greatest Blessings of Heaven, nor only to acquiesce, but be humbly thankful for our present Affluence: Yet as many may by these Means be pinched by a Stagnation of the Currency, which ever ensued in all Countries where their Produce is not in Demand, it may in Time be incumbent on us to a greater Degree abroad, that when at Market they may find a readier Sale.

I have understood that when this Colony was young, and had but little Experience, it exceeded all its Neighbours in the Fineness of its Flower and Bread, and Goodness of its Beer, which are the only Produce of our Grain. The Regulations which have already been made in the two first have greatly contributed to their Improvement, as well as the Reputation of the the Province; and it will still become the Legislature to continue their Care and Concern in a Point of Such Consequence to the whole Country; but the Abases in the last are so gross, that you cannot but be all sensible of the reproach brought on us, when you hear how we have of late been supplied by a Neighbouring Colony; and therefore I need say little to excite your most vigorous Resolutions to apply proper Remedy, which in my Opinion may very easily be found. And if besides such Measures as may render the Produce of our Grain more valuable, and consequently bring it more into Demand, Encouragement were given to raise some other Commodities that might have a constant and ready Vent in Britain, and thereby help to make Returns, it would certainly be of vast Advantage to the Publick.

In my Speech of the first Assembly choosen after my arrival, I mentioned Iron, Hemp and

Silk: In the first of these Diver proceeded with Vigour, 'till the vast Quantities unexpectedly imported into Britain from the new Works in Russia, where the poor People labour almost for nothing, has given some Damp to the Manufacture: But as Silk comes from Countries long Settled, and accustomed to the Business, where the price cannot much alter, and as no Climate in the World is found to agree better with the Silk-Worm than this, since it is impossible, that as the Inhabitants increase, the Raising of Grain should always turn to Account for Exportation, nothing in my Judgement can be more worthy of our Application than to excite the People to the planting of Mulberry Trees, and Furnish themselves with Silk-worms, since it is a Work of which the poorest and feeblest Families are capable; and Children, who can be of little other Service, may here find an Employment suitable to their Years. As the Business is new, People will naturally be backward in falling into the Practice; but if we consider that all Manufactures were so at first, that the West-Indies were for some Time before, they thought of raising Sugar, from whence they now make vast Estates, we should not be discouraged; for all Things of this Kind require only Resolution in the Beginning, of which most Things appear difficult, that afterwards become easy and familiar: therefore recommend it to-you, Gentlemen, to think of some suitable Encouragement that may prompt the Inhabitants to proper Endeavours on their Parts, and I shall use mine to Procure Persons of Skill to lead them into a Way of finishing their Labours to Advantage. The raising of Hemp, and dressing it by Water-rotting, the only Method we find rendering it truly useful, has already its Encouragement, and it is hoped in Time this also may be applied to make returns.

These are the Points I shall now recommend to you, in which, as I have nothing in View but the true Interest and Honour of the Province, and of every Subject under my Care, I cannot doubt your ready Concurrence. This Disposition will naturally lead you to unanimity and Dispatch, the only Means of giving Success to all our Counsels, and of a happy and speedy Issue to this Session; which that we may attain with sincere Expressions and real Proof of Loyalty to his Majesty, Fidelity to out Honourable Proprietors, and with the Increase of Love and Goodwill amongst all our Inhabitants, in the highest of present Wishes.   P. Gordon.

PHILADELPHIA Jan. 12. Run away the 31st of December last from John Hood of this City of Philadelphia, Shoemaker, an Irish Servant Man named John Downing, about 23 Years of Age, of a Middle Stature, long thin Visage, and dark brown Hair, Has on an old Felt Hat, an old brown jacket, a black one under it, a blue one under both; good Buckskin Breeches, blue-grey worsted Stockings, a pair of good round-toed Shoes. Whoever secures the said Runaway so as his Master may have him again, shall have Fifty Shillings Reward, and reasonable Charges paid by John Hood.

PHILADELPHIA Jan. 19. The following is a Speech of an Indian King, named Oppekhorsa, who died lately in the Jersey's, spoken just before his Death to his Successor. The Gentleman, who by Letter communicated this to us, makes the Following Remarks therein find true Greatness of Soul worthy of a King, and a deep Sense of unshaken Honesty, and a Humility which even Christians might boast of, with many other Beauties of Sense, couch'd under strong Rhetorical Figures, dictated by pure Reason and simple Nature alone.

THE SPPECH

My Brother's Son,
This Day I deliver my Heart into thy Bosom, and would have thee love that which is good and keep good Company, and to refuse that which is Evil, and to avoid Bad Company. ——— Now, in as much as I have deliver'd my Heart into thy Bosom, I also deliver my Bosom to keep my Heart therein; therefore always be sure to walk in a good path, and never depart out of it; and if any Indian should speak Evil of Indians or Christians, do not joyn with it, but look to that which is good and Joyn with the same always: Look at the Sun from the Rising of it, to the Setting of the

Same ——— in Speeches that shall be made between Indians and Christians if any thing be spoke that is Evil, do not Joyn with that, but with that which is Good. And when Speeches are made, do not thou speak first, but let all speak before thee, and take good Notice what each Man Speaks, and when thou hast heard all, Joyn with that which is good.

Brother's Son,
I would have thee to cleanse thy Ears, and take all Darkness and foulness out, that thou may'st take Notice of that which is Good and Evil, and then you Joyn with that which is good, and refuse the Evil, and also to cleanse thine Eyes, that thou may'st see both Good and Evil, and if thou see Evil, do not Joyn with it, but Joyn to that which is good.

Brother's Son,
Thou hast heard all that is past, now I would have thee to stand up (he Means by standing up to be resolute) in Time of Speeches, and to find in my Steps, and to follow my Speeches, which I have said before thee, then what thou do do'st desire in Reason will be granted thee, Why shouldst thou not follow my Example is as much as I have had a Mind which is good, therefore do thou also the same. Whereas, My Sons Sheoppy and Servampis were appointed Kings in my stead, and I understand by my Doctor, that Sheoppy, secretly advis'd him not to cure me, and that both being with me at John Hollingshead's House, there I my self saw by them, that they were more given to Drink, than to Notice of my last words, having then had a Mind to make a Speech to them, and to my Brethren the English Commissioners, therefore, I have refused them to be King after me in my stead, and have chosen the Oppekorsa my Brother's Son, to be King in their stead to succeed me, Brother's Son, I desire thee to be plain and fair, with all both Indians and Christians as I have been, I am very weak, otherwise I would have spoken more.

PHILADELPHIA Jan. 26. Last Tuesday, a Lad belonging to Israel Penburton, of this Town, Leading a calf by a string on one of the Wharfs, the Calf Junp'd into the River, hall'd the Boy in after him, and they were both Drowned.

On Tuesday morning one Joseph Ralph was found drowned at one of the Wharffs. He was seen fishing there the night before, and several circumstances is so supposed the Net pull'd him in.

PHILADELPHIA Feb. 2. No Vessel has arrived since our last, our River being lock'd up with]ce; and by Reason of this Natural Embargo, no shipping have either been Entered or Cleared out this Week.

All Persons that are indebted to Celeb Casb, sen. are desired to come forthwith and pay the same to Celeb Casb, jun. who shall give a proper Discharge for the same.

N. B. I do forbid all Persons above-mentioned to pay any Parts, to Alice my Wife, from the sate forward, or give her any Credit on my account, she being Elop'd from me,

Celeb Casb, sen.

PHILADELPHIA Feb. 9. Run away the 26th of December, 1730. from Hugh Durborow of the County of Kent, on Delaware, a Servant Man named James Caboone, aged about 18 Years, of Middle Stature, fair Complexion, round full Visage, much sign of Small-Pox, with straight Hair of a brown or a light brown colour, a small stoppage in his Speech which causeth him to shut his Lips and eyes close sometimes before he utters his Words; had on when he went away, new Shoes, new Stockings made of natural black wool, new Vest and Breeches light colour, (black Coat, which 'tis said he has not with him) an old Hat. Any Person securing the said Servant, so that his Master may have him again, shall have Twenty Shillings Reward and reasonable Charges, paid by me,

Hugh Durborow jun.

Philadelphia Feb. 16. Joseph Wild, having at Thomas Hatton's at the Lower End of Front-street has to sell, a choice Parcel of Spices, viz. Cinnamon, Cloves, Mace, Nutmeg, Pimento, Double and single refin'd London Sugar, fresh Currans, Green and Bohea Teas, Nails of most Sorts, English Saddles and Bridles, Cover-Seed, a large Copper Still and Worm, which will contain two Barrels, thread Hose Men and Women's Bleach'd and unbleach'd; with sundry other Merchandize, all which proposes to sell at reasonable Rates.

A Servant Man's Time to be dispos'd of Having Two Years and odd Months to serve, a Joyner by Trade. Enquire of the Printer hereof and know further.

NEW-YORK Feb. 22. Sometime last Week William Kerton our Pilot between the City and Sandy-Hook in his Pilot Boat near Shewsbury River, had both Thighs broke by the Firing of a small Gun which he carried in his Boat and his Life is dispaired of, to the unexpressible lost of this Port, we not knowing how to supply his Place with so honest and skillful a Pilot.

On the 19th Instant arrived here a Schooner from Barbadoes; she was within Sandy-Hook in 12 Days, and was forced out by the late hard weather and went to Rhode-Island.

PHILADELPHIA Province of Pennsylvania Feb. 24. All Persons who are Indebted to the Proprietors of the said Province on Account of Quit-Rent for the Lands they hold, or any other Account, are Required to pay the same in the next First Month (March) for Collecting whereof, James Steel, the present Receiver, hath Appointed to attend at his Office, in the Second-Street of the City of Philadelphia, from the First Day of the said Month, to the 13th (inclusive) for receiving those of the City and County of Philadelphia; at Chester, from the 24th to the 26th (inclusive) for those of that County; and at Pensbury in the Province of Bucks, from the 29th to the 31st, (inclusive) of the same Month; at which respective Times and Places, all Persons who are indebted are aforesaid, are required to bring in their several Payments in Money, or Receipts for the Mills; for such Lands who rents are to be paid in Wheat.

Run away the 4th of this Month, from his Master James Wilson of the Nothern Liberties of Philadelphia, a Servant Man named Henry Prichard, of middle Stature, dark brown Hair, aged about 22 Years, he had on a brown homespun Coat, a light colour'd Vest with Brass Buttons, and a brown Broad Cloath Vest with Brass Buttons, a pair of Cloath Breeches, a Felt Hat and Yarn Stockings. Whoever brings said Servant to his

Master, or secure him in the Work-House in Philadelphia, so that he may have him again, shall have Thirty Shillings Reward if taken within 20 Miles of Home, and Fifty Shillings of farther, and all reasonable Charges.

PHILADELPHIA March 2. We have Advice from East New-Jersey, That Capt. Downing in the Brigantine Swan, who sailed from this Port some time in November last for Madera, but last from Boston with a lading of Salt, was run ashore by distress of Weather, near the place call Squam, but its hop'd they will save some of the Cargo, also the Rigging and Sails.

Capt. Birch gives us an Account that he Spoke with a Man in Antigua, a Hatter by Trade who some time last November going with two more in an open Boat from Egg-Harbour for Lewis-Town, were blown off the Coast, but were very fortunately taken up by one Capt. Dickenson some 70 Leagues at Sea, the other two he put ashore at Bermuda, and the Hatter at Antigua.

We have an Account from Annapolis, that the Lord Baltimore and his Family designs for Maryland this Summer.

PHILADELPHIA March 9. On the 30th Day of this Instant March, will be exposed to Sale by way of Publick Vendue, at the House of John Stull, in the County of Lancaster, in the Province of Pennsylvania, the Goods, Improvements and Effects, belonging to said Stull, who hath, absented himself, and are now in the Hands of the Auditor to make Sale of: Likewise all Persons who have any Effects of aforesaid Stull's in their Hands, are to deliver them to the auditors before the Day of Sale, that they may be Sold, in order to pay his Crditors, as the Law directs. And All Persons who have any Demands on said Stull, may come at the Day of Sale, and have their Accounts adjusted by us.
Gabriel Davis, Cappenter and John Posiletbeavait.

To be Sold. A very good Tract of Land containing about 6000 Acres, scituated in the County of Hunterdon in the Western Division of the Province of New-Jersey, about 22 Miles from Brunswick, near the same distance from Elizabeth-Town, the said Tract hath on it a very good

Iron Mine, and is well accommodated with streams of Water, one of which is near the said Mine fit to set a Furnace on, and the others are suitable for fineries. The Title will be Clear. Any Person having a mind to purchase the same may Enquire Joseph Kirkbridge of Bucks-County in Pennsylvania, (the Owner) and know the Terms. If any Purchasing the said Land have a mind to set up a Furnace the said Owner is willing to hold a Share.

PHILADELPHIA March 18. Run away the 26th of February last from Peter Wren of Woodbridge, in Middlesex County in East-New-Jersey, an Irish Servant Man named Thomas Deale, of a small Stature, aged about 22 Years, he has the Letters T.D. on his left Hand done with Powder, his Hair cut off, he had on a homespun Coat of woolen and Cotton lined with striped Calminco and Pewter Buttons, Buckskin Breeches with Pewter Buttons, Yarn Stockings, a Felt Hat and Worsted Cap, also a Fannel Shirt. There is with him a likely little Woman who he calls his Wife, she had on a black Gown, a striped Pettycoat and Wastecoat of Wool and Cotton. Whoever secures the said Servant Man so that his Master may have him again shall have Three Pounds Reward and reasonable Charges.

To be Sold by William Bantoft, a Dwelling House and Lott of Ground, situated in the upper part of Front-Street, containing a breath on the said Street 24 Foot and length 213 Foot, which said Messuage and Lott of Ground is adjoining to the Lott late in Possession of George Campion, Likewise a large House and Lott of Ground in the Town of Burlington, in West-Jersey, scituated in the main Street commonly called High-Street, containing in breath on the said Street 57 Foot, and extending back Westerly 192 Foot, bounded by another Street and fronts House and Mill-House, Brewing Vessels, Kiln, a large Copper which will boil Ten Barrels, Coolers, Tuns, Backs, Malt-Mill and Mill Stones. Aslo one other Lott of Ground in the said Town of Burlington, adjoining to the before-mentioned Lott, containing in breath on High-Street 53 Foot and 21 pearches and 10 Foot in length. Likewise at the

Bantoft's House in Walnut-Street Philadelphia is to be sold, good Florence Oyl in Flasks, the beast of Teas, and also Chesire and Cloucestershire Cheese.

SALEM March 23. At the Meeting of the Justices, and Freeholders of the County of Salem (at Salem) on the 23d Day of March 1731. In Consideration of the Contagious Mortality of the Small-Pox; It was thought Expedient by the said Justices anf Freeholders that they might be somewhat Essay'd to prevent to too great and sudden Prevalency of said Mortality of Small-Pox in the County of Salem. Pursuant whereunto the said Justices and Freeholders, do hereby desire of such People as were wont heretofore to use and frequent coming to the Fairs in said County on their several Occasions, to desist their coming, because the said Justices and Freeholders have thought fit to prohibit any Fair to be kept in said County this Spring Season as usual.

John Jones, Cl.

PHILADELPHIA March 25. We hear from our Capes that some time last Week, Capt. Burrel, (one of our Pilots) his Son and Servant were all drowned as they were Fishing in a Canoe.

PHILADELPHIA March 26. Stolen or Stray'd from Edward Robinson of Philadelphia, about three Months ago; a small Grey Pacing Mare, between 12 and 13 Hands high, branded E on the near Shoulder and somewhat mottled in the Face: whoever secure the said Mare, and brings her to the above-named Edward Robinson, at his House in Walnut-Street shall have Forty Shillings Reward and reasonable Charges, paid by me

Edward Robinson.

PHILADELPHIA April 1. We hear from New-York, that the Small-pox are very brief in the High-Dutch above Albany and in Schnectady. And that many People thereaway are taken with a Violent Fever, which breaks out in red and blue spots, and very Mortal.

To be sold, a very good Tract of Land, lying on the South side of Susquehannah Lower-Ferry, on a Creek called Swan-Creek, on Navigable Water, containing 1500 Acres, the Improvements are as follows. A good Dwelling-House Shingled,

Forty Foot long, Two Brick Chimney's and all furnish'd inside, a good Kitchen, with a good Brick Chimney 25 Foot long, a good Barn 40 Foot long, Three large Tobacco Houses, 40 Foot long: 100 Acres of clear Land within good Fence, also an Orchard well Fenced in; the above Land lies on the Road, about 3 Miles from Susquehannah, to be sold by Edward Hall, living on the said Plantation.

PHILADELPHIA April 8. From Lewis-Town we have an Account of the following sorroful Accident, which happened the 9th past at Indian River, viz. One Groome who kept the Ferry there, crossing in his Flat with 3 Horses, and 8 or 9 Passengers, the Flat fill'd and sunk in the middle of the River: He and his Son who rowed with him were both drowned, together with four others who could not swim. There were two Women in the Flat, one with a Child at her Breast; this Woman was saved by a young Man who swam with her to a Stake, by which she held till a Canoe came to her Assistance, but not being able to keep the Child's Head above Water it Perished in her Arms: The other having got hold of the Tail of one of the Horses held fast while he swam and drew her safe to shore. One of the Men drowned was a Pedler, His Companion who travelled with him seeing the Flat so full refused to go in, sent his Goods, which were lost.

PHILADELPHIA April 15. Last Monday above Noon, a Waggon coming from Conestogoe to this City, laden with Flour, Hemp, Skins, &c. was set on Fire by the Bushes, which were burning near the Road. The Hemp burnt with such Violence that it was with great difficulty that they saved the Horses and Waggon. They lost all the Hemp, four Bags of Flour, and six Bags of Provender.

BURLINGTON April 18. At the Petty-Session of the Peace, held for the County of Burlington, at Burlington, the 16th Day of April, 1731. It was consider'd, that Fairs generally occasioned great Concourse of People, from the most adjacent Places, and that at present it is not to meet for keeping the Fair in Burlington, as usual, by reason of the great Mortaliti in Philadelphia and other Parts of Pennsylvania, where the Small-Pox now violently Rages: Therefore, to prevent, to the utmost Power of the Justices at the said Session, the further spreading of so Epidemical and Dangerous a Distemper, and more especially, for that the approaching Heat of the Summer may be more malignant and Fatal; it is ordered that May Fair be, and is hereby Prohibited to be kept in the said Town of Burlington, and all Persons are hereby strictly required to take Notice hereof, accordingly as they will answer for their Contempt at their Peril.

PHILADELPHIA April 22. A Choice Tract of Land, well Stored with Timber and Wood, containing 401 Acres, situated in the Northern-Liberties of the City of Philadelphia, lying between this place and Frankford, Distant three Miles and a half from this City, Bounded to the Westward above a Mile of Frankford Creek. Whoever hath a mind to purchase the said Tract of Land, may treat William Rawle, in Philadelphia.

A Tract of Land in the County of Chester, within six Miles of Samuel Nutt's Iron Works; containing about 450 Acres, 40 thereof clear'd with 20 Acres of clear'd Meadowing, part under English Grass, and conveniencies to make 20 Acres more, a new House but not finish'd; to be Sold by Ann Roberts, Widow of Owen Roberts, late of Philadelphia, deceas'd; of whom any Person disposed to purchase, may be inform'd of the Condition of Sales.

PHILADELPHIA April 29. This is to give Notice, That the House Shop and Warf, where Mr. William Parker now Dwelleth is to be Lett: there is two good dry Stores, well fitted with all things convenient for dry Goods, and three other dry Stores, and three lower Stores, convenient for Flour or any other Goods. Any Person that have any occasion for the said Premises, may inquire of John Danby, at his House in Second-street and know further; Mr. Parker remove from the above said House the 1st Day of July next ensuing.

N. B. Also, the said John Danby, hath a good Still to dispose of very cheap, which holds betwixt Eighty and Ninety Gallons.

To be Sold by the Widow Robinson, next Door to

the Coffee-House, Front-street a Brick-House and Lott, 20 Foot Front and 19 Foot Back, Men & Womens Saddles, and Saddlery Ware of all Sorts, and Household Goods.

All Persons indebted to William Attwood, are desired to pay the same, or may be expect Trouble. He intends to go to England in two Months, having sundry Sorts of European & West-India Goods, will sell at reasonable Rates, for ready Money.

All Persons indebted to the Estate of Christopher Smith, are desired to come and pay the same, to Alexander Woodrop near Carpenter's Wharf, or may depend of further Trouble in a short time.

PHILADELPHIA May 6. Last Saturday Ralph Smith, going in his Boat from this Place to Delaware-Falls, met with a hard Flow of Wind, about a Mile above this Town, the Boom gibing, knock't his Man over-board, who sunk and was not seen afterwards.

PHILADELPHIA May 10. We hear from Maryland, that Subscriptions have been lately made among the Gentlemen there, for encouraging the Manufacture of Linnen: The Mayor and Council of Annapolis, have promised pay as a Reward the sum of 5 Pounds to the Person that brings the finest Piece of Linnen, of the Growth & Manufacture of Maryland, to next September Fair; for the 2d Piece in fineness, 3 Pounds and 3d 40 Shillings, the Linnen to continue property of the Maker, Like Reward are offered in Baltimore County, and 'tis thought the Example will be followed in all the Counties in Maryland.

NEW-YORK May 10. On Saturday a young Man a Bermudian, unrigging Schooner Mast, fell from the Top and Dashed out his Brains, his Death is much lamented by his Friends.

PHILADELPHIA May 12. To be sold by Mr. Archibald Gordon and Thomas Hatton; a Choice Parcel of likely young Servants, both Men and Women, newly arrived, among which, there is a Saddler, a Millwright; Any Persons that want, may be on board the Vessel over-against Fishbourn's Dock, where they may be furnish'd, at very Reasonable Rates.

N. B. They are no Convicts.

To be Lett or Hired, a good four wheel'd chaise with two good Horses and very good Driver, Enquire of John Horton, Black-Smith in Arch-street Philadelphia.

All Persons indebted to Thomas Willing, late of this City, Merchant, are desired immediately to settle their Accounts, and pay the Balance to his Attorneys, Willing & Shippen, at their Store on Carpenter's Wharf.

PERTH-AMBOY May 13. On Saturday last one Duncan Campbell stood two Hours in the Pillory, according to his Sentence at the Superior Court of this County. To-morrow he is to receive 39 lashes at the Cart-Tail, and on Friday 31 more. His Crime is Counterfeiting and Passing Pistoles. He is to be sent to Monmouth County, to receive another Trial on the same Account.

NEW-YORK May 24. His Excellency our Governour arrived at Albany on the 12th Instant, the Indians were not come to Albany 8 Days ago but were at Schanactada 20 Miles above, and were expected in a Day or two.

NEW-YORK May 31. On Tuesday last his Excellency our Governour arrive here from Albany; The Six Nations of Indians, when they met his excellency, were very well pleased with the Presents given them, and gave the strongest Assurance of their Loyalty and Fidelity to his Majesty and the Crown of Great Britain.

PHILADELPHIA June 1. Job Rawenson being removed from his Store on Fishbourn's Wharf to his New opened Store near Dickinsons Burnt Houses in Water-Street, giveth hereby Intelligence that he hath a fine Choice of most kinds of merchandize, which he will sell at very inviting and cheap Rates, for Ready Money, or to all punctual Persons that will pay for the same any time in September or beginning of October next, being in order to make a clear store, he intending then without fail to leave this Country, this therefore is to give timely Notice.

To be Sold by Capt. Charles Hargrave, a Parcel of very likely Negroe Men, very Reasonable, they have had the Small-Pox.

ANNAPOLIS June 5. Whereas Mrs. Mary Woodward,

and Mrs. Elizabeth Ginn, of the city of London in Great Britain, Widows, have by their seperate Powers of Attorneys, impowered us the Subscibers, to Sell all the Houses and Lotts lying in the City of Annapolis, lately belonging to Amos Garrets, Esq; of the said City deceased. We do therefore herby give Notice, that on Friday the 17th Day of July next, at the House of John Lomas, the said Lotts and Houses, will be exposed to Publick Sale, by way of Auction, for Money or good Bills of Exchange: All Persons that are disposed to Buy, may be shown the said Lotts, and the said Garrets's Title thereto, by Ames Woodward, one of the Subscribers, Given under our Hands this 3d Day of June 1731.

Ames Woodward, John Gallaway.

PHILADELPHIA June 10. Run away, early this Morning, from the Sloop Maryland of Boston, Edward Sunderland Master, a Servant Man named Robert Hamock, aged about 20 Years, of a middle Stature swarthy Complexion pretty thick set, black Hair, has taken with him a dark colour'd Duroy Coat, Jacket and Breeches strip'd red, green and white, the breeches have red silk Puffs; he has also a suit of light coloured Summer Cloaths, several pair of Stockings and several other Things. Whoever takes up the said Servant and brings him to his Master, or to Mr. Peter Bayton in Philadelphia, shall have Thirty Shillings as a Reward besides reasonable Charges.

PERTH-AMBOY June 15. From New-Castle we hear, that on Tuesday the 8th Instant, the Lightning fell upon a House within a few Miles of that Place, in which killed 3 Dogs, struck several Persons deaf, and split a Woman's Nose in a surprizing Manner.

Also from the same Place we hear, that a Man and a Woman are lately committed to Prison there, on suspicion of Murdering the Woman's Husband.

About three or four Weeks ago a Servant Lad belonging to Richard Everson of Thornbury in Chester County, hanged himself in a Swamp near his Master's House. He had been missing near a Fortnight, and it was tho't he had run away; but in the late hot weather, a strong Smell Leading People to that Place, they found his Head still hanging but his Body dropp'd and lying on the Ground.

PHILADELPHIA June 17. In Third-street near the Work-House, are Thought Reading, Writing and Arithmetick. Likewise Mr. Wenton's Stenography, or New Method of Short-Hand, brought to perfection. by   Ebenezer Wikes.

Run away the 11th of this Month, from William Nichols of Calan, Turner in Chester County, a Servant Man named Henry Damsel, of a low Stature and well-set, short black Hair, red Complexion, talks thick, he has one Crocked Leg, and had on a Lincy Jacket with Pewter Buttons, a Homespun Shirt and course Drawers, brown Thread Stockings, a good pair of Shoes. Whoever shall take up the said Servant, and bring him to his said Master, or the Work-House in Philadelphia, shall have Forty Shillings Reward and all Reasonable Charges.

Stray'd or Stolen away from Joseph Claypoole of Chester Township in the County of Burlington on the 5th of this Inst. June; a bay Horse about 13 Hands and a half high, branded on the near Buttock D.S. and has lost part of his right Eye-Lid, he will Pace pretty well, with a large Bell stampt with Jos. Claypoole. Whoever takes up the said Horse, and brings him to Joseph Claypoole, sen. of Philadelphia, shall have Ten Shillings Reward and reasonable Charges.

PHILADELPHIA June 24. Last Monday we received the following Melancholy account of the loss of the Sloop Maryland, of Boston Edward Sunderland Master viz.

On Monday the 15th of this Instant June 1, I sailed from Philadelphia in the Sloop Maryland, of Boston; on Tuesday Night about 10 o'Clock I took my Departure from Cape Helopen, stearing my Course Eastward in order to make the best way for Newfoundland. Wednesday before Noon I put little Wind, and Calm; about 2 o'Clock in the Afternoon, the Wing sprung up Southerly, and by Evening blew a fresh Breeze looking Dirty like, we handed some small Sails, but still kept on my Course, E. by N. It being the Mates Watch to bring 12 o'Clock, My Watch turn'd in but I Stay'd up till about 10 o'Clock, and then laid down but could not Sleep, and perceiving it to be lighten much and the Wind failing, I went upon the Deck again, and found the Weather very Flattering, and constant Lightning and Thunder tho' at a distance. I order'd the People to lower the mainsail, then having only the Jib out, the Mate and my Self being on the Quarter-Deck, and one Man forward near the Masts, to stand by the Jib Hallards, the Candle went out in the Binicle, I desired the Mate to go down and strike a Light, in the mean time there came a prodigious Clap of Thunder and Lightning which struck down the Man forward burnt all the Cloaths off of his Back and Burnt him miserably, from the Middle of his Back to his Ancles, and also one of his Arms. The Thunder waked the People below, who immediately came upon Deck, and we brought the wounded Man aft and put him into his Cabin. Perceiving the Mast to be Splinter'd I order'd the Pump to be try'd, and taking Candle and Lanthorn, went forward and found the Mast Splinter'd in two places, and the Coat of the Mast about the Partners torn to Pieces; thinking now of no further Damage, I demanded of the Men at the Pump if she suck'd, who answer'd No, upon which going to the Side, I found the Vessel swam deeper than usual, and immediately cry'd out, The Lord have Mercy upon us, the Vessel is Sinking; this put us in the utmost Consternation, the Mate call'd to cut the Lashings of the Boat, which I finding a Hatchet, did accordingly; we had upon Deck a small Cask of Water which we put into the Boat, we also got 8 or 10 Pieces of Pork and a Bag of Bread which we got into the Boat, as also the Wounded Man; the Water being by this time to a Man's Middle in the Steerage, we got the Rudders and Tackle with all speed, and hoisted the Boat, which we had scarcely done, before the Sloop turn'd on her Side, laying with her Larboard Gunnel out of the Water: We left her the next Morning by Day Light (having no Hopes of saving anything out of her) being then about E. by N. 30 Leagues from Cape Henlopen, trusting ourselves to the Providence of God. We were Two Days and Two Nights before we made the Land, and there we came below Indian

River, about 15 Leagues to the Southward of the above Cape, and Sabbath Day Night we got to the Port of Philadelphia. The Wounded Man continues ill.

PHILADELPHIA July 1. Yesterday two Men having been to Bachelors-Hall in their return Fainted by reason of the great Heat.

Yesterday two Men and a Woman reaping in the Jerseys, it being very Hot, they unadvisidly drank Cold Water, whereof the two Men Died very suddenly and the Woman's life is dispaired of. Also a Negro Man Died suddenly in this City by drinking cold Water.

On Thursday the 8th this Instant, July, at the House of Moses Cox of Passyunk Road, a Race will be run by Mr. Chancellor's Brown Horse Now or Never, against Mr. Charles Read's Grey Mare Polley.

NEW-YORK July 5. On Thursday last at four of the Clock in the Morning, His Excellency John Montgomerie, Esq; Captain General and Commander in Chief of his Majesty's Province of New-York, New-Jersey, and the Territories thereon depending in America, and Vice-Admiral of the same, &c. Departed this Life at Fort George in this City, and was inter'd in the King's Chappel on the Evening of the Friday following.

On Wednesday last, a great Clap of Thunder happened at Morrisania, which split a great tree there all to Pieces, and killed 10 Calves, that were under the said Tree.

On Thursday last, a German in this City, being very Hot drank Cold Water, on which he died soon after.

PERTH-AMBOY July 7. By the Honourable Lewis Morris, Esq; President of his Majesty's Council for the Province of New-Jersey, &c.

A PROCLAMATION

Whereas Almighty God in his good Providence, has seen fit to take to himself John Montgomerie, Esq; late Governour of this Province, it, by virtue of his Majesty's Letters Patent under the Seal of Great Britain, devolved upon me, I have, by the Advise of His Majesty's Council for this Province, thought fit to Declare and Notify the same, that all His Majesty's Subjects inhabiting in the said Province, may take Notice thereof, and govern themselves accordingly. And I have also, by the Advice aforesaid, thought fit for His Majesty's Service, to Publish and Declare, That all Officers, Civil and Military, are to continue in their several Stations, and execute respectively their several Offices, according to the Powers given, and the several Trust reposed in them, until further Orders: And Directions shall be herein given by my Self, or the Governor or Commander in Chief of this Province for the time being.

Given under my Hand and Seal at Arms at the Council-Chamber at Perth Amboy, this seventh Day of July, in the fifth Year of the Reign of our Sovereign Lord George the Second, by the Grace of God, of Great Britain, France and Ireland, and all the Territories and Dominions thereto belonging, King, Defender of Faith &c.
Annoq. Domini: 1731.   Lewis Morris.
  By his Honour's Command Ja. Smith Secry.

ANNAPOLIS July 13. The Speech of His Excellency Benedict Leonard Calvert, Governour and Commander and Chief, in and over the Province of Maryland, to both Houses of Assembly, begun and held at the City of Annapolis, on Tuesday the Thirteenth Day of July, Annoq. Domini; 1731.

Gentlemen of the upper House and Lower House of Assembly,
As I have an Intention to visit my Native Country, upon account of my Health, which for some Time past I have very much wanted and not knowing how suddenly I might undertake the Voyage, I inclin'd to a Session of Assembly at this Time, pursuant to your last Prorogation; that I might once more at least, join with you in my best Endeavours for the real Service of the Country: A Scene wherein I shall ever be ready to act the kindest and Sincerest Part.

His Lordship the Lord Proprietory, having transmitted me his Answer to your joint address, in the late Session, I shall lay the same before you, pursuant to his Lordship's Directions.

I must renew former Recommendations, of Care and Circumspection in the Penning of our Laws; since the use, as well as the Credit of them, will much depend thereof.

I an inform'd by some of the Naval Officers, that several Persons (who in their Opinion, seem not intituled thereof,) claim the Benefit of the Laws in Favour of its intent, as to Publick Duties: And inasmuch as those Laws are by many thoughts not sufficiently clear in their Executions, an Explanation thereupon may clear all Doubts, for several other Disputes; which I hope you will therefore consider coming of.

Altho' we must principally rely of the Divine Providence, for a happy Issue to all our Consultations, yet on our Part we must not be wanting in a clam and diligent Attention thereto. Would we search after Wisdom, we must seek her in the Temple of Concord; there only she delights to dwell; there may be had Freedom of Converse with her; and Moderation only can shew us the Path that leads thereto.

And as I have such Intentions of leaving, for some Time, His Lordship's good Tenants here, they may be assur'd, that my Occasion wherein I can be serviceable to them; However the Prudence of your own Measures, may be greatly assistant to my best Inclination, in the Service of the Province of Maryland.

PHILADELPHIA July 22. A Servant Lad's Time, to be disposed of fit for Town or Country Business, has upward of Three Years to serve: if any Person has a mind to Buy the said Servant, may enquire of Evan Jones, Chymist, in Market-Street, and know further.

N. B. All Persons indebted to said Evan Jones, are desired to pay the same, or expect trouble.

PHILADELPHIA July 29. Run away, the 18th of this Instant July, from John Gordon of Freehold, in East-New-Jersey, in the Township of Middletown, an Irish Servant man Named George Tompson, by Trade a Shoemaker, aged about 21 Years, of a pale Complexion, short lightish Hair, of stature Tall and Slender, had on when he went away an old brown Ratteen Coat, an Oxenbrigs Shirt and an old Felt Hat, old Shoes and no Stockings, He writes well and is much inclined to reading and Smoaking.

Whoever takes up and secures said Servant, so

that his Master may have him again, shall have Twenty Shillings as a Reward, and all reasonable Charges, paid by me. John Gordon.

N. B. He lately Ran away from Boston, and pretends to have served his Time in Boston and Rhode Island.

Run away the 25th of June last, from the Ship John Galley, John Ball Commander, Two Sailors, the one named George Bordman, and the other John Gilline, they are both Middle Stature, they are in Sailors Habit, and have several other Cloaths. Whoever shall take up said Sailors, and bring them to the said Ship, shall have Forty Shillings reward paid by Capt. John Ball.

PHILADELPHIA Aug. 5. We hear from Evesham in West-New-Jersey, that some time last Week as two Men and a Boy were making Hay they saw a Gust Coming up, whereupon they immediately took shelter under a large Tree, there they had not been long before a sudden Flash of Lightning and a hard Clap of Thunder splinter'd the Tree from Top to Bottom, some of the splinters fell on their Heads and stun'd them, and struck one Man's Leg so that it Swell'd very much. Some of the splinters were struck above Thirty yards distant.

PHILADELPHIA Aug. 12. Run away on the 7th of this Instant July 1731, from Michael Webster of Baltimore County, in the Province of Maryland, three Servants the one a young Man named Mathew Plumley, aged about 18 Years, a slender Youth, speaks very thick, his Hair cut off close, he is of a swarthy Complexion and with Powder on one or both of his Arms with Letters or Flourishes, has a Scar burnt on one of his Hands; he is supposed to have on a Leather Jacket faced with striped Flannel, Linnen Trowsers, a Felt Hat, and old shoes and Stockings.

The other two are Women, one named Elizabeth Asmore indifferent Tall and Slender; the other named Mary Wootson, a short Woman, dark Complexion and has very light Eyes, which Servant Women have with them a Collomanco Gown, a black Quilted Petticoat and white quilted petticoat, an old Sattin Gown and a new Callocoe Gown, a pair of lace Shoes, and a pair of Spanish Leather Shoes, with sundry other sorts of wearing

Apperel. Mary Wottson has with her three Gold Rings and some English Coins.

Likewise run away with them, from Mr. Antell Deaver of the same Place, a Servant Man named John West, a White Smith by Trade, a short well set Man short light brown Hair pretty much curled, much pitted with the Small-Pox and much Belly-Busten, had with him an old Beaver Hat, with sundry other wearing Cloaths which we cannot describe.

Whoever takes up the said Servants and secures them, so that their said Masters may have them again, shall receive Twenty Shillings as a Reward for each, or Thirty Shillings for each besides, all reasonable Charges if brought to their Masters Dwellings, Paid by

Michael Webster, & Antell Deaver.

PHILADELPHIA Aug. 19. All Persons indebted to Samuel Hackney of the City of Philadelphia, are desired to come and pay the same forthwith; and they who have Demands on him, are desired to come and receive the same, he designing for Great Britain in six Weeks time: He now liveth near the Sign of the Bear's Head, Second Street.

To be Sold, By Capt. William Spafford in Front Street, a very likely Negroe Woman, fit for any House Work. A Negroe Man who speaks very good English, fit for either House or Plantation Work; a parcel of very good Green-Teas, All will be sold very reasonable for ready Money.

Just Imported, good English Beer, at Fourteen Pence per Bottle. To be sold by David Evans, at the Crown in Market-Street.

PHILADELPHIA Aug. 24. On the 12th of this Instant arrived in the River Sassafras in Maryland, the Ship Cisger, Mathew Piper Master from Dublin, which said Master in his letter to a Correspondent in this Place (confirmed by some Passengers and Servants who are come up to Philadelphia, from the said Ship) Declares, That on the 15th Day of July last, they were taken by a Spanish Pirate, in a British built Galley of 16 Guns and about an Hundred Men, of divers Nations, in the Latitude between 38 and 39 Degrees about 200 Leagues from the Capes of Virginia, by whom they were most barbarously used without any Provocation; and which the following Persons were compelled to go with them, viz. Henry Piper chief Mate, Mathew Gillat second Mate, James Peerson Carpenter, and Richard Lampreye or Lampiere a Passenger; of which this Publick Notice is given, to the end that in case the said Pirates shou'd be taken or come ashore with the said Persons, or any of them, it may be known that they were forced on board the said Pirate Ship.

NEW-YORK Aug. 25. The Speech of the Honourable Rip Van Dem. Esq; President of His Majesty's Council of the Province of New-York, to the General Assembly of the said Province, on the 25th of August 1731.

Gentlemen,

Upon the Death of our late Governour John Montgomerie Esq; the Powers and Authorities by His Majesty's Commission and Instruction given him, devolving on me, I have thought fit, by and with the Advice of his Majesty's Council to call you together, at this Time; to make such Acts and provisions, as are immediately Necessary for His Majesty's Service, the Security of the Province, and the Preservation of the Peace thereof.

I must in a particular manner recommend, that timely and effectual Provisions made for supporting the Post of Oswego and the Troops posted in it, and regulate the Indian Trade there, as the most probable Method to increase the Fur Trade, and to draw the remote Indians, and to confirm the Six Nations in the fidelity & Obedience to this Crown of Great Britain.

I must likewise recommend to your serious consideration the ruinous and bad Condition of our Frontier Garrisons, which require your Particular Care, especially the Building of the Fort at Albany, according to your Resolve in your last Session.

I need not put you in Mind, that a new Act ought to be made for Letting to Farm the Excise of Strong Liquors retailed in this Province. That Act being nigh expired, and if you think other Acts shall be immediately Necessary for His Majesty's Service, or the good of this

Province, you shall find me ready to concur with you thereon.

The Nature of the Business to be before you require Dispatch, and your own good Understanding will, I Doubt not produce a Suitable Unanimity, that neither you nor the Country may be burthened by a long Session.   Rip Van Dam.

NEW-YORK Aug. 25. There is little or no News in this Place, nothing but the melancholy scene of little Business, and less Monies, the Markets begin to grow very thin; the Small-Pox raging very violently in Town, which in a great measure hinders the Country People from Supplying the Place with Provisions. I have not yet heard that any Persons have gone out of Town for fear of it; the last Week they began to Inoculate, of which Practice I have some reason to believe will very much be followed, the Distemper has been a long time very favourable, but now begins to be of the Cofluent kind, and very Mortal.

BUCKS COUNTY Aug. 29. Last Night Broke out of Newtown Goal, two Prisoners the one named Obediah Owen, a New-England Man about 25 Years old, Committed for Horse Stealing, he is a tall well set Man, of a swarthy Complexion, short brown Hair; had on when he went away a dark Colour'd Coat, a fine Shirt, check Trowsers, black Worsted Stockings and round Toe'd Shoes with wooden Heels, He was taken at Perth-Amboy for the said Felony about 10 Weeks ago.

The other an Irish Man named George Beman, Aged about 24 Years a Felon, of middle Stature, swarthy Complexion but looks fair having lain in Goal about 5 Months; he had on a redish Camblet Coat, Cloth Breeches, of a Yellowish colour with black Puffs, an old Ozenbrigd Shirt grey Yarn Stockings and round Toe'd Leather Shoes.

Whoever secures them and brings them to Newtown Goal, shall have Five Pounds Reward for for each paid by   Timothy Smith Sheriff.

It is supposed the above felon have taken with them a Negro Man named Jo, belonging to Henry Nelson aged about 20 Years, he had a Linsey-Woolsey Coat of a gray colour, a Leather Jacket lined with white Linsey-Woolsey, a pair of Leather Breeches with blue Glass Buttons, a good

Hat, two new Shirts made of homespun Linnen, a pair of Thread Stockings and good round Toe'd Shoes. He took with him three of his Master's Horses and three Saddles and Bridles, viz. one Grey Flea bitten Horse, branded on his near Shoulder, Shod-before, about 14 Hands high and Paces well; A white Horse about 14 Hands high branded (I think) on the near Shoulder H and on the near Thigh N, a Swallow Fork in the far Ear and a Half Penny under it: The other a Dunish Bay Horse about 14 Hands high branded and Ear-mark't as before said. A new black Breasted Saddle made of Hogs-Skin; a good square Skinned black Saddle, and an old Saddle. Also two Guns with some Powder and Shot.

Whoever secures the said Negroe and the Horses &c. and bring them to their Owner near New-Town, shall have Eight Pounds Reward Paid by

Henry Nelson.

PHILADELPHIA Sept. 2. We hear also that the Sloop Maryland, Edward Sunderland Master, mentioned to be struck with Thunder and Lost at Sea was drove into Chincoteaque Bay in Virginia and most of the Goods saved.

MONMOUTH COUNTY NEW-JERSEY Sept. 2. On Tuesday last an Apprentice of one Robert White in Shewsbury, being Corrected by his Master, went home to his Parents who lived near and told them he would drown'd himself, and took his leave of his Father. His Mother went with him to his Masters, by the Way he told her that what he had he would give to her, and informed her of what he had in his Pocket Book, and some small Debts that was due him. His Mother told him that if his Master abused him he should Complain to the Justices and they would exchange him, at which he smiled, signifying that that was not to be compared to his own way of discharging himself. When he came to his Master he threatened that he would beat him the next Morning, took a Rope and a Stone of 16 Pounds Weight and went into the River in a Canoe and Tying one end of the Rope to the Stone and the other with a running Nuse about his Neck, junped Overboard and Drowned Himself.

UPPER FREEHOLD Sept. 7. Yesterday one Thomas Deacon a Servant to Robert Lawrence, and a Boy of about 11 Years of Age, coming from Meeting together heard a Dog (who for fashion sake had been to Meeting) Bark very much, sent the Child to see what was the Matter, who running back told him it was two great Bucks fast together by their Horns. The Man with much difficulty cut both their Throats their Horns being so lockt together that several have try'd to part them, since both their Heads are cut off, but find it cannot be done without breaking or cutting them.

PHILADELPHIA Sept. 9. We hear from Cranberry in the County of Middlesex in New Jersey, that one Daniel Parine taking his Gun (that his brother had charg'd unknown to him) and striking the Flint with his Knife in order to sharpen it, the Powder took fire and the Gun went off and shot his Wife with a Bullet and seven Swan shot just above the Hip Bone. The Force of the Shot was deadened by her Quilt Petticoat so that the Bullet and Wadd was taken out but an Inch in the Flesh near her Back. Her Life was at dispaired of she being with Child and near her Time; but it is now hop'd that her inwards are not hurt & that she may recover.

PHILADELPHIA Sept. 16. We hear from French Creek Iron Works, that last Friday Night, William Branson's Wagon coming from thence towards Philadelphia, laden with sixteen Hundred Weight of Iron, was unfortunately Overset, it is thought that the Wagoner lay asleep on his Face upon the Load, for when found he lay on his back with all the Iron on him, he was bruised to pieces & lay two Days before he was found.

PHILADELPHIA Sept. 23. The following piece of News from West Jersey may probably divers some of the Readers? teach Caution to others, and afford useful contemplation to the curious inquirers in Nature.

A Farmer, upon Aacocus, having fatten'd an Ox, the pamper'd Beast grey mischievous, and thereupon had a Board hung at his Horns, before his Eyes; yet he found the way to break into a Field, letting other Cattle in with him: There stood in the Field but one Tree, an Oak near the middle of the Field; Dogs being sent to drive the

Cattle out the Ox ran furiously with the rest, but not seeing what stood direct before him could not avoid the Tree; he forced off the Bark, split his Board into may Pieces, dislocated his Neck, broke his Back and some of his Ribs.

On Tuesday last, a young Man on Board the Snow Lovely Hannah, cut his Throat very deep, and fearing he had not done it effectually, jumpt overboard, but the Water being something Cold, so stagnated his Blood, that being taken up a proper Means used he is like to recover.

PHILADELPHIA Sept. 23. Last Thursday a Ship bound from the West-Indies to Virginia, Capt. Williams came into Port having lost her Masts in a great Storm of the 20th of August. She was met some days before the Storm by a large Pink, the People which came on board to request of Capt. Williams some Provisions an Anchor & Cable, and before they returned acquainted him that they having been among the Portuguese and had been Ill used, and to do themselves Justice had run away with the Pink which belong'd to the Portuguese from the Island of Tercera; and that she had a good Cargo of Merchandize on Board. Capt. Williams prevail'd with them to leave the Pink & come all on board his Ship with the most valuable Goods, which they did, and Methods were taken to sink her when they left her. They were in Number 8 but two of them left the rest afterwards, and went on board a Sloop they met at Sea, with their Share of the Plunder. The other 6 were delivered up to Authority immediately on their Landing here at Philadelphia, and are now in Irons in the Prison of this City.

NEW-YORK Sept. 27. The Small-Pox Fever and Flox prevails very much in this City, and many Children dye of said Distemper, as well as grown Persons, and the Country People are afraid to come to Town, which makes the Market thin, Provisions dear, deadens all Trade, and it goes very hard with the Poor, insomuch that a Charitable Contribution for them is promoted, one Gentleman has given Twenty Pistoles, another Twenty Pounds towards Relief, and other Charities are thrown in according to the Circumstances of the Benefactors.

PHILADELPHIA Sept. 30. On Saturday Evening, the 21st of August, a Duel was fought between Majorr Mason, formerly Major in the Tower-Guards, and Colonel Edward Chearnley, in which the latter was shot dead on the spot, the Bullet entering into his left Cheek. The coroners brought it in willing Murder. There was a very large Funeral, the Pulpit was long in Morning, and the unhappy Gentleman is very much lamented.

NEW-YORK Oct. 4. We have an Account in from Albany, dated the 25th of last Month, that the French of Canada, with about 80 Men, have built a Fort, & Enclos'd it with Stockadoes, at Crown Point, on the Southern side od Colear's-Lake, near the Carrying Point, above Sargtogo (about three days Journey from Albany) and have also built a House of Forty Feet, and are busy to Erect two more there. The Persons that brought this Account do add, That they were credibly inform,d in Canada, that the French design to enclose the said Fort and Buildings with a Stone wall next Spring, and at the same time to send up two Hundred Men to Tiedderondequat, on the South side od Caderaque Lake, above Oswego, near the Sinnechas Country, in order to stop the English from Trading with the Indians.

N. B. It is apprehended, that if these encroachments of the French are not prevented, they may prove of the last Consequence to this & the rest of his Majesty's adjacent Colonies in America.

NEW-YORK Oct. 11. It is Reported here that John Clark's Scooner, bound hither from New-Castleon Delaware, was cast away on Cape May on Wednesday or Thursday last, and is drove up on the Beach.

NEW-YORK Oct. 13. We hear that the City Hall & Prison of Perth-Amboy is burnt down to the Ground and the Prisoners forced to look out for new Quarters.

PHILADELPHIA Oct. 14. We hear from Lewis Town on Delaware, That the Ship Bristol Merchant, Joseph Maynard Commander, who sailed from this Port for Bristol the latter end of last Month, was on the First or Second Instant Founder'd near Cape Henlopen; the Men were saved, but we have not heard for certain how it is with the Ship and Cargo.

NEW-YORK Oct. 18. We hear that at Kingston in the County of Ulster, a Fire has happened there, and burnt the Grist Mill of William Borance, in which there were several Thousand Bushels of Wheat.

PHILADELPHIA Oct. 21. On Tuesday last the Five following Persons received Sentence of Death for Piracy, Capt. John MacFerson, Paul Green, John Harney and John Cole, John Smith not appearing to have consenting to any Act of Piracy was Discharged.

The same Day one Samuel Crosley, a Baker, going from this City to Burlington in a Passage Boat, fell overboard near Pennypack & was there was drowned. His Body is not yet found.

We hear from Hopewell in the Jerseys, that on the 4th past, Bucks were observed fighting near the new Meeting House there, one of them extraordinary large, supposed to be a Roe Buck the other small and the common sort. in company with them was a black Doe, who stood by to see the Engagement. The small Buck proved a full Match for the great one, giving him many violent punches in the Ribs, but in the height of the Battle the fastened their Horns so strongly together, that they were not able with all their Strength to disengage, and in that condition they were taken. The Doe retreated into the Woods, but being pursued with several Beagles Hounds, she was taken also alive, and they have put her and the great Buck into a boarded pasture together in hopes to have a Breed, if the Sizes are not unsuitable. This is the Second Brace of Bucks that have been caught by the Horns this Fall.

NEW-Castle Oct. 21. The Speech of the Honourable Patrick Gordon Esq; Lieut. Governour of the Counties of New-Castle, Kent and Sussex on Delaware, and Province of Pennsylvania, To the Representatives of the said Counties, in the General Assembly met, at New-Castle, the 21st Day of October 1731.

Gentlemen,

The good Effects naturally flowing from the Publick Peace of a Government, and the regular Administration of Justice therein, are at this time so sensibly felt throughout these Counties, that they cannot but excite an eager Desire in the minds of all good Men, to secure and perpetuate Blessings so essential to our Happiness, by doing which we not only consuly our own private Good, but likewise discharge our bounded Duty to out Sovereign, and render the most acceptable Service in our Power to out Honorouble Proprietors and our Country: I am therefore perswaded that so worthy a Choice of Representatives, as I now see before me will have nothing more at Heart, than to use their best Endeavours to maintain and improve those Blessings, the Continuance of which cannot fail of making us and our Posterity a happy People.

It is no small Satisfaction to me, that at this annual Meeting, I have an Opportunity of acquainting you, that by the Letter I have lately received for England, I am assured that the long depending Dispute, between our Honourable Proprietors and the Lord Proprietor of Maryland, was upon the Point of being amicably terminated between them, the issue whereof I expect very soon to hear. One of the Honourable Proprietors have likewise fully determined amongst us cannot fail of being acceptable to all those, who under their Government enjoy those great and valuable Privileges, for which the Name of their worthy Fathers must ever remain dear to all its Inhabitants: And as on the first of these Events, several things for the future Quiet and Security of these Counties, will naturally come to be considered, the Second will furnish an Opportunity of Completing and Adjusting the whole in the most Satisfactory manner.

As for my self, I shall esteem it a Happiness to have it in my Power, truly to represent to our Proprietors that Regard and affection, which the Assemblies of the Government have so frequently expressed for the Honourable Family, and in every Station of Life, to use my best Endeavours for serving the good People of the Counties, who have by their Representatives on all Accession, so honourably acquainted themselves to me.

PHILADELPHIA Oct. 28. Run away the 19th of this Instant October, from Isaac Norris of Fairhill, a Servant Man John Wood, a slender active Man, about 22 Years of Age, his Hair Cut off, thinish but lively Visage, born as he says at Birmingham in Great Britain, came a Servant from Britain in 1730. He is a Carpenter and Sawyer, and he has been a Sailor, and about two Weeks ago Cut his Leg with an Ax, above the side of his Instep, is well Cloathed and has taken away much others, viz. a good Leather Jacket and Breeches with Brass Buttons a Fine but worn Segathee Coat without Cuffs, several, perhaps Four or Six White and Speckled Shirts, a good Broad Cloth Coat with no Cuffs, a Riding Coat, a new lightish brown Drugget Jacket lin'd with Shalloon, strip'd Holland Jacket and Breeches, a pair of Duroy Breeches the Puffs white Silk, a new fine Hat a light brown Wigg & as is supposed several other things. Also a black Trotting Gelding about seven Years old, Mark'd E on the near Shoulder, and a Notch in the far Ear, no white about him save a snip on his upper lip, a good whole skirt Saddle, Bridle and Spirt Boots. Whoever shall take up said Servant and Horse, and bring them to me, or secure them that I may have them again, shall have Forty Shilings Reward, besides reasonable Charges, paid by
Issac Norris.

NEW-YORK Nov. 1. We hear from Back-Creek in Maryland, that on Tuesday last, a large Ship being Launched, they fear'd she would run on Shore on the other side of the Creek, to prevent which, they made fast one end of her Cable to a Tree, on the Bank side, but it going off, the Cable Slacking by misfortune, got under part of the Bilgeway, & tearing a part thereof, near 40 Foot long, swung it round with such violence that one Man was kill'd out-right & another was wounded to that degree he died presently after, and two more lir dangerously wounded; it also cast an old Man near 40 Foot up in the air, but he received no great hurt; several Women were in the Crowd but received no damage. There are in all 7 or 8 Persons very much hurt.

PHILADELPHIA Nov. 4. We hear that on the 29th of last Month, as one Gabriel Enochson was coming up the River in this City in a Canoe, in Company with John Jones. (who gave as the Account) and Eleanor Dericson, they met with Edward Nichols and John Nichols in another Canoe, who had been Fowling, and Enochson knowing there was a Hue and Cry after Edward Nichols for Horse Stealing, endeavoured to take him, and laid hold of the Canoe, but John Nichols presenting his Gun told Enochson he would shoot him if he did not quit his hold, which Enochson did, and after they had turned their Canoe John Nichols shot him in the Thigh and bottom of his Belly, whereof he lies dangerously ill. We hear also that the said Enochson has offered Ten Pounds for the Apprehending both or either of the said Fellows.

NEW-YORK NOv. 8. As to the Small-Pox, altho' there are a pretty many wholly Recovered, yet we hear not of any that was taken with the Distemper last Week, and they are very few in this City but what have had the same, so that we hope that Sickness, and the great Mortality occasioned by it, is over at this time.

PHILADELPHIA Nov. 11. To be Lett. By Mary Spay and Capt. Whreldom, the dwelling-house of Mary Spay's in Cloucester, with Stabling. Orchard and Gardens and Pasturage, Ferry-Flats and Boats. Whoever has a mind to take the same, may apply to the Persons above, and agree on reasonable Terms.

PHILADELPHIA Nov. 18. We hear from Cecil County in Maryland, that the Rev. Mr. Ormston, Minister of the Church there, is lately Dead. His Man left him in good Health sitting by the Fire, while he went to a Neighbour's House, but at his return found him lying on the Hearth, his Pipe by his Side, and his Head burnt off in the Fire. He was formerly Minister of the Church in this City.

From the same County we hear, that a Man was killed last Week, at the raising of the Masts of that Ship, whose Launching so much Mischief was done and two Men kill'd.

BURLINGTON Nov. 20. Run away from John Hutchinson of Bucks County, a Servant Man by the name of Thomas Richardson by Trade a Taylor aged about 24 Years, a short well-set fellow, full faced and a pale Complexion, had on a striped Cap bound with Blue Ferritin and tied with the same, a brown Cloth Serge Coat and a black broad Cloth Coat or Jacket, also three other Jackets whereof one is Searsukel no sleeves to any of them, a pair of black Breeches no Stockings and low heel'd Shoes. He also took with him a black pacing Mare with a long Tail, branded on the near Shoulder and Buttock I.H. and E.G. whoever takes up said Servant and secure him so that his Master may have him again shall have Fifty Shillings as a Reward and reasonable Charges.

PHILADELPHIA Nov. 22. The Speech of the Honourable Patrick Gordon, Esq; Governour of the Province of Pennsylvania, and Counties of New-Castle, Kent and Sussex upon Delaware.

To the Representatives of the Freemen of the said Province, met at Philadelphia November 22, 1731.

Gentlemen,
It is not without some uneasiness to me, that on the receipt of certain Letters from our Agent by the last Ship from Britain, I found my self under the necessary of calling you together before the Day which you stood adjourned: Those parts of them which have any relation to our Publick Affairs I now lay before you, by which you will find, that the Sugar Islands are preparing to renew, and much more vigorously than ever carry on their Attack against the Trade of these Northern Colonies, in a Branch of it, in which tho' we are not immediately & directly so deeply concerned as some others, yet if they are abridged of vending their Flour in those channels, and confined only to such as this Province has generally traffick'd in, it will in the consequence no less nearly affect our Trade in the Commodity, that it will theirs; and all who depends on that Manufacture will be equally sufferers. I was therefore unwilling, that after I had noticed thereof, one Day should be left in giving you Opportunity of considering,

what further Measures were proper to be entered into by this Government, in order to prevent, if possible, so severe a Blow to the Trade of this Place, and such a heavy Discouragement to the industrious Farmer, by whose Labours Grain is raised.

The repeal also of our last Law for Establishing Courts of Judicature, obtained by the endeavours of some Persons, on pretence that it is prejudicial to his Majesty's Interest (of which, tho' it is not notified to me in form, I have notwithstanding certain Advice) may deserve your Consideration. Thus by that Repeal, the former Law pass'd in the Year 1722 for the like purpose comes again in force, the inconveniency I hope will be less; the greatest is, the Charge that you will find both attended the Defence of it, which tho' greater than we would have wished had been incurred on that Occasion, yet as the Pains that have been in the Defence give a manifest proof of the care and vigalance of our Agent, in supporting the Rights of the Freemen of this Province, you will no doubt consider his Service, and the Necessary of a further Encouragement to one in his Station.

The late Encroachment of the French in erecting Fortifications so near Albany, and their incessant Endeavours in Practising on the Indians, to gain them over their Interest, have deservedly alarmed our Neighbours the Province of New-York, who have humbly besought his Majesty's Protection; and from his Royal Concern for the Base ans Security of all his Subjects, it is to be hoped effectual Measures may be concerted for putting a timely Stop to such dangerous Attempts in these his Majesty's Dominions. From what hath been communicated to me on these Heads, &c. the Examination of some of the Indian Traders lately taken before me, you will clearly see the Necessity of turning your thoughts to the Consideration of Indian Affairs, and of Providing by proper Regulations for the Peace and Safety of the Province, which is too frequently endangered by Persons settling on Lands not yet purchased off the Natives, and the undue Manner in which our Trade with them for these Years past has been carried on.

We have now large Expectations given us of seeing one of our Honourable Proprietors here next Spring, who as they succeed to the Honour and Estate of their much esteemed Father our late worthy Proprietor, we cannot doubt but they equally inherit his Virtues and imitate his Example in their Affection and good will from this Province, and therefore cannot fail of being cordially received by all its Inhabitants.

It may be very convenient to proceed at this Meeting to consider of such other Publick Business as may come before you, which will be an Ease to your selves and a means of lessening the Publick Expence.   P. Gordon.

PHILADELPHIA Dec. 2. We hear from the other side of the River, that a few Days ago, a House about 4 Miles back of Benj. Woods was burnt to the Ground. The Man was abroad at Labour, and the Woman gone to borrow a Sieve at a House at about a Quarter of a Mile distant; she left two young Children playing at the Door, and a third the youngest, lying on the Bed: When she was returning, to her great Surprize she saw the House on Fire, and ran to call her Husband; who came home with her, but too late to save any thing, tho' they could see all their Children at the Bed Surrounded by the Flames, & no means to be delivered: Tis thought the two went in to fetch the Youngest; A Bitch who had two Pupies, carried one of them out of the House, & 'tis suppos'd she endeavoured to fetch the other out also, her Hair being singed.

To be Sold by Edward Horne, One Eight Part of the Iron-Work, called by the name of Burlington Furnace, on Christiana-Creek, with the aforesaid Eight Part of all the Lands and Plantation and Appurtenances thereto belonging, as also a good Plantation containing 225 Acres of Land situated on Brandy-Wine-Creek, in Chester County. Any Person inclined to purchase either may apply to William Roeles, Merchant, in Philadelphia, or to the said Edward Horne, at his House near Fairhill.

NEW-YORK Dec. 7. Last Night about 12 o'Clock a Fire broke out in a Joyners House in this City, it began in the Garret when the People were all a sleep and burnt violently, but by the help of the two Fire-Engines which came from England in the Ship Beaver, the Fire was extinguished, after having burnt down the House and damaged the next.

PHILADELPHIA Dec. 14. We hear from Crowicks in West-New-Jersey, that some time ago two Brothers Quarreling the one bit off the others Ear. It is supposed they had been to free with Sir Richard Rum.

Stray'd or Stolen about a Month ago, out of Andrew Bradford's Pasture near Philadelphia, a bright Bay Cart Horse about 14 Hands high, and between six or seven Years old, with a small Star on his forehead, and branded on the near Shoulder P and the near Thigh C he is strong well creasted, and has been used only to draw in Dutch Waggon. Whoever takes him up and gives Notice, or brings him to Peter Lloyd in Second Street, Philadelphia, shall receive a reasonable Reward.

Two very likely Negroe Women to be sold by John Ripley, at Mrs. Barberry Grant in Front Street.

All Persons indebted to Richard Jayne (who married the Widow Vining) at the Sign of the Ship on William Fishbourn's Wharf, are desired to come and pay the same; and all Persons who have any demands on him, are desired to bring their Accounts, for he designs to leave this Province in a short time.

PHILADELPHIA Dec. 14. By a Letter from England of the 9th of October last via Boston, we are informed it was not then determined whether New-Jersey and New-York should have distinct Governours or not, and that it was tho't Coll. Cosby would have the Government of New-York, but not certain of it.

PHILADELPHIA Dec. 21. We hear from Maryland, that the Ship built in Back-Creek there, (as mentioned in this Paper, on the Account of two Men kill'd at her Launching & another at her Rigging) was overset lately in the Bay, as she was going from one River to another for her lading.

MARTHA'S Vineyard Dec. 23, 1731, Extract and

Translation of a Letter received from some of the Palatines who took Passage at Rotterdam in June 1731, for Philadelphia, but has been set on Shore on Martha's Vineyard, a small Island on the Coast of New-England. The Letter was directed to Michael Weis, Dutch Minister in Pennsylvania, dated Dec. 23, 1731.

Dear Mr. Weis,

We poor and miserable Creatures, who not understanding English, nor being understood by the People here, cannot, tell how or to whom to apply for Assistance, do humbly beseach you to represent our Condition to the Governour of Pennsylvania, if perhaps by this Interposition, Justice maybe done us.

Capt. Lahb made an Agreement with us in Rotterdam to carry us in his Ship to Philadelphia, and to provide sufficient Victuals for such a Voyage: But we apprehend, that from the whole of his Conduct, that he rather intended to starve and destroy us all, and make himself Master of all our Effects. We have been 24 Weeks at Sea, because when we had the fairest Winds the Ship sailed only in the Day Time. We had bought at Worms (for common use) a considerable Quantity of Rhenish Wine, which when we came to Sea was understood was stowed where we could not come to at it. The last 8 Weeks we saw no Bread at all, and a Pint of Grols was the allowance for five Persons per Day.

In great distress of Hunger and Thirst we went all together to the captain and Partitioned that we might have some of our Wine wherewith to refresh ourselves, at last in a great Rage he threw us the Key of the Hold, but sent no Body with us to shew us where the Wine lay, after long seeking we found some of the Casks but the Bungs had been drawn out and the Wine all taken away, and when we asked the Sailors what was gone with it, we received no answer but Curses. The Hunger became at length so grievous that 18 Pence was given for a Rat, and 6 Pence for a Mouse, and we sometimes could get no Water for several Days but at 6 Pence a Quart, Seven Persons died of Hunger and Thirst in one Night and were thrown naked into the Sea without any thing to sink them, nor durst, we ask any thing of the Sailors because upon the least Occasion we were beat and kickt and used like Slaves or Malefactors. Of 150 Passengers which came aboard at Rotterdam, above 100 have been miserably starved to Death; at length it pleased God that a Sloop met us and conducted our Ship into this Place called Homes's Hole in Martha's Vineyard, but after we came to Anchor the Captain kept us 6 Days on Board and suffered no Communication between us and the People on Shore, telling them that we were Turks and not Chirstians, and what Provisions was brought off he Sold to us at the rate of 8 Shillings for a loaf of Indian Corn Bread, and so for other things. In 6 Days 15 Persons more were starved to Death, and if we had been kept on board 3 or 4 Days longer we should have Perished for we were not able to help one another to a drink of Water; at length we were all in a great hurry put on board a sloop and sent on Shore, where the good People on the Island are very charitable and kind to us, giving us Bread, Meat and other Food, and doing every thing in their Power to refresh us, so that some who were near Death are likely to recover. The Capt. kept all our Goods on Board and would not suffer any to take the least thing with them, not so much as our Beds, for want of which we suffer much, tho' we are ashore, because there are but few Houses; and has since prevailed with us to sign an Engagement to pay him the full Passage as if they had landed at Philadelphia, both for the Dead and the Living; we thought to have paid the passage of the Dead out of their own Goods, but when they unloaded the Vessel and put the Chests on shore, we found that their Chests as well as ours were almost all broke open and rifled, so that there was not substance enough left among us to discharge our Obligations, and we must all alike be reduced to begging. The Time Payment in 3 Weeks from the date of Bond, we therefore pray you to have Compassion on us, and to represent our miserable Condition to those in Power, that so if possible this last Oppression of the Captain may be prevented and some Justice done to us.

We also pray God to send us Succour and help us out of our Distress we are in. We should have sent 2 or 3 Men with the Letter, but none of us are yet able to Travel, as soon as some have recovered sufficient Strength they will follow, and acquaint you with more Particulars, recommending you to the Almighty, we are Yours, &c.

The Original of this Letter is writ in High-Dutch, and Signed by 5 Passengers, Thus. Johannes Gobr, Jacob Diessenbach, John Daner, Samuel Schevacblemer, ─────────.

Everyname Index

----, Isaac 300 Lavina 68
ABBOT, Capt 168 Robert 58 170
ACTON, Benjamin 286
ADAMS, Rev 38 Thomas 283
ADAMSON, 289 Anthony 288 295
ALDRIDGE, John 277
ALEXANDER, Robert 55
ALISON, Samuel 256
ALLEN, John 245 330 Joseph 197 Richard 245 Widow 127
AMYET, John 51
ANDERSON, James 17 191
ANNE, Queen Of England 285
ANNIS, Capt 47 John 55 Tho 144
ANNON, Mr 281
ANTHONY, Capt 317 Richard 12 207
ANTROBUS, Joseph 73 190
ARNETT, Alexander 64
ARNOLD, Thomas 280-281
ARTHUR, Joseph 167-168
ASBORN, Nicholas 64
ASHENTON, Ralph 249 Robert 129
ASHTON, Thomas 156
ASMORE, Elizabeth 367
ATCHISON, William 37
ATKING, James 313
ATKINSON, Samuel 155
ATTWOOD, William 359
AUSTIN, John 256
BADCOCK, Henry 5-6
BADERK, Henry 36
BAGLEY, ---- 189 John 255 Johnael 256 Mr 35
BAINTON, Peter 331
BAIRD, Pat 126 Patrick 124 137 279-280
BALDING, Ezekiel 31

BALDWIN, William 93
BALL, Capt 173 265 John 132 209 334 367
BALTIMORE, C 148 Lord 189 354
BANCROFT, William 213
BANNET, William 144
BANTOFF, William 197
BANTOFT, 356 William 181 355
BARBER, Peter 100
BARCLAY, John 7 183
BARCROFT, Ambrose 26
BARD, Peter 297
BARGER, Isaac 56
BARNET, Peter 73 William 81 199
BARNHAM, Albert 290
BARRY, Matthias 101
BARTON, Thomas 278
BASS, Jeremiah 130
BATTELL, William 154 272
BATTIN, John 20-21 William 20 24
BAVENSON, Richard 28
BAYTON, Peter 58 213 361
BEAKS, Samuel 16
BEAN, James 333
BEAUMONT, William 28
BECKETT, Joseph 40
BECKMAN, G 178
BEDFORD, Edmund 169
BEDLOW, Peter 170
BEER, Theadola 82
BEFFET, David 173
BELL, John 256
BEMAN, George 370
BENBROOK, James 144
BENETO, Don 85
BENNET, John 65 William 126
BERMINGHAM, Richard 15
BERNET, W 206

BERRY, Richard 175
BETTISON, John 46
BETTREDGE, William 55
BICKETT, William 335-336
BICKLEY, Abraham 40 W 26
 William 243
BIEKLY, Abraham 193
BIFFET, David 185
 Margarete 186
BIGNAL, Capt 66
BILES, William 100
BILLET, William 119-120
BILLINGER, Thomas 86
BING, Thomas 130
BIRCH, Capt 354
BIRD, Robert 55
BIRMINGHAM, Col 171
BISSEL, William 112
BIVERKLO, Herman V 189
BLAKEY, Charles 336
BLOWDEN, John 283
BLUNSTON, S 46 Samuel 188
BOALS, Thomas 101
BOBBER, James V 189
BOBIN, M 220
BOELS, Thomas 247-248
BOLTON, Robert 168
BOND, Capt 154 Joseph 167
 Samuel 182
BONNY, Anne 96
BOOKS, William Dowell 312
BOON, Justice 239 Richard
 83
BOORE, Thomas 186
BORDMAN, George 367
BORROWS, Samuel 25
BOUD, Henney 6 Samuel 5-6
BOURK, 328
BOURNE, Thomas 45
BRACLEY, John 282
BRADFORD, A 172 Andrew 7
 15 32 37 66-67 69-70 74
 101 112 120 128 131 154
 161 168 175 193 197 204
 209-210 217 236 248-249
 273 282 289 291 316 319
 326 336 346 382 Mr 68
 William 7 15 31 56 94-96
 112 116 161 236 248 282
 289 291 316 336
BRADLEY, Jonathan 340
BRADWAY, Mary 303
BRAGGINGTON, William 113
BRAISER, Jane 329
BRANSON, William 216 372

BRAY, Henry 110
BREADEY, Thomas 295
BREWER, John 170
BRICE, John 313
BRICKLEY, Mr 52
BRIGHTWELL, John 245
BRINDLEY, Mrs 284
BRINGKURD, John 283
BRITAIN, Joseph 326
BRITTAIN, Joseph 221
BROCKDON, Charles 80
BROCKEN, Charles 46
BROOK, Stephen 287
BROOKE, Clement 189 Hen
 345
BROOKS, John 44
BROUGHTON, Thomas 114
BROWN, John 89 Ruth 89
 Thomas 89
BROWNE, John 154
BROWNELL, George 131 216
BROWNWELL, George 291
BRYAN, John 191 John Sr
 191
BRYANT, John 44 182
BRYARD, Mrs 189
BUCKLEY, Joseph 190
BULL, John 126 Richard
 217-218 Sarah 217-218
BULLOCK, Thomas 173
BURAT, Peter 12
BURCH, Daniel 170
BURGE, William 31
BURK, John 280 Richard 100
BURKELLO, Mr 14 Mrs 14
BURN, Roger 244
BURNE, Mathew 65 William
 103
BURNET, Gov 205 Mary 201
 Mrs 8 W 10 26 119 125
 135 159-160 William 108
 117 124 133 156 240 Wm
 201
BURNS, Thomas 119 297
BURNSIDE, James 301
BURNSIDES, James 301
BURREL, Capt 356
BURRIDGE, Thomas 10
 William 316
BURROW, John 129
BURROWS, Edward 91
BUSTEED, Jephson 67
BUSTILL, Samuel 149
BUTTERFIELD, Capt 40
BYARD, Samuel 6

BYERLY, Thomas 102
BYLLINGE, Edward 102
BYNG, Thomas 113
CABOONE, James 352
CAIN, Abel 345
CALAGHAM, Charles 303
CALDER, Thomas 54-55
CALVERT, Bernard 250
 Charles 145-146 195 317
 Edward 267 317 Benedict
 Leonard 189 194 232 252
 322 365 Lord 194 Maj-gen
 195
CAMPBELL, Duncan 360 John
 309-310
CAMPION, George 5-6 102
 128 355
CANN, John 65
CANNS, John 65
CANTHEEN, William 290
CARELON, Edward 36
CARLETON, Edward 36
CARPENTER, Edward Warner
 50 Jam 137 James Stanton
 67 Mr 128 Samuel Sr 111
CARR, Samuel 92
CARTER, Col 266 George 116
 William 71
CARVER, James 245 John 245
CARWELL, Benjamin 169
CASB, Alice 352 Caleb Jr
 352 Caleb Sr 352
CASH, Leonard 339 Martha
 339
CHALKLEY, Thomas 105
CHALMERS, James 280
CHAMBERLAND, Richard 57
CHANCELLOR, Mr 364 William
 26 62 111 126 200
CHAPMAN, Abraham 176 John
 28 Robert 335 William 39
 237
CHARLES, Ii King Of
 England 102
CHARLTON, John 290
CHARNOCK, Stephen 170
CHEARNLEY, Edward 374
CHENEY, Thomas 246
CHEYNEY, John 279
CHILD, Cephas 148
CHIT, Thomas 275
CHIVERS, Rachel 339
CHURCHELL, Mr 27
CLANPOLE, George 46
CLAPOOLE, George 244

CLARK, Charles 316 John
 374 William 54
CLARKE, Jonathan 277
CLASSEN, Nicholas 236
CLAY, Humphry 90
CLAYPOOLE, George 300 Jos
 362 Joseph 362
CLAYTON, John 26
CLIFT, George 51
CLOUD, Joseph 190 315
CLOUGH, George 244
CLYMER, Richard 287 330
COAT, Widow 325
COATS, John 112
COCK, Thomas 304
COCKRAM, Capt 201-202
CODD, Capt 6
COLDELL, C 94
COLE, John 375 William 128
 208
COLEMAN, Joseph 72
COLLET, Robert 139
COLLING, Joseph 5
COLLINS, John 181 Thomas
 183
COLVILL, Thomas 124 280
COMINGS, Robert 320
COMMING, Robert 341
CONALLY, William 218 240
CONLIFF, John 203
CONNAR, William 27
CONNOR, John 194 250 333
CONOR, Lawrence 241
CONWAY, James 203
COOK, Derick 267 Edward
 345 Richard 272
COOKE, Edward 28
COOPER, James 129 Mary 129
 William 194 204
COPSON, John 9 15 84-85
 194 218 236 Joseph 218
COPTON, John 17
CORBET, John 4
CORFEY, 291
CORNISH, Andrew 257
CORNWALLIS, Penelope 110
CORNWALLIS, 42 81 130 Tho
 109-110 William 103 109-
 110 130 133 198
CORRY, Elizabeth 345
COSBY, Col 382
COTTMAN, Benj 14 Benjamin
 14 Lawrence 14
COURE, John 198
COURTLANDT, Philip 48

388

COUTTS, James 279
COWNDEN, James 280
COX, Abraham 257 323
    Christopher 145 Moses
    364 William 16 33-34
CRAIGE, Archibald 235
CREAGH, Patrick 75-76 132
CRICHTON, James 170
CRIES, Samuel 170
CROKATT, David 255
CROSBY, John 37
CROSLEY, Charles 241
    Samuel 375
CROWDER, James 167
CRUGER, Alderman 52 John
    178
CRUMP, John 340 Magaret
    340
CUNLIFF, John 203
CURRY, James 325
CURTIS, Benjamin 133 John
    101
CYPHERS, Elizabeth 184
DAMSEL, Henry 362
DANBY, John 207 358
DANER, John 385
DANIS, David 28
DAVIES, William 24
DAVIS, Cornelius 3 Ellis
    334 Gabriel 354 James 5-
    6 275 279 John 9 Lewis
    113 Mirick 248 Philip 51
DAY, Humphry 269 William
    155
DEALE, Thomas 355
DEAVER, Antell 368
DELANY, Mathew 4
DELAVAL, John 287 Mrs John
    287
DEMPSEY, Vallentine 198
DENHAM, Thomas 31 56
DENNIS, Samuel Jr 34
DENUNE, James 281 Mr 281
DERICSON, Eleanor 378
DERRYMAN, Mary 212
DESKELE, Mr 38
DEVENPORT, Humprey 90
DICKENSON, Capt 354
DICKER, Samuel 47
DICKINSON, 360 Jonathan 46
    Mr 35 317
DIESSENBACH, Jacob 385
DIGGS, Col 74
DISWA, John 267
DOBBS, William 214

DOBSON, Richard 100
DOCKWRA, William 73
DONALDSON, James 115 316
DONNE, William 339-340
DOUBLE, John 116
DOWELL, William 312
DOWNING, Alex 331 Capt 354
    John 350
DREWRY, David 34
DRYSDALE, Hugh 69
DUCHE, Andrew 161
DUCHEE, Anthony 100
DUEBE, Anthony 221
DUNCAN, Bridget 272
DUNLOP, Wm 37
DURAN, Juan 86
DURBOROW, Hugh 352 Hugh Jr
    352
DUTTON, John 37
EANON, 284 Thomas 289
EARLE, John 15
EARLINGTON, Widow 294
EATON, Christopher 204
EDGELL, Simon 312
EDMONDS, Deborah 214 Roger
    214
EDWARDS, John 154 Thomas
    46
EILEY, John 203
ELFORD, John 182
ELLIS, Robert 58 114 167
    207 213 244 248 Widow 73
EMANS, John 27
EMPSON, Ebenezer 17
ENGLAND, Joseph 325-326
ENGLISH, Richard 344
ENOCHSON, Gabriel 378
ENOCKS, Henry 127
ENSWORTH, James 132
ESTAUGH, John 54
EUSTIST, Samuel 245
EVANS, Benjamin 85 David
    127 143 199 368 John 199
EVERSON, Richard 361
EVERTY, Isaiah 20
EYERA, John 92
FARRA, Samuel 170
FAULKER, Alexander 4
FENNING, John 161
FERGUSON, Samuel 218
FIELD, Zachariah 340
FIELDS, Zeachariah 327
FISHBOURN, Mr 277 317
    William 167 190 207 209
    214 309 315 382

FISHCURN, William 291
FISHER, Jonathan 330
FITZGERALD, Rowland 69
FITZWATER, George 58
FLEMMING, John 4
FLORNE, Edward 315 Edwr 315
FLORY, Tho 298 Thomas 297-298
FLOWER, Henry 8
FLY, William 144
FOE, Edward 160-161
FORMAN, Joseph 218 240
FORREST, Thomas 330
FORRESTER, William 69
FORRINGTON, George 127
FORTUNE, William 160
FOULKS, John 16
FOULTIS, James 50
FRAME, Alexander 198
FRANKLIN, John 65
FRASER, George 33-34
FRASET, William 47
FREELAND, Mr 161
FRENCH, Charles 8 Col 30 John 8 19 26 61 64 Mrs Aves 272
FRESNEAN, 111 Andrew 110
FUSBY, Ariana 14
GAEDOUIT, Francis 130
GAERLIN, Peter 308
GALLAWAY, John 361
GALLER, John 132
GALLEY, Sally 11
GALLOWAY, Peter 291
GAMBIE, Francis 132
GAMBLE, Francis 133
GAMITT, Isaac 286
GAMMON, Philip 161
GANDOUIT, Francis 50
GARDNER, Mr 249 Robert 199
GARIGUTS, Matthew 128
GARLACH, John Jerick 55
GARLAND, Sylvester 17 190
GARNER, John 25
GARRET, Amos 361
GARRETSON, Elizabeth 8 10-11
GARRETT, Amos 215
GARRIGUE, Mathew 71
GARRIRSON, John 311
GARRISON, John 311
GARROGUE, M 71
GARTAGE, Edward 297
GATAU, Nicholas 191

GATEAU, Nicholas 61 72
GEORGE, Ii King Of England 192 194 232 266 365 King Of England 166 220
GIBBENS, David 192
GIBBIN, John 113
GIBBS, John 334
GIBSON, Nathaniel 199
GIFF, 7
GILE, Allen 310
GILEONS, David 246
GILLAT, Mathew 369
GILLINE, John 367
GINN, Elizabeth 361
GLASCOCK, Gregory 69 Thomas 69
GLEAVES, Mrs Thomas 341 Thomas 341
GLENTWORTH, Thomas 5
GOBBS, James 246
GOBR, Johannes 385
GODFREY, Benjamin 308
GOFORTH, Arron 129
GOLD, James 161
GOLDSMITH, Joseph Best 55
GOODING, John 39
GOODMAN, Richard 313 Samuel 313
GOODSON, Job 58 176
GORDON, Archibald 359 Col 184 192 George 307 John 366-367 P 151 164 180 211 227 232 261 293 337 350 381 Patrick 144 149 151 161 164 178 180 211 224 227 230 233 258 261 273 297 333 336 347 375 379 Widow 216
GOURE, John 198
GRAFTON, Richard 92 312
GRAHAM, George 217
GRAINGER, Joshua 171
GRANGER, John 282 Joshua 172
GRANT, Mrs Barberry 382 Thomas 113
GRAYHAM, Capt 197
GREEMMAN, Capt 46
GREEN, Paul 375
GREENFIELD, Col 322
GREENMAN, Capt 45
GREENOCK, Capt 27
GREYER, 304 307
GRIFFE, Thomas 193
GRIFFING, Thomas 24

GRIFFINS, John 334
GRIFFITTS, Thomas 56
GRINES, John 245
GRUCHY, James 11
GUBB, Nathaniel 175
GUIER, Felix Mack 287
GUMLY, Nathan 18
HACKNEY, Samuel 36 127 368
HADLEY, Simon 296
HAIDON, John 133
HAILY, Capt 190
HALL, Aqualla 274 Aquilla 264 277 Archibald 140 Daniel 131 Edward 277 357 John 25 140 244
HAMBLETON, Michael 335
HAMILTON, Andrew 19 26
HAMOCK, Robert 361
HANDY, Thomas 170
HANLOCK, Thomas 301
HANNA, Andrew 289
HANSON, Jonathan 57 Timothy 285
HARBET, William 256
HARDING, Samuel 7
HARGRAVE, Charles 319 360
HARMSON, Henry 58-59
HARNEY, John 375
HARNUS, Morris 51
HARRIS, James 54 John 269 Samuel 144
HARRISON, Daniel 176 John 36 Joseph 334
HASELL, Samuel 272 275 281
HASSET, Arron 302
HASTING, Samuel 268
HATEL, Samuel 297
HATTEN, Thomas 329
HATTON, Thomas 329 352 359
HAYES, John 104 William 32
HAYMAN, S 39
HAYS, Richard 176
HEAD, Charles 27
HEAP, John 92
HEATH, James 27 197 James Paul 312 John 27 Mr 312
HEATHCOAT, John 340
HEATON, John 290 Robert 341
HENRY, James 14 John 221 329
HEPBURN, John 120
HERRING, Pickle 75
HETTON, Thomas 333
HEWES, Joseph 330

HEWES (cont.) William 330
HIDE, William 103
HIGGINS, Timothy 105
HILL, Hannah 175 John 282 Levin 284 Mrs Richard 287 Richard 19 26 39-40 175 233 237 268 286Thomas 93 William 170
HILLYARD, Benjamin 16 Capt 17
HILTON, Andrew 345
HIP, Alderman 52
HODGE, Henry 133 214 244
HODGES, Henry 54 Joseph 249
HOENE, Edward 190
HOGG, John 297
HOLLAND, Col 195 Edward 323 Richard 85
HOLLINGSHEAD, John 351
HOLT, Samuel 184
HOLY, Samuel 184
HOOD, John 350
HOPKIN, Ruth 249
HOPKINS, Capt 309 John 297 Nicholis 113
HORD, Mr 295
HORFMAN, Mary 218 236
HORNE, Edward 171 176 190 197 257 381 William 167
HORTON, John 360
HOSKINS, Ruth 192 Widow 315
HOUSMAN, John 15
HOWELL, Mordyiac 137
HUDSON, John 202 William 129 174 340
HUGGS, Joseph 194
HUGH, Ann 72 Owen 72 Thomas 25
HUGHES, John 24
HUGHS, Hugh 42
HUMPBERY, Owen 72
HUMPHREY, John 186 Thomas 73
HUMPHREYS, Rev Mr 215
HUMPHRIE, Owen 267
HUMPHRYS, John 317
HUN, Widow 334
HUNAM, John 22
HUNLOCK, Mr 35 Tho 186
HUNLOKE, Thomas 105 245
HUNT, Obediah 10 William 16 32

HUNTER, Mr 144
HUTCHINS, Zachariah 274-275 Zich 186
HUTCHINSON, John 379 Sarah 333 William 333
HYAT, Widow 264
HYNSON, Thomas 64
ILLISON, Jacob 33-34
INDIAN, Galscow 340 Glascow 339 Hannah 239 King Oppekhorsa 350 Maria 112 Peter 112
INGLIS, Mr 319
JACKMAN, Joseph 325
JACKSON, Daniel 6 Joseph 187 Stephen 186
JACOBS, Celeb 37
JAMES, James 51 John 247
JARVICE, Martyn 324
JARVIS, Martyn 310
JAYNE, Richard 382
JENNINGS, Solomon 338-339
JOBSON, Tarnell Mitchel 331
JOHN, Philip 50 Thomas 275-276
JOHNSON, Andrew 33 Chas 96 James 329 Joseph 193
JOHNSTON, Dr 4 J 3 John 3
JONES, Anne 47 Capt 81-82 85 Edward 132 198 Evan 366 Griffith 339-340 James 198 John 70 175 187 207 356 378 Jonathan 344 Joseph 4 197-198 Morgan 247 Peter 331 Samuel 199 Widow 90
JOYCE, John 66
JUERY, James 57
JUSTIN, John 183
JUSTS, Doctor 324
KANN, Conrad 209 Mariana 209
KEES, Andrew 32
KEIMER, Samuel 65-66 153
KEITH, W 26-27 60 63 99 122 156 William 12 19 29 41 57 59-60 62-63 69 75-76 78 91 97 114-115 120 122 140-142 265 327
KELAWAY, William 169
KELSEY, William 310 312
KENNY, Edmond 296
KERSEY, John 80
KERTON, William 353

KEYLL, John 56
KIETH, William 94
KING, Capt 198 George 204 Robert 35
KINLEY, William 294
KINNER, Richard 130
KIP, Jacobus 178
KIRKBRIDGE, Joseph 355
KNIGHT, Hannah 312 John 312 Joseph 137
KNOWLES, Francis 244 Frank 37
KURES, Peter 55
KWITH, William 99
LACEMAN, Isaac 90
LACY, Samuel 8 Thomas 340
LAHB, Capt 383
LAMB, Thomas 296
LAMPIERE, Richard 369
LAMPREYE, Richard 369
LAWRENCE, Mr 277 Thomas 45 128 233 284 297 Widow 34
LEA, William 203
LEADMAN, Rev Mr 267
LEDDEL, Joseph 113
LEE, John 7 Philip 264 Thomas 266
LEECH, John 174 Thomas 175-176
LEED, Titan 335
LEONARD, 149 Capt 188 James 185 John 148 187-188 191 Martha 340 Nathaniel 155 Robert 48
LESLEY, George 100
LESLIE, George 76
LETHERHAND, 197
LEWIS, John 154
LIFLER, Mary 36 Maurice 36
LILLY, Moses 169
LINCH, Cornelius 44
LINTHBICOMES, Thomas 237
LLOYD, D 230 David 102 124 143 153 166 181 212 263 274 Eleanor 319 John 29 Joseph 26 Miss 287 Peter 189 207 281 331 382 Philemon 80-81 Thomas 287
LOCKART, Alexander 193
LOFTUS, Leson 82
LOGAN, J 268 James 46 268
LOMAS, John 361
LONG, Capt 219 294 John 344

LONGFIELD, Henry 33-34
LONGSTREAT, Theophilus 174
LOW, Edward 48
LOWE, Nicholas 257
LOWMAN, Samuel 8
LOWRY, Thomas 272
LUX, Capt 80
LYALL, David 71 Mrs
    Frederick 130
LYELL, David 7
LYFORD, William 2
M'CALL, Gearge 41 George
    56 241 277
MAC'CONNEL, Alexander 325
MACANOULLY, Denis 38
MACDANIEL, Robert 64
MACFERSON, John 375
MACHADS, Capt 84-85
MACIBOY, Francis 72
MACKALL, John 323
MACKANDRES, Edmund 27
MACKDOWALL, Alexander 102
MACKEY, John 57
MACKINTOSH, Phineas 113
MACKMANNERS, Constantine
    326
MACNAYLEY, John 175
MACNISH, George 59
MACOMB, John 326
MAGAN, Juan 86
MAGIL, Daniel 37-38
MAGILL, Daniel 17
MAGNE, Capt 248-249
MAKENULTY, Denis 17
MALDIN, Daniel 310
MALLARY, Ebenezer 4
MALLONEY, Patrick 153
MALSTER, 114
MALTSBURY, John 323
MANLESTER, John 254
MANTHROPE, Samuel 139
MARKHAM, Gov 277
MARSHAL, Mr 289 291 Thomas
    28
MARSHALL, Alexander 209
    John 209
MARTIN, Daniel 7 John 92
    Robert 218
MASON, Majorr 374
MASTERS, Mr 287 Wm 199
MASTERSON, Hugh 95
MATDANIEL, Jacob 184
MATLOCK, George 35
MATTOCK, Edward 194
MAULTBY, 264 John 263

MAYNARD, John 237 Joseph
    374
MCCURDEY, James 56
MCCURDY, James 34
MELINEUX, Mary 327
MERCER, Capt 297 299
MEREDITH, William 47
MILLER, John 103 Robert
    199
MILLINER, William 311
MILLNOTS, John 297
MILLS, Samuel 175
MILNER, Nathaniel 26
MIRANDA, Mr 4
MITCHEL, 301 James 304-307
    300
MONGOMERIE, John 364
MONTGOMERIE, J 242 258 266
    276 278 313 319 332 339
    John 219-221 242-243 257
    265 276-277 312-313 338
MONTGOMERY, John 202
MONTOMERIE, John 369
MOON, William 115
MOOR, ---- 10
MOORE, Eleanor 8 10
    Elianor 10 John 126 297
    Richard 160 Simon 88
    William 145
MORALLY, William 330
MORGAN, Alexander 83 91
    Benjamin 194 Evan 103-
    104 Hogan 202 Mr 188
MORINE, Capt 46
MOROUGH, Thomas 177
MORRAY, Alexander 169
MORRILL, Thomas 129
MORRIS, Edward 194 F 339
    James 104 Lewis 113 119
    145 364-365
MOUFIELD, Thomas 91
MUGGLEWS, Charles 181
MULBELLAND, Arthur 175
MULLUN, Edward 129 Edward
    Jr 129
MUNDAY, Henry 42
MUNTGUMERY, Robert 73
MURDOCK, Capt 277
MURPHY, Margarete 191
    Richard 293-294
MURRY, John 102 Timothy
    184
NEALLS, John 59
NEEF, Francis 71
NEGRO, Archard 25 Ceazer

NEGRO (cont.)
  83 Cleo 41 Dick 245
  Franck 72 Fransh Manuel
  31 Harry 74 Jack 27 110-
  111 160 James 182 326
  Jenny 310 324 Jo 370
  Kent 41 Nan 62 Peter 216
  301 Popow 148 Qwam 16
  Rachel 111 Robin 66
  Scipio 74 Tom 41 91 Will
  185
NELSON, Henry 370
NESBITT, James 202-203
  Sarah 202-203
NESS, Samuel 216
NEVES, John 20
NEVIL, Walter 88
NEW, Thomas 221
NEWELL, Joseph 132
NEWHOUSE, Andrew 170
NEWLIN, 23 Nathaniel 22
NEWTON, Henry 216
NICHOLS, Edward 378 John
  378 Joshua 235 William
  182 362
NICHOLSON, Mr 264
NIGHTINGAL, Simon 189
NORRIS, Isaac 19 26 46 216
  218 268 377 John 325
NORTON, Ruth 89
NORWOOD, H 105
NOSTRICT, Sam 35
NUTT, Samuel 358
OADE, Joseph 89
OLIVER, Arthur 212
ONION, Stephen 17
ORION, Stephen 185 246
  326-327
ORMSTON, Rev Mr 378
ORRON, John 128
ORTON, John 326
OUGHTOPAY, Daniel 4
OVER, Thomas 8
OWEM, Mary 214
OWEN, Capt 27 Dr 44 Evan
  58 194 214 Mary 194 214
  Owen 154 Richard 48
  Roger 199
PAINE, John 4
PAINTER, Nicho 109-110
  Nicholas 103 198
PALMER, John 4 Robert 62
PARDON, Elizabeth 11
PARIER, Sarah 154
PARINE, Daniel 372

PARIS, Mrs 325
PARK, Nicholas 182
PARKE, Thomas 100-101
PARKER, Capt 65 George 345
  John 65 Mr 358 William
  358
PARKS, William 217 236 289
  316 Wm 290
PARNEL, James 111
PASCAL, Benjamin 36
PASSMORE, John 103 244
PATITE, Quinte 102
PATTISON, Sarah 202-203
PEACE, Joseph 190 221
PEARCE, Capt 265
PEARSON, Henry 174
PEELE, Samuel 237
PEERSON, James 369
PEMACH, William 340
PEMBURTON, Israel 35
PEMINGTON, Thomas 267
PENBERTON, Israel 185
PENBURTON, Israel 351
PENN, William 132 172 233
PENNEL, Joseph 93
PENNILS, Joseph 330
PERGUSON, Samuel 236
PERPOINT, Samuel 284
PERSE, Andrew 173
PETERS, Christian 301 Rese
  104 Rice 173 Thomas 104
  173
PETERSON, Andrew 27 217
PHENIX, Capt 197
PHILIPSE, Adolph 160 243
PHIPPS, Benjamin 170
  Thomas 255
PICKS, Derias 111
PIERCE, Daniel 64
PIGEON, John 58
PIGGION, Joseph 266 Mrs
  267
PIPER, Henry 369 Mathew
  368
PLUMBSTEAD, Clement 4
PLUMIN, John 4
PLUMLEY, Mathew 367
PLUMSTEAD, Mr 317-318
POLGREEN, Thomas 55 244
POLOKS, Mr 316
PORTER, Abraham 92 330
  Sarah 340
POSILETBEAVAIT, John 354
POWELL, Samuel Jr 308
PRAM, Anne 345

PRAT, John 185 Richard 187
PRESTON, Samuel 66 168 268
PRICHARD, Capt 169 Henry
    353 John 155 Joseph 170
PRICKET, William 38
PRIDE, Absaham 7
PRIEST, Widow 279
PROUSE, 301 James 111 304-
    307 300 Jimmy 304
PRYER, Thomas 182
PUGH, Edward 170 Henry 248
PULEY, Celeb 249
PURSEY, Celeb 46
PYLE, Joseph 22 Joseph Jr
    22 Ralf 22 Robert 22
QUIMBY, 49-50 Josiah 48
RABLEY, William 325 335
RADES, Mrs 44
RAKESTRAW, William 90 104
RALPH, Joseph 352
RANSTED, Caleb 269
RATSEY, Capt 168
RAWENSON, Job 360
RAWLE, Francis 106 181 184
    Joseph 316 Martha 181
    184 William 181 184 316
    Wm 315
RAWLMAN, Mary 257
RAYMOND, John 31
RAYNOLD, Philip 74
READ, Capt 64 Charles 58
    64 106 138 167 201 255
    272 281 312 329 364 Chas
    97 John 36 171 Mary 96
    William 281 Wm 296
RECORDER, Mr 52
REDMAN, Joseph 28 Sarah 28
REED, William 240
REFENDO, Capt 85
RENALDS, Robert 249
RENIER, Mrs 45
RESCARRICK, George 103
RESE, Edward 113
REUCH, Mr 277
REYLEY, John 287
REYNOLD, Philip 74
REYNOLDS, Lawrence 95 124
    Mr 103
RICE, Henry 316 John 82-83
RICHARD, Paul 248
RICHARDS, Joseph 67 199
RICHARDSON, Thomas 379
RICHMOND, John 56
RIDDLESDEN, Mr 81
RIDDLESDON, William 42

RILEY, James 156
RIPLEY, John 382
RISCARRICK, George 110
RIVES, David 32
RLLIS, Robert 45
ROACH, George 340
ROADS, Peter 15
ROBERT, John 239
ROBERTS, Ann 358 James 282
    John 237 239-240 Owen 4
    19 82 93 116 120 358
ROBERTSON, William 14
ROBINSON, Ann 102 Edward
    356 Israel 239 R 10
    Thomas 75 316-317 Widow
    358
RODES, John 172
ROE, Thomas 169
ROELES, William 381
ROGERS, Elizabeth 339
    George 124 Morgan 76
    William 75
ROLSE, Mr 83 85 Thomas 26
ROSE, Peter 335
ROSS, John 67
ROYAL, Michael 137
RUDYARD, John 182-183
RUM, Richard 382
RUMSEY, William 344
RUSCOMBE, James 209 Mr 209
RYAN, Thomas 236
RYERES, William 280
RYERSON, George 90
RYLEY, Dennis 203 Dr 27
    Margarete 216 Patrick
    216
SANDERS, James 197
SANDIFORD, Charles 329
    Ralph 186
SARTIN, Richard 154 Sarah
    154
SATTWERWALTS, George 243
SCANK, Garet 44
SCATTERGOOD, Thomas 330
SCHEVACBLEMER, Samuel 385
SCHOWTHRIP, Thomas 110
SCHUYLER, Peter 71
SCOT, Mr 14 William 288
    295
SCOTT, William 311
SCULL, Nicholas 38 116 137
SCURE, Richard Vander 48
SEAMES, Thomas 340-341
SEBOR, Thomas 175
SEDGICKK, Edward 286

SELLEN, Henry 214
SERGISSON, William 280
SHAD, George 281
SHANBURY, Nathan 309
SHARP, Thomas 345
SHARPAS, Will 52-53
SHEED, George 37 70 307 Mr 301 305 300
SHELTON, Thomas 143
SHENNAN, John 281
SHEPHARD, Robert 137
SHEPPARD, Aemy 188 Widow 188
SHERMOURS, Benjamin 257
SHIELDS, John 112
SHIPPEN, 360
SHIPPING, Edward 171
SHOWTHRIP, Thomas 103
SHRANBERY, James 56
SHURMER, Benj 8
SIMCOCK, Jacob 37
SIMES, David 245
SIMMON, Capt 2
SINTON, William 69
SITCH, John 199
SLAVE, Indian Dick 31
SLEST, Mattias 295
SLIFIELD, George 170
SLOANE, Alex 280
SLUYTER, Benj 6
SLYFIELD, Capt 55
SMART, James 127
SMEE, William 170
SMITH, 114 Capt 116 202 Christopher 359 George 168 Ja 365 James 56 116 341 Jane 188 Jo 266 John 7 75 169 335 375 Joseph 129 Joseph Jr 59 Ralph 290-291 359 Thomas 193 202 281 334 Timothy 297 370 William 37 55 325
SMOUT, Edward 192
SMYTER, John 169
SNAGGS, Richard 216
SNODEN, John 275
SOBER, Charles 186 256 Thomas 183 209 334
SOBERS, Charles 100 Thomas 59
SOLGARD, Capt 52-54 59 81 Peter 51 53
SOMERSET, Mitchell 86
SOMPER, Joseph 64
SPAFFORD, Capt 168 189

SPAFFORD (cont.) Samuel 330 William 368
SPANGLE, Widow 309
SPAY, Mary 378
SPICER, Abraham 111 C Lodwick 105 Thomas 166
SPOTTWOOD, Col 91
SPOTWOOD, Col 27
SPRIGG, 144
SPRINGER, Charles 267
SPRINYARD, John 119 Joseph 119
SPROGELL, Catharine 308
SPURLING, James 56 116
SPURVITER, Theophilus 71
SPURYORS, Theopolus 257
SQUIBB, Robert 102
STACKERS, Robert 238-239
STACY, Mahlon 330
STAPLER, Stephen 213
STAREL, Michael 255
STATTS, Richard 48
STEEL, James 8 174 190 268 353
STEELE, Gabriel 110 160 171 Newt 319
STELLE, Gabriel 7 Isaac 186
STEPHENS, Mr 73
STEVENS, George 113 Mr 35
STEWARD, James 207 Mr 298-299
STOCKDALE, Peregrine 170
STOLLARD, Capt 128
STORY, Sarah 100
STOTRE, Mr 38
STROUD, John 345
STULL, John 354
STURGIS, 307 Mrs 307
STURGUS, Joseph 269
SULLIVAN, Timothy 329
SUNDERLAND, Edward 362
SUTTON, Henry 116 John 15 Joseph 264
SWAIN, Jonathan 18
SYKES, James 101 198
SYMES, Andrew 137
TALBOT, Catherine 131 Robert 131
TAMELIN, Thomas 336
TATCHAM, 331
TAYLER, William 113
TAYLOR, 114 Col 30 John 38 189 Joseph 249 Joseph Jr 249 Philip 28

TEATMAN, Thomas 245-246
TEMPLEMAN, Henry 218
TESDALL, George 297
THIMIN, John 288
THOMAN, Rees 331
THOMAS, Frances 339 Roger 339
THOMPSON, Edmond 105 George 309
THORNBURY, Thomas 280-281
THORTON, William 80
THROCKMORTON, John 155-156
THRRAMORTON, Samuel 323
THWAITS, James 139
TIDMARSH, William 93 205 319
TIRKIE, Capt 74
TOFFO, Henry 16
TOMPSON, George 366
TOMSON, Christopher 245 Neil 65
TORTEIDED, Capt 10
TOWERS, Samuel 169
TRAFFORD, Edward 170
TREBERN, William 193
TRECHARD, George 279 Mary 279
TRENT, William 95
TRESSE, Thomas 176
TROTTER, Joseph 132
TUCK, Lawrence 20
TUFFEY, William 333-334
TUNEN, Herman 71
TYLEE, Nathaniel 217-219
UGLE, Charles 116
UNGLE, R 146
VANBURKELLO, Abel 14
VANBUSKIRK, Thomas 90
VANCOX, V 194
VANDAM, Rip 370
VANDEM, Rip 369
VANHOOK, Widow 120
VANHORNE, 111 Cornelius 91 110 John 287-288
VANREDDLESDEN, William 130 133
VANRIDDLEDEN, 81
VANTILBURG, Peter 186
VARILL, William 28
VER, Capt 81
VERSEY, John 170
VILANT, William 120
VINING, Abraham 92 Benjamin 91 Widow 382
WADER, Richard 177

WALBY, John 266
WALKER, Jonathan 178 Richard 4 Thomas 280
WALL, Ann 86 Richard 86
WALLACE, 204 David 177-178 203
WALLIS, Braden 105 Branden 105
WALTER, R 53 Robert 51-52
WALTON, John 61
WARNE, Samuel 272
WARS, Matthew Tilghman 257
WATHELL, Thomas 8
WATMORE, James 160
WATSHELL, Thomas 8
WATSON, Isaac 221 Nathan 51
WATTS, John 327
WEAVER, 328 Samuel 28
WEBB, William 18
WEBSTER, Michael 367-368
WEIS, Michael 383 Mr 383
WELDON, John 128 William 126
WELLS, Arthur 283 John 297
WELTON, Richard 131
WENTON, Mr 362
WEST, Charles 182 John 368 Robert 254
WESTWOOD, Elijah 119
WHATKINS, Thomas 204
WHITE, Henry 20 John 74
WHRELDOM, Capt 378
WIGG, Bobb 70
WIKES, Ebenezer 362
WILCOX, Thomas 236-237
WILD, Joseph 352
WILKINSON, John 300
WILLCOCKS, Edward 114
WILLIAM, Jonathan 93
WILLIAMS, Bridget 276 Capt 373 Daniel 293 George 237 Joseph 275 Rees 248 Thomas 102 William 198
WILLIAMSON, Timothy 139
WILLING, 360 Tho 236 Thomas 360
WILLINGS, David 326
WILLOCK, George 76
WILLSON, 204 David 177-178 203 Edward 139 Elizabeth 184
WILMER, Mr 264
WILSON, 264 James 294 353 John 5 18 47 74 Joseph

WILSON (cont.)
   277 Thomas 275 William 275
WINTER, Walter 237
WINTERBERRY, John 310
WINTERS, John 238 Mrs Walter 238 Walter 238-239
WOLLARD, John 57
WOOD, John 37 377 Joseph 81 Sarah 257
WOODROP, Alexander 40 359
WOODWARD, Ames 361 Mary 360
WOOTEN, Richard 40
WOOTSON, Mary 367
WORD, Caterine 161 Catherine 161 Joseph 161
WORTHINGTON, David 244 Samuel 280 Thomas 313
WOTTSON, Mary 368
WREN, Peter 355
WRIGHT, Capt 297 Jonathan 330 Richard 26 154 Thomas 193
YARD, William 31
YEILDS, Mr 94
YOUNG, William 92

Other Heritage Books by the Author:

Boston, the Redcoats, and the Homespun Patriots, 1766-1775 (1998)

New England Chronicle: News of New England from January 1722 - December 1731 (1997)

Journal of Occurrences: Patriot Propaganda on the British Occupation of Boston, 1768-1769 (1996)

Jolly Old England (1996)

1767 Chronicle (1995)

Heritage Books by Armand Francis Lucier:

1767 Chronicle

Boston, the Red Coats, and the Homespun Patriots, 1766–1775

*Central Colonies Chronicle: The Freeman, the
Servants, and the Government, 1722–1732*

*French and Indian War Notices Abstracted from Colonial Newspapers
Volume 2: 1756–1757
Volume 3: January 1, 1758 to September 17, 1759
Volume 4: September 17, 1759 to December 30, 1760
Volume 5: January 1, 1761 to January 17, 1793*

Jolly Old England

*Journal of Occurrences: Patriot Propaganda on the
British Occupation of Boston, 1768–1769*

*New England Chronicle News of New England
from January 1722–December 1731*

*Newspaper Datelines of the American Revolution
Volume 1: April 18, 1775 to November 1, 1775
Volume 2: November 1, 1775 to April 30, 1776
Volume 3: May 1, 1776 to November 1, 1776
Volume 4: November 1, 1776 to January 30, 1777*

*Pontiac's Conspiracy and Other Indian Affairs: Notices
Abstracted from Colonial Newspapers, 1763–1765*